Mute Compulsion

Søren Mau is a communist philosopher and postdoctoral researcher based in Copenhagen, Denmark. He is an Editor of the journal *Historical Materialism* and a member of the board of the Danish Society for Marxist Studies.

Mute Compulsion

A Marxist Theory of the
Economic Power of Capital

Søren Mau

Foreword by Michael Heinrich

V
VERSO
London • New York

First published in English by Verso 2023
First published as *Stummer Zwang: Eine marxistische Analyse der
ökonomischen Macht im Kapitalismus* by Dietz Berlin 2021
© Søren Mau 2021, 2023

3 5 7 9 10 8 6 4 2

Verso
UK: 6 Meard Street, London W1F 0EG
US: 388 Atlantic Avenue, Brooklyn, NY 11217
versobooks.com

Verso is the imprint of New Left Books

ISBN-13: 978-1-83976-346-5
ISBN-13: 978-1-83976-349-6 (UK EBK)
ISBN-13: 978-1-83976-350-2 (US EBK)

British Library Cataloguing in Publication Data
A catalogue record for this book is available from the British Library

Library of Congress Cataloging-in-Publication Data
Names: Mau, Søren Mads, author.
Title: Mute compulsion : a Marxist theory of the economic power of capital
  / Søren Mau ; foreword by Michael Heinrich.
Other titles: Stummer Zwang. English
Description: London ; Brooklyn, NY : Verso, 2023. | Includes
  bibliographical references and index.
Identifiers: LCCN 2022038208 (print) | LCCN 2022038209 (ebook) | ISBN
  9781839763465 (trade paperback) | ISBN 9781839763502 (ebook)
Subjects: LCSH: Marxian economics. | Capitalism. | Marx, Karl, 1818-1883.
  Kapital.
Classification: LCC HB97.5 .M35813 2023 (print) | LCC HB97.5 (ebook) |
  DDC 335.4/12—dc23/eng/20220923
LC record available at https://lccn.loc.gov/2022038208
LC ebook record available at https://lccn.loc.gov/2022038209

Typeset in Minion Pro by MJ&N Gavan, Truro, Cornwall
Printed and bound by CPI Group (UK) Ltd, Croydon CR0 4YY

Contents

A Note on Translations and References

Whenever possible, I have used official English translations of Marx's writings. When deemed necessary, I have modified these and added a footnote in case of substantial modification. All translations from German texts which are not available in English are mine.

References to Marx and Engels's *Collected Works* (MECW) look like this: (32: 421), which means volume 32, page 421. References to the *Marx-Engels-Gesamtausgabe* (MEGA2) look like this: (II.3.4: 1453); this refers to section (*Abteilung*) 2, volume 3.4, page 1453. Other references to Marx's writings follow this system of abbreviations:

Capital: A Critique of Political Economy, vol. 1, trans. Ben Fowkes (Harmondsworth: Penguin, 1978).	C1
Capital: A Critique of Political Economy, vol. 2, trans. Ben Fowkes (Harmondsworth: Penguin, 1978).	C2
Marx's Economic Manuscript of 1864–1865, ed. Fred Mosely (Chicago: Haymarket, 2017).	M
Grundrisse: Foundations of the Critique of Political Economy (Rought Draft), trans. Martin Nicolaus (Harmondsworth: Penguin, 1993).	G
'The Commodity' (chap. 1 of *Capital*, vol. 1, 1st ed.), in *Value: Studies by Karl Marx*, ed. Albert Dragstedt (London: New Park Publications, 1976).	V

'The Value-Form' (appendix of *Capital*, vol. 1, 1st ed.), trans.   A
   Mike Roth and Wal Suchting, *Capital and Class* 4 (Spring
   1978): 130–50.

'Results of the Immediate Process of Production', appendix of   R
   C1.

The Ethnological Notebooks of Karl Marx, ed. Lawrence Krader   E
   (Assen: Van Gorcum & Comp., 1974).

For more information on the volumes cited of MECW, see the appendix.
Different references within the same note are separated by a semicolon:
'G: 234, 536; 33: 324; IV.1: 43, 56; M: 788' thus means *Grundrisse*, pages
234 and 536; MECW, volume 33, page 324; MEGA2, section 4, volume 1,
pages 43 and 56; and *Marx's Economic Manuscript of 1864–1865*, page 788.

Foreword

by Michael Heinrich

I first met Søren Mau in November 2017, at the annual conference in London of the journal *Historical Materialism*. When we talked after his paper presentation, he asked me if I knew of any literature that dealt more specifically with the Marxian concept of the 'mute compulsion of economic relations'. I couldn't think of a single title. Søren then told me that he wanted to write a dissertation on this concept. At first I was a bit perplexed. I had often myself quoted the 'mute compulsion' that Marx talks about in the chapter on 'so-called primitive accumulation', and had also used it in many discussions. The idea behind it – that under certain circumstances it is not persons but economic conditions that exert compulsion on formally free workers – seemed almost self-explanatory to me. It took only two or three sentences to make clear what was meant. Until now, it had never occurred to me that this concept might need a separate analysis. My surprise was similar to that in a game of chess when, in an opening that has been analysed in most variations up to the fifteenth or twentieth move, one is confronted with an innovation on the fourth. Either such a move is terribly stupid or it is insanely good. As I realised fairly quickly, Søren's idea was not stupid at all. This 'mute compulsion' was of central importance in the contrast between personal relations of domination such as slavery or serfdom in pre-capitalist modes of production, and the impersonal domination of legally free wage labourers by which Marx characterises the capitalist mode of production. That alone should be reason enough to look at it in more detail. The only astonishing thing was that no one had done so before.

My second big surprise came about a year and a half later. I had stayed in touch with Søren, we had discussed different issues now and then, and I had agreed to participate in the defence of his thesis at the University of Southern Denmark. In the spring of 2019, I got to see his entire dissertation, written in English, for the first time. Far from being a narrow, philological discussion of the term 'mute compulsion', Søren's analysis was much broader. He presented mute compulsion as a key component of the specifically economic 'power of capital', a power based on altering the material conditions of social reproduction. For his examination of the question, already much discussed, of how capitalist relations repeatedly reproduce themselves despite all crises and contradictions, Søren had named a third type of power relations alongside those based on violence and those based on ideology. While the first two have a direct effect on people, this third type asserts itself indirectly by reshaping people's economic and social environment.

Søren's work is now available in revised form as a book. It is dedicated to a detailed investigation of this specific 'power of capital'. The various elements of a theory of this power are reconstructed from Marx's critique of political economy in his manuscripts written after 1857. The results of this reconstruction do not refer to a concrete capitalist society; they are located on the level of representation of the 'ideal cross-section' of the capitalist mode of production, namely the level of abstraction on which Marx locates his own analysis, at the end of the manuscript for the third book of *Capital*. On this level, everything is analysed that necessarily belongs to the capitalist mode of production, regardless of its respective historical manifestation – and here this 'mute compulsion' is inherent in every case.

However, Søren's investigation is not only about contributing to the elucidation of Marx's critique of political economy or completing it. This already becomes clear in the second part of his three-part work. Starting from Marx's conception of proletarians who can dispose of their life but are cut off from the necessary conditions of this life, Søren shows how biopolitical questions raised by Michel Foucault and Giorgio Agamben are inherent in Marxian analysis from the beginning, even if they are not called that. Also in the second part, the 'power of capital' based on 'mute compulsion' is examined with regard to the production of social differences on the basis of gender and racist attributions – which brings us directly to important current debates.

The third part of the work, which deals with the dynamics in which the power of capital is expressed, also shows the contemporary analytical relevance of Søren's study. The real subsumption of labour under capital is the central category here. Søren's use of this concept, however, differs considerably from the usual discussion: he deals with the real subsumption of agriculture, which highlights consequences for capital's relationship to nature; the logistics revolution of the 1970s, which was central to globalisation tendencies in the last third of the twentieth century; and capital's tendency towards crisis and production of a surplus population – all of which are issues at the heart of any fundamental confrontation with capitalism.

Reading this work is certainly not easy going. However, it soon becomes clear that the effort required does not get bogged down in the purely conceptual. It unfolds precisely the critical potential that is the necessary prerequisite for a social practice that aims to overcome domination and exploitation.

Introduction

'When the ancient slave, crucified by his master, writhed in ineffable agony, when the serf collapsed under the rod of the corvée overseer or under the burden of labor and misery, at least the crime of man against man, of society against the individual, lay open, exposed, atrocious in its nakedness, blatant in its brutality. The crucified slave, the martyred serf, died with a curse on the lips, and his dying gaze met his tormentors with hatred and a promise of revenge. Only bourgeois society draws a veil of invisibility over its crimes.'[1]

– Rosa Luxemburg

Despite more than a decade of acute crisis, a global pandemic, and resolute resistance, capitalism lingers on. In 2008, it was hit by one of the deepest crises in its history. As governments rushed to the rescue, a new cycle of struggle against the accelerating commercialisation of social life emerged. Today, our situation is still profoundly shaped by the crisis and its repercussions. The great recession of the late 2000s is only the preliminary culmination of a much larger and protracted crisis, which erupted when the post-war boom came to an end in the 1970s.[2] Since then, global capitalism has been treading water. For almost five decades, it has kept its

---

1   Rosa Luxemburg, 'Nur ein Menschenleben!', in *Gesammelte Werke*, vol. 1 (Berlin: Dietz Verlag, 1972), 468f.

2   Robert Brenner, *The Economics of Global Turbulence: The Advanced Capitalist Economies from the Long Boom to Long Downturn, 1945–2005* (London: Verso, 2006);

head above water by means of debt, outsourcing, austerity, privatisation, and wage depression, but even this comprehensive symptom treatment has not managed to stop the ongoing global stagnation.[3] A small group of hyperprofitable companies such as Apple, Alphabet, Amazon, and Meta, has ran away from a global sea of so-called zombie firms struggling with low levels of productivity and profitability and kept alive by cheap credit provided by governments desperate to avoid the political consequences of the only thing that could generate the basis for an economic recovery, namely a large-scale destruction of capital.[4] Political institutions everywhere are struggling with deep mistrust; everyone is fed up with politicians and parties, and no one any longer believes that the state could ever be something like an instrument of the will of the people. The fragile optimism of the 1990s and early 2000s has given way to a gloomy feeling of approaching disaster, not least because of the climate crisis, the existence of which everyone acknowledges, but which is nevertheless allowed to continue, since in this world, profit is more important than life.

And yet, here we are: capitalism is still with us. Or perhaps it is the other way around: we are still with *it*. In certain respects, capital's stranglehold on social life seems stronger than ever before; never have so many aspects of our existence and such large parts of the world been dependent upon the global circuits of self-valorising value. Although it is still too early to draw up a conclusive balance sheet of the post-2008 era, it is at least remarkable that, so far, the forces of capital have largely succeeded in pushing through their aims. Banks have been bailed out, taxes have been cut, austerity has been imposed, and profits have been made. Inequality keeps rising, the commodity form continues its creeping infiltration into new spheres of life, the biosphere is still heading towards the abyss, and 780 million people still live in chronic hunger. In the 1930s, after the long depression of the late nineteenth century, World War I, the Russian and German revolutions, and the Great Depression of the early 1930s, Walter Benjamin concluded: 'The experience of our generation: that capitalism will not die a natural death.'[5] Today we know that capitalism has not only *survived*, but has

---

Robert Brenner, 'What Is Good for Goldman Sachs Is Good for America: The Origins of the Current Crisis' (working paper, Institute for Social Science Research, UCLA, 2009).

3   Aaron Benanav, *Automation and the Future of Work* (London: Verso, 2020).

4   Jason E. Smith, *Smart Machines and Service Work: Automation in an Age of Stagnation* (London: Reaktion Books, 2020).

5   Walter Benjamin, *The Arcades Project*, trans. Howard Eiland and Kevin McLaughlin, (Cambridge, MA: Belknap Press, 1999), 667.

actually been *strengthened*, in and through crises, revolutions, uprisings, wars, and pandemics. *Capitalist expansion and entrenchment amid crisis and unrest*: that is our conjuncture, and it invites us to ask some important questions: How does capital manage to sustain its grip on social life? How is it even possible that a social order so volatile and hostile to life can persist for centuries? Why hasn't capitalism collapsed yet?

Coercive, Ideological, and Economic Power

In the final sections of the first volume of *Capital*, Karl Marx narrated the story of how the rule of capital was historically established: 'In actual history, it is a notorious fact that conquest, enslavement, robbery, murder, in short, violence, play the greatest part.'[6] The capitalist mode of production came into the world 'dripping from head to toe, from every pore, with blood and dirt.'[7] Marx also notes, however, that we cannot assume the forms of power required in order to *bring about* a certain state of affairs to be identical with the forms of power required for its *reproduction*. On the contrary: when violence has done its job, another form of power can take over. In a passage from which the present study derives its title, Marx describes how, once capitalist relations of production have been installed,

> the mute compulsion of economic relations seals the domination of
> the capitalist over the worker. Extra-economic, immediate violence is
> still of course used, but only in exceptional cases. In the ordinary run
> of things, the worker can be left to the 'natural laws of production', i.e.,
> it is possible to rely on his dependence on capital, which springs from
> the conditions of production themselves, and is guaranteed in perpe-
> tuity by them.[8]

Violence is thus replaced with another form of power: one not immediately visible or audible as such, but just as brutal, unremitting, and ruthless as violence; an impersonal, abstract, and anonymous form of

---

6   C1: 874.

7   C1: 926.

8   C1: 899. In English translations of *Capital*, the German *stumme Zwang* is usually – though incorrectly – rendered as 'silent' or 'dull' compulsion.

power immediately embedded *in* the economic processes themselves rather than tacked onto them in an external manner – *mute compulsion*, or, as I will also call it, *economic power*.

Although the emphasis on the importance of 'the mute compulsion of economic relations' for the reproduction of capitalism is found frequently throughout the chaotic collection of (mostly unfinished) writings which make up Marx's critique of political economy, Marx never articulated a coherent, systematic analysis of this historically novel form of social domination. Neither did his followers, although important headway has been made in the last couple of decades (studies to which I will return later). Most attempts to account for the reproduction of capitalism rely on an assumption about the nature of power which tends to obscure the workings of economic power, namely that power comes in two fundamental and irreducible forms: *violence* and *ideology*. Borrowing and slightly altering a term from Nicos Poulantzas, I will refer to this as the *violence/ ideology couplet*.[9] Alternative versions of this duality include coercion and consent, hard and soft power, dominance and hegemony, and repression and discourse. The basic – and often implicit – claim at work here is that we can explain the reproduction of capitalist social relations with reference to either the ability of rulers to employ violence or their ability to shape the way in which we (consciously or unconsciously) perceive and understand ourselves and our social world. Louis Althusser's theory of ideology is a good example of this way of thinking: according to Althusser, the reproduction of capitalist relations of production '*is ensured by the superstructure*, by the legal-political superstructure and the ideological superstructure'. In this familiar scheme, the relations of production are reproduced by the ideological and the repressive state apparatuses, which rely on ideology and violence, respectively.[10]

There is no doubt that capitalism would be impossible without the constant presence of ideological and coercive power. But there is more to the power of capital than that. Violence, as well as ideology, are forms of power that *directly* address the subject, either by immediately forcing bodies to do certain things or by shaping the way in which these bodies think. Economic power, on the other hand, addresses the subject only

---

9   See also Michel Foucault, *Discipline and Punish: The Birth of the Prison*, trans. Alan Sheridan (London: Penguin, 1991), 28.

10   Louis Althusser, *On the Reproduction of Capitalism: Ideology and Ideological State Apparatuses*, trans. G. M. Goshgarian (London: Verso, 2014), 140, 244.

indirectly, by acting on its *environment*. Whereas violence, as a form of power, is rooted in the ability to inflict pain and death, and ideology in the ability to shape how people think, economic power is rooted in *the ability to reconfigure the material conditions of social reproduction*. The concept of 'social reproduction' should here be taken in the broad sense of all the processes and activities needed in order to secure the continuous existence of social life. Economic power is thus a concept designed to capture the ways in which forms of social domination reproduce themselves through inscription in the environment of those who are subjected to it.

In this book, I will offer a theory of the economic power of capital. On the basis of a close reading and critical reconstruction of Marx's unfinished critique of political economy, I will attempt to explain why the power of capital takes the form of a 'mute compulsion of economic relations'; I will thus attempt to locate its sources, identify its mechanisms, explain its forms, distinguish between its different levels, and specify the relationship between them. What I will *not* do is to offer an analysis of a historically or geographically particular variant of the capitalist mode of production; I will, rather, be concerned with what Marx referred to as the 'core structure' or the 'ideal average' of the capitalist mode of production – that is, the logics, structures, and dynamics that constitute the *essence* of capitalism, across its historical and geographical variations.[11]

The Economy: A System of Domination

One of the reasons why Marx's critique of political economy is an indispensable starting point for developing a theory of the economic power of capital is that it firmly rejects *economistic* conceptions of the economy – that is, the idea that the economy is an ontologically separate sphere of society governed by its own distinctive 'economic' logic or rationality. For Marx, 'the economy' is *social* through and through; he 'treats the economy itself not as a network of disembodied forces but, like the political sphere, as a set of social relations', as Ellen Meiksins Wood puts it.[12] This anti-economism sets Marx radically apart from bourgeois economics and is

---

11   M: 376, 898. In the English edition of *Marx's Economic Manuscript of 1864–1865*, the German *Kernstruktur* is translated as 'basic inner structure'.

12   Ellen Meiksins Wood, *Democracy against Capitalism: Renewing Historical Materialism* (London: Verso, 2016), 21ff.

an essential precondition of a theory of the economic power of capital. Marx's critique of political economy is not an alternative or a critical political economy, but rather a critique of the entire theoretical (or ideological) field of political economy.[13] Whereas economists are engaged in the business of transforming social relations into abstract, quantifiable units which can then be inserted as variables into idealised models, Marx's critical theory does the opposite: it unravels the social relations hidden in economic categories.[14] Those social relations are *relations of domination*. Power relations are not something which is somehow superimposed on 'the economy', as in Althusser's theory of ideology, where the reproduction of property relations in the economic base occurs outside of this base. The characteristic thing about the power of capital is precisely that it has an ability to exercise itself *through* economic processes; or, put differently, that the organisation of social reproduction on the basis of capital itself gives rise to a set of powerful mechanisms which tend to reproduce the relations of production. From this anti-economistic perspective, it thus becomes possible to view the capitalist economy as a *system of power*.[15] This is why it is so terribly misguided to accuse Marx of economism; it was precisely the resolute rejection of the notion of a transhistorical 'economic' logic that allowed Marx to see and criticise the mute compulsion of capital.

As an academic discipline, economics is premised on 'the failure to recognize power relationships in society', as Robert Chernomas and Ian Hudson put it.[16] Its exponents depict the capitalist economy as the result of a set of voluntary agreements between free and equal individuals, that is, as a sphere in which domination is excluded a priori. The economy is, in other words, defined by the *absence* of power from the very outset. For economists, the expression 'the free market' is a pleonasm, whereas for

---

13   Michael Heinrich, *Die Wissenschaft vom Wert: Die Marxsche Kritik der politischen Ökonomie zwischen wissenschaftlicher Revolution und klassischer Tradition* (Münster: Westfälisches Dampfboot, 1999), pts. 1, 2; Michael Heinrich, *An Introduction to the Three Volumes of Karl Marx's Capital*, trans. Alex Locascio (New York: Monthly Review Press, 2012), 32ff.

14   Werner Bonefeld, *Critical Theory and the Critique of Political Economy* (London: Bloomsbury, 2014).

15   Giulio Palermo, 'The Ontology of Economic Power in Capitalism: Mainstream Economics and Marx', *Cambridge Journal of Economics* 31, no. 4 (2007).

16   Robert Chernomas and Ian Hudson, *The Profit Doctrine: Economists of the Neoliberal Era* (London: Pluto Press, 2017), 7.

Marx, it is a contradiction in terms. This disappearance of power is the outcome of a twofold intellectual operation.

First, the *market* is presented as the determining moment of the economic totality; what is actually a part of the economy is abstracted from the totality and made to represent the whole. This primacy of exchange was already discernible in classical political economy, but it only really came to the fore with the so-called marginal revolution in the 1870s.[17] In neoclassical economics, market exchange is presented as 'the central organizing principle of capitalist society', as Anwar Shaikh puts it.[18] In some variants of modern economics, most notably in the work of Gary Becker, the voluntary exchange of goods between rational and utility-maximising agents on the market is elevated into a prism through which all social phenomena can be understood.[19]

The second intellectual operation underpinning the disappearance of power relationships in economics is the introduction of a set of assumptions and abstractions resulting in a conception of the market which excludes the very possibility of domination. The agents who engage in transactions on the market are assumed to be isolated, hyper-rational, utility-maximising individuals with infinite and infallible information. This rational individual is the Archimedean point of the social ontology of economics; a kind of sui generis substance which accounts for everything else. Assuming this transhistorical economic rationality, the need to explain the existence of capitalism conveniently disappears: the capitalist economy appears simply as what happens if human nature is allowed to unfold without impediments. This is why, as Wood notes, in 'most accounts of capitalism and its origin, there really *is* no origin'.[20] Economists (mis)understand the market as the place where these rational individuals meet and enter into contractual relations with each other. In a

---

17 Michael Perelman, *The Invisible Handcuffs of Capitalism: How Market Tyranny Stifles the Economy by Stunting Workers* (New York: Monthly Review Press, 2011), 11; Simon Clarke, *Marx, Marginalism, and Modern Sociology: From Adam Smith to Max Weber*, 2nd ed. (Basingstoke: Macmillan, 1991), chaps. 6, 7.

18 Anwar Shaikh, *Capitalism: Competition, Conflict, Crises* (New York: Oxford University Press, 2016), 120; see also Christoph Henning, *Philosophy after Marx: 100 Years of Misreadings and the Normative Turn in Political Philosophy*, trans. Max Henninger (Chicago: Haymarket, 2015), 123.

19 Chernomas and Hudson, *Profit Doctrine*, 78ff.

20 Ellen Meiksins Wood, *The Origin of Capitalism: A Longer View* (London: Verso, 2002), 4.

competitive market, there are no barriers to entry, and hence no monopolies, apart from the (regretfully necessary) so-called natural monopolies.
The general absence of monopolies means that a market agent is never
forced to do business with a *particular* agent, and this is why every act of
exchange can be regarded as voluntary. The individuals who show up on
the market do so as owners of commodities, and as such they are completely equal. These individuals' identities and roles outside of the market
relation are regarded as irrelevant for economic theory, and the question
of why they participate in the market to begin with is equally absent;
generally, economic theory assumes that people show up on the market
to sell their commodities after having carefully weighed the possibilities
open to them and concluded that this would be the most rational thing
to do, that is, the most efficient way to satisfy their needs. This is the kind
of reasoning that makes it possible for someone like Milton Friedman to
present 'the technique of the market place' as a way of 'co-ordinating the
economic activities of millions' by means of 'voluntary co-operation of
individuals' – or, as he puts it:

> Since the household always has the alternative of producing directly
> for itself, it need not enter into any exchange unless it benefits from it.
> Hence, no exchange will take place unless both parties do benefit from
> it. Co-operation is thereby achieved without coercion.[21]

This passage is noteworthy because it explicates what is usually hidden
as an implicit assumption in economics, namely that people have the
possibility of reproducing themselves outside of the market. This is the
assumption which makes the market appear as a sphere of freedom: not
only are agents free to choose *with whom* they want to exchange their
goods, but they are also free to choose whether they want to engage in
exchange *at all*. This is why the market is usually understood as an institution providing individuals with *opportunities*, a concept which Wood
notes is 'absolutely critical to the conventional understanding of the
capitalist system'.[22]

These assumptions and abstractions form the basis of the highly idealised mathematical models so characteristic of contemporary economics.

---

21   Milton Friedman, *Capitalism and Freedom* (Chicago: University of Chicago Press,
2002), 13.

22   Wood, *The Origin of Capitalism*, 6.

The transformation of economics into a discipline fixated on the development of formalised mathematical models has allowed it to present itself as what Chernomas and Hudson call 'a non-ideological discipline, aimed at providing positive, scientific answers to the policy questions'.[23] Most economists acknowledge that reality does not always fit their models; they admit that so-called market failures exist, that we have to introduce the possibility of imperfections in order to analyse the real economy, and that some goods or services can be difficult or even impossible to distribute through competitive markets. Market failures disturb the otherwise-perfect equality of market agents, thereby making it possible for some to dominate others – and it is only in this way, through the idea of *market failure*, that power is allowed into economic theory. On this view, power signals a deviation from the norm, a failure or imperfection of a system otherwise free from such disturbances: 'Power relations emerge only when contracts are not correctly executed,' as Giulio Palermo sums up in his critique of economics.[24]

The Economy in Social Theory

While the effort to make relations of domination in the economy disappear achieves its most glaring expression in mainstream economics, it is also widespread elsewhere in the social sciences. Mainstream political science is dominated by a state-centric notion of power and generally leaves the study of the economy to economics, thereby implicitly accepting its depoliticisation of the economy. Michel Foucault's famous diagnosis, that in the field of 'political thought and analysis, we still have not cut off the head of the king', thus remains as relevant as ever.[25] Foucault is himself, however, a representative of another way of avoiding the question of economic power which has been popular among social theorists since the 1980s: the use of a sloppy critique of Marxism as an excuse for not dealing properly with the economy. Like so many before as well as

---

23   Chernomas and Hudson, *The Profit Doctrine*, 19; see also Luc Boltanski and Eve Chiapello, *The New Spirit of Capitalism*, trans. Gregory Elliott (London: Verso, 2018), 12ff.

24   Giulio Palermo, 'The Economic Debate on Power: A Marxist Critique', *Journal of Economic Methodology* 21, no. 2 (2014), 188.

25   Michel Foucault, *The History of Sexuality*, vol. 1, *The Will to Knowledge*, trans. Robert Hurley (London: Penguin, 1998), 88f.

after him, Foucault often draws a very dubious distinction between 'the economic' and 'the social', claiming – against what he perceives as Marxist economism – that 'while the human subject is placed in relations of production and of signification, he is equally placed in power relations'; as if relations of production are not power relations.[26]

Foucault shares this view of Marxism with other influential thinkers such as Pierre Bourdieu, Anthony Giddens, Bruno Latour, Jürgen Habermas, Ulrich Beck, Niklas Luhmann, Axel Honneth, Ernesto Laclau, and Chantal Mouffe.[27] One could even claim that the dominant trends in social theory over the past four decades can be seen as a reaction to what was perceived as Marxist economism. The assumption shared by these scholars and traditions is that Marxism takes 'the economy', understood as a distinct social sphere with a distinct technical or economic rationality, to be the determining moment of the social totality, thereby reducing the multifaceted nature of the social to this one factor. Bourdieu reacted to this by developing his theory of forms of capital, according to which *cultural* and *social* capital cannot be reduced to *economic* capital.[28] Habermas abandoned Marx's critique of political economy in favour of a Kantian-pragmatist theory of communication.[29] Laclau and Mouffe's post-Marxist theory of discourse broke with the economism of 'classical Marxism' by rejecting 'the distinction between discursive and non-discursive practices' and insisting 'that every object is constituted as an object of discourse', a claim that led straight into idealist constructionism.[30] Broadly speaking,

---

26   Michel Foucault, 'The Subject and Power', in *Power: The Essential Works of Michel Foucault 1954–1984*, vol. 3, ed. James D. Faubion (London: Penguin, 2002), 327; see Nicos Poulantzas, *State, Power, Socialism*, trans. Patrick Camille (London: Verso, 2014), 36, 68f.

27   For Marxist criticisms of Bourdieu, Giddens, Latour, Habermas, Luhmann, Honneth, and Laclau and Mouffe, see Alex Callinicos, *Making History: Agency, Structure, and Change in Social Theory*, 2nd ed. (Leiden: Brill, 2004); Mathieu Hikaru Desan, 'Bourdieu, Marx, and Capital: A Critique of the Extension Model', *Sociological Theory* 31, no. 4 (2013): 318–42; Henning, *Philosophy after Marx*; Andreas Malm, *The Progress of This Storm: Nature and Society in a Warming World* (London: Verso, 2018); Moishe Postone, *Time, Labor, and Social Domination: A Reinterpretation of Marx's Critical Theory* (Cambridge: Cambridge University Press, 2003); Helmut Reichelt, *Neue Marx-Lektüre: Zur Kritik sozialwissenschaftlicher Logik* (Freiburg: ça ira, 2013); Ellen Meiksins Wood, *The Retreat from Class: The New 'True' Socialism* (London: Verso, 1999).

28   Desan, 'Bourdieu, Marx, and Capital'.

29   Postone, *Time, Labor, and Social Domination*, chap. 6.

30   Ernesto Laclau and Chantal Mouffe, *Hegemony and Socialist Strategy: Towards a Radical Democratic Politics*, 2nd ed. (London: Verso, 2014), 107.

what has been called the cultural turn of social theory following the crisis of Marxism in the 1970s resulted in a tendency to exclude the economy from discussions about power, or to approach the economy through a post-structuralist lens, in which the materiality of social reproduction is dissolved in an economy of signifiers.

This familiar critique of Marxist economism was, of course, not completely unfounded; large parts of the classical Marxist tradition did indeed rely on a deeply economistic notion of the economy as the determining factor of the social totality, governed by a transhistorical tendency for the productive forces to develop. And many of those Marxists who did reject the orthodox position generally devoted their attention to other things than developing a non-economistic theory of the economy as a set of social relations of domination. The problem with most of these post-, non-, and anti-Marxist critics of Marxist economism, however, is that they fail to distinguish between Marx and Marxism, and that they treat the latter as a homogeneous intellectual tradition. As I will show in this book, Marx's critique of political economy continues to be the best resource for a critical demolition of bourgeois as well as Marxist economism.

Marx's Unfinished Critique

The aim of this study is to understand how capitalism works, or, more precisely, how capital manages to hold on to its status as the social logic everyone has to obey in order to live. In order to do so, I have turned to Marx's writings – primarily those concerned with the critique of political economy, such as the *Grundrisse* (1857–58), *A Contribution to the Critique of Political Economy* (1859), the *1861–63 Manuscripts* (1861–63), the first volume of *Capital* (1867–72), and the manuscripts for the second (1868–77) and third books (1864–65) of *Capital*.[31] As the following chapters will show, Marx's analysis of the capitalist mode of production provides an indispensable basis for developing a theory of the economic power of capital. At this point, however, a couple of clarifications are in order regarding my use of Marx's writings.

---

31   Marx intended books two and three of *Capital* – what Engels published as the second and third *volume* – to be published together in one volume, which would make up volume two. The third volume was supposed to consist of book four, which would contain a history of economic theory.

Marx's writings contain all of the basic elements for a theory of the economic power of capital, but they do not contain such a theory in anything like a finished form. This is partly because Marx had a different aim: the critique of political economy was intended as an analysis of 'the economic law of motion of modern society', and not the more specific project of developing a theory of the mute compulsion of economic relations.[32] But there is also another reason why we do not find such a theory in Marx's writings, which is that he left the critique of political economy unfinished – in more than one sense. First, he only managed to publish one of the four books which were supposed to make up *Capital* (not to mention his plan to add studies of the state, the world market, etc.). He left behind thousands and thousands of manuscript pages, some of which remain unpublished to this day. Second, his enormous research project is also unfinished in the sense that it contains unresolved theoretical problems.[33] Until the very end of his life, Marx's thinking developed constantly, but this development was not always consistent.

The unfinished character of most of Marx's writings and his frequently changing views on various matters means that the insights relevant for the construction of a theory of the economic power of capital are scattered over a large number of manuscripts, entwined not only with discussions and treatments of other theoretical issues or concrete, empirical analyses, but also with patterns of thought belonging to different and sometimes incompatible stages of the development of Marx's theories. In order to extract and make use of Marx's insights, it is therefore necessary to locate them, excavate them, reconstruct their logical interrelations, and critically examine and systematise them. That project – the condition of which has been considerably improved by the ongoing publication of a scholarly edition of Marx's writings in the *Marx-Engels Gesamtausgabe* (MEGA2) – constitutes a large part of this book.

This book is not a Marxological treatise; its ultimate aim is to understand *capitalism*, not Marx. Sometimes, however, the former presupposes the latter. For this reason, I do occasionally engage in discussions of Marx's intellectual development and other topics that might seem to be merely Marxological intricacies – but only where they ultimately help us understand capitalism.

---

32   C1: 92.
33   See Heinrich, *Die Wissenschaft vom Wert.*

The Essence of Capitalism

As I have already mentioned, my aim in this book is not to produce an analysis of a particular historical or geographical variant of the capitalist mode of production. Rather, I am concerned with the *essence* of the capitalist mode of production. So, what does it mean to construct a theory of the economic power of capital on this level of abstraction? The easiest way to explain this is to briefly consider what takes place in the first volume of *Capital*. Here, Marx proceeds from a historical fact: namely that in capitalist societies, the products of labour generally take on the form of commodities. This is a simple empirical finding which singles out a characteristic trait of the capitalist mode of production that immediately sets it apart from non-capitalist modes of production, where only a marginal share of the products of labour is produced for exchange. Marx then goes on to ask: What must be the case if the commodity is the general social form of the products of labour? What kind of social relations must be in place in order for this to be possible? From this starting point – an *essential* determination of capitalist society – he then derives the fundamental concepts and structure of his analysis, such as the distinctions between exchange value and use value, exchange value and value, concrete and abstract labour, as well as the necessity of money and its functions, the concept of capital, the theory of surplus value and exploitation, the class relation underlying all of this, and so on. This series of dialectical derivations is what Marx calls 'the method of rising from the abstract to concrete'.[34] Contrary to popular belief, this 'rising' is not simply a matter of gradually approaching the empirically observable reality.[35] It refers, rather, to a gradual increase in conceptual complexity as a result of the introduction of more and more concepts and the specification of their interrelations; by being situated within a more and more elaborate theoretical structure, the methodological abstraction of the earlier stages of the theoretical progression is gradually sublated.

Marx essentially derives all of the basic concepts of his critique of political economy from the assumption of generalised commodity exchange. What many commentators fail to notice is that Marx also

---

34   G: 101.

35   Jacques Bidet, *Exploring Marx's Capital: Philosophical, Economic, and Political Dimensions*, trans. David Fernbach (Leiden: Brill, 2007), 174; Alex Callinicos, *Deciphering Capital: Marx's Capital and Its Destiny* (London: Bookmarks, 2014), 132.

relies on certain socio-ontological presuppositions when dialectically constructing his system. Consider, for example, the role of the 'natural' length of the working day (i.e., the fact that humans need to sleep) or the 'natural' basis of surplus value (i.e., the human ability to produce more than what is necessary for the reproduction of the individual). These are two quite significant facts, and both play an important role in the conceptual progression of *Capital*. However, neither of them can be derived from the historically specific structures of capitalist society. They are, rather, characteristics of human societies as such, independently of their historical variations; they form a part of the ontology of the social (which also includes facts of nature, as Marx's examples make clear). This demonstrates that there are two independent theoretical presuppositions of Marx's analysis of the core structure of capitalism: on the one hand, socio-ontological presuppositions concerning what must be the case in *any* form of society, and, on the other hand, a historical fact, namely the generalisation of the commodity form. The dialectical reconstruction of the essential structures and dynamics of the capitalist mode of production proceeds, then, from certain assumptions about the *transhistorical* features of human societies, on the one hand, and a *historically specific* fact about an *essential feature* of the capitalist mode of production, on the other. From these two kinds of presuppositions, Marx builds the fundamental concepts of his theory.

This does not mean, however, that Marx's critique of political economy can be reduced to a pure analysis of economic form-determinations, as some scholars tend to think.[36] The critique of political economy *is* an analysis of the core structure of capitalism by means of a dialectical analysis of social forms, but it is *also* an analysis of the history of capitalism as well as, more specifically, nineteenth-century British capitalism. The empirical and historical parts of *Capital* and related manuscripts are not simply illustrations of concepts. Not only do they often contain substantial historical and empirical analyses in their own right, but at certain points, they also enter into conceptual development, as Marx's example of the natural length of the working day demonstrates.[37] The 'dialectical form of

---

36   See, for instance, Christopher Arthur, *The New Dialectic and Marx's Capital* (Leiden: Brill, 2004); Projektgruppe zur Kritik der Politischen Ökonomie, *Zur Logik des Kapitals* (Hamburg: VSA, 1973); Helmut Reichelt, *Zur logischen Struktur des Kapitalbegriffs bei Karl Marx* (Frankfurt am Main: Europäische Verlagsanstalt, 1973).

37   One of the indicators of Marx's commitment to the collection, analysis, and presentation of empirical material is the fact that he updated the data used in the first volume

presentation is right', Marx notes, 'only when it knows its limits'.[38] What prevents the empirical and historical parts of Marx's critique from collapsing into a chaotic collection of data, however, is precisely that they are presented within a systematic theoretical structure constructed by means of a dialectical development of concepts; it is this method which 'indicates the points where historical considerations must enter'.[39]

In my analysis of the economic power of capital, I will attempt to follow Marx's procedure. Rather than beginning with the commodity form, however, I will build on Marx's analysis and proceed from what I take to be the simplest definition of capitalism: *a society in which social reproduction is governed by the logic of capital to a significant degree*. This is a rather vague definition; what exactly is 'a significant degree'? However, if we wish to study historical social formations, it is neither possible nor desirable to avoid such vagueness. There are no absolute historical boundaries between pre-capitalist societies and capitalism; the question of whether a society is capitalist or not is always a question of more or less. Yet, this does not pose a problem for my analysis, because I am not concerned with the *historical emergence* of capitalism. In other words, my analysis *presupposes* that social reproduction is governed by the logic of capital to a significant degree. I will thus attempt to construct a theory which discloses the forms of power implied by the essential determinations of the capitalist mode of production. In contrast to Marx's procedure in *Capital*, I make no attempts to provide substantial empirical or historical studies. Although I will occasionally integrate empirical and historical data and studies into my presentation, these will have the status of examples and illustrations rather than exhaustive analyses.

Abstractions

The claim that it is possible to *analytically* isolate and identify the core structures that make capitalist societies capitalist does not imply the claim that there exists such a thing as a logic of capital which operates independently of its particular social context. Capitalism in its ideal

---

of *Capital* for the second edition. For a good account of Marx's method, see Heinrich, *Die Wissenschaft vom Wert*, chap. 5.

   38   29: 505.

   39   G: 460.

average is a theoretical abstraction. There is nothing mysterious about this; on the contrary, the construction of such abstractions is a completely normal analytical procedure. In 'the analysis of economic forms neither microscopes nor chemical reagents are of assistance', as Marx explains in the preface to *Capital*: 'the power of abstraction must replace both'.[40] Curiously, a number of critics of this kind of analysis seem to miss this simple point. For example, when Timothy Mitchell rejects 'the view that, regardless of local variations, at some level capitalism always does the same thing, or has the same effect', we should ask him a simple question: what makes it possible to categorise different societies as 'variants' of capitalism?[41] This obviously presupposes an abstract notion of 'capitalism'. And of course, capitalism always does the same thing: it valorises value by exploiting labour – which is why we call it capitalism.

Since my aim is to say something about the economic power of capital, I will largely ignore the role played by ideology as well as violence in the reproduction of capitalist relations of production. To prevent any misunderstanding here, I want to emphasise that this does not mean that I consider these forms of power to be secondary or unimportant. On the contrary: I regard both of them as necessary for the existence of capitalism. Marxism has a long tradition of theories of ideology – from Wilhelm Reich through Antonio Gramsci and Louis Althusser to Slavoj Žižek – which has convincingly demonstrated that capitalism would never be able to exist without shaping the way in which we think. The same is true of violence. Indeed, capitalism not only came into the world in a sea of violence; at all stages of its historical development, physical coercion has been necessary in order to enforce capital's diktat.[42] The organised violence of the state was not only necessary for the historical creation of capitalism but also continues to play a crucial role in its reproduction.

---

40   C1: 90.

41   Timothy Mitchell, *Carbon Democracy: Political Power in the Age of Oil* (London: Verso, 2013), 213.

42   See Sven Beckert, *Empire of Cotton: A New History of Global Capitalism* (London: Penguin, 2015); Heide Gerstenberger, 'The Political Economy of Capitalist Labor', *Viewpoint Magazine*, 2014, viewpointmag.com; Heide Gerstenberger, *Markt und Gewalt: Die Funktionsweise des historischen Kapitalismus* (Münster: Westfälisches Dampfboot, 2018); Heide Gerstenberger, 'Über direkte Gewalt in kapitalistischen Arbeitverhältnissen – und über Geschichtsphilosophie: Zur analytischen Konzeption von Gewalt im Kapitalismus', *PROKLA: Zeitschrift für kritische Sozialwissenschaft* 48, no. 192 (2018), 489–500; David McNally, *Blood and Money: War, Slavery, Finance, and Empire* (Chicago: Haymarket, 2020).

Without a social institution endowed with 'the privilege and will to force the totality', as Marx puts it, it is not possible to organise social reproduction on a capitalist basis.[43] This insight received a particularly acute and theoretically sophisticated articulation in the so-called state derivation debate of the 1970s, which generated a lot of important studies into the nature of the capitalist state and the ways in which the immanent contradictions of capitalist production make certain state functions necessary.[44] But violence also helps to reproduce capitalism in other ways and on other levels of the social totality. For example, feminist scholars have pointed out that sexual violence is one of the mechanisms whereby women are relegated to the sphere of reproductive labour.[45]

While it is certainly true that a capitalist system requires a state with a capacity to employ violence in order to enforce property rights, manage class relations, build infrastructure, and so on, it is also true that the state is not the primary agent in the organisation of social reproduction in capitalism. The characteristic thing about the separation between 'the political' and 'the economic' in capitalism is – as Wood eloquently puts it – that it implies 'a complete separation of private appropriation from public duties' and hence 'the development of a new sphere of power devoted completely to private rather than social purposes'.[46] In this new sphere of power, social life is subjected to the logic of valorisation primarily through mute compulsion. The choice to focus on the *economic* power of capital means that the present study will aim only at a partial understanding of the power of capital. Indeed, in order to construct a full theory of the power of capital, it would be necessary to integrate the theory of the economic power of capital with theories of ideology and violence.[47]

---

43   G: 531.

44   See Ingo Elbe, *Marx im Westen: Die neue Marx-lektüre in der Bundesrepublik seit 1965* (Berlin: Akademie Verlag, 2008), pt. 2; John Holloway and Sol Picciotto, eds., *State and Capital: A Marxist Debate* (London: Edward Arnold, 1978).

45   Maria Mies, *Patriarchy and Accumulation on a World Scale: Women in the International Division of Labour* (London: Zed Books, 1984); P. Valentine, 'The Gender Distinction in Communization Theory', *Lies: A Journal of Materialist Feminism* 1 (2012): 141–208.

46   Wood, *Democracy against Capitalism*, 31.

47   Althusserians might insist here that *ideology is a material practice*, and that my distinction between ideological and economic power is false, since both belong in the category of ideology. See Althusser, *On the Reproduction of Capitalism*, 258ff. For convincing criticisms of such an overblown and analytically useless extension of the concept of ideology among certain Althusserians, see Michèle Barrett, *Women's Oppression Today:*

My claim is not, then, that capitalism only relies on the mute compulsion of capital, or that there is a historically necessary tendency for other forms of power to gradually disappear. The theory developed in this book is rather intended to enable us to see how the power of capital is operative even when ideological and coercive domination is absent.

Overview

This book is divided into three parts, the first of which is about *conditions* in a twofold sense: on the one hand, the conceptual conditions of the theory presented in the rest of the book; and on the other, the real conditions of the economic power of capital. In the first chapter, I examine Marx's use of concepts such as power and domination and discuss the concepts of power and capital in order to specify what 'the power of capital' means. In chapter two, I provide a critical survey of the ways in which Marxist thinkers have grappled with the question of power. In the rest of part one (chapters three to five), I move on to outline the social ontology of economic power, that is, a theory of why such a thing as economic power is even possible in the first place. This involves a discussion of the role played by the notion of human nature in Marx's theories as well as an examination of Marx's frequently ignored yet highly original thoughts on the human body and the specifically human metabolism with the rest of nature.

Part two examines one of the two main sources of the economic power of capital: the relations of production. Following Robert Brenner, I distinguish between two fundamental sets of social relations, the unity of which constitutes the capitalist relations of production: on the one hand, a particular set of horizontal relations among units of production as well as among immediate producers; and, on the other hand, a particular set of vertical (class) relations between the immediate producers and those who control the conditions of social reproduction. Chapter six examines the vertical relations – that is, the form of class domination – presupposed by capitalist production, concluding with a discussion of the concept of biopolitics. This discussion of class occasions an engagement with the

The Marxist/Feminist Encounter (London: Verso, 2014), 89f; Terry Eagleton, *Ideology: An Introduction* (London: Verso, 1996), 149.

relationship between the logic of capital and the production of social differences and hierarchies based on gender and racialisation, which is the subject of chapter seven. In chapters eight and nine, I go on to examine the forms of power springing from the horizontal relations of production, including the very important yet frequently ignored question of the precise relationship between these and the vertical class relations examined in chapter six. The central concepts here are value and competition, which I argue should be understood as mechanisms of domination that subjects *everyone*, regardless of their class position, to the logic of capital.

The social relations examined in part two give rise to certain *dynamics* which are simultaneously a result and a source of the economic power of capital. Put differently: the economic power of capital turns out to be partly *the result of its own exercise*. These dynamics – the second main source of the economic power of capital – are the subject of part three.

In chapter ten, I examine capital's remoulding of the production process within the workplace. Setting off from a discussion of the metamorphosis of the abstract compulsion of the market into the despotic authority of the capitalist, I discuss the ways in which the real subsumption of labour enhances the power of capital by means of deskilling, technologies, divisions of labour, and so on. In chapter eleven, I then proceed to examine how the same dynamic is visible in capital's relation to nature. The greater part of this chapter is devoted to an analysis of a concrete example of the mute compulsion of capital, namely the real subsumption of agriculture in the twentieth and twenty-first centuries. In chapter twelve, I argue that the concept of real subsumption can also be used to understand the so-called logistics revolution in the period from the 1970s onwards, which is the latest incarnation of capital's inherent drive to 'annihilate space through time', as Marx puts it. Finally, chapter thirteen takes up the question of surplus populations and crises, arguing that capital's tendency to eject people from its circuits and regularly undermine itself should be regarded as mechanisms by means of which the logic of valorisation is imposed on social life.

These chapters provide a conceptual apparatus that allows us to understand the mute compulsion of capital: to locate its sources, identify its mechanisms, explain its forms, distinguish between its different levels, and determine the exact relation between them.

PART I
Conditions

1

Conceptualising Power and Capital

The two most fundamental concepts of the theory presented in these pages are *power* and *capital*. I thus begin with an examination and clarification of each. As a preliminary step, let us consider the terminology employed by Marx in his analyses of power and domination.

The most important concepts here are *Macht* (power) and *Herrschaft* (domination or rule). In addition to this, we also find a cluster of related terms such as *Subsumtion* (subsumption), *Disziplin* (discipline), *Kommando* (command), *Gewalt* (violence or power), *Despotismus* (despotism), *Zwang* (compulsion), *Autokratie* (autocracy), *Unterjochung* (subjugation), *Direktion* (directing or conducting), *Leitung* (management), *Aufsicht* (supervision or surveillance), *Autorität* (authority), *Kontrolle* (control), *Oberbefehl* (leadership), *Abhängigkeit* (dependency), and *Beaufsichtigung* (surveillance).

Macht, Herrschaft, Gewalt

Although it is possible to discern a pattern in Marx's use of these terms, his terminology is neither systematic nor unequivocal. *Macht*, or power, has several meanings in Marx's writings. He talks about 'the power of' things such as capital, money, the relation of exchange, the general equivalent, the state, machinery, and dead labour, to name a few examples. He frequently uses the expression 'alien power' to refer to social relations which confront human beings as something external. Generally speaking, Marx employs the concept of power in a rather broad sense, referring to the influence of social forms on the life of society, classes, and individuals. For example, he argues that with 'the extension of commodity circulation, the power of money [*die Macht des Geldes*] increases'.[1] When he uses the expression 'the power of capital', the concept of power similarly has a broad meaning, something like the degree to which the logic of capital shapes social life.

The closest we come to a definition of the power of capital in Marx's writings is found in the *1861–63 Manuscripts*: 'The power of capital vis-à-vis labour grows, or, and this is the same thing, the worker's chance of appropriating the conditions of labour is lessened.'[2] This definition, if we can call it that, has several advantages. First, it highlights the fact that the power of capital is always a form of domination, since it relies – as I will explain in detail in chapter six – on keeping apart the capacity to work and the conditions of the actualisation of this capacity. Second, it also highlights the basic thrust of Marx's critique of capitalism: it deprives people of control over their lives. A third advantage of this definition is that it poses the question of the power of capital in terms of degrees rather than an either–or. In part three, we will see how important this is for avoiding the tendency in Marxist theory to reduce the power of capital to a question of *property*, that is, a question only of whether or not capitalists own and control the means of production.

In the end, however, the definition of the power of capital as the lessening of the worker's chance of appropriating the conditions of labour is inadequate – for three reasons. First, it fails to reflect the fact that it is not only *workers*, in the narrow sense of wage labourers, that are subjected to the power of capital (more on this in chapter six). Second, it also fails to reflect that the power of capital includes a set of mechanisms to which *everyone, including the capitalists*, are subjected – something I will discuss in detail in chapters eight and nine. Finally, this definition is not representative of Marx's use of the expression 'the power of capital', as he often uses it in a sense which cannot be reduced to a question of who owns or controls the conditions of labour. In short: there is more to the power of capital than its ability to prevent workers from appropriating the conditions of social reproduction.

---

1   C1: 229.
2   33: 151.

One of the significant things to notice about Marx's use of the concept of power is that he attributes the exercise of it not only to classes and individuals but also to things and social forms such as value, money, capital, and machinery. To be sure, he does sometimes use the concept to refer to the ability of individuals to control the actions of other individuals, as when he explains that 'the power which each individual exercises over the activity of others or over social wealth exists in him as the owner of *exchange values*, of *money*'.[3] As this quote makes clear, however, Marx always considers the power of individuals as something bestowed upon them by their social context. Indeed, one of the important features of a monetised economy is precisely that 'social power becomes the private power of private persons', as Marx aptly puts it in *Capital*.[4]

Two other meanings of the concept of power should be mentioned here. In a few places, Marx employs the concept in the broad sense of an *ability* or a *potential*, as when he speaks of 'the social powers of labour [*der gesellschaftlichen Mächte der Arbeit*]', or the power of money to act as exchange value.[5] Finally, he also uses the concept to refer to powerful actors or institutions, such as 'the great powers of Europe'.[6] This is also the meaning at play when he refers to capital as 'the all-dominating economic power of bourgeois society'.[7]

Herrschaft – usually translated as 'domination' or 'rule' but sometimes also as 'predominance' or 'dominion' – is, together with power, the concept used most frequently by Marx to refer to the way in which capital shapes social life. Accordingly, he often employs the expression 'the rule of capital' (*der Herrschaft des Kapitals*) in the general sense of the influence of capital on society.[8] He describes the genesis of capitalism as the establishment of the 'general domination of capital over the countryside', and he often describes capital as 'domination of objectified labour over living labour'.[9] Marx also speaks of the domination of nature by humans, of the countryside by towns; the dominion of the bourgeoisie; the rule of dead labour, free competition, things, and products; and conditions of labour; the twelve-hour bill; and the British rule in East India. 'Domination' or 'rule'

---

3   G: 157.
4   C1: 230; see also G: 157.
5   G: 832, 30: 18.
6   12: 21.
7   G: 107.
8   G: 651.
9   G: 279, 346.

is often used synonymously with 'power', as when Marx describes how people rebel against 'the power which a physical matter, a thing, acquires with respect to men, against the domination of the accursed metal'– or when he refers to capital first as *power* over labour and then, on the very same page, as *domination* of labour.[10] Domination is also the concept on which Marx primarily relies to describe social relations of production in pre-capitalist societies, usually in combination with the adjectives 'immediate', 'personal', and 'direct', and in connection with the expression 'relations of dominance and servitude' (*Herrschafts- und Knechtschaftsver-hältnissen*).[11] The capitalist class is often described as 'the ruling class' (*die herrschende Klasse*), and Marx also uses the concept of *Herrschaft* when referring not only to the general class structure of capitalist society, but also to the more specific relation between the worker and the capitalist within the workplace, as well as the relation between colonial powers and colonised peoples.

When he wants to refer to the general subsumption of social life under capital, Marx tends to speak of 'power' or 'domination', but occasionally he also resorts to terms such as 'dependency' (*Abhängigkeit*) upon, 'sub-jugation' (*Unterjochung*) to, or 'compulsion' (*Zwang*) of capital.

Gewalt means 'violence' or 'power', depending on the context. In Marx's writings as well as in everyday language, it is often related to the state. Marx thus speaks of 'legislative power' (*gesetzgebende Gewalt*) the 'various powers' of the state, the 'division of powers' (*Teilung der Gewalten*), and in *Capital* he describes the state (*die Staatsmacht*) as 'the concentrated and organized *Gewalt* of society'.[12] The concept of *Gewalt* is often employed in order to distinguish the economic power of capital from the forms of power upon which pre-capitalist relations of production rested. This is the case, for example, in the passage from *Capital* quoted in the intro-duction to this book, where the 'mute compulsion' of capital is contrasted to 'extra-economic, immediate violence [*Gewalt*]'.[13] Another example is from the *Grundrisse*, where Marx emphasises that in the sphere of circulation, people appropriate the products of other people 'not by vio-lence' (*nicht mit Gewalt*) but rather through mutual recognition of each

10   29: 487; 32: 494.
11   C1: 173.
12   1: 241; 3: 73; C1: 551, 915. *Teilung der Gewalten* is often mistakenly translated as 'the division of responsibility' in the Penguin edition of *Capital*.
13   C1: 899.

other as proprietors.[14] In the *Grundrisse*, we also read that 'under capital, the *association* of workers is not compelled [*erzwungen*] through direct physical violence [*Gewalt*], forced labour, statute labour, slave labour; it is compelled [*erzwungen*] by the fact that the conditions of production are alien property and are themselves present as *objective association*'.[15]

When dealing with the power of the capitalist within the workplace, Marx resorts to an array of concepts, many of which bear strong connotations with the military or the pre-capitalist forms of rule: *autocracy, subsumption, direction, management, command, discipline, authority, surveillance, supervision,* and *despotism.* I will discuss the meaning of this vocabulary in chapter ten, where I take a closer look at the power of capital as it appears in the workplace.

The Concept of Power

Marx's use of the concepts of power and capital – and particularly the expression 'the power of capital' – seems to contradict a premise shared by most theories of power, namely that power, as Steven Lukes puts it, 'presupposes human agency'.[16] Some Marxists argue that capital does in fact possess agency, but since their notion of agency (or subjectivity) is rather different from that of mainstream sociology and political theory, I will set this idea aside until later in this chapter. Mainstream theories of power rely on a social ontology in which the wills, wishes, thoughts, and intentions of individual human beings constitute the ultimate foundation of any social phenomenon. While they often acknowledge the existence of *collective* agency, such theories tend to understand the collective as a mere aggregate of individuals. Almost all definitions of power in sociology and political theory are phrased in terms of 'persons' or human 'individuals' or 'actors' and their wills, desires, and intentions.[17] A famous example is

---

14 G: 243.

15 G: 590; see also 769.

16 Steven Lukes, *Essays in Social Theory* (London: Macmillan, 1977), 6.

17 See, for example, Peter Bachrach and Morton S. Baratz, 'Two Faces of Power', *American Political Science Review* 56, no. 4 (1962): 947–52; Peter Bachrach and Morton S. Baratz, 'Decisions and Nondecisions: An Analytical Framework', *American Political Science Review* 57, no. 3 (1963): 632–42; Peter M. Blau, *Exchange and Power in Social Life* (Piscataway, NJ: Transaction Publishers, 1964), 15; Robert A. Dahl, 'The Concept of Power', *Behavioral Science* 2, no. 3 (1957): 201–15; Robert A. Dahl, *Who Governs?*

Max Weber's influential definition of power as 'the chance of a man or a number of men to realize their own will in a social action even against the resistance of others who are participating in the action'.[18] Most of these theories commit the idealist mistake of assuming that the subject's active, transformative relation to its environment – its 'agency' – resides in or springs from its intellectual capacities. By abstracting from the material, corporeal, and social embeddedness of these capacities, they end up with a conception of the human being similar to the kind of idealist humanism that Marx subjected to a scathing critique in 1845 (to which I shall return in chapter three).

The mainstream literature on the concept of power is plagued by at least five common problems. The first is the individualistic social ontology just mentioned. The second is a tendency to assume that power has a *dyadic* form, as Thomas E. Wartenberg puts it in his clear-sighted critique of mainstream theories of power. On such a 'dyadic' view, power 'is 'located'' within a dual structure consisting of a dominant agent and a subordinate agent over whom they wield power.[19] The problem with this conception – epitomised in the definition of power as a relationship between an *A* and a *B* – is that it ignores how 'the power dyad is itself *situated* in the context of other social relations through which it is actually constituted as a power relationship'.[20] If there is such a thing as a form of power the source of which is the capacity to control the *material conditions of social reproduction*, we can immediately see how a dyadic conception of power would make it invisible.[21]

Democracy and Power in an American City (New Haven, CT: Yale University Press, 1961); Jeffrey C. Isaac, *Power and Marxist Theory: A Realist View* (Ithaca, NY: Cornell University Press, 1987), 9; Steven Lukes, *Power: A Radical View*, 2nd ed. (New York: Palgrave Macmillan, 2004), 72, 76; Bertrand Russell, *Power: A New Social Analysis* (London: Allen and Unwin, 1975), 25; John Scott, *Power* (Cambridge: Polity Press, 2001), 1ff; Thomas E. Wartenberg, *The Forms of Power: From Domination to Transformation* (Philadelphia: Temple University Press, 1990), 65, 76; Max Weber, *Economy and Society: An Outline of Interpretive Sociology*, trans. Ephraim Fischoff et al. (Berkeley: University of California Press, 1978), 53, 926, 942; Dennis Hume Wrong, *Power: Its Forms, Bases, and Uses* (New Brunswick, NJ: Transaction Publishers, 2009), 2. See Poulantzas's critique of the 'inter-individual' conception of power: Nicos Poulantzas, *Political Power and Social Classes*, trans. Timothy O'Hagan (London: Verso, 1978), 106.

18   Weber, *Economy and Society*, 926.

19   Wartenberg, *The Forms of Power*, 141.

20   Ibid., 142; see also Richard Newbold Adams, *Energy and Structure: A Theory of Social Power* (Austin: University of Texas Press, 1975), 9ff.

21   See also the discussions about the concept of 'structural' power (in distinction to

The third problem in mainstream theories of power is the widespread assumption that power is 'something that is exercised in discrete interactions between social agents'.[22] This 'interventional model', as Wartenberg calls it, is usually the result of an empiricist methodology, according to which power can only be an observable, causal event.[23] Such an empiricism remains trapped in the dyadic model, failing to acknowledge that 'a particular type of social context can constitute a power relationship between two social agents'.[24]

The fourth problem is that most theories of power assume that the *identities* of the *A*s and *B*s involved in a power relationship are entirely unrelated to this relationship. Again, it is Wartenberg who puts his finger on it: 'Power is conceptualized as something that exists only within specific events that take place between two *independently constituted* agents'.[25] The possibility that the very *A*-ness of *A* might be, at least partly, the result of a power relationship is precluded from the beginning; as will become clear in chapter six, this is a deeply inadequate assumption.

The fifth problem has to do with the *locus* of power. Mainstream theories of power tend to accept the familiar division of society into the state, the economy, and the social, and this leaves a clear mark on their conceptions of power. Political scientists generally take the state to be the paradigmatic locus of power, while the more sociologically orientated scholars tend to form their understanding of power on the model of intersubjective relations or non-economic social action. In either case, the result is that the economy as a sphere of power is occluded.

It is not uncommon to come across references to Marx in debates on power in social sciences. Some scholars are rather dismissive; Talcott

---

'relational' power) in the fields of international political economy and international relations: Michael Barnett and Raymond Duvall, 'Power in International Politics', *International Organization* 59, no. 1 (2005), 39–75; Pepper D. Culpepper, 'Structural Power and Political Science in the Post-Crisis Era', *Business and Politics* 17, no. 3 (2015), 391–409; Pepper D. Culpepper and Raphael Reinke, 'Structural Power and Bank Bailouts in the United Kingdom and the United States', *Politics and Society* 42, no. 4 (2014), 427–54; Jerome Roos, *Why Not Default? The Political Economy of Sovereign Debt* (Princeton: Princeton University Press, 2019), 58; Susan Strange, *States and Markets*, 2nd ed. (London: Continuum, 2004), 24f.

22   Wartenberg, *The Forms of Power*, 65.

23   Ibid., 66; Isaac, *Power and Marxist Theory*, chap. 1.

24   Wartenberg, *The Forms of Power*, 49; see also Isaac, *Power and Marxist Theory*, 33–40; Derek Layder, 'Power, Structure, and Agency', *Journal for the Theory of Social Behaviour* 15, no. 2 (1985), 131–49.

25   Wartenberg, *The Forms of Power*, 69. Emphasis added.

Parsons, for example, regards Marx's critique of capitalism as outdated, empiricist political economy.[26] Others are more sympathetic. Most of them share two misunderstandings about Marx's conception of power. First, they project an economistic conception of the economy onto Marx. The most well-known example is Weber's rejection of Marx's allegedly economic reductionism.[27] Another example is Richard W. Miller's self-professed Marxist analysis of power, which begins from the assumption that 'power' has to do with 'politics' – an assumption which then leads Miller to look for Marx's understanding of power in the so-called political writings, while completely ignoring the critique of political economy.[28] The second misunderstanding in this literature is the reduction of Marx's analysis of relations of power and domination in capitalism to a question of *class domination*. Lukes claims that for Marxists, power is 'at root, class power'.[29] Wartenberg likewise reduces 'Marx's view of domination' to a question of class domination, as do Miller and Dennis Wrong.[30] Although Jeffrey C. Isaac's attempt to construct a Marxist theory of power contains many valuable insights, he ultimately commits the same mistake. According to him, 'the primary object of explanation' for a Marxist theory of power is 'class relations under capitalism'; in accordance with this, he argues that the most important concepts of such a theory are 'class, class domination, class struggle, capitalist state'.[31] The same is true of the work of Nicos Poulantzas, Bob Jessop, and other Marxist attempts to intervene in the debates about the concept of power.[32] These authors reduce Marx's analysis of power in

---

26   Talcott Parsons, 'Power and the Social System', in Lukes, *Power*, 108ff, 489.

27   See also Wrong, *Power*, 90. Weber's straw man critique is repeated in Michael Mann, *The Sources of Social Power*, vol. 1, *A History of Power from the Beginning to A.D. 1760* (Cambridge: Cambridge University Press, 1997), 12, 24; see also Alex Callinicos, *Making History: Agency, Structure, and Change in Social Theory*, 2nd ed. (Leiden: Brill, 2004), xxxix. For critiques of Weber, see Simon Clarke, *Marx, Marginalism and Modern Sociology: From Adam Smith to Max Weber*, 2nd ed. (Basingstoke: Macmillan, 1991), chap. 8; Ellen Meiksins Wood, *Democracy against Capitalism: Renewing Historical Materialism* (London: Verso, 2016), chap. 5.

28   Richard W. Miller, *Analyzing Marx: Morality, Power, and History* (Princeton: Princeton University Press, 1984), chaps. 3, 4.

29   Parsons, 'Power and the Social System', 144.

30   Wartenberg, *The Forms of Power*, 120; Miller, *Analyzing Marx*; Wrong, *Power*, 90, 254.

31   Isaac, *Power and Marxist Theory*, 109f.

32   Poulantzas, *Political Power and Social Classes*, 99; Bob Jessop, 'Marxist Approaches to Power', in *The Wiley-Blackwell Companion to Political Sociology*, ed. Edwin Amenta, Kate Nash, and Alan Scott (Oxford: Blackwell, 2012).

capitalism to a question of the existence of a social elite with the ability to dominate workers in the workplace and influence the actions of the state, making no attempts to engage with Marx's analysis of how class structure is connected with the underlying logic of capital. What is worse, however, is that they ignore one of the most crucial aspects of Marx's analysis, namely that the power of capital includes mechanisms of domination which *transcend class*. These I will examine in chapters eight and nine.

Foucault

The concepts of power offered by mainstream sociology and political theory are thus rather useless if we want to understand the mute compulsion of capital. What about Michel Foucault's influential concept of power, then? After all, Foucault did develop his theory of power in explicit opposition to mainstream approaches.

Let me begin this discussion by saying that I consider the widespread reduction of Foucault's theory of power to a theory of discourse to be an unproductive simplification. Foucault does not belong in the same category as Ernesto Laclau and Chantal Mouffe, Norman Fairclough, (the early) Judith Butler, and other constructivist idealists. Discursive power is certainly a theme that pervades Foucault's writings, but they have much more to offer than that.[33] Foucault's preoccupation with discursive power is strongest in his writings from the 1960s, such as *The Order of Things*, *The Archaeology of Knowledge*, and *The Discourse of Language*. In his later writings, he is more interested in non-discursive forms of power, even if he continues to insist that 'power cannot be exercised unless a certain economy of discourses of truth functions in, on the basis of, and thanks to, that power'.[34] I will not go into a discussion of his views on discursive power here, as they are not immediately relevant for my purposes; they should rather be regarded as belonging to the field of theories of ideology.[35] Foucault would undoubtedly object to this and insist that he

---

33   It should thus come as no surprise that Laclau and Mouffe criticised Foucault for maintaining a distinction 'between discursive and non-discursive practices'. See Ernesto Laclau and Chantal Mouffe, *Hegemony and Socialist Strategy: Towards a Radical Democratic Politics*, 2nd ed. (London: Verso, 2014), 107.

34   Michel Foucault, *'Society Must Be Defended': Lectures as the Collège de France, 1975–1976*, trans. David Macey (London: Penguin, 2004), 24.

35   The same is true of other kinds of discourse analysis, such as those of Laclau and

explicitly rejected the concept of ideology. It does not require more than a quick glance, however, to see that this rejection is not so much a critique as a superficial dismissal and an attempt to position himself in relation to Marxist orthodoxy in general and Althusser(ianism) in particular. If Foucault is right that the concept of ideology inevitably presupposes 'a human subject on the lines of the model provided by classical philosophy, endowed with a consciousness which power is then thought to seize on', or if the concept really is inextricably caught up in an opposition to 'truth' or science, it would indeed make sense to abandon this concept; but this is obviously not the case.[36] Foucault's hostility towards the notion of ideology is nothing more than a rejection of vulgar Althusserianism and a crude Enlightenment notion of ideology, and neither of those can be identified with the concept of ideology *tout court*.

His dismissal of the notion of ideology is only one example of Foucault's well-known animosity towards Marxism – an attitude that has led many Marxists to reject his work as just another example of postmodern anti-Marxism. Foucault is notoriously unclear about who precisely he is criticising when he attacks 'Marxism'; the reader is always left with vague references to 'a certain contemporary conception that passes for the Marxist conception' or 'a particular version of academic Marxism'.[37] Given the intellectual and political context of his writings, the most likely targets of his critique are the Althusserians, French Maoism, and the orthodox Marxism of the French Communist Party (PCF).[38] Foucault was mostly preoccupied with the 'dispersed and discontinuous offensives' proliferating in the wake of 1968, including what he referred to as 'the insurrection of subjugated knowledges' in prisons and psychiatric institutions.[39] Many

Mouffe, Norman Fairclough, and Edward Said. For an account of the trajectory which led from Althusser's theory of ideology over Foucault to so-called postmodern discourse theory, see Jan Rehmann, *Theories of Ideology: The Powers of Alienation and Subjection* (Chicago: Haymarket, 2013), chap. 7.

36   Michel Foucault, 'Body/Power', in *Power/Knowledge: Selected Interviews and Other Writings 1972–1977*, ed. Colin Gordon (New York: Vintage, 1980), 58; Michel Foucault, 'Truth and Power', in *Power: The Essential Works of Michel Foucault 1954–1984*, vol. 3, ed. James D. Faubion, (London: Penguin, 2002), 119.

37   Foucault, *'Society Must Be Defended'*, 13; Michel Foucault, 'The Mesh of Power', trans. Christopher Chitty, *Viewpoint Magazine*, no. 2 (2012), viewpointmag.com; Michel Foucault, 'Truth and Juridical Forms', in Faubion, *Power*, 15.

38   Nicos Poulantzas, *State, Power, Socialism*, trans. Patrick Camille (London: Verso, 2014), 146.

39   Foucault, *'Society Must Be Defended'*, 5ff.

of the parties and groups who identified as Marxists – the Stalinist PCF and the Maoists – were unable or unwilling to acknowledge and engage in these struggles, which they could not control, and which did not fit with their idea of what a proper proletarian class struggle should look like. This was, of course, especially true of the PCF, which was a downright reactionary force.[40]

Seen in this light, Foucault's attitude towards Marxism is not completely incomprehensible. This is the perspective from which we must read Foucault's statement that 'what has happened since 1968 ... is something profoundly anti-Marxist'.[41] In addition to this, Foucault's critique of Marxism is, as we will see in the next chapter, quite to the point if we read it not as a critique of Marxism *as such*, but rather as a critique of traditional and orthodox Marxism: the latter were indeed state centric and economistic in their understanding of power, and they did indeed tend to reduce every concrete instance of domination to an example of the universal and homogeneous domination of the working class by the bourgeoisie.[42]

What about Marx, then? Foucault is – perhaps intentionally – ambiguous. On the one hand, he dismisses Marx as an outdated political economist who belongs in the nineteenth century. In *The Archaeology of Knowledge*, for example, he claims that Marx's theory was governed by the same 'rules of formation' as the political economy of David Ricardo, something he repeated on several occasions.[43] This says more about Foucault's lack of understanding of Marx's project than it says about the relation between Marx and Ricardo. On the other hand, he is often careful to exempt Marx

---

40   Geoff Eley, *Forging Democracy: The History of the Left in Europe, 1850–2000* (New York: Oxford University Press, 2002), chaps. 21–23.

41   Foucault, 'Body/Power', 57.

42   See ibid., 58f; Foucault, 'Truth and Juridical Forms', 1ff; Foucault, 'Truth and Power', 117; Foucault, *Society Must Be Defended*', 13f, 29ff; and Foucault, 'The Mesh of Power'. In 1960, Sartre aired similar opinions in *Critique of Dialectical Reason*: he accused 'contemporary Marxism' of 'neglecting the particular content of a cultural system and reducing it immediately to the universality of a class ideology'. His own Marxist existentialism 'reacts by affirming the specificity of the historical event, which it refuses to conceive of as the absurd juxtaposition of a contingent residue and an a priori signification'. See Jean-Paul Sartre, *Search for a Method*, trans. Hazel E. Barnes (New York: Vintage, 1968), 115, 126.

43   Michel Foucault, 'Questions on Geography', in Gordon, *Power/Knowledge*, 76; Michel Foucault, 'Interview with Michel Foucault', in Faubion, *Power*, 269f; Michel Foucault, *The Order of Things: An Archaeology of the Human Sciences* (London: Routledge, 2007 [1966]), 194.

from the accusations he levels against Marxism.[44] Occasionally he also refers to Marx in a very positive manner, especially in the context of his analyses of disciplinary power, which has rather obvious points of intersection with Marx's analysis of factory work.[45]

Let us set aside Foucault's polemical references to Marx(ism) and take a look at the more substantial issues. One of the great merits of Foucault's theory of power is that it avoids the five problems in mainstream theories of power outlined earlier. Foucault does not rely on an individualist social ontology; rather than treating the individual 'as a sort of elementary nucleus [or] a primitive atom', he regards it as a 'power-effect' and a 'relay' through which power passes.[46] For this reason, he also avoids presupposing that the subjects involved in a relationship of power are constituted independently of that relationship. His theory likewise implies a rejection of the dyadic conception of power; rather than a relation between an *A* and a *B*, Foucault holds that power is a 'conduct of conducts', which means that it should be understood 'as a way in which certain actions may structure the field of other possible actions'.[47] Furthermore, his emphasis on institutional structures and the myriad of practices through which relations of domination are produced on the micro-level of everyday life is clearly opposed to the 'interventional model', which assumes the exercise of power to take the form of discrete events. Finally, Foucault's resolute break with state-centric conceptions of power – summed up in his famous injunction to 'cut off the head of the king' in political thought – allowed him to avoid assuming the state to be the paradigmatic locus of power; 'power relations are rooted in the whole network of the social', as he puts it.[48]

44   See, for instance, Foucault, 'Questions on Geography', 72; Michel Foucault, 'The Confession of the Flesh', in Gordon, *Power/Knowledge*, 208; Foucault, 'The Mesh of Power'.

45   See Foucault, 'Body/Power', 58; Michel Foucault, *Discipline and Punish: The Birth of the Prison*, trans. Alan Sheridan (London: Penguin, 1991), 163, 175, 221; Foucault, 'The Mesh of Power'; see also David Harvey, *A Companion to Marx's Capital* (London: Verso, 2010), 148; Pierre Macherey, 'The Productive Subject', trans. Tijana Okić, Patrick King, and Cory Knudson, *Viewpoint Magazine*, no. 5 (2015), viewpointmag.com. For a good discussion of the Marx–Foucault (dis)connection (in Danish), see Mikkel Bolt, 'På råbeafstand af marxismen: Et bidrag til kritik af kritikken af kritikken (Latour, Foucault, Marx)', *K&K: Kultur og Klasse* 44, no. 122 (2016): 143–80. See also Jacques Bidet, *Foucault with Marx*, trans. Steven Corcoran (London: Zed Books, 2016); and Rehmann, *Theories of Ideology*, chap. 7.4, 11.

46   Foucault, *'Society Must Be Defended'*, 29f.

47   Michel Foucault, 'The Subject and Power', in Faubion, *Power*, 341, 343.

48   Michel Foucault, *The History of Sexuality*, vol. 1, *The Will to Knowledge*, trans. Robert Hurley (London: Penguin, 1998), 89; Foucault, 'The Subject and Power', 345.

Another strength of Foucault's conception of power is his critique of economism. In one of his jabs against Marxism (presumably Althusser), he insists that 'there are not first of all relations of production, and then, in addition, alongside or on top of these relations, mechanisms of power that modify or disturb them, or make them more consistent, coherent, or stable'.[49] This remark not only touches upon a central weakness of Althusser's theory but also articulates a fundamental premise for a theory of the economic power of capital, namely that relations of power do not somehow exist *outside* of economic relations – rather, economic relations *are* relations of power. Foucault does not treat the economy as an onto-logically separate sphere, and he clearly saw that the historical emergence of capitalism required 'a set of political techniques, techniques of power, by which man was tied to something like labor'.[50]

In one of his attempts to distance himself from Marxism, Foucault defends a 'nominalistic' theory of power.[51] He presents this as a matter of method-ology; when studying power, we should avoid the kind of analysis which proceeds from social structures on the level of the totality, such as classes and property relations, and aim instead for 'an ascending analysis of power, or in other words begin with its infinitesimal mechanisms'.[52] Instead of deducing every concrete instance of domination from the rule of the bourgeoisie, we should direct our attention to the 'micro-physics of power', or the multiplicity of concrete techniques and mechanisms of power. This idea is perhaps the hallmark of Foucault's approach to power, and, as we will see in chapter ten, it is indeed impossible to understand the economic power of capital without paying very close attention to the way in which capital moulds the labour process on its most minute levels (which is what Marx refers to as 'real subsumption'). Without understanding the 'meticulous control of the operations of the body', which takes place in capitalist production, we will not be able to understand the economic power of capital as a whole.[53]

---

49   Michel Foucault, *Security, Territory, Population: Lectures at the College De France, 1977–78*, trans. Graham Burchell (Basingstoke: Palgrave Macmillan, 2009), 2.

50   Michel Foucault, 'Truth and Juridical Forms', 86. Foucault was not always con-sistent on this point, however. Occasionally he apparently forgets his important insight about power relations being embedded in economic relations, which leads him to re-erect the opposition between 'relations of production' and 'power relations'. See Foucault, 'Truth and Juridical Forms, 17; Foucault, 'The Subject and Power', 327; Poulantzas, *State, Power, Socialism*, 36.

51   Foucault, *The History of Sexuality*, 93.

52   Foucault, 'Society Must Be Defended', 30.

53   Foucault, *Discipline and Punish*, 137.

However, this nominalism comes at a price, and so does the refusal to take questions of class and property into consideration. Foucault tends to simply ignore property relations, perhaps because they do not fit very well the notion of power as a process or as something that only exists in the concrete mechanisms and techniques employed in the subjection of bodies to rules and regulations. The power derived from property is not a process, and it cannot be grasped by examining concrete social practices. While it is certainly true to say that a 'web of microscopic, capillary political power had to be established at level of man's very existence' in order to transform people 'into agents of production, into workers', it is also true that certain property relations – and thus a certain class structure – was also required.[54] As Andreas Malm has noted, the 'systematic division' of human beings into 'direct producers and exploiters that must relate to each other' is 'a property at the level of the whole', but there is no room for such a level in Foucauldian nominalism.[55] Foucault is therefore incapable of identifying the underlying social logic of precisely those 'infinitesimal mechanisms' of power which he is so eager to place under the microscope. His preoccupation with the concrete turns out to be incredibly *abstract* because it isolates the micro level from its wider social context. In his analysis of factory discipline, Foucault is therefore unable to answer the question of *why* workers show up at the factory gates in the first place. In order to answer that question, it is necessary to examine property relations and class structures – in other words, to take into account social relations of domination which are *not* a 'web of microscopic, capillary political power', but rather a set of totalising social structures permeating the entire social field. Foucault's insistence that power 'can never be appropriated in the way that wealth or a commodity can be appropriated' might have allowed him to escape the dead ends of orthodox Marxism and mainstream political science, but it also led to an abstract nominalism which is ultimately unable to account for the phenomena it wants to explain.[56]

---

54   Foucault, 'Truth and Juridical Forms', 86.

55   Andreas Malm, *The Progress of This Storm: Nature and Society in a Warming World* (London: Verso, 2018), 162.

56   Foucault, *'Society Must Be Defended'*, 29. See also Foucault, *The History of Sexuality*, 94; and Foucault, *Discipline and Punish*, 26.

Capital: A Social Logic

What is power, then? The discussion in the previous pages has provided some clues, but before we can come up with a meaningful answer, we first have to examine what *capital* is. In mainstream economics, capital is a transhistorical and rather vague concept which refers to a so-called factor of production, alongside labour and land. This 'trinity formula' of capital, labour, and land as the three necessary elements in any process of production has its origin in classical political economy and was subjected to a devastating critique by Marx in the manuscripts for the third book of *Capital*. Here, Marx demonstrates how the juxtaposition of land, labour, and capital naturalises what is in fact 'a definite *social* relation of production pertaining to a particular historical formation of society'.[57] In opposition to this apologetic (and analytically useless) concept of capital, Marx understands capital as a historically specific social logic – a logic in the sense that it refers not to a specific category of things, but rather to a certain way of using things. Capital is a concept which refers to the social *form* of wealth, not its *content*, analogously to the discipline of philosophical logic, which (at least in its non-Hegelian sense) is concerned with forms of thought rather than their content. This social form is captured in Marx's simple and brilliant 'general formula of capital': $M–C–M'$, where M stands for money and C for commodity, and the prime symbol (') next to the second M indicates that the second sum of money is larger than the first. This formula represents a 'process' or a 'movement' in which value, in its incarnations as money and commodities, is augmented.[58] Marx often speaks of the 'valorisation of value' (*Verwertung des Werts*), which means not only that something is given value in a broad sense, but refers more specifically to the process whereby value is *augmented*. Capital is a valorisation of value, and can thus 'only be grasped as a movement, and not as a static thing'.[59] Everything capable of assuming the commodity form – be it coats, fantasies, humans, promises, land, or abilities – can be integrated into this movement and thereby be transformed into the 'body' of the 'processing value'.[60]

---

57 M: 888.
58 30: 11, 12, 17; 32, 490.
59 C2: 185.
60 II.11: 57.

Capital, in the simple sense of a process of exchange undertaken with the aim of pocketing a profit, has existed for thousands of years prior to the advent of capitalism. Aristotle called it 'chrematistics' and condemned it as unnatural, Saint Paul warned that the 'love of money is the root of all evil' (1 Timothy 6:10), and throughout the middle ages, the church consistently looked upon profit-seeking activities with suspicion. What distinguishes capitalism from pre-capitalist systems is not the mere existence of capital, but rather its social function. In pre-capitalist societies, the processes governed by the logic of capital were always marginal to social reproduction. From the sixteenth century onwards, however, a fundamental transformation took place: the logic of capital began to weave itself into the very fabric of social life, eventually reaching the point where people had become dependent upon it for their survival. Capital became 'the all-dominating economic power', or, put differently: *society became capitalist.*[61]

If capital is a social logic, to what extent does it then make sense to speak of 'the power of capital'? Do 'social logics' belong to the category of entities capable of having or exercising power? If we want stick to this notion of 'the power of capital' – as I think we should – two options are available: either we accept that capital is not a social actor and give up the idea that power presupposes agency, or we hold on to the idea that power presupposes agency and affirm that it does make sense to regard capital as a social actor. Let us begin by examining the second option. One way to construct such an argument would be to draw on Latourian actor–network theory, Graham Harman's object-oriented ontology, or other strands of so-called new materialism and their insistence that 'non-human objects are crucial political actors'.[62] Despite Harman's and Latour's not very original animosity towards Marxism, a concept of agency as broad as theirs could easily accommodate capital. In that way, our problem would be solved: power presupposes agency, and capital is a social actor. The problem is, however, that this deflation of the concept of agency also obscures the difference between the natural and the social – a distinction which is, as Malm has convincingly demonstrated in his critique of new materialisms, absolutely crucial to hold on to.[63] The Latourian definition of agency as 'making a difference' is, in other words, *too broad.*[64]

---

61   G: 107.

62   Graham Harman, *Object-Oriented Ontology: A New Theory of Everything* (London: Penguin, 2018), 146.

63   Malm, *The Progress of This Storm.*

64   Latour quoted in ibid., 89.

Is Capital a Subject?

What about the idea that capital is a *subject* in a Hegelian sense, then? What if we rephrase the question of 'agency' in terms closer to the German philosophical tradition out of which Marxism grew? Is this what we need in order to forge a conceptual link between 'power' and 'capital'? One thing is for sure: Marx very often refers to value circulating in the form of capital as a 'subject'.[65] His description of capital as an 'automatic subject' is often accepted at face value, for example by Werner Bonefeld, Michael Heinrich, Helmut Reichelt, Anselm Jappe, Robert Kurz, Jacques Cammatte, Moishe Postone, and Chris Arthur.[66] We should be cautious here, however: as several commentators have pointed out, Marx's use of the phrase 'automatic subject' is intended to highlight the fetishistic appearance of capital on the surface of the capitalist economy, not its inner nature.[67] When Marx employs this expression, he is always referring either to capital 'as it immediately appears in the sphere of circulation' or to interest-bearing capital, that is, the 'most estranged and peculiar form' of capital.[68] What is characteristic about both of these forms is that

---

65   See, for example, G: 266, 311, 470, 585, 620, 745f; 30: 12f, 17; 33: 91; M: 494; II.6: 53; and C1: 255.

66   Werner Bonefeld, *Critical Theory and the Critique of Political Economy* (London: Bloomsbury, 2014), 43; Michael Heinrich, *Die Wissenschaft vom Wert: Die Marxsche Kritik der politischen Ökonomie zwischen wissenschaftlicher Revolution und klassischer Tradition* (Münster: Westfälisches Dampfboot, 1999), 252; Michael Heinrich, *An Introduction to the Three Volumes of Karl Marx's Capital*, trans. Alex Locascio (New York: Monthly Review Press, 2012), 89; Helmut Reichelt, *Zur logischen Struktur des Kapitalbegriffs bei Karl Marx* (Frankfurt am Main: Europäische Verlagsanstalt, 1973), 76; Anselm Jappe, *Die Abenteuer der Ware: Für eine neue Wertkritik* (Münster: Unrast Verlag, 2005), 83; Robert Kurz, *Geld ohne Wert: Grundrisse zu einer Transformation der Kritik der politischen Ökonomie* (Berlin: Horlemann, 2012), 33; Jacques Cammatte, *Capital and Community*, trans. David Brown (New York: Prism Key Press, 2011), 379ff; Moishe Postone, *Time, Labor, and Social Domination: A Reinterpretation of Marx's Critical Theory* (Cambridge: Cambridge University Press, 2003), 75; Christopher Arthur, *The New Dialectic and Marx's Capital* (Leiden: Brill, 2004), 117.

67   See Helmut Brentel, *Soziale Form und Ökonomisches Objekt: Studien zum Gegenstands- und Methodenverständnis der Kritik der politischen Ökonomie* (Wiesbaden: Springer Fachmedien Wiesbaden, 1989), 267f; Ingo Elbe, *Marx im Westen: Die neue Marx-lektüre in der Bundesrepublik seit 1965* (Berlin: Akademie Verlag, 2008); Harvey, *A Companion to Marx's Capital*, 90; Nadja Rakowitz and Jürgen Behre, 'Automatisches Subjekt? Zur Bedeutung des Kapitalbegriffs bei Marx', 2001, rote-ruhr-uni.com/cms/texte/Automatisches-Subjekt; Karl Reitter, 'Vorwort', in *Karl Marx: Philosoph der Befreiung oder Theoretiker des Kapitals? Zur Kritik der 'Neuen Marx-Lektüre'*, ed. Karl Reitter (Wien: Mandelbaum Verlag, 2015), 15.

68   C1: 257, M: 896.

they obscure the origin of surplus value, which is why the valorisation of value 'appears to derive from occult qualities that are inherent in capital itself'.[69] When Marx refers to capital as an 'automatic subject', '*self*-moving substance', or '*self*-valorising value', he is describing a fetishistic inversion, not the actual functioning of capital.[70]

One might still argue, however, that even if capital is not an *automatic* (i.e., self-moving) subject, it can nevertheless still be said to be a subject in another and less radical sense. In addition to this, one could of course argue that Marx was simply wrong when he rejected the idea that capital is a subject. There is indeed, as several commentators have noted, a strong similarity between the logic of capital and Hegel's concept of subjectivity – a similarity which goes beyond the fetishistic appearances.[71] For Hegel, subjectivity is *self-relating negativity*, or 'the "I"'s pure reflection into itself', which is tantamount to the ability 'to abstract from everything … to extinguish all particularity, all determinacy'.[72] The subject posits itself by externalising itself, only in order to sublate this difference – it is 'the doubling which sets up opposition, and then again the negation of this indifferent diversity and of its anti-thesis [*Gegensatzes*]'.[73] Acquisition of

---

69   M: 98. See also 33: 71, 74; M: 492, 500, 896; and C1: 256. It is interesting to note that Marx deleted the word 'subject' from chapter four of *Capital* in the French edition (II.7: 123f).

70   C1: 256; M: 492; emphasis added. This touches upon the question of the meaning of 'appearance' in Marx's writings. As has been pointed out many times, Marx often employs this concept in the Hegelian sense of a *real* and *necessary* – though potentially obscuring – reflection of essence. This is the case, for example, when he refers to profit as 'the form of appearance of surplus value' (M: 98). In other cases, however, it simply signals an *ideological mystification*, as when he writes that social relations 'appear as eternal natural relations' (33: 71). I have written about the meaning of 'appearance' in Marx's writings elsewhere: Søren Mau, 'Den dobbelte fordrejning: Fetichismebegrebet i kritikken af den politiske økonomi', *Slagmark: Tidsskrift for Idéhistorie*, no. 77 (2018): 106f. In the descriptions of capital quoted in this paragraph, Marx uses 'appearance' in the sense of ideological mystification.

71   See Patrick Murray, *Marx's Theory of Scientific Knowledge* (New York: Humanity Books, 1990), 216f; Postone, *Time, Labor, and Social Domination*, 75; Reichelt, *Zur logischen Struktur des Kapitalbegriffs bei Karl Marx*, 76; Slavoj Žižek, *The Sublime Object of Ideology* (London: Verso, 2009), 28f. For a discussion of this analogy, see Frank Engster, *Das Geld als Mass, Mittel und Methode: Das Rechnen mit der Identität der Zeit* (Berlin: Neofelis Verlag, 2014), 95ff.

72   G. W. F. Hegel, *Elements of the Philosophy of Right*, trans. H. B. Nisbet (Cambridge: Cambridge University Press, 2003), 38f; Dieter Henrich, *Between Kant and Hegel: Lectures on German Idealism* (Cambridge, MA: Harvard University Press, 2008), 290.

73   G. W. F. Hegel, *Phenomenology of Spirit*, trans. A. V. Miller (Oxford: Oxford University Press, 1977), 10.

status as a subject in this sense is precisely what is at stake in the struggle of life and death in the transition from consciousness to self-consciousness in the *Phenomenology of Spirit*; each consciousness must demonstrate that it is 'the pure negation of its objective mode'.[74]

It is evident that Marx was deeply influenced by this concept of subjectivity. In the *1844 Manuscripts*, he praised Hegel's 'dialectic of negativity', which 'conceives the self-creation of the human being as a process, conceives objectification as de-objectification, as externalisation and sublation of this externalisation'.[75] At the same time, Marx is deeply critical of Hegel's idealist misunderstanding of this dialectic, which equates labour with *intellectual* labour.[76] In the theses on Feuerbach, Marx radicalises the critique of idealism, but he holds on to the idealist emphasis on 'the *active* side' of human existence which had been neglected by 'all previous materialism'.[77] To cut a long story short: rather than reject Hegel's notion of subjectivity in toto, Marx extracts its essential core and excavates it from its idealist shell by reconceptualising it as a social, material, and productive practice.

The resemblance between capital and the subject in this Hegelian sense comes out very clearly in Marx's analysis of capital. For him, capital is fundamentally a *movement*, or 'value-in-process'.[78] The beginning and the end of this movement are qualitatively identical: with capital, value 'enters into a private relationship with itself', thereby elevating its being-for-*others* – that is, being-for-consumption in the case of simple circulation (C–M–C) – to 'being-for-itself'.[79] In distinction to the 'concept-less form' (*begriffslose Form*)[80] of interest-bearing capital (M–M'), capital proper (M–C–M') establishes its 'identity with itself' by relating itself to *an other* in the form of the mediating C in the middle.[81] Insofar as the doubling of the commodity into commodity and money is an externalisation of the dual nature of the commodity, we can say that capital posits a

---

74   Ibid., 113.

75   3: 332f. The translation of this passage in the MECW is rather unfortunate.

76   3: 333.

77   5: 3; Étienne Balibar, *The Philosophy of Marx*, trans. Gregory Elliot and Chris Turner (London: Verso, 2014), 25ff.

78   30: 12.

79   C1: 256, G: 452.

80   Mistakenly translated as 'irrational' in the English translation of *Marx's Economic Manuscript of 1864–1865*. For Marx's explanation of what 'concept-less' means, see II.11: 582.

81   M: 493; C1: 255.

difference – the difference between commodity and money – *as well as sublates it*: the universalisation of the commodity form necessarily leads to the 'autonomisation' of value in money, and it is precisely this doubling which makes it possible for commodities and money to circulate in the form of capital.[82] When they do that – that is to say, when they circulate in the form $M-C-M'$ – their difference and the change of forms (*Formwechsel*) are, however, reduced to subordinate moments of the process through which value affirms itself as 'the essence which remains equal to itself' (*das sich gleichbleibende Wesen*).[83]

Capital sustains itself by means of its constant change of form and its continuous movement through the spheres of circulation and production. With capital, the entry of money into the sphere of circulation – that is, the act of *buying*, or *giving up* the money for a commodity – is merely 'a moment of its staying-with-itself' (*Beisichbleiben*);[84] *it stays with itself by renouncing itself*. By performing this deeply tautological movement, capital constantly re-establishes the conditions of its own repetition: it contains what Marx calls 'the principle of self-renewal', or, in Hegelian terms, it 'posits' its own presuppositions.[85] By transforming the circulation of commodities and money into this spiral-like form, capital transforms the 'bad infinite process' of simple circulation ($C-M-C$) into a self-referential infinity.[86] As a social *form*, capital is completely indifferent to its *content*; the only thing that counts is whether or not value can be valorised.[87] For this reason, the self-relating movement of capital is truly a self-relating *negativity*: it negates any particular content by transforming it into real abstractions in order to absorb it into the vortex of value.

On the basis of this structural similarity, Postone proclaims capital to be a 'historical Subject in the Hegelian sense.'[88] In contrast to Hegel's subject, however, capital is 'historically determinate and blind'. While it is 'self-reflexive', it 'does not possess self-consciousness'.[89] Chris Arthur argues that the crux of the matter is capital's ability to transform heterogeneous commodities into bearers of surplus value; it is this 'capacity to range

---

82 C1: 153.
83 G: 312.
84 G: 234.
85 29: 480; G: 542.
86 G: 197; C1: 253.
87 G: 452.
88 Postone, *Time, Labor, and Social Domination*, 75.
89 Ibid., 77.

things under their universal concept' which, according to him, justifies the categorisation of capital as a subject.[90] Contra Postone, Arthur also attributes *consciousness* to capital in the form of its personifications – that is, the capitalists.[91] Stavros Tombazos goes even further, claiming that 'capital must be understood as a living organism endowed with a body (use-value) and a soul (value), its own will and logic (profit, expanded reproduction, and so on)'.[92] Similar interpretations of capital as an absolute and omnipotent subject are defended by Robert Kurz, Anselm Jappe, and Jacques Camatte.[93]

Capital as an Emergent Property

I do not find these attempts to conceptualise capital as a subject convincing – for several reasons. First, capital is bound to do certain things in a way that a subject – at least in the Hegelian sense – is not. For Hegel, subjectivity involves the potential suspension of *all* determinacy. This is why 'natural consciousness' – the protagonist of the *Phenomenology* – must engage in a struggle of life and death; it has to prove 'that it is not attached to any determinate *being-there* [*Dasein*]', not even to *life*.[94] Capital is not like that; even though it exhibits a dynamic very similar to the self-relating negativity of the subject, it is always bound to pursue the same action: *to valorise value*. Capital does not possess the kind of irreducible freedom implied by Hegel's notion of subjectivity – *if it ceases to do what it does, it ceases to be*. It cannot veer off course, even when it partially negates itself in order to preserve itself as a totality, which is what happens in crises (more on this in chapter thirteen). Another reason why I think we should reject the notion of capital as a subject is the inextricable tie between

---

90   Christopher Arthur, 'Subject and Counter-Subject', *Historical Materialism* 12, no. 3 (2004): 95f; Arthur, *The New Dialectic and Marx's Capital*, chap. 8; see also Riccardo Bellofiore, 'A Ghost Turning into a Vampire: The Concept of Capital and Living Labour', in *Re-Reading Marx: New Perspectives after the Critical Edition*, ed. Riccardo Bellofiore and Roberto Fineschi (Basingstoke: Palgrave Macmillan, 2009), 180ff.

91   Arthur, 'Subject and Counter-Subject', 96.

92   Stavros Tombazos, *Time in Marx: The Categories of Time in Marx's* Capital (Chicago: Haymarket, 2014), 80.

93   Kurz, *Geld ohne Wert*; Jappe, *Die Abenteuer der Ware*; Cammatte, *Capital and Community*.

94   Hegel, *Phenomenology of Spirit*, 113.

capital and its underlying social relations and practices. Capital is value in motion, and value is a social relation which gains an autonomous form in money, thereby making it possible for value to circulate in the form of capital. Capital is, as Marx and Engels eloquently put it, a 'fixation of social activity' or a 'consolidation of what we ourselves produce into a material power above us'.[95] What the 'power of money' reveals, they explain in *The German Ideology*, is 'the autonomisation of relations of production'.[96] Capital is a process consisting of a purchase and a sale, and, as Marx observes, 'commodities cannot themselves go to the market and perform exchanges', which is why 'their guardians' must be mobilised if value is to be valorised.[97] In other words, capital can never free itself from the subjective praxis that undergirds it.

My disagreement with Postone and Arthur is partly a matter of emphasis and terminological preferences. Arthur acknowledges that capital 'pre-supposes both labour and nature as conditions of its existence'.[98] Postone also admits that capital 'consists of objectified relations', which leads Callinicos to conclude that Postone simply reinterprets 'subject' as structure.[99] Similar considerations have led others to describe capital as a 'quasi-' or a 'pseudo-subject'.[100] Another way to conceptualise this 'autonomisation' of social relations is offered by the concept of *emergence*. As Malm explains, an emergent property is 'a property of the system *resulting from the organisation of its parts*'.[101] Emergent properties are irreducible to their parts and 'exert causal powers in their own right'.[102] This seems to me to capture Marx's apt description of capital as 'the existence of social labour … as itself existing independently opposite its real moments – hence itself a *particular* existence apart from them'.[103] Conceptualisation of capital as an emergent property of social relations thus allows us to avoid the

---

95   5: 47; I.5: 37.

96   5: 396; I.5: 453; see also G: 471; 34: 128.

97   C1: 178.

98   Postone, 'Subject and Counter-Subject', 99.

99   Postone, *Time, Labor, and Social Domination*, 76; Alex Callinicos, *Deciphering Capital: Marx's* Capital *and Its Destiny* (London: Bookmarks, 2014), 219.

100   Brentel, *Soziale Form und Ökonomisches Objekt*, 268; Tony Smith, 'The Chapters on Machinery in the 1861–63 Manuscripts', in Bellofiore and Fineschi, *Re-Reading Marx*, 124.

101   Malm, *The Progress of This Storm*, 67.

102   Ibid., 163; see also Roy Bhaskar, *Dialectic: The Pulse of Freedom* (London: Routledge, 2008), 373.

103   G: 471.

hyperbolic and ultimately unconvincing depiction of capital as a living subject endowed with consciousness, will, and intentionality, while still holding on to the crucial insight that it does indeed exert causal power in its own right.

So: capital is neither a social actor in the sense in which mainstream theories of power would require it to be, nor is it a subject in a materialist-Hegelian sense. Does that mean that we are forced to relinquish the notion of 'the power of capital'? No. Rather, it invites us to question the assumption that power is always a relation between 'subjects' or 'actors' or 'agents'. What we need to do, in other words, is to broaden the concept of power. But how much, exactly?

In its broadest sense, to have power is simply 'to be able to make a difference to the world'.[104] As a synonym for 'capacity' or 'ability', 'power' can refer to human as well as non-human processes and potentials which have nothing to do with social domination, such as the power of gravity, electrical power, horse power, labour power, and so on.[105] Scholars writing about power usually mention this broad sense of the term in order to specify that they are exclusively concerned with *social* power, which they then proceed to define in terms of relations between social actors. This is where we should intervene, not in order to obliterate the difference between natural and social power – which is indeed, contrary to the claims of new materialists, crucial to insist on – but rather in order to question the arbitrary constriction of the concept of power to refer *exclusively* to relations between social actors. If we define social power as something which can only be possessed or exercised by social actors or subjects, we introduce an artificial conceptual cleavage between social relations and their emergent properties, with the result that the ways in which those emergent properties shape the field of possible actions of social actors become theoretically invisible. Power is not only a relation between social actors; it can also be a relation between actors on the one hand and an emergent property of social relations on the other. The concept of power should thus be extended to refer to relations among social actors *as well as* the emergent properties of these relations. These emergent properties

---

104   Steven Lukes, 'Introduction', in *Power*, 5.

105   Thomas Hobbes, *Leviathan* (Oxford: Oxford University Press, 2008), 58; Lukes, *Power*, 61f; Andreas Malm, *Fossil Capital: The Rise of Steam Power and the Roots of Global Warming* (London: Verso, 2016), 17ff; Mann, *The Sources of Social Power*, 6; Scott, *Power*, 1; Wartenberg, *The Forms of Power*, 3; Wrong, *Power*, xix.

are purely *social*, but they cannot be grasped as relations among social *actors*, even though the latter are *necessary conditions* of their existence. The *power of capital* can thus be defined as *capital's capacity to impose its logic on social life*; a capacity which includes and ultimately relies upon, yet is not reducible to, relations among social actors in a traditional sense, such as the relationship between capitalists and proletarians or the relationship between an employer and an employee.

This definition of the power of capital has at least two implications for how we should think about social power in general. First, we should avoid defining power as a dyadic relation between an *A* and a *B*.[106] This eliminates all of the mainstream theories examined earlier in this chapter. Second, we should also avoid defining power as something which can only be possessed or exercised by 'actors', 'agents', 'humans', 'persons', 'groups', 'classes', and/or 'subjects'.[107] At the same time, however, we also want to avoid a concept of power so broad that it makes it impossible to distinguish social domination from natural processes or simple capacities; in other words, a definition of power as something along the lines of 'the ability to make a difference' will not suffice. Among the definitions which meet these criteria is Foucault's: 'The exercise of power is a "conduct of conducts" and a management of possibilities.'[108] Another definition which would fit here is the one provided by Michael Barnett and Raymond Duvall: 'Power is the production, in and through social relations, of effects on actors that shape their capacity to control their fate.'[109] In order to settle on a particular definition of power, however, we would have to take into consideration a number of factors and issues which are not immediately relevant for our purposes, such as the question of whether power is a *capacity* or the actual *exercise* of a capacity. (If power were a capacity, the two definitions just mentioned would have to be modified.)[110] This is not the place to delve

---

106   Among the definitions which meet this requirement are Adams, *Energy and Structure*, 12; Barnett and Duvall, 'Power in International Politics', 45; Foucault, 'The Subject and Power', 341f; Isaac, *Power and Marxist Theory*, 80; Poulantzas, *Political Power and Social Classes*, 104; Wartenberg, *The Forms of Power*, 85.

107   This eliminates the definitions proposed by Adams, *Energy and Structure*, 12; Isaac, *Power and Marxist Theory*, 80; Poulantzas, *Political Power and Social Classes*, 104; Wartenberg, *The Forms of Power*, 85.

108   Michel Foucault, 'The Subject and Power', in Faubion, *Power* (London: Penguin, 2002), 341.

109   Barnett and Duvall, 'Power in International Politics', 45.

110   See Isaac, *Power and Marxist Theory*, chap. 3; Lukes, *Power*, 109; Peter Morriss,

into these debates. At this point in our discussion, we have what we need as far as the clarification of the concepts of power and capital goes.

Before we move on to a consideration of how the Marxist tradition has grappled with the issue of power, a terminological clarification is in order. In the literature on power, one often comes across a distinction between power and domination. Power is then understood either in the broad sense as the capacity of an actor to influence its environment (regardless of whether or not this involves the subjection of other actors) or in a narrower sense that also encompasses forms of power acknowledged as legitimate (sometimes referred to as 'authority'). Domination, on the other hand, is taken to be a more specific form of power which involves some kind of conflict between the principal and the subaltern, to use John Scott's terms.[111] This distinction sometimes overlaps with the popular distinction between *power to* (the capacity to do something) and *power over* (the capacity to subjugate someone). These distinctions might be useful in other contexts, but they are irrelevant for our purposes for the simple reason that the power of capital always involves and relies on domination. Or, put differently: the 'power to' of capital is always a 'power over'.

Power: A Philosophical Analysis, 2nd ed. (Manchester: Manchester University Press, 2002); Scott, *Power*, 5; Wrong, *Power*, 6ff.

111   Scott, *Power*, 2.

2
Power and Marxism

In the last chapter, we saw that mainstream social science has little to offer if we want to understand how the logic of capital imposes itself on our lives. What about the Marxist tradition, then? It is safe to say that no intellectual tradition has posed the question of the power of capital as persistently as Marxism. If there is one thing that unites this otherwise extremely heterogeneous tradition, it is the insight that capitalism is an oppressive system based on the exploitation and domination of the working class. Despite this promising point of departure, however, Marxist attempts to explain how capital holds on to its power have generally left much to be desired – at least prior to the 1960s, when the renewal and proliferation of Marxist theory resulted in new tendencies and perspectives which overcame some of the crucial weaknesses of traditional Marxism. I will return to these more recent trends in Marxist scholarship later in this chapter. To begin with, however, let us take a brief look at the dominant conception of power in Marxist theory in the period from Marx's death until the rediscovery of the critique of political economy in the 1960s.

Historical Materialism

A survey of the prevalent understandings of power in the Marxist tradition has to begin with the complex of ideas known as 'the materialist conception of history' or 'historical materialism'. Developed by Engels and other important Marxists – especially Karl Kautsky – in the decades following Marx's death, this doctrine offered a philosophy of history solidly grounded in a technicist conception of the economy. Its founding document was Marx's 1859 preface to *A Contribution to the Critique of Political Economy*, lauded by leading Marxist intellectuals as a 'brilliant and monumental' (Bukharin) exposition of 'the fundamental principles of materialism as applied to human society and its history' (Lenin).[1] In this brief preface, Marx explains how 'the economic structure of society' forms the basis of 'a legal and political superstructure' as well as corresponding 'forms of social consciousness'. At some point in the history of any mode of production, he writes, 'the material productive forces of society come into conflict with the existing relations of production', thereby inaugurating 'an era of social revolution'.[2] Another locus classicus routinely cited by traditional Marxists is a remark from *The Poverty of Philosophy* according to which the 'hand-mill gives you society with the feudal lord; the steam-mill, society with the industrial capitalist'.[3] In influential writings such as *Socialism: Utopian and Scientific* (1880), Engels codified this as 'the materialist conception of history', according to which 'the final causes of all social changes and political revolutions are to be sought, not in men's brains, not in man's better insight into eternal truth and justice, but in changes in the modes of production and exchange'.[4]

---

1   Nikolai Bukharin, 'Marx's Teaching and Its Historical Importance' (1933), in Bukharin et al., *Marxism and Modern Thought* (London: Routledge, 1935); Vladimir Ilyich Lenin, 'Karl Marx: A Brief Biographical Sketch with an Exposition of Marxism' (1914), in *Lenin's Collected Works*, vol. 21, ed. Stewart Smith, trans. Clemence Dutt (Moscow: Progress Publishers, 1974), 43–91. See also Antonio Labriola, *Essays on the Materialistic Conception of History*, trans. Charles H. Kerr (New York: Cosimo Classics, 2005); Eduard Bernstein, *Evolutionary Socialism*, trans. Edith C. Harvey (New York: Schocken, 1961), 3; Franz Mehring, *On Historical Materialism*, trans. Bob Archer (London: New Park, 1975); Joseph Stalin, 'Dialectical and Historical Materialism' (1938), available at marxists.org.

2   29: 263.

3   6: 166.

4   24: 306. Recall that many of Marx's writings were unavailable to the first generation of Marxists – not only because many of them had not been published at all, but also because many of those published in Marx's own lifetime were not reprinted until well into the twentieth century. In addition to this, Marx 'was read mainly by movement intellectuals', as Geoff Eley puts it. See Geoff Eley, *Forging Democracy: The History of the Left in Europe, 1850–2000* (New York: Oxford University Press, 2002), 43. Among the most widely read works in the era of the Second International were Engels's *Socialism: Scientific*

The doctrine of historical materialism was further developed by influential Marxists such as Kautsky, Franz Mehring, and Georgi Plekhanov. The economy, conceived as a distinct social sphere, was proclaimed to be the basis or infrastructure and thus *primary* in relation to the ideological, political, and legal 'superstructures'. This basis was a 'mode of production', a totality made up of the (unstable) unity of two moments: the productive forces and the relations of production. Historical development was, then, conceived as a succession of modes of production driven forward by a dialectic of productive forces and relations of production. The contradiction between these arises because of the immanent and necessary progress of technology, understood as a transhistorical force necessarily colliding with the historically specific social relations attempting to hold it back. Historical materialism was, in other words, a determinist philosophy of history in which specific social formations were, in the last instance, reduced to a stage in the unfolding of a transhistorical technological rationality. 'The productive forces at man's disposal determine all his social relations', as Plekhanov put it.[5] Kautsky likewise held the *'development of technology'* to be 'the motor of social development', providing a scientific basis for proletarian struggle:

> With the progress of technology not only the material means are born that make socialism possible but also the driving forces that bring it about. This driving force is the proletarian class struggle ... It must finally be victorious due to the continuous progress of technology.[6]

The determinism of historical materialism was exacerbated by scientistic positivism. In the preface to *A Contribution*, Marx had claimed that economic analysis could be conducted with 'the precision of natural science'. Likewise, in the preface to *Capital*, he had written about the 'iron necessity' of 'the natural laws of capitalist production'.[7] Marx's understanding of nature was shaped in a context influenced by German idealism which saw no opposition between speculative philosophy and natural science. However, by

and Utopian, August Bebel's *Woman under Socialism*, and Kautsky's *The Economic Doctrines of Karl Marx*. See Eley, chap. 2; and Lise Vogel, *Marxism and the Oppression of Women: Toward a Unitary Theory* (Chicago: Haymarket, 2014), 100.

5   G. V. Plekhanov, *Fundamental Problems of Marxism*, trans. Julius Katzer (New York: International Publishers, 1971), 115.

6   Karl Kautsky, 'Nature and Society' (1929), trans. John H. Kautsky, *International Journal of Comparative Sociology* 30, nos. 1–2 (1989).

7   C1: 91.

the time these remarks were taken up by the early Marxists, the intellectual milieu had changed. Speculative *Naturphilosophie* had been replaced with empirical science, and 'nature' had come to mean an 'objective' world outside of human thought, ruled by transhistorical laws. At Marx's funeral, Engels famously compared Marx to Darwin. While the latter had 'discovered the law of development of organic nature on our planet', Marx was cast as 'the discoverer of the fundamental law according to which history moves'.[8] This similitude was picked up by Kautsky, who pushed historical materialism further in the direction of an evolutionist philosophy of history. In this context, Marx's remarks about the 'natural laws' of capitalism were taken as justification for the introduction of a positivist paradigm of social science.

The *productive force determinism* of orthodox historical materialism precluded the development of an understanding of the economic power of capital for the simple reason that economic relations were seen as the result of a transhistorical technological drive rather than as struggles about power and domination.[9]

Theories of the State

Even if productive force determinism led these early Marxists to view the rule of the bourgeoisie as the outcome of a necessary historical development, they nevertheless still considered the relationship between the

---

8   24: 463.

9   For critical discussions of the shortcomings of traditional historical materialism, see Daniel Bensaïd, *Marx for Our Times: Adventures and Misadventures of a Critique*, trans. Gregory Elliot (London: Verso, 2009), chaps. 1–2; Alex Callinicos, *Making History: Agency, Structure, and Change in Social Theory*, 2nd ed. (Leiden: Brill, 2004); Lucio Colletti, *From Rousseau to Lenin: Studies in Ideology and Society*, trans. John Merrington and Judith White (New York: Monthly Review Press, 1973), pt. 1; Ingo Elbe, 'Between Marx, Marxism, and Marxisms – Ways of Reading Marx's Theory', trans. Alex Locascio, *Viewpoint Magazine*, 21 October 2013, viewpointmag.com; John Bellamy Foster, *Marx's Ecology: Materialism and Nature* (New York: Monthly Review Press, 2000), 226ff; Richard Gunn, 'Against Historical Materialism: Marxism as a First-Order Discourse', in *Open Marxism*, vol. 2, *Theory and Practice* (London: Pluto Press, 1992); Andreas Malm, *Fossil Capital: The Rise of Steam Power and the Roots of Global Warming* (London: Verso, 2016); S. H. Rigby, *Marxism and History: A Critical Introduction* (Manchester: Manchester University Press, 1998); Alfred Schmidt, *History and Structure: Essays on Hegelian-Marxist and Structuralist Theories of History*, trans. Jeffrey Herf (Cambridge, MA: MIT Press, 1983); Ellen Meiksins Wood, *Democracy against Capitalism: Renewing Historical Materialism* (London: Verso, 2016), pt. 1.

bourgeoisie and the proletariat to be a relation of domination. In their attempts to understand this, they tended to view the state and its means of violent oppression as the ultimate locus of capitalist power. Even those who rejected orthodox productive force determinism accepted the reified opposition between *politics* and *economy*, in which the latter was emptied of social content.[10] Power was thus taken to be something that had to do with the state, understood as an instrument of the bourgeoisie – a critique of the capitalist state which tended to ignore the *form* of the state in favour of a focus on the *content* of policy and state action.[11]

The tendency to ignore mechanisms of power embedded in the economy and regard the control over the state as the primary means of capitalist class domination was also a result of the idea – almost universally accepted among classical Marxists – that capitalism had entered a 'monopoly stage' distinct from the 'competitive' capitalism of the nineteenth century. According to Rudolf Hilferding and Lenin, the capitalist economies of the early twentieth century had become dominated by large monopolies engaged in imperialist exploitation through a fusion of finance capital and the state.[12] The rule of the bourgeoisie was now ensured by a 'capitalist oligarchy' in control of the state.[13] Lenin spoke of a 'personal union' within the upper echolons of the banks, the monopolies, and the state, resulting in a 'sort of division of labour amongst several hundred kings of finance who reign over modern capitalist society'.[14] The concentration and centralisation of capital, and the pressure to expand, had – Hilferding and Lenin argued – led to an amalgamation of finance-controlled monopolies and of the state in order to secure new outlets for capital through imperialism. In other words: state monopoly capitalism had become the order of the day. The 'blatant seizure of the state by the

---

10   Simon Clarke, *Marx, Marginalism, and Modern Sociology: From Adam Smith to Max Weber*, 2nd ed. (Basingstoke: Macmillan, 1991), 309; Christoph Henning, *Philosophy after Marx: 100 Years of Misreadings and the Normative Turn in Political Philosophy*, trans. Max Henninger (Chicago: Haymarket, 2015), 42ff.

11   Elbe, 'Between Marx, Marxism, and Marxisms'; John Holloway and Sol Picciotto, 'Introduction: Towards a Materialist Theory of the State', in *State and Capital: A Marxist Debate*, ed. John Holloway and Sol Picciotto (London: Edward Arnold, 1978), 1.

12   Rudolf Hilferding, *Finance Capital: A Study of the Latest Phase of Capitalist Development*, trans. Morris Watnick and Sam Gordon (London: Routledge & Kegan Paul, 1981); Vladimir Illich Lenin, *Imperialism: The Highest Stage of Capitalism* (London: Penguin, 2010).

13   Henning, *Philosophy after Marx*, 109ff.

14   Lenin, *Imperialism*, 47.

capitalist class' had led to a replacement of the anarchy of competition with the planned production of the monopolies.[15] Marx's analysis of capitalism – or at least parts of it, and especially the theory of value – was consequently considered obsolete, as it concerned itself with a supposedly bygone form of capitalism.

This kind of analysis had tremendous consequences for how the power of capital was understood. First, capital's ability to reproduce its dominant position was now seen as a result of the *absence* of competition. Second, its dominance was primarily guaranteed by the ability of the state to employ violence in order to subjugate subaltern nations and secure profitable outlets for the export of capital. Additionally, the power of capital was assumed to be equivalent to the personal power of financial oligarchs. Here is Lenin in *State and Revolution*:

> Imperialism in particular – the era of banking capital, the era of gigantic capitalist monopolies, the era of the transformation of monopoly capitalism into state monopoly-capitalism – shows an unprecedented strengthening of the 'state machinery' and an unprecedented growth of its bureaucratic and military apparatuses, side by side with the increase of repressive measures against the proletariat, alike in the monarchical and the freest republican countries.[16]

In short, the picture of capitalist power painted by Lenin and Hilferding is dominated by militarism, violence, and corruption. This is certainly a reflection of their historical context, but this does not change the fact that it made them incapable of grasping the mute compulsion of economic relations, which reproduce the power of capital even in the *absence* of corruption and violence.

In 1966, Paul A. Baran and Paul Sweezy published their immensely influential *Monopoly Capital*. Although they differ from Lenin and Hilferding in many respects, their analysis was nevertheless an updated version of the same basic idea: capitalism had undergone a transformation from a competitive to a monopolistic form. Thus, because Marx had based his analysis of capitalism on a competitive model, that analysis was regarded as obsolete. The theory of monopoly capital has – in its older as well as

---

15   Hilferding, *Finance Capital*, 368.

16   Vladimir Illich Lenin, *State and Revolution* (New York: International Publishers, 2012), 29.

its more recent versions – been subjected to criticism from various points of view, on conceptual as well as empirical grounds. Many commentators have pointed out that the analysis relies on a conflation of Marx's concept of competition with that of neoclassical economics and a projection of the latter onto the capitalist economy of the nineteenth century.[17] This led to an all-too-abstract opposition between competition and monopoly, ignoring the fact that capitalism is characterised by what Steve Zeluck calls the 'dynamic interaction' between the 'constant struggle for monopoly position and the constant *loss* of that monopoly position through competition'.[18] In addition to this, it should also be kept in mind that the elimination of *intra*-branch competition does not mean that *inter*-branch competition thereby also disappears. David Harvey has criticised the monopoly capital analysis on the basis of an important observation regarding changes in structures of management in large, monopolistic corporations. As he explains with reference to Alfred Chandler's classic study of the history of American firms, 'what appears on the outside as a steady and seemingly irreversible movement towards centralisation has been accompanied by a progressive, controlled decentralization in the structure of management'.[19] This means that the formation of monopolies is actually compatible with a kind of 'internalization of competition' through decentralisation of management.[20] For this reason, monopoly is not equivalent to a lessening of competition; it can also signal a change in the *form* of competition. In addition to these theoretical problems, critics have also demonstrated that the theory of monopoly capitalism stood on shaky empirical grounds. Christoph Henning and Michael Heinrich point out that Lenin and Hilferding built their analyses on insufficient data, and Robert Brenner argues that Baran and Sweezy generalised from a number of tendencies which turned out to be 'quite *temporary* and specific aspects of the economy of the US in the 1950s'.[21]

17   David Harvey, *The Limits to Capital* (London: Verso, 2006), 142ff; Christel Neusüss, *Imperialismus und Weltmarktbewegung des Kapitals* (Erlangen: Politladen, 1972); Anwar Shaikh, *Capitalism: Competition, Conflict, Crises* (New York: Oxford University Press, 2016), 355; Steve Zeluck, 'On the Theory of the Monopoly Stage of Capitalism', *Against the Current* 1, no. 1 (1980); Jonas Zoninsein, *Monopoly Capital Theory: Hilferding and Twentieth-Century Capitalism* (New York: Praeger, 1990), 20.

18   Zeluck, 'On the Theory of the Monopoly Stage of Capitalism', 45.

19   Harvey, *The Limits to Capital*, 148; Alfred Dupont Chandler, *The Visible Hand: The Managerial Revolution in American Business* (Cambridge, MA: Belknap Press, 2002).

20   Harvey, *The Limits to Capital*, 148.

21   Henning, *Philosophy after Marx*, 109; Michael Heinrich, *An Introduction to the Three Volumes of Karl Marx's Capital*, trans. Alex Locascio (New York: Monthly Review

Monopoly Capital was written in the 1950s and published in 1966, just as the *intensification* of competition on a global scale began to undermine the post-war boom and usher in the neoliberal era. The loss of popularity that the concept of monopoly capitalism has experienced in the last four decades may be related to the advent of neoliberalism, with its general intensification of competitive pressures. The deregulation of international trade and finance, the development of new communication technologies, and the revolution in logistics have all contributed to the globalisation and intensification of competition. The collapse of the Eastern bloc, the integration of China into the capitalist world market, and the wave of structural adjustments in the global South have opened up vast new fields into which capital can enmesh itself. The transition from the vertically integrated corporations, characteristic of the Fordist era, to the horizontally integrated networks of lean production has also contributed to the intensification of competition, as have the consistent waves of privatisation and outsourcing of state functions in what were once called welfare states.

In short, there are many good reasons why the idea of monopoly capitalism seems so unconvincing in the current conjuncture. But for our purposes, one is most salient: namely that this theory inhibited the acknowledgement of the economic power of capital because it led to a one-sided focus on the state and a simplistic model of class domination. In this way, the theory replaced the mute compulsion of capital with the violent regime of a 'personal union' in control of the state.

Productive force determinism and the base/superstructure model continued to haunt Marxist debates about the state until the 1970s, when scholars such as Nicos Poulantzas, Ellen Meiksins Wood, members of the Conference on Socialist Economics, and the participants in the German state-derivation debate parted ways with orthodox Marxism, opening up new theoretical perspectives.[22] They all attempted to carve out a path between the crude instrumentalism of classical Marxism and the social

---

Press, 2012), 215f; Robert Brenner, *The Economics of Global Turbulence: The Advanced Capitalist Economies from Long Boom to Long Downturn, 1945–2005* (London: Verso, 2006), 54.

22   Nicos Poulantzas, *Political Power and Social Classes*, trans. Timothy O'Hagan (London: Verso, 1978); Nicos Poulantzas, *State, Power, Socialism*, trans. Patrick Camille (London: Verso, 2014); Wood, *Democracy against Capitalism*; Simon Clarke, ed., *The State Debate* (Basingstoke: Macmillan, 1991); John Holloway and Sol Picciotto, eds., *State and Capital: A Marxist Debate* (London: Edward Arnold, 1978); Ingo Elbe, *Marx im Westen: Die neue Marx-lektüre in der Bundesrepublik seit 1965* (Berlin: Akademie Verlag, 2008), chap. 2.

democratic view of the state as a neutral arena, and many of them did so by
moving beyond the exclusive occupation with the *content* of state policy –
that is, the question of who benefits from this policy. Instead, they posed
the more fundamental question of the very *form* of the state, a question
which was aptly formulated by Evgeny B. Pashukanis as early as 1924:

> Why does class rule not remain what it is, the factual subjugation of
> one section of the population by the other? Why does it assume the
> form of official state rule, or – which is the same thing – why does
> the machinery of state coercion not come into being as the private
> machinery of the ruling class; why does it detach itself from the ruling
> class and take on the form of an impersonal apparatus of public power,
> separate from society?[23]

The great advantage of such an approach is that it allows us to circumvent the conceptual gulf between the *economic* and the *political* taken for
granted in both classical Marxism and Poulantzas's Althusserian social
ontology, in which the base/superstructure model and the distinction
between an economic and a political 'level' or 'instance' were taken to be a
feature of *all* modes of production.[24] In an important contribution to these
debates, Wood demonstrated the inadequacy of the base/superstructure
model and proposed to conceptualise the separation of the political and
the economic in capitalism as 'the differentiation of political functions
themselves and their separate allocation to the private economic sphere
and the public sphere of the state'.[25] Bernhard Blanke, Ulrich Jürgens,
and Hans Kastendiek likewise rejected 'the commonplace (scientific)
notion of the relation between politics and economics [that] contains the
assumption that only politics has to do with domination, that economics
on the other hand has to do with "material laws"'.[26] In general, the participants in the state-derivation debate proceeded from 'an interpretation
of Marx's *Capital* not as a theory of the "economic" but as a theory of the

---

23   Evgeny B. Pashukanis, *Law and Marxism: A General Theory*, trans. Barbara
Einhorn (London: Pluto Press, 1983), 139.

24   Poulantzas, *Political Power and Social Classes*, 13.

25   Wood, *Democracy against Capitalism*, 31.

26   Bernhard Blanke, Ulrich Jürgens, and Hans Kastendiek, 'On the Current Marxist
Discussion on the Analysis of Form and Function of the Bourgeois State', in Holloway and
Picciotto, *State and Capital*, 121f.

social relations of capitalist society', in the words of Simon Clarke.[27] This acknowledgement of the social nature of the political and the economic is a fundamental prerequisite not only of a theory of economic power but also of a theory of the state.

The most sophisticated attempts to come up with an answer to Pashukanis's question were developed in German state-derivation debates of the 1970s, where a number of scholars carefully demonstrated how capitalist relations of production presuppose the existence of an institution not directly involved in the organisation of social reproduction and endowed with the ability to 'force the totality', as Marx put it in the *Grundrisse*.[28] For example, it can be shown that the universalisation of the 'cell form' of capitalism – the commodity – presupposes an institution with the ability to guarantee property rights.[29] Furthermore, the separation of the units of production into competing capitals makes it impossible for these capitals individually to secure the *general conditions* of production as a totality; it is for this reason that capitalist production presupposes an institution with the ability to secure these conditions (such as infrastructure, currency, education, research, etc.) by imposing certain rules on *all* capitals.[30] Joachim Hirsch puts it well:

> The bourgeois state is in its specific historical shape a social form which capital must necessarily create for its own reproduction, and, just as necessarily, the state apparatus must assume an existence formally separated from the ruling class, the bourgeoisie.[31]

For our purposes, the decisive lesson from these debates is that the organisation of social reproduction on the basis of the valorisation of

---

27   Simon Clarke, 'The State Debate', in *The State Debate* (Basingstoke: Macmillan, 1991), 9.

28   G: 531.

29   C1: 90.

30   See Claudia von Braunmühl et al., *Probleme einer materialistischen Staatstheorie* (Frankfurt am Main: Suhrkamp, 1973); Clarke, 'The State Debate'; Elbe, *Marx im Westen*, chap. 2; Heinrich, *An Introduction*, 203ff; Holloway and Picciotto, *State and Capital*; Dieter Läpple, *Staat und Allgemeine Produktionsbedingungen, Grundlagen zur Kritik der Infrastrukturtheorien* (Berlin: VSA, 1973); Gert Schäfer, 'Nogle problemer vedrørende forholdet mellem "økonomisk" og "politiske" herredømme', in *Til rekonstruktionen af den marxistiske statsteori*, ed. Eike Hennig et al. (København: Rhodos, 1974).

31   Joachim Hirsch, 'The State Apparatus and Social Reproduction: Elements of a Theory of the Bourgeois State', in Holloway and Picciotto, *State and Capital*, 97f.

value presupposes an institution formally separated from the immediate processes of social production endowed with the capacity to enforce rules upon everyone by means of coercive force. I agree with Max Weber, along with Poulantzas, Hirsch, and many others, that *violence* is the distinctive form of power pertaining to the state.[32] This identification is important for the theory of the economic power of capital since it reveals how *the mute compulsion of capital presupposes the coercive force of the state.* The state is, in Marx's words, 'the political engine for forcibly perpetuating the social enslavement of the producers of wealth by its appropriators, of the economic rule of capital over labour'.[33] State violence is not only one of the means by which the conditions of capital accumulation were originally established; it also *continues* to be a necessary moment of the reproduction of the capitalist relations of production. Despite this necessity, it remains the case that social production under capitalism is organised by means of the mute compulsion of capital. As Blanke, Jürgens, and Kastendiek put it, 'The movement of value as material-economic nexus represents a type of societization free from personal, physical force.'[34] At the same time, in capitalism, the social regulation of economic activity is, to use Wood's term, 'privatized'. This privatisation results in the emergence of 'the development of a new sphere of power', and in order to theorise this sphere of power, we need a theory of economic power alongside the theory of the state.[35]

Theories of Ideology

Apart from theories of the state, the most persistent preoccupation with the question of power in the Marxist tradition is found in theories of ideology.[36] The Marxists of the Second International era used the term 'ideology' in the broad sense of 'any kind of socially determined

---

32   Hirsch, 'State Apparatus', 62, 65; Poulantzas, *Political Power and Social Classes*, 225ff; Poulantzas, *State, Power, Socialism*, 80; Blanke et al., 'On the Current Marxist Discussion', 124; Wood, *Democracy against Capitalism*, 32.

33   22: 535.

34   Blanke et al., 'On the Current Marxist Discussion', 122.

35   Wood, *Democracy against Capitalism*, 29, 31.

36   For an overview of Marxist theories of ideology, see Terry Eagleton, *Ideology: An Introduction* (London: Verso, 1996); Jan Rehmann, *Theories of Ideology: The Powers of Alienation and Subjection* (Chicago: Haymarket, 2013).

thought'.[37] Here, however, I am only interested in ideology insofar as it has to do with power. Theories of ideology in this sense began to appear in the 1920s, as a response to at least two problems. On a theoretical level, classical Marxism had, as we have just seen, focussed excessively on the coercive force of the state, thereby neglecting the role of ideology. On a conjunctural level, the enthusiasm for World War I among European working classes and the subsequent advent of fascism called for the development of theories capable of understanding what was referred to as the 'subjective factor' – that is, the question of how it was possible to for reactionary forces to mobilise proletarians against their 'objective' interests. 'Anyone who underestimates the material power of ideology will never achieve anything,' warned Wilhelm Reich in 1934. 'In our historical period, it has shown itself to be stronger than the power of material distress: otherwise, the workers and the peasants, and not Hitler and Thyssen, would be in power.'[38] In contrast to those who emphasised the importance of the coercive power of the state in the reproduction of class society, Reich insisted that 'it is only seldom that the owners of the social means of production resort to the means of brute violence in the domination of the oppressed classes; its main weapon is its ideological power'.[39]

Western Marxists such as Georg Lukács, Antonio Gramsci, Theodor Adorno, and Louis Althusser responded to this practical and theoretical need for a theory of ideology. Although this is a diverse group of thinkers, they share one basic idea, which underpins all theories of ideology: namely that one of the means by which capitalism reproduces itself is through affecting the concepts, imageries, myths, and narratives through which we (consciously or unconsciously) represent, interpret, and understand social reality. Broadly speaking, ideology addresses how we *think*, and this is why Reich, Gramsci, Althusser, and others distinguish it from *violence* or *coercion*, which directly addresses the body.

Perry Anderson's category of 'Western Marxism' is often criticised for lumping together a number of very diverse thinkers under a somewhat vague heading. Although I partly agree with this criticism, I nevertheless

---

37   Eagleton, *Ideology*, 89; Rehmann, *Theories of Ideology*, chaps. 2, 3.

38   Wilhelm Reich, *Was ist Klassenbewusstsein? Ein Beitrag zur Neuformierung der Arbeiterbewegung von Ernst Parell* (Copenhagen: Verlag für Sexualpolitik, 1934), 28.

39   Wilhelm Reich, *The Mass Psychology of Fascism*, trans. Vincent R. Carfagno (New York: Farrar, Straus & Giroux, 1970), 25.

find the categorisation useful for one specific reason: the general lack of attention to economic power in the works of thinkers such as Lukács, Gramsci, Adorno, and Althusser, as well as Karl Korsch, Max Horkheimer, Herbert Marcuse, Henri Lefebvre, Jean-Paul Sartre, and Guy Debord. It is certainly possible to find exceptions, but on the whole, Western Marxism has generally been occupied with other forms of power – especially *ideological power*. Anderson presents the emergence of Western Marxism as a turn to philosophy at the expense of economics, and though this description certainly captures something significant, it implies a problematic subdivision of Marxist theory: Anderson seems to regard Marx's critique of political economy as an economic theory rather than a critical theory of capitalist social relations (and thus a *critique* of economic theory), a misunderstanding which leads him to reproduce the familiar division of Marx's writings into the early 'philosophical' works and the later 'economic' works.[40] As I hope will become clear in the course of this book, this is an impoverished reading of the critique of political economy, which cannot be opposed to something like 'Marx's philosophy'. What *is* true in Anderson's account, however, is that Western Marxism failed to engage seriously with the critique of political economy – a failure that was to a large degree a result of their (often implicit) acceptance of the idea that Marx's later writings are concerned with 'economics' and thus only relevant to engage with systematically if one was interested in 'economic theory' or wanted to undertake an 'economic analysis' of a concrete situation.[41]

The claim that Western Marxists failed to properly appreciate Marx's critique of political economy requires some qualifications. One of the strengths of Lukács's Marxism is its rejection of the interpretation of Marx's later works as a turn away from philosophy.[42] His appreciation of the philosophical richness of *Capital* allowed him to develop a highly original reading of Marx's analysis of the commodity and to reach the astonishing conclusion that the section on fetishism in the first chapter of *Capital* – which had been virtually ignored until the publication of *History and Class Consciousness* in 1923 – 'contains within itself the whole

40   Perry Anderson, *Considerations on Western Marxism* (London: Verso, 1987), 49ff, 99, 115f.

41   Elbe, 'Between Marx, Marxism, and Marxisms'; Heinrich, *An Introduction*, 26; Wood, *Democracy against Capitalism*, 6.

42   Georg Lukács, *The Ontology of Social Being: 2. Marx*, trans. David Fernbach (London: Merlin Press, 1978), 11.

of historical materialism'.[43] Lukács was, unfortunately, not particularly interested in power; insofar as he discusses it, he is primarily interested in 'reified consciousness', that is, ideology.[44] In addition to his preoccupation with aesthetics and methodology, he was chiefly occupied with a Weber-inspired and deeply romantic critique of the 'capitalist process of rationalisation', which 'disrupts every organically unified process of work and life'.[45] Weber's influence is also visible in the connection Lukács draws between the critique of fetishism and Weber's 'rationalisation' thesis, according to which modern society is increasingly dominated by instrumental rationality.[46] This led Lukács, paradoxically, to invert the critical insight of Marx's analysis of fetishism, namely that bourgeois society – which conceives of itself as enlightened and free from superstition – treats the products of labour as supernatural entities endowed with their own will. In other words: capitalism is not a *disenchanted*, but rather an *enchanted* world.

Karl Korsch is probably the sole thinker among the Western Marxists to have undertaken the most serious engagement with Marx's critique of political economy. In *Karl Marx* – written in 1935–36, but first published in an English translation in 1938 – he recognised that Marx's theory of value is not a quantitative theory of prices but is rather intended to reveal 'the real social nature of the *fundamental human relations* underlying the so-called "value" of the classicists'.[47] Korsch's critique of traditional Marxist orthodoxy in *Marxism and Philosophy* and his interpretation of the critique of political economy in *Karl Marx* definitely cleared some ground for a theory of the economic power of capital, even if he did not himself venture down that road.[48]

Antonio Gramsci is rightfully considered one of the great thinkers of power in the Marxist canon. His fundamental insight was that the power of the bourgeoisie relied not only on *coercion*, but also – perhaps even primarily so in Western Europe – on the creation of *consent* on the part of the working classes; a consent produced in and through institutions of

---

43   Georg Lukács, *History and Class Consciousness: Studies in Marxist Dialectics*, trans. Rodney Livingstone (London: Merlin Press, 2010), 171.

44   For a good discussion of Lukács on ideology, see Eagleton, *Ideology*, 94–106.

45   Lukács, *History and Class Consciousness*, 102f.

46   Clarke, *Marx, Marginalism and Modern Sociology*, 315; See also Elbe, 'Between Marx, Marxism, and Marxisms'.

47   Karl Korsch, *Karl Marx* (Chicago: Haymarket, 2017), 19.

48   Karl Korsch, *Marxism and Philosophy*, trans. Fred Halliday (London: Verso, 2013).

'civil society' such as churches, schools, and the media. This insight was a decisive advance compared to the state-centric conceptions of power in classical Marxism. In the most common reading, Gramsci's theory of hegemony is intended as a theory of how the ruling classes maintain their position by means of culture and ideology. Gramsci is often charged with neglecting the economy, for example by Anderson, who claims that 'Gramsci's silence on economic problems was complete'.[49] In recent years, several scholars have pointed out that Gramsci was more complex than that. Alex Callinicos, Michael R. Krätke, and Peter D. Thomas have all demonstrated that Gramsci was quite attentive to 'economic' questions, and that Gramsci's 'integral concept of civil society' does not, in Thomas's words, exclude 'the economic' but rather insists that it must be 'theorised in *political* terms' – a crucial precondition for a theory of economic power.[50] As Krätke's discussion of the engagement with political economy in the *Prison Notebooks* makes clear, however, Gramsci's knowledge of political economy as well as Marx's critique of it had very clear limits. The same is true of his attempts to analyse the economic structure and dynamics of capitalism. Although he clearly grasps the difference between David Ricardo's ahistorical mode of thought and Marx's consistent historicisation of Ricardo's concepts, he is, as Krätke puts it, 'not clear about what constitutes the specific difference between Marx's "critical" economics and "classical" economics'.[51] Gramsci seems to think that the theories of Ricardo and Marx are basically variants of the same type of theory, and there is nothing to suggest an awareness on the part of Gramsci of the fundamental difference between their concepts of value.

Similar points can be made with regards to Adorno. Contrary to the widespread perception of Adorno's critical theory as 'a totalizing one-dimensional cultural theory', there is in fact a 'Marxian core of Adorno's late work', as Chris O'Kane puts it.[52] This core consists of a consistent

---

49   Perry Anderson, *Considerations on Western Marxism* (London: Verso, 1987), 75.

50   Peter D. Thomas, *The Gramscian Moment: Philosophy, Hegemony, and Marxism* (Chicago: Haymarket, 2010), 175; Alex Callinicos, 'Continuing "Capital" in the Face of the Present' (paper presented at Capital.150: Marx's *Capital* Today, King's College, London, 2017); Michael R. Krätke, 'Antonio Gramsci's Contribution to a Critical Economics', *Historical Materialism* 19, no. 3 (2011): 63–105.

51   Michael R. Krätke, 'Antonio Gramsci's Contribution to a Critical Economics', *Historical Materialism* 19, no. 3 (2011): 80; Antonio Gramsci, *Prison Notebooks*: vol. 3, trans. Joseph A. Buttigieg (New York: Columbia University Press, 2011), 308f.

52   Chris O'Kane, '"The Process of Domination Spews Out Tatters of Subjugated

emphasis on the universal domination of the logic of *exchange* in bourgeois society, an insight which became an important point of departure for what eventually became the *Neue Marx-Lektüre*.[53] It is also worth recalling, however, that it was precisely the inadequacy of Adorno's (and Horkheimer's) engagement with the critique of political economy that spurred his students to go back to the *Grundrisse* and *Capital* to reconstruct Marx's critical theory.[54] Adorno's analysis of exchange value as a form of *domination* was an important step towards a theory of the economic power of capital, but his one-sided emphasis on the implementation of the logic of identity in the sphere of circulation (inherited from Alfred Sohn-Rethel) led him to ignore that the exchange of equivalences is only one side of the coin, the other being the appropriation of surplus labour *without* an exchange of equivalents.[55] For this reason, Adorno and Horkheimer's claim that 'bourgeois society is ruled by equivalence' is actually quite misleading.[56] We could just as well say the opposite: bourgeois society is ruled by non-equivalence. Given the intimate connection between the exchange of equivalents in the sphere of circulation and the exploitation of labour in the sphere of production, however, what we need is rather a Hegelian sublation of these two abstract moments: bourgeois society is ruled by the unity of equivalence and non-equivalence.

My discussion of Lukács, Korsch, Gramsci, and Adorno demonstrates

---

Nature": Critical Theory, Negative Totality, and the State of Extraction', in *Black Box: A Record of the Catastrophe*, vol. 1, ed. Black Box Collective (Oakland: PM Press, 2015), 191.

53   O'Kane, 'Critical Theory', 191.

54   See Hans-Georg Backhaus, *Dialektik der Wertform: Untersuchungen zur marxschen Ökonomiekritik* (Freiburg: ca ira, 1997), 76; Endnotes, 'Communisation and Value-Form Theory', in *Endnotes 2: Misery and the Value Form* (London: Endnotes, 2010), 83ff; Jan Hoff, *Marx Worldwide: On the Development of the International Discourse on Marx since 1965*, trans. Nicholas Gray (Leiden: Brill, 2017), 27ff; O'Kane, 'Critical Theory', 196f; Helmut Reichelt, 'From the Frankfurt School to Value-Form Analysis', trans. Michael Eldred, *Thesis Eleven* 4, no. 1 (1982), 166–69; Helmut Reichelt, 'Marx's Critique of Economic Categories: Reflections on the Problem of Validity in the Dialectical Method of Presentation in *Capital*', trans. Werner Strauss, *Historical Materialism* 15, no. 4 (2007).

55   See Gerhard Hanloser and Karl Reitter, *Der bewegte Marx: Eine einführende Kritik des Zirkulationsmarxismus* (Münster: Unrast Verlag, 2008), 14f; Georg Klauda, 'Von der Arbeiterbewegung zur Kritischen Theorie: Zur Urgeschichte des Marxismus ohne Klassen', in *Karl Marx: Philosoph der Befreiung oder Theoretiker des Kapitals? Zur Kritik der 'Neuen Marx-Lektüre'*, ed. Karl Reitter (Wien: Mandelbaum Verlag, 2015); Chris O'Kane, 'Critical Theory'; Reichelt, 'Marx's Critique of Economic Categories'.

56   Max Horkheimer and Theodor W. Adorno, *Dialectic of Enlightenment: Philosophical Fragments*, trans. Edmund Jephcott (Stanford: Stanford University Press, 2002), 4.

that Western Marxism as a tradition is not completely devoid of attempts to draw on insights from Marx's critique of political economy. Yet, it also makes it clear that these attempts leave much to be desired. The primary contribution of Western Marxists, as far as advancing our understanding of the power of capital goes, is to be found in their theories and analyses of ideology. To be sure, this is a decisive step forward compared to the state-centric conceptions of power in classical Marxism. Theories of ideology have convincingly shown that ideological power is necessary for the reproduction of capitalist relations of production. But they do not tell us much about the mute compulsion of economic relations.

Theories of Economic Power

We have now seen how classical Marxists as well as Western Marxists generally remained within the confines of the violence/ideology couplet – or, put differently, that neither of them managed to bring the *economic power* of capital to the fore. With the renaissance of Marxist theory in the 1960s, however, a number of theoretical currents emerged which succeeded in breaking with this couplet, even if they did not articulate it in those terms. I will discuss in detail the advantages of this scholarship, as well as its shortcomings, in the following chapters; therefore, I will limit myself here to a brief overview of what I take to be the most significant contributions to the project in which this book aims to partake: the uncovering of the workings of capital's mute compulsion.

One of the most important and original currents in the contemporary Marxist landscape is what sometimes goes by the name of value-form theory.[57] As already mentioned, Hans-Georg Backhaus and Helmut

---

57 This somewhat broad term refers to the early representatives of the Neue Marx-Lektüre: Backhaus, *Dialektik der Wertform*; Hans-Jürgen Krahl, *Konstitution und Klassenkampf: Zur historischen Dialektik von bürgerlicher Emanzipation und proletarischer Revolution* (Frankfurt: Verlag Neue Kritik, 1971); Helmut Reichelt, *Zur logischen Struktur des Kapitalbegriffs bei Karl Marx* (Frankfurt am Main: Europäische Verlagsanstalt, 1973); Alfred Schmidt, *The Concept of Nature in Marx*, trans. Ben Fowkes (London: Verso, 2013). Later works within that strand include Helmut Brentel, *Soziale Form und Ökonomisches Objekt: Studien zum Gegenstands- und Methodenverständnis der Kritik der politischen Ökonomie* (Wiesbaden: Springer Fachmedien Wiesbaden, 1989); Elbe, *Marx im Westen*; Sven Ellmers, *Die formanalytische Klassentheorie von Karl Marx: Ein Beitrag zur 'neuen Marx-Lektüre'*, 2nd ed. (Duisburg: Universitätverlag Rhein-Ruhr, 2009); Frank Engster,

Reichelt originally developed what eventually became the *Neue Marx-Lektüre* as a reaction to the lack of engagement with Marx's critique of political economy in the work of Adorno and Horkheimer.[58] Perhaps the most fundamental contribution of value-form theory is the reinterpretation of Marx's critique of political economy as precisely that – not an *alternative* political economy but a *critique* of political economy; not an economic theory intended to produce quantifiable concepts which can be operationalised in empirical economic analysis but a qualitative theory of social forms aimed at uncovering and criticising the social relations

---

Das Geld als Mass, Mittel und Methode: Das Rechnen mit der Identität der Zeit (Berlin: Neofelis Verlag, 2014); Michael Heinrich, *Die Wissenschaft vom Wert: Die Marxsche Kritik der politischen Ökonomie zwischen wissenschaftlicher Revolution und klassischer Tradition* (Münster: Westfälisches Dampfboot, 1999); and Nadja Rakowitz, *Einfache Warenproduktion: Ideal und Ideologie* (Freiburg: ca ira, 2000). On the 'critique of value', see Anselm Jappe, *Die Abenteuer der Ware: Für eine neue Wertkritik* (Münster: Unrast Verlag, 2005); Robert Kurz, *Geld ohne Wert: Grundrisse zu einer Transformation der Kritik der politischen Ökonomie* (Berlin: Horlemann, 2012); Neil Larsen et al., eds., *Marxism and the Critique of Value* (Chicago: MCM' Publishing, 2014); and Ernst Lohoff and Norbert Trenkle, *Die Große Entwertung* (Münster: Unrast Verlag, 2013). On 'new' or 'systematic' dialectics, see Christopher Arthur, *The New Dialectic and Marx's Capital* (Leiden: Brill, 2004); Patrick Murray, *Marx's Theory of Scientific Knowledge* (New York: Humanity Books, 1990); Geert Reuten and Mike Williams, *Value Form and the State: The Tendencies of Accumulation and the Determination of Economic Policy in Capitalist Society* (London: Routledge, 1989); and Tony Smith, *The Logic of Marx's Capital: Replies to Hegelian Criticisms* (New York: SUNY Press, 1990). Predecessors include Pashukanis, *Law and Marxism*; Roman Rosdolsky, *The Making of Marx's 'Capital'*, trans. Pete Burgess (London: Pluto Press, 1977); I. I. Rubin, *Essays on Marx's Theory of Value*, trans. Miloš Samardžija and Fredy Perlman (Delhi: Aakar Books, 2008). Associated scholarship includes Riccardo Bellofiore, 'A Ghost Turning into a Vampire: The Concept of Capital and Living Labour', in *Re-Reading Marx: New Perspectives after the Critical Edition*, ed. Riccardo Bellofiore and Roberto Fineschi (Basingstoke: Palgrave Macmillan, 2009); Werner Bonefeld, *Critical Theory and the Critique of Political Economy* (London: Bloomsbury, 2014); Moishe Postone, *Time, Labor, and Social Domination: A Reinterpretation of Marx's Critical Theory* (Cambridge: Cambridge University Press, 2003); Projektgruppe Entwicklung des Marxschen Systems, *Das Kapital vom Geld: Interpretation der verschiedenen Entwürfe* (Hamburg: VSA, 1973); Projektgruppe zur Kritik der Politischen Ökonomie, *Zur Logik des Kapitals* (Hamburg: VSA, 1973); Guido Starosta, *Marx's Capital: Method and Revolutionary Subjectivity* (Chicago: Haymarket, 2016); and Dieter Wolf, *Der dialektische Widerspruch im Kapital: Ein Beitrag zur Marxschen Werttheorie* (Hamburg: VSA, 2002). For overviews, see Elbe, *Marx im Westen*; Hoff, *Marx Worldwide*; Anselm Jappe, 'Towards a History of the Critique of Value', *Capitalism Nature Socialism* 25, no. 2 (2014): 25–37; and Neil Larsen et al., 'Introduction', in *Marxism and the Critique of Value*, ed. Neil Larsen et al. (Chicago: MCM' Publishing, 2014).

58   Reichelt, 'From the Frankfurt School to Value-Form Analysis', 166–9.

underlying the capitalist mode of production. This opened up the possibility of re-reading Marx's theory of value as a theory of the transformation
of capitalist social relations into real abstractions imposing themselves
on social life through an impersonal form of power – an interpretation
that has been taken up with particular acuteness in the work of Michael
Heinrich, who will be a central interlocutor in the following chapters.
Another important work in this tradition is Moishe Postone's reinterpretation of the critique of political economy as a theory of a historically
unique 'abstract form of social domination'.[59]

Another important strand of contemporary Marxist thought is the political Marxism of Robert Brenner and Ellen Meiksins Wood. In a seminal
essay from 1981, Wood forcefully argues that '*economic* categories express
certain *social* relations'.[60] Her firm rejection of the economism so often
imputed to Marx allows her to conceptualise the specificity of capitalism
in terms of the forms of power employed by ruling classes in their effort
to extract surplus labour from producers; whereas pre-capitalist rulers
had to rely on personal relations of dependence upheld by extra-economic
coercion, capitalists can, under normal circumstances, rely on a purely
economic form of power. As in the case of value-form theory, the crucial
advance made by Brenner and Wood had to do with the resolute break
with the idea of the economy as an ontologically separate sphere governed
by sui generis, transhistorical laws.

The effort to break with economism in order to reveal the social
constitution of the economy is a project which also sits at the core of
Marxist-feminist attempts to grasp the relation between the formal
economy and the life-making activities which take place outside of the
immediate circuits of capital. In recent years, the insights gained during
the domestic-labour debates of the 1970s have been taken up, expanded,
and clarified by scholars working within social reproduction theory.[61]
This important branch of Marxist theory takes up a crucial question
almost completely ignored by Marx: 'What kinds of processes enable the
worker to arrive at the doors of her place of work every day so that she can

---

59   Postone, *Time, Labor, and Social Domination*, 3.

60   Wood, *Democracy against Capitalism*, 23.

61   Tithi Bhattacharya, ed., *Social Reproduction Theory: Remapping Class, Recentering
Oppression* (London: Pluto Press, 2017); Cinzia Arruzza, 'Remarks on Gender', *Viewpoint
Magazine*, no. 4 (2014), viewpointmag.com; Susan Ferguson, *Women and Work: Femi-
nism, Labour, and Social Reproduction* (London: Pluto Press, 2019).

produce the wealth of society?'[62] As Tithi Bhattacharya emphasises, such a perspective requires us to accept Marx's invitation 'to see the "economic" as a social relation: one that involves domination and coercion, even if juridical forms and political institutions seek to obscure that'.[63]

The once-widespread caricature of Marx's work as a promethean pan-egyric to the subjugation of nature has been effectively refuted by the Marxist ecologists Paul Burkett and John Bellamy Foster.[64] One of the great merits of Marxist ecology is to have emphasised the *materiality* of the capitalist economy, that is, the fact that capitalist social relations are part of a natural world which is *not* a product of capitalism and which does not always obey its commands. The critique of political economy is not merely an analysis of economic form-determinations but also a theory which 'deals with *the interrelation between economic forms and the concrete material world*', as Kohei Saito has recently formulated it.[65] Likewise, Andreas Malm has convincingly demonstrated that it is impossible to fully understand the power of capital without understanding its relations to nature, and that in order to understand those relations, it is necessary to reject economistic and technicist obfuscations of what the economy is.[66]

The tradition of labour process theory inaugurated by Harry Braver-man's *Labor and Monopoly Capital* is another important source of insights for the development of a theory of the economic power of capital. It involves a crucial shift from a view of technological development as the outcome of a transhistorical march forward of the productive forces – and hence as a potentially liberating force (recall Lenin's embrace of Taylorism) – to an acknowledgement of the ways in which it works as a means of domination used by employers in order to break the power of the workers. Such a perspective on technology, which aligns well with

---

62   Tithi Bhattacharya, 'Introduction: Mapping Social Reproduction Theory', in *Social Reproduction Theory*, 1.

63   Tithi Bhattacharya, 'How Not to Skip Class: Social Reproduction of Labour and the Global Working Class', in *Social Reproduction Theory*, 71.

64   Paul Burkett, *Marx and Nature: A Red and Green Perspective* (Chicago: Haymar-ket, 2014); Foster, *Marx's Ecology*.

65   Kohei Saito, *Karl Marx's Ecosocialism: Capital, Nature, and the Unfinished Critique of Political Economy* (New York: Monthly Review Press, 2017), 16.

66   Malm, *Fossil Capital*; Andreas Malm, *The Progress of This Storm: Nature and Society in a Warming World* (London: Verso, 2018); Andreas Malm, 'Marx on Steam: From the Optimism of Progress to the Pessimism of Power', *Rethinking Marxism* 30, no. 2 (2018), 166–85.

the emphasis on materiality in Marxist ecology, is a *condicio sine qua non* for understanding the power of capital as it manifests itself within the workplace.

Finally, I should also mention a number of important studies which do not fit neatly into any of the above-mentioned traditions. Lucio Colletti's trenchant critique of traditional Marxism was one of the earliest successful attempts to reject Marxist economism on the basis of a methodologically careful interpretation of the critique of political economy, including the theory of value.[67] David Harvey's oeuvre has provided many key insights to the present work about the spatiality of capitalist power, in addition to clarifying a number of issues related to Marx's methodology and his theory of accumulation and crisis. William Clare Roberts's interpretation of the first volume of *Capital* as a political theory provides several clear-sighted interventions into contemporary debates and underlines the 'novel form of domination' characteristic of capitalism.[68] Jasper Bernes's writings on logistics and agriculture are both essential points of reference for understanding the contemporary bases of capital's power, as is Aaron Benanav's study of the global surplus population since 1950 and his work with other members of the Endnotes collective.[69]

---

67   Lucio Colletti, *From Rousseau to Lenin: Studies in Ideology and Society*, trans. John Merrington and Judith White (New York: Monthly Review Press, 1973); Raya Dunayevskaya also made important headway with her interpretation of *Capital* as 'a critique of the very foundations of political economy'. More than two decades before Diane Elson, she suggested that we should speak of the 'value theory of labour' rather than the 'labour theory of value'. Raya Dunayevskaya, *Marxism and Freedom: From 1776 until Today*, 3rd ed. (London: Pluto Press, 1971), 106, 138; Diane Elson, 'The Value Theory of Labour', in *Value: The Representation of Labour in Capitalism*, ed. Diane Elson (London: Verso, 2015).

68   William Clare Roberts, *Marx's Inferno: The Political Theory of* Capital (Princeton: Princeton University Press, 2017), 17.

69   Jasper Bernes, 'Logistics, Counterlogistics, and the Communist Prospect', in *Endnotes 3: Gender, Class and Other Misfortunes* (London: Endnotes, 2013); Jasper Bernes, 'The Belly of the Revolution', in *Materialism and the Critique of Energy*, ed. Brent Ryan Bellamy and Jeff Diamanti (Chicago: MCM' Publishing, 2018); Aaron Benanav, 'A Global History of Unemployment: Surplus Populations in the World Economy, 1949–2010' (PhD diss., UCLA, 2015); Aaron Benanav and John Clegg, 'Crisis and Immiseration: Critical Theory Today', in *The SAGE Handbook of Frankfurt School Critical Theory*, ed. Beverly Best, Werner Bonefeld, and Chris O'Kane (London: SAGE, 2018), 1629–48; Endnotes and Aaron Benanav, 'Misery and Debt: On the Logic and History of Surplus Populations and Surplus Capital', in *Endnotes 2: Misery and the Value Form* (London: Endnotes, 2010); Aaron Benanav, *Automation and the Future of Work* (New York: Verso, 2020).

All of these scholars have contributed to the uncovering of the mute compulsion of capital in important ways. Some of them zoom in on specific aspects of this power; others have a more general scope. Some of them proceed from empirical analyses, others from a dialectical analysis of concepts. However, none of them provide a comprehensive account of the economic power of capital, and many of them reveal theoretical shortcomings of various kinds. In the course of the following chapters, I will do my best to single out and integrate the most relevant parts of this scholarship into a systematic theory of the economic power of capital based on a close reading of Marx's critique of political economy.

3

The Social Ontology of Economic Power

What is it about human beings that makes it possible for them to organise their reproduction through hierarchies and logics which impose themselves on social life by means of mute compulsion? Why is it that these peculiar beings are capable of getting caught up in something like economic power? In order to answer these questions, it is necessary to outline what I will call the social ontology of economic power. If ontology is the study of being *qua* being, as the Aristotelean definition goes, social ontology is the study of a particular kind of being, namely that of the social or of society. Its first question is thus: what is society? Social ontology is the examination of 'the nature of social reality', as Carol C. Gould puts it, and is therefore concerned with determinations common to all societies, regardless of their historical and geographical context.[1] To provide a social ontology of economic power thus means to trace the possibility of economic power back to the nature of social reality – which is what I will do in this and the following two chapters.

---

1   Carol C. Gould, *Marx's Social Ontology: Individuality and Community in Marx's Theory of Social Reality* (Cambridge, MA: MIT Press, 1980), xv; see also Daniel Krier and Mark P. Worrell, 'The Social Ontology of Capitalism: An Introduction', in *The Social Ontology of Capitalism*, ed. Daniel Krier and Mark P. Worrell (New York: Palgrave Macmillan, 2017); Michael J. Thompson, 'Social Ontology and Social Critique: Toward a New Paradigm for Critical Theory', in Krier and Worrell, *The Social Ontology of Capitalism*.

The Necessity of Social Ontology

In classical Marxism, social ontology went by the name of 'the materialist conception of history'. In the subdivisions of Marxist doctrine, this was understood as the application of the philosophy of dialectical materialism 'to the social life of mankind', as Lenin put it.[2] As I explained in the last chapter, this was a social ontology in which the economy was taken to be a distinct sphere within a social totality governed by a transhistorical tendency for the productive forces to develop. Although it might be possible to explain or perhaps even justify orthodox historical materialism as 'a force of moral resistance, of cohesion, of patient perseverance' for 'those who do not have the initiative in the struggle', as Gramsci once claimed, it is clearly philosophically flawed.[3] This much was clear to early Western Marxists such as Korsch, Lukács, Gramsci, Marcuse, and Adorno, all of whom rejected the determinism and positivism of orthodox historical materialism.[4] Since the 1960s, there has been a broad consensus among Marxist scholars to reject productive force determinism in favour of an emphasis on the primacy of the relations of production.

Perhaps the most resolute rejection of orthodox historical materialism in the contemporary Marxist landscape is found among scholars belonging to the value-form theoretical tradition. As mentioned in the previous chapter, they have rightly pointed out that Marx was first of all engaged in a critical study of a historically specific mode of production, not in the construction of a philosophy of history. In accordance with this reading, most of them have endeavoured to 'expel from Marx's work everything that smells of an "unscientific" philosophy of history'.[5] Chris Arthur, for example, opposes *historical* dialectics – the classical idea of historical development as a dialectical process – to *systematic* dialectics, which he understands as a method 'concerned with the articulation of categories designed to conceptualise

---

2   Vladimir Illich Lenin, 'Karl Marx: A Brief Biographical Sketch with an Exposition of Marxism' (1914), in *Lenin's Collected Works*, vol. 21, ed. Stewart Smith, trans. Clemence Dutt (Moscow: Progress Publishers, 1974), 43–91.

3   Antonio Gramsci, *Prison Notebooks*, vol. 3, trans. Joseph A. Buttigieg (New York: Columbia University Press, 2011), 353.

4   Perry Anderson, *Considerations on Western Marxism* (London: Verso, 1987), 60; Ingo Elbe, *Marx im Westen: Die neue Marx-lektüre in der Bundesrepublik seit 1965* (Berlin: Akademie Verlag, 2008), 25f; John Bellamy Foster, *Marx's Ecology: Materialism and Nature* (New York: Monthly Review Press, 2000), 244f.

5   Endnotes, *Endnotes 2: Misery and the Value Form* (London: Endnotes, 2010), 100.

an existent concrete whole'.[6] From this perspective, dialectics is neither a universal ontological structure (as in dialectical materialism) nor a logic of history (as in historical materialism), but a mode of presentation, that is, a method for constructing a coherent conceptual apparatus.[7] Some scholars, such as Robert Kurz and Moishe Postone, accept the idea that there is in fact a *real* dialectic of productive forces and relations of production, but rather than understanding this as a transhistorical dynamic, they reinterpret it as a specifically capitalist phenomenon.[8]

The resolute break with orthodox historical materialism was necessary and important. However, it is also inadequate to simply insist that all the categories of the critique of political economy are only valid in relation to the capitalist mode of production.[9] In their eagerness to emphasise the historicity of Marx's concepts, value-form theorists tend to neglect social ontology, but there is no way out; the very idea of something being historically specific presupposes a concept of that which is *not* historically specific, and, for this reason, concepts which refer to historically specific social forms always carry certain assumptions about the ontology of the social. An absolute historicism, according to which the concepts by means of which we perceive social reality are completely immanent to a specific historical situation, would, paradoxically, end up representing this historical situation as something *eternal*, since it would make it impossible to conceptualise other situations and compare them with the current one. The philosophical lesson here is that difference and identity presuppose each other, or, as Hegel put it, 'Comparing has meaning only

---

6   Christopher Arthur, *The New Dialectic and Marx's* Capital (Leiden: Brill, 2004), 4.

7   See, for example, Werner Bonefeld, Critical Theory and the Critique of Political Economy (London: Bloomsbury, 2014), 5f, 68; Michael Heinrich, *Die Wissenschaft vom Wert: Die Marxsche Kritik der politischen Ökonomie zwischen wissenschaftlicher Revolution und klassischer Tradition* (Münster: Westfälisches Dampfboot, 1999), 171ff; Moishe Postone, *Time, Labor, and Social Domination: A Reinterpretation of Marx's Critical Theory* (Cambridge: Cambridge University Press, 2003), 142; Tony Smith, *Globalisation: A Systematic Marxian Account* (Chicago: Haymarket, 2009), 6ff.

8   Robert Kurz, *Geld ohne Wert: Grundrisse zu einer Transformation der Kritik der politischen Ökonomie* (Berlin: Horlemann, 2012), 284; Postone, *Time, Labor, and Social Domination*, 18.

9   Some scholars, like Moishe Postone, Anselm Jappe, and Robert Kurz, reject a transhistorical notion of labour. For an analysis of Marx's concepts of labour and a non-essentialist defence of a transhistorical concept of labour, see Søren Mau, 'Fra væsen til stofskifte: Marx' arbejdsbegreber', *Slagmark: Tidsskrift for Idéhistorie*, no. 76 (2017). Kurz is even critical of using such concepts as 'economy' and 'relations of production' outside of a capitalist context; see *Geld ohne Wert*, 37, 58, 86f.

on the assumption that there is a distinction, and conversely, likewise ... distinguishing has a meaning only on the assumption that there is some equality.'[10] In other words, the emphasis on the specificity of capitalism implies the identification of the difference between capitalist and non-capitalist societies, and this, in turn, implies the identification of elements common to capitalist and non-capitalist societies.[11] If we insist on absolute difference, we inevitably lose sight of the specificity of capitalism, and hence also its historicity.[12]

Relations and Relata

In the *Grundrisse*, Marx provides the following answer to the basic question of social ontology: 'Society does not consist of individuals, but expresses the sum of interrelations, the relations within which these individuals stand.'[13] While this statement clearly sets Marx apart from the atomism of bourgeois thought, it does not really identify the precise relation between 'individuals' and their 'relations'. At first sight, it seems obvious that *relations* always presuppose certain *relata*. This is essentially the idea that leads Gould to conclude that Marx regards individuals as ontologically primary.[14] But is not the opposite also true? If humans are

10   G. W. F. Hegel, *The Encyclopedia of Logic. Part I of the Encyclopedia of Philosophical Sciences with the Zusätze*, trans. T. F. Geraets, W. A. Suchting, and H. S. Harris (Indianapolis: Hackett, 1991), 184; see also *The Science of Logic*, trans. George di Giovanni (Cambridge: Cambridge University Press, 2010), 368.

11   See also the critique of Postone in Joseph Fracchia, 'On Transhistorical Abstractions and the Intersection of Historical Theory and Social Critique', *Historical Materialism* 12, no. 3 (2004): 125–46.

12   When Marx began to write the *Grundrisse* in August 1857, he planned to begin with 'the general, abstract determinants which obtain in more or less all forms of society' (G: 108), but he dropped this plan shortly thereafter, in October 1857 (see G: 227). In the preface to *Contribution*, he explains that he omitted the introduction of 1857 because it 'seems confusing to anticipate results which still have to be substantiated' (29: 261). The preface nevertheless proceeds to outline some of 'the general, abstract determinants which obtain in more or less all forms of society'. In the *1861–63 Manuscript*, Marx holds that 'it is entirely certain that human production possesses definite *laws* or *relations* which remain the same in all forms of production' (34: 236). Marx sketches out some of the basic elements of a social ontology in chapter seven of *Capital*, where he examines 'the labour process independently of any specific social formation' (C1: 283).

13   G: 265.

14   Another attempt to construct a kind of Marxism on the basis of the ontological primacy of the individual can be found in Jean-Paul Sartre's *Critique of Dialectical Reason*,

inherently social, as Marxists have always agreed, do individuals not also presuppose their social relations? Given its antagonistic relationship with bourgeois atomism, it is not surprising that the dominant trend in Marxism has been to insist on what Callinicos describes as 'the ontological primacy of relations' over subjects.[15] Bertell Ollman, for example, argues that Marx developed a 'philosophy of internal relations', according to which 'relations are internal to each factor (they are ontological relations), so that when an important one alters, the factor itself alters; it becomes something else'.[16] Put differently: *relations are constitutive of the relata*. A similar perspective has been formulated by David McNally in his attempt to conceptualise the relations between different forms of oppression through the lens of Hegel's 'dialectical organicism'. In his view, the 'distinct parts of a social whole ... mediate each other and in so doing constitute each other'.[17] As McNally's phrasing makes clear, this way of attributing primacy to relations is strongly associated with the idea of the primacy of the *whole* or of the *totality*, concepts which are both crucial in Hegelian readings of Marx, such as those of Lukács and, more recently, Arthur.[18] According to the latter, the object of Marx's theory is 'a *totality* where every part has to be complemented by others to be what it is; hence internal relations typify the whole. A thing is internally related to another if this other is a necessary condition of its nature.'[19]

While such philosophies of internal relations obviously capture an essential aspect of Marx's social ontology, the mere declaration that things are internally related does not get us very far and can even be misleading if not further developed. The claim that everything *is what it is* by virtue of

---

vol. 1, *Theory of Practical Ensembles*, trans. Alan Sheridan-Smith (London: Verso, 2004). See also Perry Anderson, *Arguments within English Marxism* (London: Verso, 1980), 50ff; and Alex Callinicos, *Making History: Agency, Structure, and Change in Social Theory*, 2nd ed. (Leiden: Brill, 2004), 70. Callinicos reads Sartre as a precursor for another form of individualist Marxism: Jon Elster's analytical Marxism.

15   Alex Callinicos, *Deciphering* Capital: *Marx's* Capital *and Its Destiny* (London: Bookmarks, 2014), 317.

16   Bertell Ollman, *Alienation: Marx's Conception of Man in Capitalist Society*, 2nd ed. (Cambridge: Cambridge University Press, 1976), 15.

17   David McNally, 'Intersections and Dialectics: Critical Reconstructions in Social Reproduction Theory', in *Social Reproduction Theory: Remapping Class, Recentering Oppression*, ed. Tithi Bhattacharya (London: Pluto, 2017), 104.

18   Georg Lukács, *History and Class Consciousness: Studies in Marxist Dialectics*, trans. Rodney Livingstone (London: Merlin Press, 2010), 9.

19   Arthur, *The New Dialectic*, 24f.

its relation to *everything else* leads to absurd consequences; if I move the book in front of me two centimetres, its (spatial) relation to everything else has changed, with the consequence that *everything* has literally become something new because of that change. This essentially leaves us with two equally untenable options: either we assume that change occurs, which would force us to accept some kind of Heraclitean ontology where everything is in constant flux and identity does not exist, since we would have to conclude that everything changes all of the time. Or we begin with the assumption that identity exists, which would then force us to accept the opposite: a Parmenidean ontology where change is impossible.

The way to avoid both of these positions is not to give up on the idea that relations are (or at least can be) constitutive of relata, but rather to allow for the existence of different kinds of relations with different degrees of significance for their relata. So, while we should stick to the idea that moments of a totality cannot be understood in complete abstraction from this totality, we also have to insist that not *all* aspects of that totality are equally constitutive of any given part. This is also – at least implicitly – acknowledged by Ollman in the passage quoted above, where the word 'important' seems to imply that relations can be more or less constitutive of a given 'factor'. Similarly, McNally acknowledges the existence of what he calls 'partial totalities', and Lukács emphasises that 'the category of totality does not reduce its various elements to an undifferentiated uniformity, to identity'.[20]

The Essence of the Human Being

We cannot, then, remain content with a social ontology which takes social relations to be ontologically primary on the basis of a vague reference to the immanent relationality of everything. In order to get a better idea of the relation between individuals and their social relations, as well as the relative importance of the different kinds of relations in which those individuals find themselves, I propose to begin by examining a controversial issue: the theoretical status of the concept of the human being in Marx's writings. This has been the subject of endless debates

---

20   McNally, 'Intersections and Dialectics', 105; Lukács, *History and Class Consciousness*, 12; see also Slavoj Žižek, *Less Than Nothing: Hegel and the Shadow of Dialectical Materialism* (London: Verso, 2012), 398.

since the early 1930s, when the first publication of Marx's *1844 Manu-scripts* led to a wave of humanist readings of his critique of capitalism.[21] When Siegfried Landshut first published the manuscripts in 1932, he declared that they demonstrated how Marx's real aim was the 'realisation of Man', not the abolition of private property.[22] This interpretation was followed up the same year by those of Herbert Marcuse and Henri de Man, who discovered the 'ethical-humanist motives' of Marx's socialism in the *1844 Manuscripts*.[23] The publication of an English translation of the manuscripts in 1956 likewise led many to discover 'in Marx a champion of liberal values and of the dignity and freedom of the individual', as one commentator puts it.[24] With its heavy use of concepts such as the human essence, the individual, and alienation, and the absence of tedious eco-nomic theory, the *1844 Manuscripts* seemed to offer a convenient Marxist escape route from orthodox Marxism. The French version of this Marxist humanism bore a theological imprint, with commentators emphasising the common ethical foundations of Marxism and Christianity – an inter-pretation which was also intended to support the Communist Party's attempt to appeal to Catholic voters.[25]

---

21   For an overview of the publication and different editions of the manuscripts, as well as the reception of them, see Marcello Musto, 'The "Young Marx" Myth in Interpre-tations of the Economic–Philosophic Manuscripts of 1844', *Critique* 43, no. 2 (2015). In MEGA2 they are published in volumes I.2 and IV.2, which, according to critics, reflect an undue separation of what should actually belong together in the fourth section of the MEGA2. See Jürgen Rojahn, 'Die Marxschen Manuskripte aus dem Jahre 1844 in der neuen Marx-Engels-Gesamtausgabe (MEGA)', *Archiv für Sozialgeschichte*, no. 25 (1985), 647–63.

22   Siegfried Landshut, *Karl Marx* (Lübenk: Charles Coleman, 1932); Marcello Musto, '"Young Marx" Myth', *Critique* 43, no. 2 (2015): 241f.

23   Herbert Marcuse, *Studies in Critical Philosophy*, trans. Joris De Bres (Boston: Beacon Press, 1972), 1–48; Henri de Man, 'Der neu entdeckte Marx', *Der Kampf* XXV, no. 5–6 (1932); Marcello Musto, 'The "Young Marx" Myth', *Critique* 43, no. 2 (2015), 242. See also Jakob Hommes, *Der technische Eros: Das Wesen der materialistischen Geschichtsauf-fassung* (Freiburg: Herder, 1955); Heinrich Popitz, *Der entfremdete Mensch: Zeitkritik und Geschichtsphilosophie des jungen Marx* (Basle: Verlag fur Recht und Gesellschaft, 1953); and Erich Thier, *Das Menschenbild des Jungen Marx* (Göttingen: Vandenhoeck, 1957).

24   Donald Clark Hodges, 'Marx's Contribution to Humanism', *Science and Society* 29, no. 2 (1965), 173. See Erich Fromm, ed., *Socialist Humanism: An International Sym-posium* (New York: Doubleday, 1965); Erich Fromm, *Marx's Concept of Man* (London: Continuum, 2004); and Robert C. Tucker, *Philosophy and Myth in Karl Marx* (London: Transaction, 2001).

25   G. M. Goshgarian, 'Introduction', in Louis Althusser, *The Humanist Controversy and Other Writings*, ed. François Matheron (London: Verso, 2003), xxivf; Pierre Bigo,

This was the conjuncture in which Althusser intervened with his famous essay 'Marxism and Humanism' in the early 1960s.[26] Althusser argued that Marx's early writings (1842–44) were permeated by a Feuerbachian humanism which he then broke with in 1845 (in the *Theses on Feuerbach* and *The German Ideology*). With this 'epistemological break', Marx opened up 'the continent of history' by building 'a theory of history and politics based on radically new concepts: the concepts of social formation, productive forces, relations of production, superstructure, ideologies, determination in the last instance by the economy, specific determination of the other levels, etc'.[27] Althusser concluded that 'in respect to theory, therefore, one can and must speak openly of *Marx's theoretical anti-humanism*'.[28] The core of this anti-humanism is 'a refusal to root the explanation of social formations and their history in a concept of man with theoretical pretensions – that is, a concept of man as an *originating subject*'.[29] Althusser also referred to this position as 'theoretical *a*-humanism'.[30] I will not go into a comprehensive discussion of the debates spurred by Althusser's intervention here, but in order to understand the social ontology of economic power, it is necessary to briefly indicate why Althusser was right in his core claim: that Marx broke with a certain form of humanist thought in 1845, and that this break was an important step forward.

The critique of bourgeois society and the modern state developed by Marx in 1843 and 1844 is firmly based on a concept of human nature. By this, I mean that the concept of the essence of the human being is the *basis* of Marx's critique; it is the standard against which social reality is

---

Marxisme et humanisme (Paris: Presses universitaires de France, 1953); Jean-Yves Calvez, *La Pensée de Karl Marx* (Paris: Seuil, 1956); Roger Garaudy, *From Anathema to Dialogue: The Challenge of Marxist-Christian Cooperation* (London: Collins, 1967); Maurice Merleau-Ponty, *Sense and Non-Sense*, trans. Hubert L. Dreyfus and Patricia Allen Dreyfus (Evanston: Northwestern University Press, 1964).

26   See Anderson, *Arguments within English Marxism*, 106ff; Gregory Elliott, *Althusser: The Detour of Theory* (Leiden: Brill, 2006), 20ff; Kate Soper, *Humanism and Anti-Humanism* (London: Hutchinson, 1986), chap. 4.

27   Louis Althusser, *For Marx*, trans. Ben Brewster (London: Verso, 2005), 227.

28   Ibid., 228.

29   Louis Althusser, 'Is It Simple to Be a Marxist in Philosophy?', in *Philosophy and the Spontaneous Philosophy of the Scientists*, trans. Ben Brewster (London: Verso, 2011), 239; Louis Althusser et al., *Reading* Capital: *The Complete Edition*, trans. Ben Brewster and David Fernbach (London: Verso, 2015), 290.

30   Louis Althusser, 'The Humanist Controversy', in *The Humanist Controversy*, 232; Althusser et al., *Reading* Capital, 268.

measured.[31] The critical apparatus in these texts consists of a complex
theoretical constellation combining elements from Hegel, the young Hegelians, and classical political economists. From Feuerbach, Marx inherits
a humanist critique of religion and speculative philosophy, according to
which the latter represents the alienation of the human species-being.[32]
Although Marx praised Feuerbach in his writings from 1843 and 1844, he
was never uncritical; in a March 1843 letter to Arnold Ruge, he complained
that Feuerbach 'refers too much to nature and too little to politics'.[33] In
the *Critique of Hegel's Philosophy of Right*, written the same year, Marx
borrowed heavily from Feuerbach in an effort to demystify Hegel's
'hypostasised abstractions'.[34] However, when he turned his attention to
the critique of bourgeois society and its apologists (the economists) in
1844, the tables had turned; here, Marx replaces Feuerbach's abstract
notions of love, reason, and will with Hegel's notion of '*labour* as the
essence of man', a move which allows him to inject Hegel's emphasis on
historicity into the concept of the human essence.[35] This is not to deny that
the *1844 Manuscripts* are deeply Feuerbachian; on the contrary, they are
likely the most Feuerbachian texts Marx ever wrote. But Feuerbach and
Hegel are not the only sources of inspiration; the manuscripts also bear
witness to the impact of Engels's *Outline of a Critique of Political Economy*
and Moses Hess's *On the Essence of Money*, both from 1843.[36] In the *1844
Manuscripts*, Marx praises these texts as the 'only *original* German works
of substance in this science [i.e., political economy]'.[37] In *On the Essence*

---

31   Heinrich, *Die Wissenschaft vom Wert*, 103.

32   Bruno Bauer was another important source of inspiration for Marx's analysis of
the inversion of the human essence. See Zvi Rosen, *Bruno Bauer and Karl Marx: The Influence of Bruno Bauer on Marx's Thought* (The Hague: Martinus Nijhoff, 1977); Hans-Martin
Sass, 'Bruno Bauer's Critical Theory', *Philosophical Forum* 8, no. 2 (1976). Feuerbach's
influence on Marx dates from 1843, when he read Feuerbach's *Preliminary Theses on the
Reform of Philosophy* and *Principles of Philosophy of the Future*, not from the publication
of *The Essence of Christianity* in 1841, as Engels claimed many years later. See 26: 364;
Heinrich, *Die Wissenschaft vom Wert*, 94; Stathis Kouvelakis, *Philosophy and Revolution:
From Kant to Marx* (London: Verso, 2003), 247, 260; David McLellan, *The Young Hegelians
and Karl Marx* (London: Macmillan, 1970), 93ff.

33   1: 400.

34   3: 15; see also 11, 23, 29.

35   3: 333. Heinrich, *Die Wissenschaft vom Wert*, 113; Soper, *Humanism and Anti-
Humanism*, 34.

36   Hess's text was not published until 1845, but Marx read it as an editor in 1843.

37   3: 232. See especially 3: 421, 427. In 1859, Marx still referred to Engels's *Outlines*
as a 'brilliant sketch of a critique of economic categories' (29: 264).

of Money, Hess unveiled money as 'the product of mutually alienated man' and argued, in a truly Feuerbachian manner, that 'what God is to the theoretical life, money is to the practical life in this inverted world: the externalised capacity of men'.[38] In a very similar fashion, Marx wrote in *On the Jewish Question* (also from 1843) that

> under the domination of egoistic need [man] can be active practically, and produce objects in practice, only by putting his products, and his activity, under the domination of an alien being, and bestowing the significance of an alien entity – money – on them.[39]

As David McLellan notes, the similarity of these two texts is 'more than enough to justify the claim that Marx copied Hess's ideas at this stage'.[40]

With his emphasis on labour as the essence of the human being, Hegel had, so Marx argues, reached the 'standpoint' of modern political economy.[41] The problem is, however, that 'the only labour which Hegel knows and recognises is *abstractly mental* labour'.[42] In order to undermine this idealist obfuscation, Marx reaches out for two antidotes: on the one hand, Feuerbach's 'real, corporeal *man*', and, on the other, the prosaic, down-to-earth understanding of labour in political economy.[43]

This mixture of Hegel, political economy, Hess, and Feuerbach (under the auspices of the latter) constitutes the basis of Marx's critique of modern society in 1843 and 1844. His simple and fundamental charge against this society is that it *alienates human beings from their essence*. The essence of the human being is labour, which Marx understands as the self-creation of the human being through objectification.[44] Through 'work upon the

---

38   Moses Hess, 'The Essence of Money', 1845, available at marxists.org.

39   3: 174.

40   McLellan, *The Young Hegelians*, 158; see also Kouvelakis, *Philosophy and Revolution*, 180f.

41   3: 333.

42   Ibid.

43   3: 336. It should be noted that this reading of Hegel is not unproblematic. It is not obvious why the *Phenomenology of Spirit* should be read as philosophical anthropology, as Marx tends to do. In Hegel's own view, phenomenology is 'the Science of the *experience of consciousness*'. Hegel's theory of human nature is found in his *anthropology* in the first section of the philosophy of spirit in the *Encyclopaedia*. In addition to this, it should also be noted that Hegel never declares labour to be the essence of the human being (see Althusser, 'The Humanist Controversy', 250).

44   3: 332f.

objective world', man also 'proves himself to be a *species-being*'; he 'relates to himself as a *universal* and therefore a free being'.[45] There is a certain ambivalence in Marx's description of this 'species-being'. On the one hand, he constantly stresses that the human being is a *natural* and *corporeal* being; like plants and animals, humans must engage in a 'continuous interchange' with other parts of nature in order to live.[46] On the other hand, he also insists that there is a fundamental scission between humans and animals – that humans are *conscious* beings, which is why they are species-beings:

> The animal is immediately one with its life activity. It does not dis-
> tinguish itself from it. It is its life activity. Man makes his life activity
> itself the object of his will and of his consciousness. He has conscious
> life activity. It is not a determination with which he directly merges.
> Conscious life activity distinguishes man immediately from animal life
> activity. It is just because of this that he is a species-being. Or it is only
> because he is a species-being that he is a conscious being, i.e., that his
> own life is an object for him. Only because of that is his activity free
> activity.[47]

Because of this crucial difference between humans and animals, Marx regards it as degrading for humans to be treated as animals. He thus con- demns political economy on the grounds that it 'knows the worker only as a working animal', and he similarly laments the fact that in bourgeois society, 'what is animal becomes human and what is human becomes animal'.[48]

A Romantic Critique of Alienation

In the *1844 Manuscripts*, Marx repeatedly emphasises the *social* nature of the human being. For instance, he praises Feuerbach for having estab- lished 'the social relationship of "man to man" [as] the basic principle of the theory'.[49] With regards to the basic question of social ontology,

---

45   3: 277; 3: 275.
46   3: 337f, 276.
47   3: 276.
48   3: 243; 3: 275.
49   3: 328; see also 206, 299.

then, it would seem that here, in 1844, Marx considers *relations* to be ontologically primary, rather than individuals. As Michael Heinrich has noted, however, Marx actually remains firmly on 'Feuerbachian terrain' here, inasmuch as he grasps society 'as the objectification of an essence immanent in the individual'.[50] In a certain sense, this is already implied by the very notion of alienation. In order for something to be *alienated*, it first has to *exist*, or put differently: to say that something (the human essence, for example) is *alienated* is not the same as saying that it *no longer exists*. Bourgeois society *alienates* the essence of the human being; it does not *abolish* it. In other words, this essence continues to exist despite being held back and thwarted by a certain set of social relations. Humans are treated *like* animals in this society, but they are not thereby *transformed into* animals – their humanity, their essence, persists underneath their animal-like conditions. What this simple analysis tells us is that the notion of alienation carries with it the idea of an unrealised potential; it implies a concept of the human essence as something which continues to exist even when a given set of social relations prevents it from unfolding.

The alienation of the human essence in bourgeois society is fourfold: humans are alienated from the *products* of their labour as well as the productive *activity* itself, and consequently they are also alienated from their *species-being* as well as *each other*.[51] In bourgeois society, man has consequently 'lost himself and is dehumanised'.[52] Communism thus comes to represent the *reappropriation of the human essence*: the '*social* revolution', writes Marx, 'represents man's protest against a dehumanised life'.[53] Communism will prevail when humans demand to be treated as *humans* rather than animals; it will thus take the form of a restoration of *a natural order*, or as Marx puts it, it would be 'the true resolution of the strife between existence and essence'.[54] Communism is 'the real *appropriation* of the *human* essence by and for man', the 'complete return of man to

---

50   Heinrich, *Die Wissenschaft vom Wert*, 114f, 118. For this reason, Gould's Aristotelian reading of *Grundrisse*, according to which Marx considered the 'social individual' to be 'the primary ontological subject', actually fits better with the *1844 Manuscripts*.

51   See 3: 274ff; Heinrich, *Die Wissenschaft vom Wert*, 107f; David Leopold, *The Young Karl Marx: German Philosophy, Modern Politics, and Human Flourishing* (Cambridge: Cambridge University Press, 2007), 230f; McLellan, *The Young Hegelians*, 133; Ollman, *Alienation*, chaps. 19–22.

52   3: 212; see also 274, 284, 303; 4: 36.

53   3: 205.

54   3: 296.

himself' as well as the emancipation of labour, which will then become 'a *free manifestation of life,* hence an *enjoyment of life*'.[55]

As we can see from these considerations and quotations, Marx's early critique of bourgeois society is deeply *humanist* and *romantic* – humanist in the sense that the concept of the essence of the human being occupies a central role as the basis of critique,[56] and romantic because it is based on an idea of an original, lost, and natural unity which ought to be restored.[57] This kind of critique presupposes typical romantic ideals such as immediacy, naturalness, and wholeness. In turn, the political project which follows from such a critique necessarily takes the form of *the reconstitution of a natural order*, that is, the emancipation of human nature or the abolition of capitalism in order for humans to *become what they really are* underneath their alienated existence.

This kind of romanticism can be found in most forms of humanist Marxism. Lukács, for example, denounced the division of labour on the grounds that it 'disrupts every organic unified process of work and life'.[58] In his view, capitalism brings 'the essence of man into conflict with his existence' and creates a 'fragmented', 'deformed and crippled' human being.[59] Stavros Tombazos reads Marx's political project as 'nothing other than that of the reconciliation of the individual with himself, who by his own initiatives must search for his own fragments, recover the lost time and return "home", purified from slavery thanks to a long journey through the maze of alienation'.[60] Ollman similarly accuses capitalism of reducing the human being to 'a mere rump' and conceives of communism as 'a kind of reunification'.[61] In the words of a more recent Marxist humanist:

---

55   Ibid.; 3: 308.

56   In his account of Marx's development – to which I refer extensively in the preceding paragraphs – Heinrich prefers to talk of 'anthropologism' rather than 'humanism' (Heinrich, *Die Wissenschaft vom Wert*, 82, 111, 118). For a good overview of the different meanings of 'humanism' and 'anti-humanism' in discussions concerning these terms, see Kate Soper, *Humanism and Anti-Humanism* (London: Hutchinson, 1986), chap. 1.

57   For discussions of Marx and romanticism, see Shlomo Avineri, *The Social and Political Thought of Karl Marx* (Cambridge: Cambridge University Press, 1980), 55f; Michael Levin, 'Marxism and Romanticism: Marx's Debt to German Conservatism', *Political Studies* 22, no. 4 (1974): 400–413; Michael Löwy, 'The Romantic and the Marxist Critique of Modern Civilization', *Theory and Society* 16, no. 6 (1987): 891–904.

58   Lukács, *History and Class Consciousness*, 103.

59   Ibid., xxiv, 90.

60   Stavros Tombazos, *Time in Marx: The Categories of Time in Marx's* Capital (Chicago: Haymarket, 2014), 107.

61   Ollman, *Alienation*, 134f.

'Liberation from capital requires that the proper relationship between subject and object be established.'[62] Such romantic criticisms rarely specify what it would mean to establish such a 'proper' relationship. As Kate Soper eloquently puts it, quoting Marx's *1844 Manuscripts*: 'To be told that "man himself should be the intermediary between men" or that "men should relate to each other as men" is not, in fact, to be told anything specific about the form their interaction should take.'[63] John Mepham's account of the pitfalls of romantic humanism is even more to the point:

> The phrases 'man himself' and 'as people' trade on some *untheorised* ideal of the *really human*, some vision of *true humanity* being expressed in social life. They are functioning as metaphors in which idealised relations between *individuals* are illicitly mapped onto a utopian scheme of patterns of relations in general, relations in which social organisations (political organisations, institutions, collectivities of all kinds) have entirely disappeared. The disjunction between 'the human' and 'the dehumanized' as forms of social mediation, is empty of cognitive content, for the valorization of the former is based on nothing more than an implicit, essentialist individualist philosophical imperative.[64]

Indeed, critiques of capitalism in the name of human nature rarely go beyond solemn invocations of an ideal of the truly human; and when they do, they tend to depoliticise the critique by conceiving the abolition of capitalism as the restoration of a natural harmony. Such inadequacies plagued Marx's writings from 1843 up to and including *The Holy Family* (late 1844). Then he changed his mind.

The Settling of Accounts

It is apparent that Engels developed a critical distance towards Feuerbach's humanism before Marx did. Having read Max Stirner's *The Ego and Its Own* in November 1844, he wrote to Marx: 'Stirner is right in

---

62   John Roche, 'Marx and Humanism', *Rethinking Marxism* 17, no. 3 (2005): 346. See also Raya Dunayevskaya, *Marxism and Freedom: From 1776 until Today*, 3rd ed. (London: Pluto Press, 1971), 93, 107; Kohei Saito, *Karl Marx's Ecosocialism: Capital, Nature, and the Unfinished Critique of Political Economy* (New York: Monthly Review Press, 2017), 14.

63   Soper, *Humanism and Anti-Humanism*, 103.

64   Quoted in ibid., 103.

rejecting Feuerbach's "man", or at least the "man" of *The Essence of Christianity*. Feuerbach deduces his "man" from God, it is from God that he arrives at "man", and hence "man" is crowned with a theological halo of abstraction.'[65] In following years, Marx and Engels developed this critique of Feuerbach further. As previously mentioned, Marx was already critical of the *content* of Feuerbach's conception of the human essence in 1844, which is why he replaced notions like love, reason, and will with a materialist version of Hegel's concept of labour. In the course of 1845 and 1846, Marx not only abandoned this concept of labour; he also turned against the very *structure* of Feuerbach's critical model – that is, the idea that the human being has an essence which can be alienated, reappropriated, and made to function as the basis of critique.[66] In a March 1845 draft for a review of Friedrich List's *The National System of Political Economy*, Marx resolutely abandons the idea of labour as the essence of the human being. Instead, he now regards it as a 'by its very nature ... unfree, unhuman, unsocial activity', arguing that it is 'one of the greatest misapprehensions to speak of free, human, social labour'.[67] This point is repeated in *The German Ideology*, where Marx and Engels insist that 'the communist revolution ... does away with *labour*'.[68] It is still, however, possible to find Feuerbachian motives in the critique of List, as when Marx accuses the

---

65   38: 12; Althusser, 'The Humanist Controversy', 258. Marx's reply to this letter has, unfortunately, not been preserved. January 1845, Engels wrote to Marx: 'As regards Stirner, I entirely agree with you. When I wrote to you [i.e., in November 1844], I was still too much under the immediate impression made upon me by the book' (38: 16). This indicates that Marx was critical of Engels's reading of Stirner. In the same letter, Engels reports that he presented Marx's letter to Hess, who apparently agreed with Marx's reading of Stirner and claimed to have written a similar critique of Stirner. Engels left Marx's letter with Hess, who 'wished to use some things out of it', but Engels later got the letter back (38: 26). In 1845, Hess published the essay *The Last Philosophers*, in which he criticised Feuerbach in a manner similar to Marx's critique in the sixth thesis on Feuerbach; see Moses Hess, 'The Recent Philosophers', in *The Young Hegelians: An Anthology*, ed. Lawrence S. Stepelevich (Cambridge: Cambridge University Press, 1983), 363; and Heinrich, *Die Wissenschaft vom Wert*, 124. Note that the English translation of the relevant passage of Hess's essay is quite confusing. See McLellan, *The Young Hegelians*, 121; and Althusser, 'The Humanist Controversy', 258.

66   Heinrich, *Die Wissenschaft vom Wert*, 103, 119.

67   4: 278f.

68   5: 52, 205; I.5: 44, 259. Later, in 1857, Marx returned to a transhistorical concept of labour, but as we will see later in this chapter, it is radically different from the concept of labour in the *1844 Manuscripts*. See Mau, 'Fra væsen til stofskifte'; Amy E. Wendling, *Karl Marx on Technology and Alienation* (London: Palgrave Macmillan, 2009), chap. 2.

bourgeois of seeing in the proletarian 'not a *human being*, but a *force* capable of creating wealth'.[69]

Marx confronts Feuerbachian humanism head on in the *Theses on Feuerbach* and *The German Ideology*. In the sixth thesis, the precise meaning of which has been the subject of countless discussions, Marx criticises Feuerbach for resolving 'the essence of religion into the essence of *man*. But the essence of man is no abstraction inherent in each single individual. In its reality it is the ensemble of the social relations.' He then adds two corollaries: first, he notes that Feuerbach abstracts from 'the historical process' and presupposes 'an abstract – *isolated* – human individual'. This is merely a restatement of a critique of Feuerbach which was already present in the *1844 Manuscripts*, where Marx emphasised the *social* nature of the human being and integrated Hegel's emphasis on *historicity* into his critical model. In the second corollary, he then criticises Feuerbach for being unable to understand 'essence' as anything other than 'as "species", as an inner, mute, general character which unites the many individuals *in a natural way*' – a description that fits Marx's own notion of essence in 1844 quite well. Many commentators have pointed out that in the sixth thesis, strictly speaking, Marx does not *deny* the existence of a human essence, and that it is even possible to read the second corollary as a call for the development of an improved concept of the 'essence' of the human being.[70]

While this is true, such an interpretation becomes decidedly less plausible if we read it in the light of *The German Ideology*.[71] Here, Marx and

---

69   4: 286.

70   See, for example, Norman Geras, *Marx and Human Nature: Refutation of a Legend* (London: Verso, 2016); Piotr Hoffmann, *The Anatomy of Idealism: Passivity and Activity in Kant, Hegel and Marx* (The Hague: Martinus Nijhoff Publishers, 1982), 104; Mehmet Tabak, *Dialectics of Human Nature in Marx's Philosophy* (New York: Palgrave Macmillan, 2012), 11f.

71   The manuscripts known under this title did not comprise a 'work'. They are, rather, an edited collection of separate manuscripts put together by David Riazanov, the editor of the first MEGA who originally published them in 1932. The original manuscripts have only recently (October 2017) been published in MEGA2 I.5, although parts were published in *Marx-Engels-Jahrbuch 2003*. For the sake of convenience, I will continue to refer to these manuscripts as *The German Ideology*. I have compared all quotes from MECW with MEGA2 I.5. See Terrell Carver, 'The German Ideology Never Took Place', *History of Political Thought* 31, no. 1 (2010): 107–27; Terrell Carver and Daniel Blank, *A Political History of the Editions of Marx and Engels's 'German Ideology' Manuscripts* (New York: Palgrave Macmillan, 2014).

Engels repeatedly distance themselves from the concepts of alienation and
'the essence of man', making fun of the 'speculative-idealistic' conception
of revolution as 'self-generation of the species' – which was precisely how
Marx understood revolution in the *1844 Manuscripts*.[72] In accordance with
the *Theses*, Feuerbach is accused of replacing 'real' human beings with the
abstraction 'man' as such.[73] Marx and Engels furthermore admit that the
introduction to the *Critique of Hegel's Philosophy of Right* as well as *On the
Jewish Question* were tainted by 'philosophical phraseology [and] the traditionally occurring philosophical expressions such as "human essence" [and]
"species"'.[74] We can thus see why it makes perfect sense that Marx later (in
1859) described *The German Ideology* as a 'self-clarification' in which he and
Engels 'settled the accounts' with their 'former philosophical conscience'.[75]

With regards to Marx's changing views on these matters, it is also worth
considering the critique of the 'true socialism' of Karl Grün and Moses
Hess in the *Communist Manifesto*. Recall that Hess's analysis of money
as the alienation of the human essence had been a powerful influence on
Marx in 1843. In 1848, however, Marx writes:

> Since it [French socialism] ceased in the hands of the German to
> express the struggle of one class with the other, he felt conscious of
> having overcome 'French one-sidedness' and of representing, not true
> requirements, but the requirements of Truth; not the interests of the
> proletariat, but the interests of Human Nature, of Man in general, who
> belongs to no class, has no reality, who exists only in the misty realm
> of philosophical fantasy.[76]

The true socialists are similarly accused of transforming 'the French
criticism of the economic functions of money' into the 'Alienation of
Humanity'.[77] It is indeed striking how this ridicule of Hess and Grün's
Feuerbach-inspired socialism is couched in terms very similar, if not
identical, to the core concepts of the *1844 Manuscripts*.

---

72   5: 48; I.5: 37; 5: 54, 160, 293; I.5: 46, 210, 348; 5: 52; I.5: 42.

73   5: 39, 41; I.5: 19, 25.

74   5: 236; I.5: 291.

75   29: 264. In 1867, Marx reread *The Holy Family* and wrote to Engels: 'I was pleas-
antly surprised to find that we have no need to feel ashamed of the piece, although the
Feuerbach cult now makes a most comical impression upon one' (42: 360).

76   6: 511; see also 6: 330.

77   6: 511.

Based on these considerations, I agree with Althusser and Heinrich that Marx did in fact break with a theoretically untenable humanism in 1845. From that point onwards, Marx no longer criticised capitalism in the name of the essence of the human being. To be sure, he did hold on to certain aspects of his Feuerbachian critical apparatus, a tendency that cannot simply be dismissed as a remnant of youthful aberrations. Perhaps the clearest example of Feuerbach's (and Bruno Bauer's) continuing influence on Marx's later writings is the theme of 'inversion'. In the *Grundrisse* and the manuscripts of the 1860s, Marx constantly makes the point that under capitalist relations of production, the conditions of production confront workers as an 'alien power'. In *Capital*, he even draws a deeply Feuerbachian analogy between capitalism and religion: 'Just as man is governed, in religion, by the products of his own brain, so, in capitalist production, he is governed by the products of his own hand.'[78] His use of terms such as the 'inverted' or 'topsy-turvy' world and 'mystification' in the 1860s also testifies to the lasting influence of Feuerbach on his thought. Even the concept of alienation occasionally crops up. After the break with romantic humanism, however, these terms and expressions no longer refer to *human nature*; it is rather *social relations* that confront proletarians as an alien power. Marx has retained a Feuerbachian understanding of inversion, but he has replaced human nature with social relations and thereby emptied it of romantic humanism.[79]

While I think the core of the Althusserian thesis of a 'break' with humanism in 1845 is convincing, I do not find Althusser's periodisation of Marx's overall development convincing. The year 1845 marks an important break with regards to the question of *humanism*, but if we look at the development of Marx's thought on ecology, crisis, history, the state, technology, value, the division of labour, or pre- and non-capitalist societies, for example, other years would stand out as important.[80] Marx's

---

78   C1: 772; compare with 3: 29, 274.

79   Some authors have attempted to rescue the concept of alienation by detaching it from some of the core ideas of romanticist-essentialist humanism. See for example Simon Clarke, *Marx, Marginalism, and Modern Sociology: From Adam Smith to Max Weber*, 2nd ed. (Basingstoke: Macmillan, 1991); Postone, *Time, Labor and Social Domination*; Wendling, *Karl Marx on Technology and Alienation*. While I agree that it is, in principle, possible to use the concept of alienation without falling prey to the shortcomings of romantic humanism, the concept is so strongly associated with the latter that I prefer not to use it.

80   For accounts of Marx's development with regards to these topics, see Kevin B. Anderson, *Marx at the Margins: On Nationalism, Ethnicity, and Non-Western Societies*,

thinking developed constantly until the very end of his life; therefore, rather than discussing the continuities and breaks in Marx's thought *as a whole*, it would be more fruitful to focus these discussions on specific problems and different aspects of his enormous research programme.[81]

2nd ed. (Chicago: Chicago University Press, 2016); Rob Beamish, *Marx, Method, and the Division of Labor* (Urbana: University of Illinois Press, 1992); Simon Clarke, *Marx's Theory of Crisis* (Basingstoke: Macmillan, 1994); John Bellamy Foster and Paul Burkett, *Marx and the Earth: An Anti-Critique* (Leiden: Brill, 2016); Heinrich, *Die Wissenschaft vom Wert*; Michael Heinrich, 'Crisis Theory, the Law of the Tendency of the Profit Rate to Fall, and Marx's Studies in the 1870s', trans. Alex Locascio, *Monthly Review* 64, no. 11 (2013), monthlyreview.org; Andreas Malm, 'Marx on Steam: From the Optimism of Progress to the Pessimism of Power', *Re-thinking Marxism* 30, no. 2 (2018): 166–85; Ali Rattansi, *Marx and the Division of Labour* (London: Macmillan, 1982); Saito, *Karl Marx's Ecosocialism*; Peter D. Thomas and Geert Reuten, 'Crisis and the Rate of Profit in Marx's Laboratory', in *In Marx's Laboratory: Critical Interpretations of the Grundrisse* (Chicago: Haymarket, 2014).

81   Regarding the development of Marx's thought in the last fifteen years of his life, see Anderson, *Marx at the Margins*; Endnotes, 'A History of Separation', in *Endnotes 4: Unity in Separation* (London: Endnotes, 2015), 186ff; Heinrich, 'Crisis Theory'; Marcello Musto, *The Last Years of Karl Marx, 1881–1883: An Intellectual Biography* (Stanford: Stanford University Press, 2020); Saito, *Karl Marx's Ecosocialism*.

4

The Human Corporeal Organisation

There are some very interesting things about the body in Marx's writings.

–Michel Foucault

For Althusser, it was Marx's break with theoretical humanism that enabled him to found historical materialism, a new science of history whose central categories do not rely on a concept of human nature.[1] Since the critique of capitalism is nothing but the application of this science of history to a particular mode of production, neither could the concept of human nature have any place there. Marxist humanists, on the other hand, usually make the exact opposite claim: that the concept of human nature does play a role in Marx's general theory of history, and that for this reason, it also has a role to play in the analysis and critique of particular modes of production, such as capitalism.[2] In this and the following

---

1   Louis Althusser, *For Marx*, trans. Ben Brewster (London: Verso, 2005), 227; Louis Althusser, 'The Humanist Controversy', in *The Humanist Controversy and Other Writings*, trans. G. M. Goshgarian (London: Verso, 2003), 263f.

2   See, for instance, Shlomo Avineri, *The Social and Political Thought of Karl Marx* (Cambridge: Cambridge University Press, 1980); Harry Braverman, *Labor and Monopoly Capital: The Degradation of Work in the Twentieth Century* (New York: Monthly Review Press, 1974); Kevin M. Brien, 'Marx's Radical Humanism', *International Critical Thought* 1, no. 2 (2011); Raya Dunayevskaya, *Marxism and Freedom: From 1776 until Today*, 3rd ed. (London: Pluto Press, 1971); John G. Fox, *Marx, the Body, and Human Nature* (London: Palgrave Macmillan, 2015); Norman Geras, *Marx and Human Nature: Refutation of a Legend* (London: Verso, 2016); Carol C. Gould, *Marx's Social Ontology: Individuality and Community in Marx's Theory of Social Reality* (Cambridge, MA: MIT Press, 1980); David

chapter, I will defend a position that cuts across these two positions. Against Althusser, I will argue that the social ontology underlying Marx's critique of political economy does imply and rely on a notion of human nature, and that this concept is worth defending. Against the humanists, however, I will argue that this notion of human nature cannot possibly function as the basis of a critique of capitalism. What is more important for our purposes, however, is that this notion of human nature will ultimately allow us to explain what economic power is and why it is possible.

Metabolism and Needs

Few would deny that it is possible to speak of human beings in the same way as we speak of snails, mosquitoes, horses, or killer whales. Even Althusser concedes that a 'materialist, scientific theory of human palaeontology certainly does matter to historical materialism'.[3] Insofar as we can single out a number of characteristic traits that distinguish *Homo sapiens* from other species, it also seems unproblematic to say that there is such a thing as a 'human nature'. The controversies only arise when we begin to make claims about the role such a concept can or should play in social theory. Therefore, before we go into that discussion, let us begin by examining the human being as an animal on a par with other animals and the rest of nature.

The emphasis on the *naturalness* of the human being is a constant in Marx's thought.[4] In the *1844 Manuscripts*, he stresses that 'the human

---

Harvey, *Seventeen Contradictions and the End of Capitalism* (London: Profile Books, 2014); Georg Lukács, *History and Class Consciousness: Studies in Marxist Dialectics*, trans. Rodney Livingstone (London: Merlin Press, 2010); Ernest Mandel, *The Formation of the Economic Thought of Karl Marx: 1843 to Capital*, trans. Brian Pearce (London: Verso, 2015); Bertell Ollman, *Alienation: Marx's Conception of Man in Capitalist Society*, 2nd ed. (Cambridge: Cambridge University Press, 1976); John Roche, 'Marx and Humanism', *Rethinking Marxism* 17, no. 3 (2005); Kohei Saito, *Karl Marx's Ecosocialism: Capital, Nature, and the Unfinished Critique of Political Economy* (New York: Monthly Review Press, 2017); Mehmet Tabak, *Dialectics of Human Nature in Marx's Philosophy* (New York: Palgrave Macmillan, 2012); E. P. Thompson, *The Poverty of Theory; or, An Orrery of Errors* (London: Merlin Press, 1995); Stavros Tombazos, *Time in Marx: The Categories of Time in Marx's Capital* (Chicago: Haymarket, 2014).

3   Althusser, 'The Humanist Controversy', 291.

4   Joseph Fracchia, 'Organisms and Objectifications: A Historical-Materialist Inquiry into the "Human and Animal"', *Monthly Review* 68, no. 10 (2017).

being is a part of nature' and rejects traditional conceptions of the human being, and that of Hegel in particular, with his emphasis on the corporeality and materiality of human existence.[5] Nature is the 'inorganic body' of the human being, Marx writes, 'with which it must remain in continuous interchange if it is not to die'.[6] Later, he re-conceptualises this 'continuous interchange' as a *metabolism* (*Stoffwechsel*) with the rest of nature, which is the 'natural condition' common to 'all particular social forms of human life'.[7] Marx's use of this concept was deeply influenced by the agricultural chemist Justus von Liebig, who used it to refer to the 'incessant process of organic exchange of old and new compounds through combinations, assimilations, and excretions' without which living organisms would die.[8] The notion of *Stoffwechsel* thus highlights the materiality of human existence: the fact that the human being is a moment of a material totality, an organism indissolubly inscribed in a flow of matter, just like plants, bacteria, fungi, or other animals.[9]

If the human being is such a moment in a metabolic flow of matter, then it has certain *needs*; inputs are required in order for this metabolism to continue to exist. However, the apparently obvious concept of need can be treacherous, so we have to tread carefully here: any talk of 'natural' needs risks slipping into reductive ideas about a hierarchy of needs, according to which a set of allegedly 'basic' needs (food, clothes, shelter, etc.) are

---

5   3: 276; see also 336. Four decades later, in the *Critique of the Gotha Programme* (1875), Marx reasserts that human labour power is 'a force of nature' (24: 81). See also Paul Burkett, *Marx and Nature: A Red and Green Perspective* (Chicago: Haymarket, 2014), pt. 1; and Amy E. Wendling, *Karl Marx on Technology and Alienation* (London: Palgrave Macmillan, 2009), chap. 2.

6   3: 276.

7   30: 63. See also G: 489, 640; 30: 40; M: 197, 885, 889; C1: 283, 290, 637. It was Alfred Schmidt who first drew attention to the importance of this rich concept, but its significance for Marx's thought and ecological critique was not fully appreciated until John Bellamy Foster's *Marx's Ecology: Materialism and Nature* (New York: Monthly Review Press, 2000). For a more recent and detailed analysis, see Saito's *Karl Marx's Ecosocialism.* Jason W. Moore has recently criticised the concept of metabolism for being unable to break with Cartesian dualism, but this has been convincingly repudiated by Andreas Malm. See Jason W. Moore, *Capitalism in the Web of Life: Ecology and the Accumulation of Capital* (London: Verso, 2015), 75ff; Andreas Malm, *The Progress of This Storm: Nature and Society in a Warming World* (London: Verso, 2018), 177ff; and Andreas Malm, 'Against Hybridism: Why We Need to Distinguish between Nature and Society, Now More than Ever', *Historical Materialism* 27, no. 2 (2019): 156–87.

8   Saito, *Karl Marx's Ecosocialism*, 69.

9   See Wendling, *Karl Marx on Technology and Alienation*, chap. 2.

accorded 'primacy' in relation to 'socially produced' needs, wants, or desires.[10] Marx was very attentive to this problem, and he clearly saw that 'needs must be understood as historic and specific contents rather than as mere forms of a pre-given essence', as Kate Soper puts it in her excellent discussion of the subject.[11] There is no such thing as a set of natural needs which inevitably override needs, wants, and desires stemming from historically specific social relations. The mere fact that every year hundreds of thousands of people commit suicide should make us think twice about postulating the existence of something like an irrepressible need for survival, for example. Human beings regularly display their willingness to sacrifice themselves for all kinds of reasons, and they do dangerous things while well aware of the dangers involved. As psychoanalysis has taught us, they even do dangerous, unhealthy, risky, and hazardous things *because* they are dangerous, unhealthy, risky, and hazardous. We must recognise, in the words of Soper, that

> even our so-called basic biological needs for food, shelter and the like, must be seen as specific, socially mediated contents, the principle of whose explanation is not our common physiological nature but the social relations of production, distribution and exchange.[12]

The really important thing to note here, however, is that such a notion of socially mediated needs is *not* incompatible with a concept of some sort of fundamental biological needs. Despite the socially mediated character of every human need, and despite the fact that people harm, kill, starve, and sacrifice themselves, it remains the case that *in order for there to be human beings at all, certain biological requirements have to be met.* Yet, the claim that human beings have certain biological needs does *not* imply that these needs will always and inevitably *override* social mediations, or that they will tend to do so. For this reason, it is perfectly possible to hold on to a concept of natural needs as what Agnes Heller calls 'a limit concept: a limit (different for different societies) beyond which human

---

10   Theodor W. Adorno, 'Theses on Need', trans. Martin Shuster and Iain Macdonald, *Adorno Studies* 1, no. 1 (2017): 100–5.

11   Kate Soper, *On Human Needs: Open and Closed Theories in a Marxist Perspective* (Brighton: Harvester Press, 1981), 87; see also Agnes Heller, *The Theory of Need in Marx* (London: Verso, 2018).

12   Soper, *On Human Needs*, 88.

life is no longer reproducible as such, beyond which the limit of bare existence is passed.'[13] Such a limit might be 'extremely elastic,' but it is nevertheless there – and to deny it would be to deny the corporeality of human existence.[14] Humans must, as Marx and Engels put it, 'be in a position to live in order to "make history".'[15]

The Structure of the Human Body

If the fact of being a natural organism in a metabolic totality is what humans share with other animals, what then sets them apart from the latter? What distinguishes the specifically *human* form of metabolism from other metabolisms? As we have seen, Marx endorsed a rather traditional distinction between humans and animals in the *1844 Manuscripts* – one that sits rather uneasily with the emphasis on the corporeality of human nature in those very same manuscripts. Marx argues that the human being is a 'species-being,' a 'being for itself' (*für sich selbst seiendes Wesen*) endowed with the capacity to relate to itself in a universal manner by virtue of its *consciousness*.[16] He is quite unequivocal on this point: 'Conscious life activity distinguishes man immediately from animal life activity. It is just because of this that he is a species-being.'[17] In *The German Ideology*, however, he completely abandons this emphasis on consciousness, species-being, and 'being for itself' while retaining the materialist emphasis on corporeality. In a crucial and famous passage, Marx and Engels write that

> the first premise of all human history is, of course, the existence of living human individuals. Thus the first fact to be established is the corporeal organisation [*körperliche Organisation*] of these individuals and their consequent relation to the rest of nature … Humans can be distinguished from animals by consciousness, by religion or anything else you like. They themselves begin to distinguish themselves from

---

13 Agnes Heller, *The Theory of Need in Marx* (London: Verso, 2018), 32.

14 Soper, *On Human Needs*, 59; Kate Soper, *What Is Nature? Culture, Politics, and the Non-Human* (Oxford: Blackwell, 1995), 133f.

15 5: 41; I.5: 26.

16 3: 337.

17 3: 276.

animals as soon as they begin to *produce* their means of subsistence, a step which is conditioned by their corporeal organisation.[18]

Marx and Engels are really breaking new ground here; instead of *consciousness* and *species-being*, they now point to *production* as the specific trait of the human being. Humans *produce* rather than merely *consume* their means of subsistence. It is of course perfectly possible for *individual* human beings to consume without ever producing anything, but they can only do so if *someone else* produces for them. To be sure, 'animals also produce. They build themselves nests, dwellings, like the bees, beavers, ants, etc.', as Marx argues in the *1844 Manuscripts*.[19] The distinction at play here is not an absolute distinction, then: human animals are not the *only* animals that produce, but they do so to a much higher degree than other species.

The really crucial element in this passage from *The German Ideology*, however, is the notion of *corporeal organisation*.[20] This is the condition, we are told, of human production.[21] Yet, after stating that the corporeal organisation of human individuals is the 'first premise of all human history', Marx and Engels go on to state that 'of course, we cannot here go into either the actual physical nature of human beings [*die physische Beschaffenheit der Menschen selbst*], or into the natural conditions in which humans find themselves'. This, they tell us, is a premise which 'all historical investigation must set out from'.[22]

It is remarkable that despite the canonical status of these passages from *The German Ideology*, the concept of corporeal organisation has been 'almost universally neglected', as Joseph Fracchia – who is, to my knowledge, the only one who has attempted to come up with an interpretation of this concept – puts it.[23] Most commentators seem to regard

---

18   5: 31; I.5: 8.

19   3: 276.

20   *Körperliche* is usually translated as 'physical' in the *Collected Works*, but 'corporeal' is more accurate ('physical' would be *physische*, a word also used by Marx in the same paragraph).

21   See also G: 734.

22   5: 31; I.5: 8.

23   Joseph Fracchia, 'Beyond the Human-Nature Debate: Human Corporeal Organisation as the First Fact of Historical Materialism', *Historical Materialism* 13, no. 1 (2005): 39. Among those who quote the passage without providing an interpretation of this concept are Avineri, *The Social and Political Thought of Karl Marx*, 73; Burkett, *Marx and Nature*, 269; Foster, *Marx's Ecology*, 115; Fox, *Marx, the Body, and Human Nature*, 156;

the features of the human body as a simple premise, that is, as something that lies outside of the concerns of Marxist theory. Despite their emphasis on materiality and (re)production, Marxists have therefore been oddly silent on the issue of the body.[24] Not only have they thereby reproduced the problematic tendency so prevalent in philosophy and social theory to ignore the body; they have also overlooked what in fact amounts to a 'corporeal turn' in Marx's thought.

What is the 'corporeal organisation' of human beings? How is the human body organised? Drawing on Marx's other writings, Fracchia suggests that we think of the human body as involving, on the one hand, a 'set of corporeal capabilities' and, on the other hand, a 'set of corporeal constraints'.[25] Constraints, in his formulation, set the limits for the capacity of humans to 'make history' and refer to 'bodily needs' as well as limits such as mortality, terrestriality, diurnality, and the limits of human sense organs.[26] Fracchia divides the *capabilities* into two subcategories. The first is what he calls 'bodily instruments' – organs which can be used as instruments, such as the hand, 'the uniquely flexible supra-laryngeal tract which is the absolute prerequisite for all human languages and thus human cultures … the human "perceptual systems", and, of course, the unique human brain'.[27] The second subcategory is the corporeal *dexterities* to which the flexibility of the bodily instruments give rise, such as bipedality.[28]

Fracchia's interpretation of the notion of corporeal organisation highlights some very important and interesting features of the human body, but it misses an absolutely crucial aspect of the specifically human metabolism: *the use of extra-somatic tools* – not the 'bodily instruments' of which Fracchia speaks, but those tools which are not immediately linked to the body. This, I will argue, is *the* most essential aspect of the corporeal organisation of the human being. Indeed, while it is widely acknowledged

---

Piotr Hoffmann, *The Anatomy of Idealism: Passivity and Activity in Kant, Hegel and Marx* (The Hague: Martinus Nijhoff Publishers, 1982), 79ff, 96, 106; David McNally, *Bodies of Meaning: Studies on Language, Labor, and Liberation* (Albany: State University of New York Press, 2001), 77; Alfred Schmidt, *The Concept of Nature in Marx*, trans. Ben Fowkes (London: Verso, 2013), 91; Tabak, *Dialectics of Human Nature in Marx's Philosophy*, 38.

24 Fracchia, 'Beyond the Human-Nature Debate', 34f; Fox, *Marx, the Body, and Human Nature*, chap. 1.

25 Fracchia, 'Beyond the Human-Nature Debate', 43.

26 Ibid., 51.

27 Ibid., 47.

28 Ibid., 48f.

that Marx stressed the centrality of tools in human (re)production, the significance of tools for a Marxist social ontology, in general, and the social ontology of economic power, in particular, is seldomly discussed. Rather, most accounts of Marx's analysis of the human use of tools discuss it in connection with the analysis of the labour process in chapter seven of the first volume of *Capital*. In these discussions, the analysis of tools is for the most part completely overshadowed by interpretations of this famous passage:

> We presuppose labour in a form in which it is an exclusively human characteristic. A spider conducts operations which resemble those of the weaver, and a bee would put many a human architect to shame by the construction of its honeycomb cells. But what distinguishes the worst architect from the best of bees is that the architect builds the cell in his mind before he constructs it in wax. At the end of every labour process, a result emerges which had already been conceived by the worker at the beginning, hence already existed ideally.[29]

Many commentators lay great stress on this distinction between the instinctual actions of animals and the properly human form of 'purposeful activity' governed by a prior mental conception.[30] As a result of this focus, tools tend to fade into the background.[31] I do not intend to deny that the human capacity for intellectual anticipation of the labour process is an important and distinctive feature of the human metabolism. It is, however, only part of the story, and for our purposes – namely,

---

29   C1: 283f.

30   See also G: 298, 311; 29: 278.

31   Examples of this include Avineri, *The Social and Political Thought of Karl Marx*, 81f; Braverman, *Labor and Monopoly Capital*, 46; Lucio Colletti, *From Rousseau to Lenin: Studies in Ideology and Society*, trans. John Merrington and Judith White (New York: Monthly Review Press, 1973), 67; Gould, *Marx's Social Ontology*, 41f; David Harvey, *A Companion to Marx's* Capital (London: Verso, 2010), 111ff; Michael Heinrich, *Wie das Marxsche 'Kapital' lesen? Leseanleitung und Kommentar zum Anfang des 'Kapital' Teil 2* (Stuttgart: Schmetterling Verlag, 2013), 153ff; Hoffmann, *The Anatomy of Idealism*, 81ff; Georg Lukács, *The Ontology of Social Being: 3. Labour*, trans. David Fernbach (London: Merlin Press, 1980), 3, 105; Martin McIvor, 'Marx's Philosophical Modernism: Post-Kantian Foundations of Historical Materialism', in *Karl Marx and Contemporary Philosophy*, ed. Andrew Chitty and Martin McIvor (Basingstoke: Palgrave Macmillan, 2009), 44; Ollman, *Alienation*, 110f; Saito, *Karl Marx's Ecosocialism*, 65; Tabak, *Dialectics of Human Nature in Marx's Philosophy*, 21.

for understanding the socio-ontological presuppositions of economic power – the use of tools is more important. Intellectual capacities and the use of tools are in fact closely connected, not only because they are a part of the same evolutionary development, but also because the complexity of human toolmaking requires certain intellectual capacities, including communication of complex information.[32]

Social Toolmakers

The important thing about human tool use is that it is *necessary*. Humans do not use tools simply because it is convenient; they are *dependent* upon them. As I have already noted, other animals use tools too, but they do not come close to the complexity and scale of human tools. The 'use and construction of instruments of labour' should therefore, in Marx's words, be regarded as 'characteristic of the specifically human labour process'.[33] The anatomy of *Homo sapiens sapiens* is even partly a *result* of the ability of its predecessors to produce simple tools, such as the hand axes of *Homo erectus*.[34] Tools are an integral part of the human body, and it is this aspect of human corporeal organisation which makes it necessary for humans to *produce* their means of subsistence. The details of the evolutionary trajectory that led to this need not concern us here; they belong to the set of facts that 'all historical investigation must set out from'.[35]

Because of this dependency upon tools, Marx refers to the latter as *organs*: 'Thus nature becomes one of the organs of his [i.e., the worker's] activity, which he annexes to his own bodily organs, extending his shape [*Gestalt*] in spite of the Bible.'[36] Tools are a *prolongation* of the body or, in

---

32   McNally, *Bodies of Meaning*, 92, 88. Alfred Schmidt even holds that 'there can be hardly any doubt that the most basic and abstract concepts have arisen in the context of labour-processes, i.e. in the context of tool-making.' Schmidt, *The Concept of Nature in Marx*, 102. See also the contributions in Kathleen R. Gibson and Tim Ingold, eds., *Tools, Language, and Cognition in Human Evolution* (Cambridge: Cambridge University Press, 1993).

33   C1: 286; see also Malm, *The Progress of This Storm*, 165; McNally, *Bodies of Meaning*, 100.

34   McNally, *Bodies of Meaning*, 92.

35   See Foster, *Marx's Ecology*, 200ff; McNally, *Bodies of Meaning*, chap. 3.

36   C1: 285, 493; see also 30: 58.

the words of Lewis Mumford, an extension of 'the powers of the otherwise unarmed organism' known as the human being.[37] They are not, however, the kind of extension that one can simply decide not to use: 'Just as the human being requires lungs to breathe with, so it requires something that is the work of human hands in order to consume the forces of nature productively.'[38] *Just like the lungs, tools are a part of the human body, a necessary part of the specifically human metabolism*, and for this reason, Marx approvingly quotes Benjamin Franklin's definition of the human being as a 'tool-making animal'.[39] This obviously harks back to the idea of nature as the 'inorganic body' of the human being in the *1844 Manuscripts*.[40] There, Marx conceptualised nature *as such* as the 'body' of the human being in order to highlight the corporeality of human existence against Hegel's idealist notion of labour.[41] The analytical value of such an extremely broad notion of the human body is, however, somewhat doubtful. An echo of this idea can be found in *Capital*, where Marx notes that in 'a wider sense we may include among the instruments of labour ... all the objective conditions necessary for carrying on the labour process' such as 'the earth'.[42] In general, however, when Marx speaks of 'tools', it is not in this 'wider sense' but in the narrower sense of 'things through which the impact of labour on its object is mediated'.[43]

Tools may be organs, but at the same time they are much easier to separate from the rest of the body than are other organs, such as the lungs, the liver, or the skin. They occupy a peculiar position on the threshold between the material of labour on the one hand and Fracchia's 'bodily instruments' on the other. Among the few Marxists who have appreciated this ambiguity we find Plekhanov and Kautsky, who argued that

37   Lewis Mumford, *Technics and Civilization* (Chicago: University of Chicago Press, 2010 [1934]), 10.

38   C1: 508. See also Foster, *Marx's Ecology*, 200f; John Bellamy Foster and Paul Burkett, 'The Dialectic of Organic/Inorganic Relations: Marx and the Hegelian Philosophy of Nature', *Organization and Environment* 13, no. 4 (2000): 413; Andreas Malm, *Fossil Capital: The Rise of Steam Power and the Roots of Global Warming* (London: Verso, 2016), 280; McNally, *Bodies of Meaning*, 91; and Schmidt, *The Concept of Nature*, 102.

39   30: 98; C1: 286.

40   For a comprehensive analysis of this concept, see Foster and Burkett, 'The Dialectic of Organic/Inorganic Relations'.

41   3: 276.

42   C1: 286.

43   C1: 286.

the artificial organs created by man are distinguished from animal organs in that they are not part of his body, but exist outside it. They are thus of an ambiguous nature. They belong to man as his organs and are yet at the same time part of his environment.[44]

Kautsky and Plekhanov's technicist misunderstanding of the relation between the human being, its tools, and its environment prevented them from harvesting the potential of this line of thought, but they did capture the essential thing, namely that *human tools are at the same time a part of the body – an organ – and separated from it.*[45] Tools are partially free-floating organs, only precariously connected to the bodies whose necessary metabolism with the rest of nature they mediate. Because of human dependence on tools, the constitutive moments of the human metabolism are much easier to separate and temporarily dissolve than the metabolisms of other animals (and plants, for that matter) – a circumstance which is, as I will discuss in the next chapter, absolutely crucial for understanding how such a thing as economic power is possible.

At this point, we have to introduce yet another fact from which 'all historical investigation must set out': the *social* nature of human production. To begin with this merely means that humans are dependent upon other humans for their reproduction. 'A human body cannot,' as Malm puts it, 'regulate her *Stoffwechsel* in solitude, any more than she could speak in a private tongue: she must do it as a communal being. Her relation to the rest of nature is therefore mediated through her relations to other human beings.'[46] Marx consistently treats the human being as 'a social animal', which is to say that 'human life has from the beginning rested on … social production'.[47] In opposition to 'the unimaginative conceits of the eighteenth-century Robinsonades', so dear to classical political economy as well as contemporary economics, Marx insists that 'all production is appropriation of nature on the part of an individual within and through

---

44   Karl Kautsky, 'My Book on the Materialist Conception of History', *International Journal of Comparative Sociology* 30, no. 1 (1989): 69; G. V. Plekhanov, *In Defence of Materialism: The Development of the Monist View of History*, trans. Andrew Rothstein (London: Lawrence & Wishart, 1947), 146ff.

45   See also S. H. Rigby, *Marxism and History: A Critical Introduction* (Manchester: Manchester University Press, 1998), 63; Wendling, *Karl Marx on Technology and Alienation*, 31.

46   Malm, *Fossil Capital*, 160; see also Burkett, *Marx and Nature*, 28f.

47   C1: 444; 34: 329.

a specific form of society'.[48] Marx regarded this as a *fact* whose explanation is the business of empirical studies of human evolution rather than social theory. An explanation of this kind would have to account for such evolutionary processes as the origins and effects of bipedality, which freed the hands for carrying and toolmaking; the ways in which increased effectivity of hunting and gathering created new and complex forms of social interaction as well as freeing up time for social activities not immediately related to the provision of food; how fire made it possible to externalise digestion, enormously increase energy efficiency, and develop larger brains; and how larger brains, in turn, combined with a narrow birth canal as a result of bipedality led to the peculiar phenomenon of prematurely born human animals.[49]

We are now finally in a position to return to the question posed in the beginning of chapter three: whether the individual or the social relations in which individuals find themselves are ontologically primary. The preceding analysis of the human body reveals that *already at the level of their 'corporeal organisation', human individuals are caught up in a web of social relations mediating their access to the conditions of their reproduction.* Some of their organs even circulate as tools in their social environment. For this reason, it does not make sense to ascribe primacy to *either* individuals *or* social relations. As Étienne Balibar puts it, Marx's perspective 'establishes a complete reciprocity between these two poles, which cannot exist without one another'.[50] In order to express this reciprocity, Balibar borrows the notion of 'transindividuality' from Gilbert Simondon; thus, we might say that the notion of corporeal organisation reveals the corporeal roots of transindividuality.[51] We can, of course, speak of individuals in a corporeal sense: it is certainly possible to identify human individuals as relatively tightly knit bundles of functionally coupled organs spatially separated from other similar bundles. But the boundaries of the body are blurry, and for this reason we should avoid positing the kind of absolute division between individuals and their social relations implied by claims about the 'primacy' of one or the other.[52]

---

48   G: 87; see also G: 83; C1: 269; 5: 35; and 30: 98.

49   See McNally, *Bodies of Meaning*, chap. 3; James C. Scott, *Against the Grain: A Deep History of the Earliest States* (New Haven, CT: Yale University Press, 2017), chap. 1.

50   Étienne Balibar, *The Philosophy of Marx*, trans. Gregory Elliot and Chris Turner (London: Verso, 2014), 32.

51   Étienne Balibar, 'Philosophies of the Transindividual: Spinoza, Marx, Freud', *Australasian Philosophical Review* 2, no. 1 (2018), 5–25.

52   See also Luca Basso's concept of singularity, which is likewise an attempt to

The *double mediation* at the heart of the human metabolism – the mediation of tools and the mediation of social relations – explains why it can take infinite different forms. To be sure, the human corporeal organisation also implies certain limits, as emphasised by Fracchia, but within these limits, the possibilities are virtually endless. Humans are bound to mediate their metabolism through tools, but there is no *necessary* way to organise this mediation. There is no specific set of tools which every individual must necessarily use, and for this reason there is an infinity of ways in which a division of labour can be organised. Human corporeal organisation opens up an immense space of *possibility* founded on a *necessity*: a metabolism must be established, but its social form is never simply given. There is no natural form of human metabolism, in the sense that the natural characteristics of the human animal do not entail a specific form of metabolism. The organisation of the human body implies, as Piotr Hoffmann puts it, 'that human life cannot flow in a ready-made channel'.[53]

The Original Cleavage

These considerations allow us to grasp the poverty of the notion of an 'original unity' of humans and nature – a common figure in romantic critiques of capitalism. A recent example is Kohei Saito's otherwise-impressive account of Marx's ecosocialism. In Saito's reading, the core of Marx's political project is the abolition of capitalist alienation and 'the conscious rehabilitation of the unity of humanity and nature'.[54] What does it mean to say that there is a 'unity' of humanity and nature? Such a claim can be understood in two different ways. First, it can be interpreted in the banal sense that humans are natural beings, that is, a part of the totality we refer to as nature. If this is what it means to speak of the unity of humans and nature, however, it makes absolutely no sense to say that such a unity has been broken by capitalism. Sure, people die of starvation because of capitalist relations of production, but it is hardly the general condition of existence – partly because capital needs people to stay alive so they can

conceptualise Marx's overcoming of what Basso refers to as 'individualism' and 'holism'. Luca Basso, *Marx and Singularity: From the Early Writings to the* Grundrisse (Leiden: Brill, 2012), 2.

53   Piotr Hoffmann, *The Anatomy of Idealism: Passivity and Activity in Kant, Hegel and Marx* (The Hague: Martinus Nijhoff Publishers, 1982), 96.

54   Saito, *Karl Marx's Ecosocialism*, 177.

produce surplus value. Capital *organises* the human metabolism with the rest of nature; it does not abolish it. The second possible interpretation of the idea of a unity of humanity and nature is a variant of the romantic ideal of an authentically human life we encountered in chapter three. Such a notion relies on an implicit ideal of an authentic or immediate way for humans to relate to nature. This is the notion which runs through Saito's book and so many other romantic criticisms of the capitalist destruction of the biosphere.[55] In its worst forms, such a romanticism turns into New Age mysticism or reactionary *Schwärmerei* for rural life.

Marx's analysis of the human body allows us to see just how misguided it is to speak of an original unity of humans and nature. We should rather speak of an *original disunity* or an *original cleavage* between humans and the rest of nature. What characterises the human animal is that it is, in the words of Soper, 'biologically underdetermined'.[56] At the centre of its being is what Piotr Hoffmann calls a 'loss of immediacy', which far from being the result of capitalist alienation is rather an ontological and constitutive feature of this peculiar animal.[57] Living all of your life staring into a smartphone in a megacity and eating prepared fast food without ever knowing where it comes from and how it is produced does not mean that some holy bond between you and nature has been broken; it just means that your individual metabolism is mediated by a complex system of infrastructures, data, machines, financial flows, and planetary supply chains.[58] Marx's critique of capitalism is, as Postone puts it, a critique 'of forms of social mediation, not a critique of mediation from the standpoint of immediacy'.[59] Here, Marx shows himself to be a true student of Hegel, for whom immediacy always reveals itself to be mediated.[60]

---

55   Another example is Foster and Burkett, 'The Dialectic of Organic/Inorganic Relations', 416.

56   Soper, *What Is Nature?*, 126.

57   Hoffmann, *The Anatomy of Idealism*, 79.

58   In some passages, Marx seems to slip into such a romanticism, as when he speaks of an 'original unity between the worker and the conditions of labour' (33: 340; see also G: 489; 32: 492; and 20: 129). It is possible, however, to read these passages as a reference not to some authentic or natural bond, but rather to *socially constituted* and relatively stable pre-capitalist connections between labour and its conditions.

59   Moishe Postone, Time, Labor, and Social Domination: A Reinterpretation of Marx's Critical Theory (Cambridge: Cambridge University Press, 2003), 49.

60   See, for example, G. W. F. Hegel, *The Encyclopedia of Logic: Part I of the Encyclopedia of Philosophical Sciences with the Zusätze*, trans. T. F. Geraets, W. A. Suchting, and H. S. Harris (Indianapolis: Hackett, 1991), 115.

At this juncture, we immediately face the danger of slipping into a different but equally untenable romanticism, namely a call for humans to be humble and come to terms with or appreciate their finitude. The acknowledgement of the inherent lack of unity in the metabolism of humans and the rest of nature should not lead us to conceive of humans as fragile, vulnerable, and ontologically homeless creatures destined to remain caught in opaque mediations. Such a mode of thinking amounts to a secularisation of the religious demand for humans to display their submissiveness and obedience to God. One finds examples of this in existentialist philosophies of the Heideggerian variant or in Arnold Gehlen's conservative philosophical anthropology, according to which the natural incompleteness of human beings justifies the call for stable social institutions (i.e., the shepherd God is replaced with the shepherd state).[61] The key to avoiding such an ideology of finitude is to recall that it is the very fragility and porosity of the human metabolism which has made humans so evolutionarily successful. Indeed, human corporeal organisation is the source of an immense flexibility and has enabled this animal to 'break out of a narrow ecological niche', as Fracchia points out.[62] Far from being the sign of an inherent finitude of the human being, the loss of immediacy at the centre of its being is rather a sign of its *infinity* in the sense that it enables humans to socially mediate their relation to the rest of nature in an infinite number of ways.

---

61   Arnold Gehlen, *Man, His Nature and Place in the World*, trans. Clare McMillan and Karl-Siegbert Rehberg (New York: Columbia University Press, 1988).

62   Fracchia, 'Beyond the Human-Nature Debate', 49; Hoffmann, *The Anatomy of Idealism*, 79f.

5

Metabolic Domination

The biologically underdetermined nature of the human being makes it important to insist on a distinction which has been under sustained attack from various strands of critical theory in the last couple of decades: that between the *social* and the *natural*. The conception of the human defended in the preceding chapter obviously entails that humans and their social relations cannot be thought of as something existing *outside* of nature. Nevertheless, relations between human animals are significantly different from relations between other natural things and organisms, and we need a conceptual apparatus which is capable of reflecting that difference. In a ridicule of economists in *Capital*, Marx writes that 'so far no chemist has ever discovered exchange-value either in a pearl or a diamond'.[1] What does he mean by that? That the *value form* is a 'purely social' property which has nothing to do with 'natural qualities' of a commodity, such as its chemical composition.[2] Similarly, Marx insists that 'to be a slave, to be a citizen, are social determinations, relations between human beings A and B. Human being A, as such, is not a slave. He is a slave in and through

---

1 C1: 177,

2 C1: 139; 20: 121. See Patrick Murray and Jeanne Schuler's analysis of the meaning of the expression 'purely social' in Marx's text: Patrick Murray and Jeanne Schuler, 'Social Form and the "Purely Social": On the Kind of Sociality Involved in Value', in *The Social Ontology of Capitalism*, ed. D. Krier and M. P. Worrell (New York: Palgrave Macmillan, 2017). They distinguish between two meanings. Here, I am concerned with what they refer to as the 'first' meaning, which is that value is '*strictly* a consequence of a specific social form of labor' (134).

society.'[3] To say that having a value or being a slave is a *social* property is to say that these phenomena have their roots in relations between human beings.[4] The reason why Marx finds it important to underline the *social* nature of things such as value and slavery is, of course, that he wants to stress that they are *not necessary* – that is, that they fall within the domain of what can actually be *changed* by human beings. This is the core of the distinction between the natural and the social on which Marx's denaturalising critique of social forms rests: the social is that which can be changed by humans, and the natural is that which is necessary from the point of view of human society. As Kate Soper puts it in her brilliant discussion of this distinction, nature is

> those material structures and processes that are independent of human activity (in the sense that they are not human created product), and whose forces and causal powers are the necessary condition of every human practice, and determine the possible forms it can take.[5]

Only by insisting on such a distinction is it possible to conceptualise the crucial and real difference – systematically obliterated by economists and other ideologues – between the value of a commodity and its chemical composition or the enslavement of a human being and the possibility of its emancipation.

A distinction between the natural and social does not imply the claim that their boundaries are fixed. Social relations give rise to technologies which enable humans to control and manipulate natural processes which were hitherto outside their reach. Nor does the distinction between the natural and the social imply positing an absolute difference between them. Andreas Malm has convincingly demonstrated that it is perfectly possible to insist on a 'substance monism' while acknowledging that human social relations have certain 'emergent properties' which cannot be found in the rest of nature. Drawing on contemporary philosophy of mind as a kind of template, Malm dubs this position 'substance monism property dualism'.[6] Another way to put it is that there is a *dialectical*

---

3   G: 265; see also G: 259; 9: 211; and C1: 273.

4   6: 321.

5   Kate Soper, *What Is Nature? Culture, Politics, and the Non-Human* (Oxford: Blackwell, 1995), 132f.

6   Andreas Malm, *The Progress of This Storm: Nature and Society in a Warming World* (London: Verso, 2018), chap. 2.

relation between the natural and the social. The concept of dialectics is often used in an extremely sloppy manner; more often than not, it simply means 'that everything is dependent upon everything else and is in a state of interaction and that it's all rather complicated,' as Michael Heinrich aptly puts it.[7] But dialectics is neither interaction, mutual presupposition, reciprocity, nor simply contradiction. Dialectics is, rather, a process in which a concrete totality reveals itself to contain its own negation as one of its moments.[8] This is the sense in which the relation between the natural and the social is dialectical: nature is the totality out of which emerges an animal whose corporeal organisation opens up a new field of possibility which sets these animals apart from the rest of nature.

Modes, Relations, Forces, History

For Marx, 'mode of production' refers to a relatively stable way of organising the human metabolism. He employs this term in at least two different senses. First, he uses it to refer to the specific social and technical structure of the labour process. Second, a broader sense where it refers not only to the labour process but to all the significant aspects of the economic structure of a given society – this is the sense in which we can speak of the feudal or the capitalist mode of production.[9] Here, I am concerned only with this broad sense of the term. A mode of production, in turn, consists of a combination of a set of *relations of production* and a set of *productive forces*.[10] 'Productive forces' refers to all the elements which enter into the production of a use value: means of production, raw materials, energy, and labour, including knowledge and skills.[11] The

7   Michael Heinrich, *An Introduction to the Three Volumes of Karl Marx's* Capital, trans. Alex Locascio (New York: Monthly Review Press, 2012), 36f.

8   A paradigmatic example is Hegel's account of the dialectic of sense certainty in the *Phenomenology of Spirit*: sense certainty posits 'this' as the truth, but it turns out that one of the moments of 'this', namely 'now', in fact amounts to 'not-this'. G. W. F. Hegel, *Phenomenology of Spirit*, trans. A. V. Miller (Oxford: Oxford University Press, 1977), 59ff.

9   David Harvey, *The Limits to Capital* (London: Verso, 2006), 25f; S. H. Rigby, *Marxism and History: A Critical Introduction* (Manchester: Manchester University Press, 1998), 24.

10   Alex Callinicos, *Making History: Agency, Structure, and Change in Social Theory*, 2nd ed. (Leiden: Brill, 2004), 41; Louis Althusser, *On the Reproduction of Capitalism: Ideology and Ideological State Apparatuses*, trans. G. M. Goshgarian (London: Verso, 2014), 20.

11   See Althusser, *On the Reproduction of Capitalism*, 22ff; Callinicos, *Making*

'relations of production' refers to the social relations under which the forces of production are employed.

The primacy ascribed to productive forces in orthodox historical materialism is, as I have already mentioned, also possible to find in many of Marx's writings. In *The German Ideology*, he and Engels are quite unambiguous: 'In the development of productive forces there comes a stage when productive forces and means of intercourse are brought into being which, under the existing relations, only cause mischief, and are no longer productive but destructive forces.'[12] In this familiar scheme, the relations of production are the variable which adapts to the immanently developing productive forces. This position is restated in writings such as *The Poverty of Philosophy* and the *Communist Manifesto*, achieving its paradigmatic formulation in the preface to the *Contribution to the Critique of Political Economy* (quoted in chapter three). As he delved into a detailed study of technology in the early 1860s, however, Marx changed his views.[13] He now began to regard the development of the productive forces as a *result* of the relations of production. Apparently, Marx did not realise just how significant a theoretical change this was, and he continued to hold on to some of the core ideas of productive force determinism in some of his writings from the 1860s.[14] Perhaps the best example is a famous passage from chapter thirty-two of the first volume of *Capital*, where he claims that 'capitalist production begets, with the inexorability of a natural process, its own negation'.[15] As Heinrich has rightly pointed out, however, this passage is merely 'declamatory' and does not constitute a 'prerequisite for [the] essential arguments of the critique of political economy'.[16] Marx's

---

History, 43ff; Harvey, *The Limits to Capital*, 98ff; Rigby, *Marxism and History*, 17ff; and Goran Therborn, *Science, Class and Society: On the Formation of Sociology and Historical Materialism* (London: Routledge, 1976).

12   5: 52; I.5: 43.

13   Andreas Malm, *Fossil Capital: The Rise of Steam Power and the Roots of Global Warming* (London: Verso, 2016), 274ff; Andreas Malm, 'Marx on Steam: From the Optimism of Progress to the Pessimism of Power', *Rethinking Marxism* 30, no. 2 (2018): 166–85; Rob Beamish, *Marx, Method, and the Division of Labor* (Urbana: University of Illinois Press, 1992).

14   See Malm, *Fossil Capital*, 276; Rigby, *Marxism and History*, 148; William H. Shaw, '"The Handmill Gives You the Feudal Lord": Marx's Technological Determinism', *History and Theory* 18, no. 2 (1979): 158f; Chris Wickham, 'Productive Forces and the Economic Logic of the Feudal Mode of Production', *Historical Materialism* 16, no. 2 (2008): 6f.

15   C1: 929.

16   Michael Heinrich, 'Geschichtsphilosophie bei Marx', in *Geschichtsphilosophie oder Das Begreifen der Historizität*, ed. Diethard Behrens (Freiburg: ca ira, 1999).

productive force determinism relies on the unwarranted assumption of a transhistorically necessary tendency for the productive forces to develop, regardless of the specific relations of production under which they are put to use – an assumption which is essentially *external* to Marx's general theoretical framework. After the publication of the French edition of the first volume of *Capital* (1872–75) – the last edition Marx prepared – productive force determinism disappears entirely from his writings.[17] Towards the end of his life, he even explicitly opposed determinist readings of his work. In a 1877 letter to the editors of a Russian journal, Marx stressed that the sections on so-called primitive accumulation in *Capital* was no more than a 'historical sketch of the genesis of capitalism in Western Europe', not 'a historico-philosophical theory of general development, imposed by fate on all peoples, whatever the historical circumstances in which they are placed'.[18] He restated this point in his letter to Vera Zasulich from 1881, where he underlined that his analysis of 'the "historical inevitability" of this process is *expressly* limited to the *countries of Western Europe*'.[19]

What drives history is not the immanent and necessary development of the productive forces, but human beings acting within a set of determinate social structures from which certain tendencies arise. Some modes of production thwart certain forms of technological development; others – such as capitalism – accelerate some forms of it. As Marx explains in an absolutely crucial passage from the *1861–63 Manuscripts*:

> *Natural laws of production!* Here, it is true, it is a matter of the *natural laws of bourgeois production*, hence of the laws within which production occurs at a particular historical stage and under *particular historical conditions of production*. If there were no such laws, the *system of bourgeois production* would be altogether incomprehensible [*unbegreiflich*]. What is involved here, therefore, is the presentation of *the nature* of this particular mode of production, hence its *natural laws*. But just as it is itself *historical*, so are its *nature* and the *laws of that nature*. The natural laws of the Asiatic, the ancient, or the feudal mode of production were essentially different.[20]

---

17   See Kevin B. Anderson's important study on Marx's preoccupation with non-Western and pre-capitalist societies in the last decade of his life and its impact on his understanding of history: *Marx at the Margins: On Nationalism, Ethnicity, and Non-Western Societies*, 2nd ed. (Chicago: University of Chicago Press, 2016), chap. 6.

18   24: 200.

19   46: 71; see also Anderson, *Marx at the Margins*, 224ff.

20   34: 236.

So, the expression 'natural laws' refers to the *essential* and *historically specific* determinations of a mode of production, not to the way in which a transhistorical technological drive smashes through the fetters of historical particularities. Every mode of production has its own laws, and as we have seen, there is no such thing as a *natural* mode of production. The historicity of the human being 'is not superimposed upon man's physical organisation but grows directly out of it,' as Piotr Hoffman puts it – not because a sequence of modes of production is inscribed in the essence of the human being but precisely because of the *absence* of such an inscription.[21] This is how we must understand Marx's claim in *The German Ideology* that 'humans have history because they must *produce* their life, and because they must produce it moreover in a *certain* way: this is determined by their corporeal organisation'.[22] Only because the corporeal organisation of the human being opens up an immense space of possibility is something like a succession of modes of production – that is, *history* – possible. The translation of this *possibility* into *actuality* – the processes that decide on the specific social relations under which people live – is what we call *politics*.

The Meaning of Materialism

One might object that my description of the human being in this and the preceding chapter has been somewhat reductive, with its narrow focus on the reproduction of corporeal existence. Is a Marxist social ontology really committed to a conception of humans as beings whose sole or primary goal in life is to procure the means of subsistence? Is human life not so much more than that? What about thought, language, meaning, affects, culture, art, religion, beauty? This would undoubtedly be a reasonable objection if what I have presented in this and the preceding chapter claimed to be a full-fledged philosophical anthropology. But that is not the case. The analysis of the human being presented in the preceding pages is intended only to help us get a better understanding of what economic power is – and more specifically, how it is possible in the first place.

At the same time, however, it should also be noted that the social ontology defended here does ascribe a special importance to social relations

---

21 Piotr Hoffmann, *The Anatomy of Idealism: Passivity and Activity in Kant, Hegel and Marx* (The Hague: Martinus Nijhoff Publishers, 1982), 81.

22 5: 43.

of *production*, compared to other aspects of the social totality. It *is* a *materialist* social ontology. What does that mean? Unfortunately, orthodox historical materialism and the innumerable straw-man criticisms of Marx's 'economism' have obfuscated the meaning of Marx's materialism. In order to grasp the core of Marx's materialism, it is therefore useful to consider the positions Marx tried to avoid.

Marx was, first of all, concerned with overturning idealism. The primary (though not exclusive) target of his criticism was not idealism as general ontology or as a philosophical system, but more specifically the philosophical anthropology of the idealists and the resulting (mis)understanding of society and history. As discussed earlier in relation to the critique of Hegel in the *1844 Manuscripts*, Marx accused idealist philosophers – including most of the Young Hegelians – of subscribing to 'a spiritualistic view of what it means to be human', as Patrick Murray puts it.[23] According to Marx, idealists tend to think of humans as 'ethereal beings ... able to live on the ether of pure thought', a view which results in a conception of social and historical change as something originating in thought, abstractly understood.[24] This, in turn, leads – at least in Young Hegelian criticism – to a one-sided emphasis on *critique* as the driving force of social change.[25] Marx had himself defended such a position in 1843, when he underlined the urgent need for a 'reform of consciousness' through a 'ruthless criticism of all that exists'.[26] As we have seen, Feuerbach's humanism, with its emphasis on the naturalness and corporeality of human existence, helped Marx to transcend this idealism a year later, in 1844.

However, the materialist philosophies of the eighteenth and nineteenth century were equally fraught with reductive abstractions. Marx regarded post-Baconian British materialism as 'one-sided' because of its mechanical ontology, which reduced 'concepts, notions, and ideas' to mere 'phantoms of the real world'.[27] The materialism of the French Enlightenment represented, as Murray puts it, 'only an abstract negation, a *mere* turning-upside-down, of the idealist position. That is, they retained the same logical dualism but altered the order of priority.'[28] Like Feuerbach's, such

---

23   Patrick Murray, *Marx's Theory of Scientific Knowledge* (New York: Humanity Books, 1990), 64.

24   4: 53.

25   Ibid.

26   3: 144, 142.

27   4: 128.

28   Murray, *Marx's Theory of Scientific Knowledge*, 69. Marx was well versed in the

a form of materialism is *ahistorical* and *asocial*. Marx's social ontology is an attempt to sail safely between the Scylla of idealist anthropology and the Charybdis of ahistorical materialism; to avoid an *abstract dualism* of thought and being *as well as reducing* the one to the other; to insist, that is, on the identity-in-difference of thought and being. In order to do that, Marx mobilised elements of both traditions against each other. This is particularly clear in the *Theses on Feuerbach*, where Marx attacked 'all previous materialism (that of Feuerbach included)' for its failure to appreciate the significance of subjectivity and human practice. The '*active* side' of human existence was thus 'set forth abstractly by idealism'.[29] Marx's materialism is an attempt to hold on to the idealist emphasis on activity and subjectivity as well as the materialist insistence on the corporeality of human beings and the primacy of their *practical* rather than theoretical relationship to their surroundings.

Such a materialism does not amount to a reductive claim about consciousness being an immediate reflection of 'matter'. To be sure, Marx does occasionally express himself in a manner which suggests such a crude 'reflection theory' of knowledge and ideology. These passages are mostly found in highly polemical or programmatic texts such as *The German Ideology* and the preface to the *Contribution*, where he famously claims that 'it is not the consciousness of men that determines their existence, but their social existence that determines their consciousness'.[30] In orthodox historical materialism, such passages and expressions became the canonical basis for what was effectively a regression to a pre-Marxian abstract materialism – as with Lenin, who insisted that 'consciousness is only the reflection of being, at best an approximately true (adequate, perfectly exact) reflection of it'.[31] Such a view, and the one-sided quips by

---

history of materialism, having written his doctoral dissertation on Epicurus and Democritus. See his outline of the history of modern materialism in *The Holy Family* (4: 124–34), from which I have just quoted, his critique of the ahistorical materialism of the physiocrats in the *1861–63 Manuscripts* (30: 353), and the 'abstract materialism of natural science' in *Capital* (C1: 494).

29   5: 3; Étienne Balibar, *The Philosophy of Marx*, trans. Gregory Elliot and Chris Turner (London: Verso, 2014), 23ff.

30   29: 263. See also 5: 36 and I.5: 135, where Marx and Engels speak of 'echoes', 'reflexes', and 'direct efflux' (*Ausfluß*). Murray notes – correctly, in my view – that these passages should be read as polemical jabs rather than well-considered theoretical concepts (*Marx's Theory of Scientific Knowledge*, 69). See also Terry Eagleton, *Ideology: An Introduction* (London: Verso, 1996), 73.

31   Vladimir Illich Lenin, *Materialism and Empirio-Criticism: Critical Comments on*

Marx on which it relies, does not, however, do justice to the inner logic of Marx's materialist social ontology. The 'point is not', as Murray explains, 'that consciousness is just an epiphenomenon of being (or life) but that it never exists apart from, as an independent entity detached from, being (or life). Consciousness is always the *consciousness-of* some determinate life practice.'[32] The whole thrust of Marx's materialist view of human intellectual activity is to see it as an integrated part of human social practice. Human beings are 'thinking bodies', in Joseph Fracchia's words; 'the "spirit" is from the outset infested with curse of being "burdened" with matter', as Marx and Engels write in *The German Ideology*, and for this reason the 'production of ideas, of conceptions, of consciousness is from the beginning immediately interwoven [*verflochten*] with the material activity and the material intercourse of humans.'[33]

One of the most fundamental claims of Marx's materialism, in addition to the emphasis on the socio-material embeddedness of intellectual activity, concerns the relative significance of different sets of social relations within the social totality. The centrality ascribed to relations of production by Marx derives from the simple fact that relations of production are the social relations through which people gain access to the necessary conditions of their life. The procurement of means of subsistence is something

---

a Reactionary Philosophy, trans. Abraham Fineberg, in *Lenin Collected Works*, vol. 14 (Moscow: Progress Publishers, 1972), chap. 6.2; Karl Korsch, *Marxism and Philosophy*, trans. Fred Halliday (London: Verso, 2013), 81.

32   Murray, *Marx's Theory of Scientific Knowledge*, 70; see also Rigby, *Marxism and History*, 275ff; Alfred Schmidt, *The Concept of Nature in Marx*, trans. Ben Fowkes (London: Verso, 2013), 107ff.

33   5: 43f; I.5: 30; 5: 36; I.5: 135. Joseph Fracchia, 'Beyond the Human-Nature Debate: Human Corporeal Organisation as the First Fact of Historical Materialism', *Historical Materialism* 13, no. 1 (2005): 58. Marx's hostility to idealist hypostatisations led him to adopt a somewhat empiricist attitude in *The German Ideology* and other writings from the mid-1840s. Later, however, he discovered that abstractions also occur in social reality itself. This development can be seen, for example, by comparing his ridicule in *The Holy Family* of the Hegelian idealist who thinks that *the fruit* as such really exists, with the passage from the first edition of *Capital* where he notes that with money, it is as if *the animal* as such exists right next to all of the particular animals. His changing views on methodology also led him to appreciate the value of theoretical abstractions. Whereas one of Marx's earliest criticisms of Ricardo was that he was too abstract, he later accused him of not being abstract enough. See Louis Althusser et al., *Reading Capital: The Complete Edition*, trans. Ben Brewster and David Fernbach (London: Verso, 2015), 146; Alex Callinicos, *Deciphering Capital: Marx's Capital and Its Destiny* (London: Bookmarks, 2014), 47; Amy E. Wendling, *Karl Marx on Technology and Alienation* (London: Palgrave Macmillan, 2009), 67.

most people tend to regard as rather important; if they do not, they risk their life. Once certain social relations have established themselves at this level, they result in what Robert Brenner calls 'rules for reproduction', that is, they act as limits on how people can gain access to life's necessities.[34] As is hopefully clear by now, this does not imply an economistic view of social life. Indeed, the economy is not, as I have repeatedly stressed, a separate social sphere governed by an economic rationality. The economy in Marx's sense is, rather, the sum of activities and processes through which social reproduction is organised; and the logics which govern these processes are inherently social and historical: 'Historical materialist approaches begin,' as Brenner puts it, 'from a denial of any notion of trans-historical individual economic rationality'.[35] It is this denaturalisation of the economy which radically distinguishes Marx from political economy (as well as contemporary economics). The relations of production are not something 'out there' in a separate economic sphere; they are nothing but the relations through which people reproduce their lives, relations which are an immediate part of daily life. What is characteristic about the economic sphere, if we want to call it that, is not the logics which governs it but the social function of the activities which constitute it, that is, the fact that the very existence of society depends on them. This is the basic idea of Marx's materialism. The latter does not claim that the social relations which govern social reproduction also automatically govern other spheres of life, or that social forms of consciousness are mere reflections of it. What it does claim, however, is that relations of production exert a very powerful influence on other aspects of social life by virtue of their absolutely fundamental role in the reproduction of the very existence of social life.[36]

---

34   Robert Brenner, 'Property and Progress: Where Adam Smith Went Wrong', in *Marxist History-Writing for the Twenty-First Century*, ed. Chris Wickham (Oxford: Oxford University Press, 2007), 59.

35   See also 34: 329. Brenner, 'Property and Progress', 57.

36   The doctrinaire codification of the so-called primacy of production took the form of the base/superstructure model, according to which the economic structure of a society unilaterally determined the forms taken by the state, law, culture, ideology, and so on. Although there is certainly a rational kernel in this model, I agree with Wood that it 'has always been more trouble than it is worth' (*Democracy against Capitalism: Renewing Historical Materialism* [London: Verso, 2016], 49). The state and the law, for example, cannot simply be placed in as 'superstructure', as some of their functions are necessary for the structures of the economic 'base' (27f; see also Rigby, *Marxism and History*, chap. 9). For this reason, she suggests replacing it with a conception of the social totality as 'a

How to Extract Surplus Labour

At this point, in order to finally approach the question of *power*, it is necessary to introduce yet another one of those facts on which social ontology is based: *the fateful capacity of human beings to produce more than what is necessary for their own survival*. Without this capacity, Marx explains, class society would be impossible:

> If the worker needs to use all of his time to produce the necessary means of subsistence for himself and his family, he has no time left in which to perform unpaid labour for other people. Unless labour has attained a certain level of productivity, the worker will have no such free time at his disposal, and without superfluous time there can be no surplus labour, hence no capitalists, as also no slave-owners, no feudal barons, in a word no class of large-scale landed proprietors.[37]

The mere *possibility* of surplus labour – which is dependent upon certain favourable natural conditions – can only explain the *possibility* of class domination, never its *actuality*.[38] In order for this potential to be realised, some people have to succeed in extracting surplus labour from others. If we now consider the ways in which this can happen, the relation between human corporeal organisation and power becomes clear. One option is to force other people to do surplus labour by means of (the threat of) direct violence. Another possibility is to psychologically or ideologically manipulate people into doing it. These strategies can of course be, and have probably always been, combined. Given the precarious nature of the human metabolism, however, there is also a third possibility, which is to *exploit this ontological fragility and insert oneself in the gap between life and its conditions*. This is exactly what economic power does. Malm describes it well:

> No other species can be so flexible, so universal, so omnivorous in relation to the rest of nature – *but for the very same reason, no other species can have its metabolism organised through such sharp internal*

---

continuous structure of social relations and forms with varying degrees of distance from the immediate processes of production and appropriation' (25f.).

37   C1: 646f.
38   C1: 649f.

divisions. If a broad set of extra-somatic tools is a distinctive feature of Homo sapiens sapiens, it is also the point where that species ceases to be a unity … A material, a machine, a prime mover can become private property. The individual might need them like she needs her own lungs, but they are outside of her body, caught by others in a net, versatile *and* off-limits, and so she may have no choice but to go via a master to access them: she is snared in property relations.[39]

The fact that parts of the human body can be concentrated as property in the hands of other members of the species has the consequence that *power can weave itself into the very fabric of the human metabolism.* Instead of attaching itself externally to the metabolism and violently pumping out surplus labour like a leech, the dominant part in a power relation can inject itself into the heart of social reproduction. The use of violence thus becomes less necessary, since power is now transferred to things. The phenomenon of economic power thus reveals the 'unique propensity' of humans 'to *actively order matter so that it solidifies their social relations*'.[40] As Alf Hornborg notes, human beings embody social relations in artefacts, with the consequence that 'the management of artifacts is tantamount to the management of relations'.[41] This is why property relations is such an important factor in human existence, and, as we will see in the next chapter, one of the characteristic features of capitalism is that it is the only mode of production to have been able to fully exploit the possibility of this mode of domination. Elaine Scarry, who is one of the few to have appreciated this intimate connection between power and the structure of the human body, explains the significance of property well:

It is the identification of the materials of earth as 'a prolongation' of the worker's body that leads Marx to designate 'private property' as a key problem for civilization: through private property, the maker is separated from the materials of earth, from the inorganic prolongation of his own activity, and therefore enters into the process of artifice as one who cannot sell what he makes (coats, bricks) but can only sell his own now truncated activity of making … Thus the disturbingly

39   Malm, *Fossil Capital*, 280.
40   Malm, *The Progress of This Storm*, 143.
41   Alf Hornborg, *Global Magic: Technologies of Appropriation from Ancient Rome to Wall Street* (Basingstoke: Palgrave Macmillan, 2016), 93, 104, 162.

graphic concept of the severing of the worker from his own extended body becomes central to *Capital*, though it usually occurs in the more abstract phrasing of 'the separation of the worker from the means of production'.[42]

The porosity of the human being makes this peculiar animal extremely susceptible to property relations. It opens up the possibility of a new form of power defined by the ability of social logics, such as capital, to transform it into the mediator between life and its conditions.

In my account of human corporeal organisation, I have written a lot about 'tools' – a term which might conjure up the image of artefacts such as axes, spears, spoons, hammers, and the like. To be sure, even the simplest human tools are vastly more complex than those used by apes – not only because 'apes do not use heat, adhesives, knots or weaving to permanently join two or more separate objects,' but also because of the social character of the production and use of tools.[43] Humans are able to join together tools, and to produce tools with the help of other tools. Because of the separability of the body and its tool-organs, the latter can also be coupled to motive forces other than the human body; 'the unity of the motive force of labor and the labor itself is not inviolable,' as Harry Braverman puts it.[44] An important aspect of the human use of tools is thus what Malm calls the 'peculiar human capacity for energetic division'.[45] In one sense, even a simple task such as dropping a stone on a shell in order to crack it open is a utilisation of a force of nature, namely gravity. Humans can also use the bodies of each other as well as animals as sources of energy.[46] At a later point in human history came inventions such as mills, powered first by water and later by wind, and even later coal and oil became the energetic basis of social reproduction. Over time, tools developed into *machinery*.

42   Elaine Scarry, *The Body in Pain: The Making and Unmaking of the World* (New York: Oxford University Press, 1985), 250. The quote continues with the claim: 'and as a difference between the capacity to "sell the products of labour" and to sell "labour power"'. This is not very precise. A more appropriate difference would be that between selling labour power and being independent of the market.

43   David McNally, *Bodies of Meaning: Studies on Language, Labor, and Liberation* (Albany: State University of New York Press, 2001), 100.

44   Harry Braverman, *Labor and Monopoly Capital: The Degradation of Work in the Twentieth Century* (New York: Monthly Review Press, 1974), 50.

45   Malm, *Fossil Capital*, 315.

46   30: 97; 33: 392; C1: 493.

During his studies of technology in 1863, Marx broached the question of the distinction between tool and machine, a subject about which the 'crude English mechanics' and the 'German jackasses' had created considerable confusion.[47] 'Once the tool is itself driven by a mechanism … [i.e.,] is converted into the tool of a mechanism,' Marx explains, 'the machine has replaced the tool'.[48] This is so regardless of whether or not the motive force is human bodies.[49] Taken together, the capacity for energetic division and the advent of the machine greatly enhanced the degree to which human bodies could get caught in vast material infrastructure imbued with social relations of domination (the concrete effects of which will be explored in chapter ten). Power relations are embedded in the material structures of production in tools, machines, and energy – not because these structures carry an immanent technical rationality, imposing themselves on society, but because they are a part of the social relations of production.

At this point, the outline of the socio-ontological framework necessary for understanding the mute compulsion of economic relations is complete. What I have presented in the preceding chapters is not a social ontology *tout court* but a social ontology of economic power, and in order to do that I proposed to begin from the disputed question of human nature. As we have seen, when Marx turned away from the romantic humanism of his most Feuerbachian period (1844), he did not simply dismiss the idea that there is such a thing as a human nature. Instead, he turned his attention to the human *body*, on the basis of which he crafted a new, materialist conception of human nature. I have argued that we should integrate Marx's analysis of human use of tools into this notion of corporeal organisation. This synthesis allows us to see how the structure of the human body implies a certain porosity and flexibility in its metabolism with the rest of nature: rather than an original unity of humans and nature, there is a natural *cleavage*, since parts of the human body – the tool-organs – are only loosely connected to the rest of the body, allowing them to circulate in the social environment.

---

47   41: 449; 33: 389; C1: 492f. It is interesting to note that Marx begins his long and rich discussion of tools and machines in the *1861–63 Manuscripts* with a quote of Darwin on the 'differentiation of organs' (33: 387).

48   33: 423; C1: 495; see also Beamish, *Marx, Method, and the Division of Labor*, 102ff.

49   C1: 495.

The interpretation of human corporeal organisation provided in this chapter implies that there is in fact such a thing as a human nature – it even implies a *transhistorical* notion of human nature. On the face of it, this seems to place us firmly in the humanist camp, against Althusserian anti-humanism. The position defended here does not, however, fit seamlessly into the usual categories of the debate. Contrary to Althusser's claims, the turn away from the humanism of the *1844 Manuscripts* did not lead Marx to discard the notion of the human being as such; in fact, the social ontology of Marx's later works is actually *built* on a notion of human nature. Despite this disagreement with Althusser, the conception of human nature presented here supports what I take to be the core of the spirit of Althusserian anti-humanism: the rejection of a romantic critique of capitalism in the name of a human essence. Capitalism does not contradict or repress the essence of the human being any more than any other mode of production, and communism will not be the realisation of that essence.[50] Marx's social ontology implies the rejection of the existence of an essence which can be thwarted or realised by particular social formations. Romantic essentialism amounts to a depoliticisation of critique, as it construes anti-capitalist politics as the restoration of a natural order. In contrast to this, the social ontology presented in the preceding pages insists on the political by refusing the possibility of a transcendent anchor for the critique of capital. Human nature explains why it is possible for human beings to organise their social reproduction in so many different ways, but it can never serve as the normative basis for the rejection of a specific form of society, just as it can never explain why a specific form of society exists; in other words, the concept of human nature presented here rules out the possibility of assigning to it an explanatory or critical function with regards to historically specific social formations.

While the concept of human nature does not, then, have a place in the analysis of *specific* modes of production, it is a central component of Marxist social ontology. The corporeal organisation of the human being is a crucial part of the explanation for why human social reproduction can take so many different forms. It explains how the social emerges dialectically from nature, and thus how natural history itself gives rise to human history, without reducing the logic of the latter to that of the former. It reveals the poverty of economism by demonstrating that what we call 'the

---

50   See also Jason Read, *The Micro-Politics of Capital: Marx and the Prehistory of the Present* (Albany: State University of New York Press, 2003), 23.

economy' is *social* through and through, and that there is no such thing as a natural mode of production. Furthermore, such an understanding of corporeal organisation explains why humans have the peculiar capacity to delegate the reproduction of the social relations through which they regulate their metabolism to their material environment. Coupled with the capacity for surplus labour, it also explains how social relations of *domination* can reproduce themselves by becoming enmeshed in the reproduction of social life. Therefore, this conception explains the *possibility* of economic power. In the rest of the book, we shall see how capital has exploited this possibility.

PART II
Relations

6

Transcendental Class Domination

The fountains of your life are sealed by the hand of capital, that quaffs its golden goblet to the lees and gives the dregs to you. Why are you locked out of life when you are locked out of the factory? ... What gives the capitalist this tremendous power?

–Ernest Jones[1]

Capital in the broadest sense – the exchange of goods with the aim of making a profit – has, as I have already mentioned, existed for centuries. What distinguishes capitalism from other modes of production is not the mere existence of capital but its social significance; only in this peculiar mode of production is the accumulation of abstract wealth the basis of social reproduction. In order for this to be possible, a set of certain social relations of production has to be in place. Following Robert Brenner's useful distinction, we can divide these relations into two sets: *vertical* relations between the immediate producers and the exploiters, and *horizontal* relations among producers themselves and exploiters themselves.[2] These distinct yet tightly interwoven relations form the basis of equally

---

1   12: 462.

2   Robert Brenner, 'Property and Progress: Where Adam Smith Went Wrong', in *Marxist History-Writing for the Twenty-First Century*, ed. Chris Wickham (Oxford: Oxford University Press, 2007), 58; see also Alex Callinicos, *Making History: Agency, Structure, and Change in Social Theory*, 2nd ed. (Leiden: Brill, 2004), 51f; Alex Callinicos, *Deciphering* Capital: *Marx's* Capital *and Its Destiny* (London: Bookmarks, 2014), 175f.

distinct yet tightly interwoven forms of domination, and, taken together, they explain why the power of capital takes the form of a mute compulsion. I will return to these horizontal relations, and the relationship between the horizontal and the vertical relations, in chapters eight and nine respectively. In this chapter, however, I want to zoom in on the vertical class relations constitutive of the capitalist mode of production.

The Creation of Dependency

In the second part of the first volume of *Capital* (chapters 4–6), Marx poses the question of how capital can be the dominant form of the circulation of money and commodities without systematically violating the law of exchange of equivalents (since if it did that, stable market relations could not exist). The answer is that in order for this to be possible, a commodity 'whose use value possesses the peculiar property of being a source of value, whose actual consumption is therefore itself an objectification of labour' has to be available on the market.[3] In other words: it must be possible to purchase labour power as a commodity in order for $M-C-M'$ to be the dominant form of circulation. This 'historical pre-condition comprises a world's history', aspects of which Marx examines in part eight of *Capital*.[4] The commodification of labour power is the condition of possibility of what Marx calls the *capital relation*, which is the relationship between the proletarian who sells her labour power and the capitalist who buys it.[5] At first glance, this relationship seems to be a purely voluntary market transaction, that is, a simple relationship between a buyer and a seller – which is indeed how it is treated by mainstream economics. If we examine the conditions under which this relationship exists, however, we will discover that it is in fact a relationship of domination. Because I am not concerned with the historical emergence of capitalism, but rather with 'bourgeois society as something that has already come into being, moving itself on its own basis', the focus of this chapter will be on the conditions under which labour power *continues* to be available on the market and not the conditions under which it originally became available.[6] Nevertheless,

---

3   C1: 270.
4   C1: 274.
5   C1: 724.
6   G: 253.

a brief sketch of some of the main conclusions of historical research on the origins of the capital relation will help us understand the form of domination it implies.

Mainstream economics treats the market as an institution providing individuals with *opportunities* – a view corresponding to what Brenner and Ellen Meiksins Wood refer to as *the commercialisation model* of the historical origins of capitalism. According to this narrative, the emergence of capitalism appears as 'a maturation of age-old commercial practices (together with technical advances) and their liberation from political and cultural constraints', as Wood puts it.[7] If only people are allowed to exchange freely, so the story goes, a market economy will automatically establish itself. This is the view with which Marx resolutely broke in the sections on the 'so-called primitive accumulation' in *Capital*, where he described the violent origins of capitalism. Violence was necessary, in his view, because peasants had to be deprived of the possibility to reproduce themselves outside of the market – something they did not give up voluntarily. In other words: market dependence had to be *created*, since peasants generally did what they could to avoid relying too much on the market. Rather than producing exclusively for the market, they preferred to produce for their own subsistence. Producing for the market required specialisation in order to remain competitive, and because of the unpredictable nature of agricultural production, among other factors, specialisation meant vulnerability. As Brenner explains:

> Given the uncertainty of the harvest and the unacceptable cost of 'business failure' – namely the possibility of starvation – peasants could not afford to adopt maximising exchange value via specialization as their rule of reproduction and adopted instead the rule of 'safety first' or 'produce for subsistence'.[8]

Production exclusively for the market also conflicted with the dominant family structures in the early modern period, when large families were necessary in order to 'secure insurance against illness and old age in a society in which there was no institution upon which they could rely

---

7   Ellen Meiksins Wood, *The Origin of Capitalism: A Longer View* (London: Verso, 2002), 12.

8   Brenner, 'Property and Progress', 68.

outside the family'.[9] Peasants thus had good reasons to resist becoming market dependent, and this was exactly what they did.[10] Even the dispossession of peasants was not enough, however, to secure a steady flow of exploitable labour power into the market. Instead of selling their ability to work, the propertyless were, in Marx's words, 'more inclined to become vagabonds and robbers and beggars'.[11] 'In the 16th and 17th centuries', as Silvia Federici explains, 'the hatred of wage-labor was so intense that many proletarians preferred to risk the gallows'.[12] The state therefore had to step in and punish beggars, vagabonds, and others who refused to work. Here is Marx's summary: 'Thus were the agricultural folk first forcibly expropriated from the soil, driven from their homes, turned into vagabonds, and then whipped, branded and tortured by grotesquely terroristic laws accepting the discipline necessary for the system of wage-labour.'[13] However, it was not only those needed for wage labour who were violently forced to adapt to capitalist production. What Federici calls a 'war against women' also had to be undertaken in order to subject them to the capitalist separation of the production of commodities and reproduction of labour power, a separation in which women were assigned to the domestic sphere and the 'double dependence' upon capital through the male wage.[14]

Historical studies of the origin of capitalism demonstrate that the latter was not a result of the voluntary acts of individuals. Capitalism did not emerge because human nature was finally allowed to unfold its 'propensity to truck, barter, and exchange one thing for another', as Adam Smith put it, but rather because some people violently forced others to become dependent upon markets. The analysis of the *reproduction* of capitalism demonstrates, as we will see, that once capitalism has been established, it systematically prevents individuals from opting out of it.

---

9   Ibid.

10   Robert Brenner, 'Agrarian Class Stucture and Economic Development in Pre-Industrial Europe', in *The Brenner Debate*, ed. T. H. Aston and C. H. E. Philpin (Cambridge: Cambridge University Press, 1987); Brenner, 'Property and Progress'; Wood, *The Origin of Capitalism*.

11   G: 736.

12   Silvia Federici, *Caliban and the Witch: Women, the Body and Primitive Accumulation* (New York: Autonomedia, 2004), 136.

13   C1: 899.

14   Federici, *Caliban and the Witch*, 88, 97.

The Concept of Class

In the dialectical progression of categories in *Capital*, classes only enter into the picture in chapter six, after the introduction of the concept of capital. Marx begins, in other words, with the analysis of the horizontal relations between the units of production, expressed in the commodity form of the products of labour, before proceeding to the vertical class relations underlying the capital form. In chapter nine, we will see how this has led some Marxists to erroneously conclude that capitalist class domination is merely the form of appearance of a more primary form of social domination, namely the domination of *everyone* by the value form. In reality, however, class domination is already implied by the commodity form. As Marx repeatedly stresses: 'Only where wage-labour is its basis does commodity production impose itself upon society as a whole.'[15] This is what he demonstrates by conceptually deriving the necessity of the commodification of labour power from the generalisation of the commodity form through a set of interconnected dialectical arguments.[16]

The capitalist mode of production presupposes the 'existence of a class which possesses nothing but its capacity to labour'; only when such a class exists will the capitalist *in spe* be able to purchase labour power on the market. But what exactly does 'class' mean here?[17] Many scholars have noted that 'Marx's own discussion of the concept of class is notoriously unsystematic'.[18] It is common to distinguish between 'objective' and 'subjective' conceptions of class, or class 'in itself' and class 'for itself', as Marx puts it in *The Poverty of Philosophy*.[19] As a subjective concept, 'class' refers to a group of people who identify as such on the basis of shared experiences and/or interests. As an objective concept, it refers to a position in the social order, regardless of whether people identify with the position they occupy or not. In addition to this distinction, it is common to distinguish

---

15   C1: 733; see also 274, 557.

16   See Sven Ellmers, *Die formanalytische Klassentheorie von Karl Marx: Ein Beitrag zur 'neuen Marx-Lektüre'*, 2nd ed. (Duisburg: Universitätverlag Rhein-Ruhr, 2009); Michael Heinrich, *Die Wissenschaft vom Wert: Die Marxsche Kritik der politischen Ökonomie zwischen wissenschaftlicher Revolution und klassischer Tradition* (Münster: Westfälisches Dampfboot, 1999), 263ff; Søren Mau, 'The Transition to Capital in Marx's Critique of Political Economy', *Historical Materialism* 26, no. 1 (2018): 68–102.

17   9: 213.

18   Callinicos, *Making History*, 52.

19   6: 211.

between empirical and structural conceptions of class: whereas the former distinguishes between classes on the basis of purely empirical criteria such as income or wealth, the latter defines classes with reference to the social structure of a given society.[20] These concepts need not be mutually exclusive, and rather than looking for *one* correct concept of class, we should let the precise meaning of it depend on *what* we want to study and *how* we want to study it. What I am interested in here is the form of class domination presupposed by the core structure of the capitalist mode of production and not, for example, classes as conscious political actors or a historically specific class composition; I am, in other words, concerned with class in an objective and structural sense. Therefore, the kind of question I am interested in is: If the power of capital presupposes a specific form of class domination, who is the dominant part, and who is dominated? What is the criterion for distinguishing between them? And how is this domination exercised?

Capital needs workers. A steady supply of labour power presupposes that the people needed as wage labourers are deprived of the possibility of reproducing themselves outside of the market. This, in turn, presupposes the dispossession of everyone who could potentially support those needed by capitalists as wage labourers. The set of *people dependent on the market* is, in other words, not necessarily identical with the set of *people capital needs as wage labourers*; the latter is only a subset of the former. If we want to grasp the fundamental class domination underlying the capitalist mode of production, we therefore have to avoid defining class in terms of *exploitation*. Wood, for example, consistently centres her analysis on the relation between the direct producers and the appropriators of their surplus labour.[21] Taking her cue from an oft-quoted passage from volume three of *Capital*, according to which the 'specific *economic* form

---

20   For discussions of these distinctions and related issues in Marxist theories of class, see Perry Anderson, *Arguments within English Marxism* (London: Verso, 1980); Callinicos, *Making History*, 52ff; G. E. M. De Ste. Croix, *The Class Struggle in the Ancient Greek World: From the Archaic Age to the Arab Conquests* (Ithaca, NY: Cornell University Press, 1989); Ellmers, *Die formanalytische Klassentheorie von Karl Marx*; Heinrich, *Die Wissenschaft vom Wert*, 263ff; Michael Heinrich, 'Welche Klassen und welche Kämpfe? Eine Antwort auf Karl Reitters "Kapitalismus ohne Klassenkampf?"', *grundrisse: zeitschrift für linke theorie & debatte*, no. 11 (2004); E. P. Thompson, *The Making of the English Working Class* (London: Penguin, 2013), 8ff; Ellen Meiksins Wood, *Democracy against Capitalism: Renewing Historical Materialism* (London: Verso, 2016), chap. 3; Erik Olin Wright, *Classes*, 2nd ed. (London: Verso, 1998).

21   Wood, *Democracy against Capitalism*, 33.

in which unpaid surplus labour is pumped out of the *direct producers* determines the relationship of domination and servitude', she treats class as a relation between exploiters and exploited.[22] This is, of course, an enormously important aspect of class domination in capitalism, but it is also too narrow. The relation of exploitation is premised on a broader class domination rooted not in the extraction of surplus labour but in *the relation to the means of production*. This is not to deny the centrality of the relation of exploitation. In chapter ten, I will examine the specific form of class domination involved in the relation of exploitation at the point of production. Here, however, I am concerned with the class structure presupposed by the relation of exploitation. In this context, class domination therefore refers to the relation between *those who control the conditions of social reproduction* and *those who are excluded from the direct access to the conditions of social reproduction*. 'Class' thus denotes *the relation of a group of people to the conditions of social reproduction*. From such a perspective, the central thing is that capitalism relies on a power relationship between the 'possessors of the conditions of production, who rule, and on the other side the propertyless', and that the ruling class rules because it is the class 'whose conditions are the conditions of the whole society'.[23]

Not only is a definition of class in terms of exploitation inadequate for the development of an understanding of the class domination presupposed by capitalism; it also risks reinforcing the tendency to regard the struggles of wage labourers – and especially industrial workers – as the only real class struggle. An understanding of class as a shared relation to the conditions of social reproduction, on the contrary, allows us to broaden our notion of class struggle and see how struggles across the entire social field can be a part of the same political project: wrenching the conditions of life from the grip of capital. It thus allows us to see that the crisis of classical workers' movements in the neoliberal era does not necessarily amount to the disappearance of class struggle, but rather signals a change in class composition and forms of class struggle.[24]

---

22   M: 778.

23   30: 196; 5: 413; I.5: 470. In MECW, *Besitzer*, which means 'possessor', is translated as 'owners', which obscures the fact that actual control rather than formal ownership is the crucial issue for the establishment of a relation of class domination. *Besitzlosen* is likewise translated as 'propertyless'.

24   See Tithi Bhattacharya, 'How Not to Skip Class: Social Reproduction of Labour and the Global Working Class', in *Social Reproduction Theory*; Joshua Clover, *Riot. Strike. Riot: The New Era of Uprisings* (London: Verso, 2016); David McNally, '"Unity of the

Proletarians and Workers

The subsumption of social reproduction under the logic of valorisation presupposes the subjection of those deprived of access to the means of production outside of the market to those who control these means of production – that is, the subjection of proletarians to the capitalist class. Because not everyone who depends on capital for their survival *works* (or has the ability to do so), I prefer to speak of 'proletarians' and 'the proletariat' rather than 'workers' and 'the working class'. Indeed, *what defines the proletarian condition is not work but the radical split between life and its conditions*. The proletarian subject is, in Marx's words, a 'naked life' or a 'mere subject' cut off from its objective conditions.[25] Marx also refers to this as '*absolute poverty*', by which he means 'poverty not as shortage, but as total exclusion of objective wealth'.[26] The notion of poverty involved here is not merely a matter of living standards in a straightforward quantitative sense. It is rather a *qualitative* concept of poverty which refers not to *how much* you have, but to *how* you have what you have. Capitalism is the institutionalisation of insecurity; even a relatively well-paid employee who lives in a social democratic welfare state depends on an economic system which is systematically prone to violent convulsions, sudden crashes, and protracted depressions. This is what absolute poverty means.

Proletarianisation is necessary in order to establish the capital relation, that is, the relation between proletarians who sell their labour power and the capitalists who purchase it. However, as mentioned above, not all proletarians sell their labour power, and many of those who do also work outside of the wage relation. It is the great merit of Marxist feminists to have shown that capitalism has always relied on an enormous amount of unwaged reproductive labour which takes place outside of the immediate circuits of capital yet is necessary for the latter to function. The historically unique split between the production of commodities and production of people is an important source of the oppression of women in capitalist

---

Diverse": Working-Class Formations and Popular Uprisings from Cochabamba to Cairo', in *Marxism and Social Movements*, ed. Colin Barker et al. (Leiden: Brill, 2013). Regarding the primacy accorded to struggles at the point of production in the history of the left, see Geoff Eley, *Forging Democracy: The History of the Left in Europe, 1850–2000* (New York: Oxford University Press, 2002); Endnotes, 'A History of Separation', in *Endnotes 4: Unity in Separation* (London: Endnotes, 2015).

25   6: 499; 30: 38.
26   G: 296; 30: 39f.

society, and we will take a closer look at it in the next chapter. Before we get to that, however, we have to examine the mechanisms that force a part of the proletariat to sell their capacity to work.

As previously mentioned, mere dispossession is not enough to secure a steady flow of labour power into the market. In a significant passage in the *Grundrisse*, which I have already quoted in parts, Marx notes that

> the propertyless are more inclined to become vagabonds and robbers and beggars than workers. The last becomes normal only in the developed mode of capital's production. In the prehistory of capital, state coercion to transform the propertyless into *workers* at conditions advantageous for capital, which are not yet here enforced upon the workers by competition among one another.[27]

The important thing to notice here is the distinction between being *propertyless* and being a *worker*: proletarians do not automatically become workers – they have to be *made into* workers.[28] Here, we see why it is important to reject one of the assumptions common to many of the mainstream theories of power which I discussed in chapter one, namely that the identity of the subjects involved in a power relationship is constituted independently of that relationship. If we examine the relationship between the worker and the capitalist without asking *why the worker is a worker* in the first place, we lose sight of an important aspect of the power of capital. The worker is not simply a negative remnant; it is rather a specific form of subjectivity, a positive result of capitalist relations of production: 'The positing of the individual as *worker*, in this nakedness, is itself', as Marx puts it in the *Grundrisse*, 'a product of *history*'.[29] So how does this transformation take place?

In a certain sense, this entire book can be read as an answer to that question. In the following chapters, we will see that it is partly the result of mechanisms and processes such as the competitive pressures of the market (chapters eight and nine), real subsumption of labour and nature (chapter ten and eleven), and the threat of unemployment and crises (chapter

---

27   G: 736.

28   Another important element in this quote is the juxtaposition of *competition* and *violence* as two different mechanisms of domination. I will come back to this in chapter nine.

29   G: 472.

thirteen). Underlying all of these forms of power through which humans are transformed into workers, however, is a fundamental condition of the capitalist mode of production: the radical separation between life and its conditions which allows capital to insert itself as the mediator between them. The proletarian is a 'mere possibility' or a 'bare living labour capacity', and by isolating capacities from the conditions of their realisation, capital becomes the logic which governs the translation of possibility into actuality.[30] This is the most fundamental level of the economic power of capital: 'the free worker can', as Marx explains, 'only satisfy his vital needs to the extent that he sells his labour [power]; hence is *forced into this by his own interest, not by external compulsion*'.[31] The valorisation of value *injects itself into the human metabolism*, making *the reproduction of capital the condition of the reproduction of life*. This is why workers 'are *compelled* to sell themselves *voluntarily*', as Marx puts it in a formula which nicely captures the paradoxical and deceptive nature of capitalist power.[32] In 1786, the British physician and economist Joseph Townsend clearly grasped the utility of this mute compulsion:

> Hunger will tame the fiercest animals, it will teach decency and civility, obedience and subjection, to the most perverse. In general it is only hunger which can spur and goad them [the poor] onto labour; yet our laws have said they shall never hunger. The laws, it must be confessed, have likewise said, they shall be compelled to work. But then legal constraint is attended with much trouble, violence and noise: whereas hunger is not only peaceable, silent, unremitting pressure, but, as the most natural motive to industry and labour, it calls forth the most powerful exertions; and, when satisfied by the free bounty of another, lays lasting and sure foundations for goodwill and gratitude.

We might speculate whether this quote from Townsend's *Dissertation on the Poor Laws*, with its opposition between 'violence and noise' on the one side and 'silent, unremitting pressure' on the other, was the source of inspiration for the passage in *Capital* from which this book derives its title.[33] Marx quotes it in several manuscripts spanning a period of almost

---

30 G: 454, 604.
31 30: 198. Emphasis added.
32 C1: 899. Emphasis added.
33 See also Karl Polanyi's comments on Townsend, from where this is quoted:

two decades. In a notebook from 1851, he excerpted this passage, under-lining the part where Townsend writes that 'hunger is not only peaceable, silent, unremitting pressure, but, as the most natural motive to industry and labour, it calls forth the most powerful exertions'.[34] He later used this 'thoroughly brutal' quote in the *Grundrisse*, the *1861–63 Manuscripts*, and volume one of *Capital*.[35] In the *1861–63 Manuscripts*, it appears immedi-ately following a paragraph in which Marx emphasises the specific nature of economic power:

> The relation which compels the worker to do surplus labour is the fact that the conditions of his labour exist over against him as capital. He is not subjected to any external compulsion, but in order to live – in a world where commodities are determined by their value – he is compelled to sell his labour capacity as a commodity, whereas the val-orisation of this labour capacity over and above its own value is the prerogative of capital.[36]

This tells us two important things about power. First, it makes visible the inadequacy of the assumption that power is an immediate relation-ship between two social agents. In opposition to violence or ideology, the 'silent, unremitting pressure' of property relations does not directly address the worker; it rather addresses the material environment of the worker, or, more specifically, the material conditions of reproduction. It thus highlights that power can also be exercised through the control over anything which '*constitute[s] part of the meaningful environment of another actor*', as anthropologist Richard Adams puts it.[37] Second, it also demonstrates that power is, in Foucault's words, 'exercised only over free subjects'.[38] The power of capital does not just *prevent* the worker from following their will (although it often does that); it also facilitates a certain

Karl Polanyi, *The Great Transformation: The Political and Economic Origins of Our Time* (Boston: Beacon Press, 2001), 116ff.

34   IV.9: 215.

35   G: 845; 30: 205; C1: 800.

36   30: 204.

37   Richard Newbold Adams, *Energy and Structure: A Theory of Social Power* (Austin: University of Texas Press, 1975), 12; see also Thomas E. Wartenberg, *The Forms of Power: From Domination to Transformation* (Philadelphia: Temple University Press, 1990), 85.

38   Michel Foucault, 'The Subject and Power', in *Power: The Essential Works of Michel Foucault 1954–1984, Volume Three*, trans. Leslie Sawyer (London: Penguin, 2002), 342.

way in which they can actually follow that will. Mute compulsion only works because the worker *wants to live*. Only because of this can capital succeed in demanding surplus labour in exchange for the means of life.

Transcendental Indebtedness

The worker exists as a mere possibility '*outside of the conditions of its existence*'. The worker 'has his needs in *actuality*', but 'the activity of satisfying them is only possessed by him as a non-objective [*gegenstandslose*] capacity (a *possibility*) confined within his own subjectivity'.[39] This conjunction of *potentiality* and *actuality* allows capital to insert itself as 'the *social mediation* as such, through which the individual gains access to the means of his reproduction'.[40] The worker is not merely a *nothing*, but in a sense, they are *less than nothing*: not only are they excluded from the conditions of their existence (they are absolutely poor); they also *owe their future* to capital. The worker-subject is an *indebted* subject; under capitalism, life itself comes with an obligation to valorise value, and for this reason 'the worker belongs [*gehört*] to capital *before* he has sold himself to the capitalist'.[41] As Marx perceptively notes, the accumulation of capital is 'a stockpiling of property titles to labour',[42] or, put differently,

> a *draft on future labour*. As such, it is a matter of indifference whether this exists in the form of tokens of value, debt claims, etc. It may be replaced by any other title. Like the state creditor with his coupons, every capitalist possesses a draft on future labour in his newly acquired value, and by appropriating present labour he has already appropriated future labour. The accumulation of capital in the money form is by no means a material accumulation of the material conditions of labour. It is rather an *accumulation of property titles to labour*.[43]

At the most basic level, then, capital engages not only with *present*, but also with *future* labour, and 'by means of the appropriation of ongoing

---

39   30: 40. Emphasis added.
40   G: 609, 607.
41   C1: 723. Emphasis added.
42   G: 367.
43   34: 12. This passage from the later parts of the *1861–63 Manuscripts* seems to be a further development of a passage from the *Grundrisse* (G: 367).

labour [it] has already at the same time appropriated future labour'.[44] The debt incurred by the worker at birth is thus a kind of *transcendental debt* in the sense that it forms a part of the necessary conditions of possibility for social reproduction in a society ruled by the logic of capital. This debt is the continuing presence of the historical origins of capitalism; it is the existence of the past *in* the present. The historical creation of the capital relation can thus be seen as the original incurment of a debt which is inherited by every new generation of proletarians. On its most basic level, debt is a *promise to pay*.[45] From this perspective, surplus labour is a kind of interest the worker has to pay in order to live: 'The wage-worker has permission ... *to live* only insofar as he works for a certain time gratis for the capitalist', as Marx puts it.[46] This transcendental debt is the basis of interest-bearing capital, in which

> all wealth that can ever be produced belongs to capital ... and every-
> thing that it has received up till now is only a first instalment for its 'all
> engrossing' appetite. By its own inherent laws, all surplus labour that
> the human race can ever supply belongs to it, *Moloch*.[47]

At its root, capital is thus a debt relation, and debt is therefore not only 'a new technique of power' belonging to the financialised capitalism of the neoliberal era. It might be true that 'the indebted man' is 'the subjective figure of modern-day capitalism', and it is certainly true that debt has taken on new forms and functions in the neoliberal era, but it is crucial to acknowledge that the transcendentally indebted subject has been a part of capitalism from its very beginning.[48]

As a *promise* to pay, debt involves a certain configuration of temporality. Any debt relation is an attempt to 'neutralize time', that is, to reduce 'the future and its possibilities to current power relations'.[49] A debt relation is thus a power relation in which the *future* is subjected to the present. In addition to this, however, we should bear in mind that capital is 'the rule of past, dead labour over the living', or as Marx puts it in the *Manifesto*: 'In

---

44   G: 367.
45   Maurizio Lazzarato, *The Making of the Indebted Man: An Essay on the Neoliberal Condition*, trans. Joshua David Jordan (Los Angeles: Semiotext(e), 2012), 39.
46   24: 92.
47   M: 498.
48   Lazzarato, *The Making of the Indebted Man*, 38.
49   Ibid., 45f.

bourgeois society, the past dominates the present.'[50] *The power of capital is, in other words, based upon a temporal displacement in which the past appropriates the future in order to subjugate and neutralise the present.*

Impersonal Class Domination

The transformation of people into absolutely poor and transcendentally indebted workers binds them to *capital as such*, not to a particular capitalist. This is why the power of capital is an *impersonal* form of power, in distinction to the *personal* relations of dependence so prevalent in pre-capitalist modes of production; whereas the slave, for example, 'is the property of a particular *master*; the worker must indeed sell himself to capital, but not to a particular capitalist'.[51] As Marx explains in *Wage Labour and Capital*:

> The worker leaves the capitalist to whom he hires himself whenever he likes, and the capitalist discharges him whenever he thinks fit, as soon as he no longer gets any utility out of him, or not the anticipated utility. But the worker, whose sole source of livelihood is the sale of his labour[power] cannot leave the *whole class of purchasers*, that is, the *capitalist class*, without renouncing his existence. *He belongs not to this or that bourgeois, but to the bourgeoisie, the bourgeois class,* and it is his business to dispose of himself, that is to find a purchaser within this bourgeois class.[52]

Here we begin to get a glimpse of the way in which the *horizontal* relations among capitalists mediate the *vertical* class relationship between the worker and the capitalist: since the ruling class is split into autonomous and competing units of production, the worker can choose who she wants to sell her labour power to. I will analyse these horizontal relations in chapter eight and nine; for now, the important thing to notice is that the *impersonal* character of capitalist *class* domination is partly the result of the intersection of the split between life and its conditions and the split between different units of production in a market system. Because of this

---

50   R: 988; 6: 499; see also M: 500.
51   R: 1032; 6: 499.
52   9: 203.

overlapping of two splits, capitalism is a system of *class* domination in a stronger sense than were pre-capitalist societies; only in capitalism are producers subjected to a *class as such*, and not only the particular members of the ruling class. The capital relation is, as Marx puts it, 'a *relation of compulsion* [*Zwangsverhältnis*] not based on personal relations of domination and dependency, but simply on differing economic functions'.[53]

Capitalist class domination presupposes and reproduces a historically unique form of individuality; the proletarian is 'an abstraction ... stripped of all objectivity'.[54] This is a result not only of the split between life and its conditions and the impersonal relation to the ruling class but also of the centrifugal forces of competition and the booms and busts of business cycles. The atomism of bourgeois society is a recurrent theme in Marx's writings – from the early critique of human rights as the rights of the 'abstract citoyen' in *On the Jewish Question* to the analysis of the 'purely atomistic' relationships among market agents in *Capital*.[55] Marx always ridicules the Robinsonades populating the writings of political economists, but not simply in order to dismiss their individualist social ontology as a false perception of reality; the point is, rather, that what they perceive as 'posited by nature' is instead a 'historic result', and that the individual created by 'this society of free competition' is just as embedded in social relations as people were in pre-capitalist societies.[56] In a certain sense, we could even say that in capitalism people are embedded in social relations to a historically unique degree, since the individual is not only entangled in personal relations in a local community, town, region, or country – they are immediately, and on a daily basis, integrated into a global economic system where things taking place on the other side of the planet might very well affect their life in a much more significant way than what happens next door. Marx therefore emphasises that modern individuals are 'abstract individuals, who are, however, by this very fact put into a position to enter into relation with one another as individuals'.[57] The individual is not a residue of the dissolution of pre-capitalist social bonds; it is a socially constituted form of subjectivity.[58] Capital strives to

---

53 R: 1021.
54 G: 295f.
55 3: 167; C1: 187.
56 3: 167; C1: 187.
57 5: 87; I.5: 111.
58 Patrick Murray, *The Mismeasure of Wealth: Essays on Marx and Social Form* (Leiden: Brill, 2016), 37; Martha Campbell, 'The Objectivity of Value versus the Idea

dissolve any bond that inhibits its movement in order to re-connect the parts according to the logic of valorisation; it isolates the naked life of the proletarian in order to re-connect it to its conditions by means of money, which thereby becomes 'the *procurer* [*Kuppler*] between the need and the object, between life and the means of life of the human being'.[59] The *rule of capital is not the dissolution of community as such, but a historically novel form of community based on the amputated proletarian body (i.e., cut off from its objective conditions) as its smallest component*; 'Money thereby directly and simultaneously becomes the *real community* [*Gemeinwesen*], since it is the general substance of survival for all, and at the same time the social product of all'.[60]

Unity in Separation

Just as we should avoid understanding the bourgeois individual as the absence of sociality, we should also avoid understanding the difference between capitalist and pre-capitalist relations of production as a simple opposition between *separation* and *non-separation* (or *unity*) of the immediate producers and the means of production. The idea that capitalism is based on such a separation is one of the most universally accepted claims among Marxists. Sentences such as the following can be found all over Marx's writings: 'The capital-relation presupposes a complete separation between the workers and the ownership of the conditions for the

---

of Habitual Action', in *The Constitution of Capital: Essays on Volume I of Marx's Capital*, ed. Riccardo Bellofiore and Nicola Taylor (Basingstoke: Palgrave Macmillan, 2004), 80ff.

59   3: 323.

60   G: 225f; see also 509. Note that this does not entail the claim that capitalism implies a tendency to eradicate cultural differences and transform everyone into homogeneous proletarians. Capitalism is compatible with a wide array of different cultural forms, and as long as they do not interfere with the basic prerequisites of capital accumulation, there is no reason to assume that capitalism contains an immanent drive to dissolve them. In fact, capital will often find it advantageous to strengthen traditional social hierarchies and pre- or non-capitalist cultural forms. See also Vivek Chibber's critique of the widespread misunderstanding of Marx's concept of 'abstract labour' in post-colonial theory, a topic I will briefly return to in chapter five (*Postcolonial Theory and the Specter of Capital* [London: Verso, 2013], chap. 6.). While Chibber makes a strong argument in this case, there are several problems with other elements of his *Postcolonial Theory and the Specter of Capital*, especially his methodological individualism, his rational-choice framework, and his defence of an 'Enlightenment notion of universal interests' (179).

realization of their labour.'[61] This is usually contrasted to pre-capitalist modes of production, and especially feudalism, where there was a *unity* of producers and the means of production. While I do not intend to dispute this, it is crucial to be precise about the meaning of 'unity' and 'separation' involved in these claims.

As we saw in the last chapter, human beings are, on an ontological level, constitutively separated from the conditions of their reproduction. There is no such thing as a natural unity of humans and the rest of nature, and for this reason it is important to acknowledge that the relation between the producers and the means of production under feudalism was every bit as socially mediated as it is under capitalism. If there was a relatively stable connection between life and its conditions in feudalism, this was not because of the naturalness of such a connection. As Brenner explains, feudal peasant possession was only possible because of 'villagers' self-organization ... in a conscious political community'.[62] The connection between life and its conditions was much more stable and secure in feudalism than it is in capitalism, but, rather than being a result of the natural and immediate character of such a connection, it was the outcome of political struggles. We should therefore avoid depicting the transition from feudalism to capitalism as a kind of economic re-telling of Aristophanes' love myth in Plato's *Symposium*, that is, as a dissolution of an original unity of man and earth. The key to avoiding this is to see how the capitalist separation and the pre-capitalist non-separation are nothing but different ways of organising the necessary *connection* between labour and its conditions. Marx puts this well in a draft manuscript for the second book of *Capital*:

> Whatever the social form of production, workers and means of production always remain its factors. But if they are in a state of mutual separation, they are only potentially factors of production. For any

---

61   C1: 874. Brenner points out that the core of this argument is not so much about the access to the *means of production* as the access to the *means of subsistence*: the crucial thing for capital is that people are dependent on the market for their survival ('Property and Progress', 60). This is a useful clarification insofar as we want to know how the *individual* is subjected to capital; but on the level of the social totality separation from the means of production and separation from the means of subsistence is the same thing, since production is necessary for obtaining means of subsistence (see 30: 40; C2: 116; and II.11: 694).

62   Brenner, 'Property and Progress', 63.

production to take place, they must be connected. The particular form and mode in which this connection is effected is what distinguishes the various economic epochs of the social structure. In the present case, the separation of the free worker from his means of production is the given starting point, and we have seen how and under what conditions the two come to be united in the hands of the capitalist – i.e., as his capital in its productive mode of existence.[63]

This emphasis on the necessary and historically variable connections between labour and its conditions allows us to specify the difference between the mute compulsion of the capital relation and the mechanisms of power through which pre-capitalist class hierarchies were upheld. In the case of slavery, the power of the exploiter is based on the intimate and permanent *connection* between the producer (the slave) and the means of production; the slave is the immediate property of the slave-owner in the same way as the means of production are. The power of the feudal lord was likewise based on a stable *connection* between the peasants and the means of production; 'lords could not, as a rule, find it in their own interests to separate their peasants from the means of subsistence', in Brenner's words.[64] For this reason, they had to employ (the threat of) direct physical coercion in order to make the peasants perform surplus labour. In distinction to these pre-capitalist modes of domination, the power of the capitalist class is based on the permanent *separation* of the producers from the means of production and subsistence (as well as from each other). However, this separation is also the 'starting point' of their temporary and precarious re-connection through capital, as Marx makes clear in the passage just quoted. Capitalism is thus based on a 'unity in separation', to use Endnotes' phrase.[65] In this mode of production, *proletarians are temporarily connected to the conditions of their life through the very same social relations that ensure their permanent separation from them.*

---

63   C2: 120; II.11: 672.

64   Brenner, 'Property and Progress', 64.

65   Endnotes, 'A History of Separation', 180; Aaron Benanav and John Clegg, 'Crisis and Immiseration: Critical Theory Today', in *The SAGE Handbook of Frankfurt School Critical Theory*, ed. Beverly Best, Werner Bonefeld, and Chris O'Kane (London: SAGE, 2018), 1629–48.

Transcendental Power

Because of this peculiar unity of separation and unity, the ruling class does not need to employ violence in order to force workers to perform surplus labour:

> The slave only works under the impulse of external fear, but not for *his own existence,* which does not belong to him, and yet it is *guaranteed.* The free worker, in contrast, is driven by his wants … The *continuity of the relation* between slave and slave holder is preserved by the direct compulsion exerted upon the slave. The free worker, on the other hand, must preserve it himself, since his existence and that of his family depend upon his constantly renewing the sale of his labour capacity to the capitalist.[66]

So, whereas the 'Roman slave was held by chains', the 'wage-labourer is bound to his owner by invisible threads'.[67] This kind of domination operates on what Michael Hardt and Antonio Negri have called *the transcendental plane of power.* According to them, there is a tendency in 'contemporary conceptions of power' – their primary target is Giorgio Agamben – to think of power in the way Foucault warned against: as something *transcendent,* governing society from above or the outside.[68] Instead of Foucault's turn to the *immanence* of power, however, Hardt and Negri invite us to replace 'the excessive focus on the concept of sovereignty' with an analysis of the *transcendental* plane of power, by which they mean the social relations through which 'the conditions of possibility of social life' are structured.[69] They explicitly understand this shift of perspective as analogous to Kant's Copernican revolution. For Kant, the *transcendent* realm is what lies *beyond* the field of possible experiences, that is, the metaphysical problems he deals with in the transcendental dialectic in the *Critique of Pure Reason.* The *transcendental,* on the other hand, concerns *the conditions of possibility* of the field of possible

---

66   34: 98f. 'Wants' is in English in the original. The same passage appears in R: 1031.
67   C1: 719; see also 30: 197.
68   Michael Hardt and Antonio Negri, *Commonwealth* (Cambridge, MA: Belknap, 2011), 3.
69   Ibid., 4, 6.

experiences. Space and time, for example, are transcendental forms of intuition, which means that they are conditions of possibility of what can appear to us in experience. In other words, whereas the *transcendent* lies *beyond* the field of immanence, the *transcendental* is what is logically *prior* to this field. Hardt and Negri transpose this conceptual scheme to power relationships, arguing that our primary focus should be on 'the transcendental plane of power, where law and capital are the primary forces'.[70] It is by no means clear why they locate the *law* on this level – after all, it is merely 'the juridical expression of class relations'.[71] Be that as it may, their utilisation of the Kantian scheme nevertheless captures something important about the economic power of capital. Whereas the power of the feudal lord was a *transcendent* power in the sense that it attached itself to production in an external manner without directly intervening in the labour process, the power of capital operates by *cleaving up the human metabolism in order to govern the conditions of the re-connection of its moments* – a mechanism of power which allows it to dispense with the use of immediate violence in the extraction of surplus value. 'Such transcendental powers', Hardt and Negri explain, 'compel obedience not through the commandment of a sovereign or even primarily through force but rather by structuring the conditions of possibility of social life'.[72] *The economic power of capital thus rests upon the ability of capital to seize life by the roots and entangle it in the logic of valorisation.*[73]

Hardt and Negri reduce *all* aspects of the power of capital to the transcendental level. However, as we will see in part three, capital also operates on what we could call the immanent level. Capital not only structures the conditions of possibility of social reproduction; it also actively intervenes in the processes and activities that make up social reproduction, from the most minute level in the workplace to global restructurings of the entire capitalist system.

---

70   Ibid., 6.

71   5: 342; I.5: 397.

72   Hardt and Negri, *Commonwealth*, 6.

73   See also Kurz, who likewise suggests to think of the logic of capital as a kind of 'transcendental a priori' setting the limits of what can take place in social reality: Robert Kurz, *Geld ohne Wert: Grundrisse zu einer Transformation der Kritik der politischen Ökonomie* (Berlin: Horlemann, 2012).

A Biopolitical Fracture

If one is familiar with the work of Foucault and Agamben, it is difficult not to think of the concepts of *biopower* and *biopolitics* when reading Marx's descriptions of the proletarian as a 'naked life' cut off from its conditions. Is this merely a terminological coincidence, or does it tell us something about the relationship between biopolitics and the capitalist mode of production?

In Foucault's analysis, biopower is one of the two forms of power characteristic of modernity, alongside *discipline*.[74] Both are opposed to *sovereign power*, the essence of which is 'the right to decide life and death'.[75] Sovereign power corresponds *mutatis mutandis* to the power of the feudal lord as described by Marx; it is, in Foucault's word, a 'right to seizure' based on the law, which in turn is based on violence: 'The law always refers to the sword'.[76] As I mentioned in chapter one, Foucault reproaches the political theory of his own time for being trapped in a sovereign paradigm of power. If we want to understand modern forms of power, Foucault urges us to 'abandon the model of Leviathan' in favour of an analysis of the concrete 'techniques and tactics of domination'.[77] If we do so, we will see that the modern world is built upon forms of power which do not fit easily into the paradigm of sovereignty.

Disciplinary power is a set of techniques and methods 'which made possible the meticulous control of the operations of the body, which assured the constant subjection of its forces and imposed upon them a relation of docility-utility'.[78] Discipline is *individualising* and targets the *body*.[79] According to Foucault, it emerged in the sixteenth century and was later, in the eighteenth century, supplemented with biopower or biopolitics, a technology of power which is not directed at the *individual* body, but rather

---

74   Michel Foucault, *'Society Must Be Defended': Lectures as the Collège de France, 1975–76*, trans. David Macey (London: Penguin, 2004), 243ff.

75   Michel Foucault, *The History of Sexuality*, vol. 1, *The Will to Knowledge*, trans. Robert Hurley (London: Penguin, 1998), 135.

76   Ibid., 136, 144.

77   Foucault, 'Society Must Be Defended', 34.

78   Michel Foucault, *Discipline and Punish: The Birth of the Prison*, trans. Alan Sheridan (London: Penguin, 1991), 137.

79   Ibid., 136; Foucault, *The History of Sexuality*, 139; Foucault, 'Society Must Be Defended', 242; Michel Foucault, 'The Mesh of Power', trans. Christopher Chitty, *Viewpoint Magazine*, no. 2 (2012), viewpointmag.com.

at the *species* body. In contrast to the sovereign right to kill, biopolitics is concerned with the positive management, control, and regulation of the life of the population.[80] Biopolitics thus marks the historical juncture at which the life of the population became the target of political power through techniques and mechanisms connected to problems such as 'birthrate, longevity, public health, housing, and migration'.[81]

One of the paradoxes of Foucault's analysis of biopolitics is that it tends to re-erect the kind of state-centred analysis the concept of discipline was designed to dispel. To be sure, Foucault does make the point that biopolitical measures take place not only on the level of the state, but also 'at the sub-State level, in a whole series of sub-State institutions such as medical institutions, welfare funds, insurance, and so on'.[82] However, in a fashion typical for him, he simply mentions this in passing without specifying what institutions he has in mind and how they are related to the state. The biopolitical techniques, measures, and institutions most often mentioned, – such as housing, public hygiene, statistics, migration, rate of reproduction, fertility, and longevity – are all issues which have traditionally belonged to the realm of the state.[83] Seen in connection with Foucault's description of biopolitics as 'State control of the biological' and a form of 'governmental practice', I think it is fair to conclude that biopolitics in Foucault's sense refers to a form of *state* power.[84]

Foucault draws an explicit connection between discipline, biopower, and capitalism. The connection between disciplinary power and industrial capital is quite obvious, and Foucault actually goes so far as to conclude that it was the 'growth of a capitalist system [which] gave rise to the specific modality of disciplinary power'.[85] He also holds that there is a close relationship between biopower and capitalism:

---

80   Foucault, *The History of Sexuality*, 137.

81   Ibid., 140; Foucault, *'Society Must Be Defended'*, 243ff; Foucault, 'The Mesh of Power'.

82   Foucault, *'Society Must Be Defended'*, 250.

83   Foucault, *The History of Sexuality*, 140; Foucault, *'Society Must Be Defended'*, 243; Foucault, 'The Mesh of Power'.

84   Foucault, *'Society Must Be Defended'*, 240; Michel Foucault, *The Birth of Biopolitics: Lectures at the Collège de France, 1978–79*, trans. Graham Burchell (Basingstoke: Palgrave Macmillan, 2008), 317.

85   Foucault, *Discipline and Punish*, 221; Michel Foucault, 'Truth and Juridical Forms', in *Power: The Essential Works of Michel Foucault 1954–1984*, vol. 3, ed. James D. Faubion (London: Penguin, 2002), 68f, 86; Foucault, *'Society Must Be Defended'*, 36.

This bio-power was without question an indispensable element in the development of capitalism; the latter would not have been possible without the controlled insertion of bodies into the machinery of production and the adjustment of the phenomena of population to economic processes.[86]

Foucault is very unclear, however, about what he means by 'capitalism'. He occasionally refers to 'accumulation of capital' and 'profits', but, generally, he seems to identify capitalism with the industrial capitalism of the late eighteenth and the nineteenth centuries.[87] The only place where the logic of capital really appears in Foucault's analyses is when he examines the factory as a disciplinary space. By identifying capitalism with a specific work regime defined by a certain technology and the concrete character of the corresponding labour process, however, Foucault misses the *social logic* which governs these processes. Here we see the consequences of Foucault's refusal (discussed in chapter one) to take property relations into account in his analysis of modern forms of power. Because of this omission, he artificially separates the expressions of the power of capital in the factory (discipline) and the state (biopower) from their underlying cause: capitalist property relations.

Federici rightly notes that Foucault 'offers no clues' as to what led to the emergence of biopower, but that 'if we place this shift in the context of the rise of capitalism the puzzle vanishes, for the promotion of life-forces turns out to be nothing more than the result of a new concern with the accumulation and reproduction of labour-power'.[88] This is why it is fruitful to combine the insights of Foucault and Marx. What Marx's analysis of capitalism tells us is *why* the life of the population had to become a central concern of state policy. In this light, biopolitics can be seen as an answer to the radical separation of life from its conditions at the root of the capitalist relations of production. Capitalism introduces a historically unique insecurity at the most fundamental level of social reproduction, and for this reason the state has to assume the task of administering the life of the

---

86   Foucault, *The History of Sexuality*, 140f; see also Michel Foucault, 'Truth and Power', in Faubion, *Power*, 125; Michel Foucault, 'The Birth of Social Medicine', in Faubion, *Power*, 137.

87   Foucault, 'The Subject and Power', in Faubion, *Power*, 344; Foucault, 'Truth and Juridical Forms', 86f.

88   Federici, *Caliban and the Witch*, 16.

population. Since the aim of capitalist production is the accumulation of wealth in its monetary form rather than the fulfilment of human needs, capitalist production frequently leads to the undermining of the life of the workers on whose lives it ultimately depends. A good example is the struggle over the length of the working day in mid-nineteenth-century British industry, which Marx narrates in chapter ten of the first volume of *Capital*: the capitalists' 'voracious appetite for surplus labour' threatened the reproduction of the labour force to such a degree that the state had to step in and impose legal limits on the length of the working day. Other historical examples could be given – for instance, public hygiene, housing, education, and poor relief, all of which arose in response to the rapid urbanisation brought about by capitalist industrialisation.

In order to grasp the relation between capitalism and biopolitics more clearly, let us turn to Agamben's influential analysis of Western biopolitics. Agamben presents his grandiose *Homo Sacer* project, which consists of nine books published from 1995 to 2014, as an 'inquiry into the genealogy – or, as one used to say, the *nature* – of power in the West'.[89] In his own understanding, this project is essentially a continuation of Foucault's work. According to Agamben, Foucault's theory of power contains two parallel 'directives for research': on the one hand, the analysis of political techniques and, on the other, 'the *technologies of the self*'. Agamben argues that both of these parallel directives refer back to a hidden or unexamined 'common center' in Foucault's writings.[90] What Agamben discovers in this hidden centre is the problem of *sovereignty*, which he – following Carl Schmitt – defines as the ability to decide on the state of exception. Already at this point, it becomes clear that Agamben's conception of biopolitics diverges quite dramatically from Foucault's. For Foucault, biopolitics is a distinctively *modern* form of power which historically succeeds sovereign power. For Agamben, however, biopolitics is inextricably tied to sovereign power: '*the production of a biopolitical body is*', as he puts it, '*the original activity of sovereign power*'.[91] Rather than a modern phenomenon, biopolitics is, according to Agamben, 'as old as the sovereign exception' itself.[92]

89 Giorgio Agamben, *The Kingdom and the Glory: For a Theological Genealogy of Economy and Government*, trans. Lorenzo Chiesa and Matteo Mandarini (Stanford: Stanford University Press, 2011), xi.

90 Giorgio Agamben, *Homo Sacer: Sovereign Power and Bare Life*, trans. Daniel Heller-Roazen (Stanford: Stanford University Press, 1998), 5.

91 Ibid., 6.

92 Ibid.

What *is* distinctive about modernity, nonetheless, is that 'the exception everywhere becomes the rule', as he writes with reference to Walter Benjamin's theses on the concept of history.[93]

What Agamben discovers in the logic of sovereignty is the apparatus through which life becomes entangled in power. In the state of exception – which is, according to him, the essence of sovereignty – the subject is exposed to the law by being *abandoned* by it; it is included in the sphere of law by virtue of being excluded from it. This relation of inclusionary exclusion, or abandonment, is the mechanism through which life is integrated into the law: *'The originary relation of law to life is not application but Abandonment.'*[94] The life that gets caught up in the web of the law through the sovereign exception is what Agamben refers to as a *naked* or *bare* life, by which he means a life separated from its form, reduced to the mere fact of being alive in a biological sense. This is paradigmatically captured in the *homo sacer*, a legal category of Roman law referring to people 'who *may be killed and yet not sacrificed*'.[95] The essence of sovereignty is thus the ability to institute the exception through which the subjects of the law are stripped naked and exposed to sovereign violence.

This brief summary of Agamben's conception of biopolitics and sovereignty is enough to allow us to identify its fundamental problems and to see how we can avoid these by drawing on Marx's critique of political economy. Agamben correctly points out that the isolation of something like a bare life is an important element in the constitution of modern relations of power, but he fails to identify the causes and nature of modern biopolitics; rather than being the result of an ancient logic of sovereignty, *the biopolitical isolation of bare life is a consequence of capitalist relations of production*. The obstacle that prevents Agamben from seeing this is his

---

93   Ibid., 9. For discussions of the relation between Foucault's and Agamben's notions of biopower and biopolitics, see Katia Genel, 'The Question of Biopower: Foucault and Agamben', *Rethinking Marxism* 18, no. 1 (2006): 43–62; Mika Ojakangas, 'Impossible Dialogue on Bio-Power: Agamben and Foucault', *Foucault Studies* no. 2 (2005): 5–28; Paul Patton, 'Agamben and Foucault on Biopower and Biopolitics', in *Giorgio Agamben: Sovereignty and Life*, ed. Matthew Calarco and Steven DeCaroli (Stanford: Stanford University Press, 2007). A third influential use of these concepts is that of Hardt and Negri. For them, 'biopolitics' is 'the power of life to resist', a use of the concept which is – contrary to what they claim – fundamentally in opposition to Foucault as well as Agamben, for whom biopolitics is always a form of domination. See Hardt and Negri, *Commonwealth*, 57.

94   Agamben, *Homo Sacer*, 29; Giorgio Agamben, *State of Exception*, trans. Kevin Attell (Chicago: University of Chicago Press, 2005).

95   Agamben, *Homo Sacer*, 8.

abstract, essentialist, and ahistorical conception of the sovereign power of the state. What Marx said about the German Social Democrats in 1875 is even more true of Agamben: instead of examining the way in which the state in its very form is shaped by the relations of production, he 'treats the state rather as an independent entity'.[96] Or, as Marx puts it in the early 1880s, in his critical notes on the deeply ahistorical conception of sovereignty in the work of the British jurist and historian Henry Sumner Maine: 'The basic mistake is ... that *political superiority*, whatever its peculiar shape, is taken as something which stands above society, something that is based only on itself'.[97] The same could be said of Agamben. Relations of production are 'the hidden basis of the entire social edifice, and hence also the political form of the relationship of sovereignty and dependence, in short, the specific form of the state'.[98] In contrast to such a historically sensitive perspective on the state, Agamben identifies the state with a logic of sovereignty which dates back at least to ancient Greece. History is thereby cleansed of ruptures and development, and transformed into a history of the gradual and uninterrupted unfolding of the logic of sovereignty. But: 'state power does not hover in mid air'.[99] The fact that Agamben subsumes ancient modes of production based on slavery together with feudalism and capitalism under the same logic of power bears witness to his lack of sensitivity towards the specificity of different modes of production. On this point, Foucault's understanding of biopower exhibits a much more nuanced awareness of the historical specificity of modern forms of power and their connection to capitalist production. Agamben's concept of sovereignty is truly the night in which all cows are black, and this abstraction is only possible because his exclusive focus on the state and sovereignty makes him blind to the relations of production.[100]

96   24: 94.

97   E: 329f; see also Kevin B. Anderson, *Marx at the Margins: On Nationalism, Ethnicity, and Non-Western Societies*, 2nd ed. (Chicago: Chicago University Press, 2016), 207f.

98   M: 778.

99   11: 186.

100   See also Hardt and Negri's critique of Agamben, to which I referred in the last section (Hardt and Negri, *Commonwealth*, 3ff). Another problem with Agamben's notion of sovereignty is his denial of the possibility of a form of sovereignty which is not biopolitical. For a powerful defence of 'a political and democratic conception of sovereignty' against Agamben's 'extremely abstract' political strategy, see Nicolai von Eggers, 'Reappropriating Sovereignty. A Critique of Giorgio Agamben's Abandonment of Sovereignty', *Trópos* 8, no. 1 (2015).

Agamben's inadequate conception of sovereignty should not, however, lead us to discard his analysis of biopolitics in its entirety. Let us attempt to leave aside his abstractions and consider what the analysis of capitalist class domination presented in this chapter might tell us about the relation between modern biopolitics and capitalism. I want to approach this question by beginning with an examination of Arne De Boever's attempt to make Agamben and Marx think together.[101] De Boever holds that the proletarian is a figure of bare life in Agamben's sense, and that the capital relation is a relation of sovereignty. He substantiates the first claim through an interesting observation about the word *vogelfrei* (literally 'free as a bird'), which Marx frequently uses in his descriptions of the proletariat. In the Penguin edition of *Capital*, *vogelfrei* is translated as 'free', 'rightless', 'unattached', or 'unprotected', but De Boever points out that it could also be translated as 'outlaw', since in Marx's time, *vogelfrei* referred to people who were excluded from the protection of the law in a manner similar to *homo sacer* in Roman law.[102] A mere terminological convergence might not be the strongest argument for the claim that the proletarian is a paradigmatic example of bare life on a par with the werewolf, the *Friedlos*, the *Muselman*, the refugee, and similar figures populating the Agambenian universe, but, as we have seen throughout this chapter, it is not difficult to find more substantial arguments for such a claim in Marx's analysis of the proletarian subject. On this point, I agree with De Boever, but the rest of his attempt to fuse Marx and Agamben is plagued by a number of serious misunderstandings.

First, De Boever fails to distinguish between the *creation* and the *reproduction* of the capital relation, a failure which leads him to implicitly assume that his discussion of so-called primitive accumulation also tells us something about the forms of power involved in the reproduction of capitalism. Second, his account of the historical emergence of capitalism is incredibly misleading. In order to support his claim that the sovereign exception is the operative logic of the capital relation, he claims that 'capitalists actually acted like little sovereigns ... side-stepping the legal and political order'.[103] He bases this on Marx's observation that 'the landed and capitalist profit-grubbers' who seized state lands in the period following

---

101   Arne De Boever, 'Agamben and Marx: Sovereignty, Governmentality, Economy', *Law and Critique* 20, no. 3 (2009).

102   Ibid., 263f.

103   Ibid., 265.

the English revolution did so 'without the slightest observance of legal etiquette'.[104] There are two problems with De Boever's interpretation: first, the circumvention of *parts* of the law is not a state of exception, in other words, the suspension of the law as such in its entirety; second, the seizure of English state lands in the late seventeenth century cannot be used as a general description of the transition to capitalism. In fact, the historical evidence presented by Marx in his examination of so-called primitive accumulation points in the opposite direction of De Boever's conclusions; the capital relation was not established by capitalists side-stepping the law, but rather by the active intervention of the state in support of the emerging capitalist class, and the *intensification* of the legal regulation of the life of what was to become rural wage labourers (enclosures, 'bloody legislation' against vagabonds and beggars, restriction of mobility, etc.). It is thus misleading to claim that 'the proletariat is a figure of a legal and political abandonment' – not only because the *historical* creation of the worker-subject involved an intensification of legal regulation, but also because the *continuous* reproduction of capitalism is compatible with legal equality. An economic system based on the exchange of commodities presupposes that market agents – including the proletarian who sells her labour power as a commodity – must 'recognize each other as owners of private property', as Marx puts it in *Capital*.[105] The peculiar thing about capitalism is precisely that it does not require legal inequality in order to reproduce a system of class domination; by treating everyone as equal and free proprietors, the state contributes to the reproduction of the subjection of one class to another. In other words, De Boever is right in his claim that the proletarian is a figure of abandonment, but this abandonment is *economic* rather than *legal*.

The upshot of these considerations is that we should follow Foucault and insist that the historical entrance of bare life on the scene of politics is not the result of the logic of sovereignty. The modern state can only relate to its subjects as a population whose biological life has to be administered, controlled, and regulated because capitalist relations of production have already isolated the naked life of the proletarian subject in order for the accumulation of abstract wealth to take place. *Bare life is the result not of sovereign violence but of the mute compulsion of economic relations: the separation of life and its conditions is the original biopolitical fracture and*

---

104   C1: 884.
105   C1: 178.

the root of modern biopolitics. This is not to suggest that we can immediately derive all of the concrete examples of modern biopolitics examined by Agamben (Nazi concentration camps, contemporary refugee camps, etc.) from the capital relation. My argument is situated on a more general level; as I have sought to show in this chapter, the isolation of bare life required by the subjection of social life to the imperative of valorisation is the background against which it becomes possible to understand the relation between law and life.[106]

---

106   If the capital relation is indeed the original biopolitical fracture, we should perhaps reconsider Agamben's claim that the camp is 'the biopolitical paradigm of the modern' (*Homo Sacer*, viii.). Perhaps it is rather the mega-slums populated by surplus populations deemed useless for the valorisation of value? See Aaron Benanav, 'A Global History of Unemployment: Surplus Populations in the World Economy, 1949–2010' (PhD diss., UCLA, 2015); Mike Davis, *Planet of Slums* (London: Verso, 2017); and Endnotes, 'An Identical Abject-Subject?', in *Endnotes 4.*

7

Capitalism and Difference

In order to secure the inflow of exploitable labour power onto the market, proletarian life has to be isolated from its conditions. As I noted in the last chapter, however, not all proletarians sell their labour power, and many of those who do also perform socially necessary labour *outside* of the wage relation. Throughout the history of capitalism, most of the labour required to reproduce labour power on a daily as well as an intergenerational basis has been performed by proletarian women as unwaged domestic labour. The emergence of the capitalist mode of production introduced a historically unique split between the production of goods and the reproduction of labour power, a split in which proletarian women were forced to undertake the unwaged and invisible labour necessary for the capitalist system to function.

Marx's failure to examine this kind of labour and its role in the capitalist economy is probably the most damaging blind spot in his critique of political economy.[1] A comprehensive treatment of this issue did not

---

1 See Heather A. Brown, *Marx on Gender and the Family: A Critical Study* (Leiden: Brill, 2012); Silvia Federici, 'Notes on Gender in Marx's *Capital*', *Continental Thought and Theory: A Journal of Intellectual Freedom* 1, no. 4 (2017), 19–37; David Harvey, *The Limits to Capital* (London: Verso, 2006), 163; Holly Lewis, *The Politics of Everybody: Feminism, Queer Theory, and Marxism at the Intersection* (London: Zed Books, 2016), 110ff; Lise Vogel, *Marxism and the Oppression of Women: Toward a Unitary Theory* (Chicago: Haymarket, 2014), chaps. 4, 5; Amy E. Wendling, 'Second Nature: Gender in Marx's *Grundrisse*', in *In Marx's Laboratory: Critical Interpretations of the* Grundrisse, ed. Riccardo Bellofiore, Guido Starosta, and Peter D. Thomas (Chicago: Haymarket, 2014).

emerge until the domestic-labour debates in the 1970s, in the course of which Marxist feminists fleshed out how the capitalist separation of the production of commodities from the reproduction of workers has acted, and continues to act, as an important source of the oppression of women under capitalism. From the early 1980s onwards, however, the debate petered out; in a conjuncture of neoliberal reaction and growing fatigue with Marxist theory in general, post-structuralist theories of gender gradually pushed Marxist feminism into the background and replaced the materialist emphasis on labour and social reproduction with more or less idealist conceptions of discursive power.[2]

In recent years, however, there has been a refreshing resurgence of interest in Marxist feminism. Under the rubric of *social reproduction theory*, scholars have integrated the insights of earlier generations of Marxist feminists into a more comprehensive theoretical framework.[3] Social reproduction theory begins from a question similar to that which animated the domestic-labour debates, but with a broader scope: what is the relationship between the production of commodities and all of the activities which take place *outside* of the immediate circuit of capital yet are *necessary* for the reproduction of the capitalist totality? By framing the question of social reproduction in this way – that is, by avoiding the presumption of a specific *site* of reproductive labour (the home) and a specific *identity* of those who perform it (women) – social reproduction theory has been able to overcome many of the limitations of earlier Marxist feminism and produce a framework within which the role of racism,

---

2   Susan Ferguson and David McNally, 'Capital, Labour-Power, and Gender Relations: Introduction of the *Historical Materialism* Edition of *Marxism and the Oppression of Women*', in Lise Vogel, *Marxism and the Oppression of Women* (Chicago: Haymarket, 2013), xxxiv; Cinzia Arruzza, 'Functionalist, Determinist, Reductionist: Social Reproduction Feminism and Its Critics', *Science and Society* 80, no. 1 (2016): 9–30.

3   See, for example, Cinzia Arruzza, *Dangerous Liaisons: The Marriages and Divorces of Marxism and Feminism* (Pontypool: Merlin Press, 2013); Cinzia Arruzza, 'Remarks on Gender', *Viewpoint Magazine*, no. 4 (2014), viewpointmag.com; Arruzza, 'Functionalist, Determinist, Reductionist', 9–30; Cinzia Arruzza, Tithi Bhattacharya, and Nancy Fraser, *Feminism for the 99 Percent: A Manifesto* (London: Verso, 2019); Tithi Bhattacharya, ed., *Social Reproduction Theory: Remapping Class, Recentering Oppression* (London: Pluto Press, 2017); Susan Ferguson, *Women and Work: Feminism, Labour, and Social Reproduction* (London: Pluto Press, 2019); Martha E. Giménez, *Marx, Women, and Capitalist Social Reproduction: Marxist-Feminist Essays* (Leiden: Brill, 2018); Holly Lewis, *The Politics of Everybody: Feminism, Queer Theory, and Marxism at the Intersection* (London: Zed Books, 2016).

sexism, transphobia, heteronormativity, and other forms of oppression in the reproduction of capitalism can be examined.[4]

The Marxist-feminist perspective on the capitalist system is absolutely crucial for a theory of the economic power of capital. By examining how all of those processes and activities which usually go by the name of 'the economy' are systematically related to activities and process which are usually categorised as belonging to the 'private' sphere of the home and the family, Marxist feminism has dealt a tremendous blow to bourgeois economism. The de-naturalising historicisation of the capitalist separation of spheres allows us, in the words of Tithi Bhattacharya, 'to see the "economic" as a social relation: one that involves domination and coercion, even if juridical forms and political institutions seek to obscure that'.[5]

The Necessary Outside

It is unquestionable that throughout the history of capitalism, the tasks necessary for the reproduction of labour power have primarily taken place outside of the immediate control of capital, and that they have been and still are conferred primarily upon women. But why is this the case? How do we explain it? Is it a result of the interaction of mutually irreducible social forms, or can we logically derive it from the core structure of capitalism? Or, more precisely: Is the separation of the reproduction of labour power from the production of commodities *necessary* for capitalism, and if so, does this separation necessarily overlap with social identities such as gender? What can we say about the relationship between capital and gender on this level of abstraction?

Let us begin with the question of whether capitalist production necessarily implies that some of the activities required to reproduce labour power are performed *outside* of the immediate circuits of capital. Can we imagine a situation in which capital internalises all of its presuppositions? Following Lise Vogel and others, let us distinguish between the *daily* maintenance of proletarians and the *generational* replacement of the labour force.[6]

---

4   Arruzza, 'Remarks on Gender'.

5   Tithi Bhattacharya, 'How Not to Skip Class: Social Reproduction of Labour and the Global Working Class', in *Social Reproduction Theory*, 71; see also Arruzza, 'Functionalist, Determinist, Reductionist'.

6   Lise Vogel, *Marxism and the Oppression of Women: Toward a Unitary Theory* (Chicago: Haymarket, 2014), 188.

It is almost impossible to pin down exactly what kind of activities are necessary for the daily maintenance of the ability to work. Workers need something to eat, something to wear, and a place to sleep, so someone has to cook, clean, do the dishes and the laundry, and so on. Most workers also get ill once in a while and will then need help from others. Then there are social and psychological needs: a certain degree of care, company, love, and recognition is needed in order to prevent workers from becoming so depressed that it will impair their ability to produce surplus value. But what exactly does that mean? Is going out for drinks with friends repro-ductive labour if it helps them endure their shitty jobs? What about sex? Capital 'has made and makes money out of our cooking, smiling, fucking', as Silvia Federici once noted.[7] The list of activities which have to be per-formed in order to make it possible for a worker to show up for work the next day can be extended almost indefinitely, and the concept of the daily reproduction of labour power threatens to explode in meaninglessness or simply merge with the concept of life.

Nevertheless, it is still possible to single out some essential physical and emotional needs which will have to be met in order for the ability to produce surplus value to be maintained on a daily basis, regardless of the historical, geographical, and cultural context. Many of the tasks necessary to meet these needs can be made superfluous by new technologies or lifted out of the privatised sphere of reproduction by being transformed into commodities or public services – and this is indeed what has happened to many of them in the course of the history of capitalism: dishwashers, washing machines, refrigerators, and robot vacuum cleaners diminish the time needed to clean; online supermarkets, takeaway food, and ready-made meals replace grocery shopping and cooking; sex has always been a commodity; public health care can replace personal nursing; and so on. The question is: Is there a limit to the commercialisation and socialisation of reproductive tasks? Would it in principle be possible to automate, social-ise, or commercialise *all* of the tasks required for the daily reproduction of labour power? The elasticity of this concept makes it impossible to give a conclusive answer, but judging from historical developments, it seems likely that most tasks can indeed be commodified or provided by the state. The best candidates for exceptions are probably some of the emotional and psychological aspects of reproduction; although the mental health of

---

7   Silvia Federici, *Revolution at Point Zero: Housework, Reproduction, and Feminist Struggle* (Oakland: PM Press, 2012), 19.

workers can be partially commercialised or socialised by means of profes-
sional therapists and psychologists, it nevertheless seems highly doubtful
that this could replace all of the personal relations on which most people
rely for psychological and emotional support.[8]

What about the *generational* reproduction of labour power, then? Here
things stand a bit differently. Although it is perhaps in principle possible
to imagine the establishment of private or public child-factories, it seems
unlikely that pregnancy, childbirth, and all aspects of child-rearing can
be completely commercialised or transformed into a state task. What
would commercialisation mean here? One extreme model would be the
establishment of a kind of worker factories, where capitalists would hire
people to give birth to children which would then be sold to capitalists.
However, such a system of universal slavery would not really be a capitalist
system anymore.[9] Another commercial model would be the universalisation of surrogacy – in other words, the transformation of pregnancy
into a commodified service (which it already is, of course). It seems a bit
far fetched to imagine the entire generational reproduction of the labour
force being organised by means of commercial surrogacy, but, in principle, it might be compatible with capitalist relations of production. Other
tasks connected to birth and child-rearing have been transformed into
commodified services, such as child care and lactation (think of the use
of commercial wet nurses among the upper classes in nineteenth-century
Europe). What about *socialisation*, then – how could that look? In another
extreme scenario, this would involve state employees producing children
who would eventually be released as free proletarians (if they were sold
directly to capitalists, it would again amount to universal slavery). A less
extreme model would be a partial socialisation of generational reproduction, of which we get a partial glimpse in so-called 'welfare states' such
as Denmark, where most parents have the right to eight months' paid
parental leave, free hospitals, and relatively cheap day care (depending
on income level).[10]

---

8   Jean Gardiner, 'Women's Domestic Labor', in *Capitalist Patriarchy and the Case for
Socialist Feminism*, ed. Zillah R. Eisenstein (New York: Monthly Review Press, 1979), 185.

9   Maya Andrea Gonzalez, 'Communization and the Abolition of Gender', in *Communization and Its Discontents: Contestation, Critique, and Contemporary Struggles*, ed.
Benjamin Noys (Wivenhoe: Minor Compositions, 2011), 227.

10   Having children nevertheless has substantially negative effects on Danish women.
A recent study of wage inequality reports that despite extensive socialisation of child
care and a labour force participation rate of 80 per cent, 'the arrival of children creates a

These thought experiments do not seem to get us very far. Indeed, it is difficult to pin down these boundaries conceptually – a circumstance which indicates that we are approaching the limits of what an analysis of the core structure of capitalism can tell us. Perhaps it would in principle be possible to fully automate, socialise, or commercialise the reproduction of labour power. Perhaps it is simply not possible to reach a conclusion on this level of abstraction. However, based on the considerations above, I am inclined to agree with scholars such as Roswitha Scholz, the Endnotes collective, Maya Andrea Gonzalez and F. T. C. Manning when they claim that there will always be an indivisible remainder of reproductive labour which will have to be performed outside of the immediate control of capital or the state.[11] *Someone* will have to do this labour; but who? Can we say anything about their identity on this level of abstraction – their gender, for example?

Of What Is 'Woman' the Name?

Among those who claim that there is a necessary relationship between reproductive labour and the (gender) identity of those who perform this labour, two main argumentative strategies can be identified. The first is to rely on a purely biological definition of woman as a human being endowed with the capacity to bear children. The most consistent and explicit representative of this position is Vogel. Her argument proceeds from the fact that pregnancy, birth, and lactation imply 'several months of somewhat reduced capacity to work', which means that women – 'the 51 percent of human beings who have the capacity to bear children' – are

---

gender gap of around 20% in the long run' (Henrik Jacobsen Kleven, Camille Landais, and Jakob Egholt Søgaard, 'Children and Gender Inequality: Evidence from Denmark', CEBI Working Paper Series [Copenhagen: Center for Economic Behaviour and Inequality, University of Copenhagen, 2018]).

11   Roswitha Scholz, *Das Geschlecht des Kapitalismus: Feministische Theorien und die postmoderne Metamorphose* (Bad Honnef: Horlemann, 2011); Roswitha Scholz, 'Patriarchy and Commodity Society: Gender without the Body', in *Marxism and the Critique of Value*, ed. Neil Larsen et al. (Chicago: MCM' Publishing, 2014); Endnotes, 'The Logic of Gender', *Endnotes 3: Gender, Class, and Other Misfortunes* (London: Endnotes, 2013), 56–90; Maya Andrea Gonzalez, 'Communization and the Abolition of Gender', in Noys, *Communization and Its Discontents*; F. T. C. Manning, 'Closing the Conceptual Gap: A Response to Cinzia Arruzza's "Remarks on Gender"', *Viewpoint Magazine*, 4 May 2015, viewpointmag.com.

dependent upon others in order to gain access to means of subsistence in those periods.[12] In addition to the dependence on capital shared by all proletarians, women are thus, because of their (biologically determined) role in intergenerational reproduction of labour power, subjected to an extra level of dependence.

The reduced capacity to work due to pregnancy and birth requires mothers to rely on other people, and historically that role has been filled by proletarian men. Vogel can thus conclude that 'the provision by men of means of subsistence to women during the child-bearing period ... forms the material basis for women's subordination in class-society'.[13] However, there is nothing about the mothers' reduced capacity to work which necessitates that their survival is guaranteed by *men*. It is possible to imagine, for example, that the state or a community of women could take care of non-working mothers. Accordingly, Vogel notes that 'the existence of women's oppression in class-societies is, it must be emphasised, a historical phenomenon. It can be analysed, as here, with the guidance of a theoretical framework, but it is not itself deducible theoretically'.[14] Given that only some people have the capacity to bear children and that pregnancy and childbirth imply relying on other people's labour for several months, it is necessarily the case that people who have children are structurally made dependent upon others. But we cannot derive the necessity of the identity of those upon whom they rely.

Vogel is not the only Marxist feminist who equates 'humans with the capacity to bear children' and 'women', although she is more explicit than most in her argument about the role of biological differences. Even though she and other Marxist feminists such as Maria Mies, Zillah R. Eisenstein, Johanna Brenner, and Maria Ramas stress that social relations of gender cannot be explained by biological differences, they nevertheless use the term 'women' in a completely ahistorical sense of 'humans who can have children'.[15] As Holly Lewis rightly notes, Marxist feminists have tended to

---

12   Vogel, *Marxism and the Oppression of Women*, 151, 173.

13   Ibid., 153.

14   Ibid., 154.

15   Johanna Brenner and Maria Ramas, 'Rethinking Women's Oppression', in *Women and the Politics of Class*, by Johanna Brenner (New York: Monthly Review Press, 2000), 25; Zillah R. Eisenstein, 'Developing a Theory of Capitalist Patriarchy and Socialist Feminism', in *Capitalist Patriarchy and the Case for Socialist Feminism*, ed. Zillah R. Eisenstein (New York: Monthly Review Press, 1979), 19, 25; Martha E. Giménez, 'Capitalism and the Oppression of Women: Marx Revisited', *Science and Society* 69, no. 1 (2005): 22; Maria

treat 'the collective subject "woman" as transparently obvious'.[16] Many scholars simply assume that only women can have children, and that all women are equipped with a uterus. In order to see why such a concept of 'woman' is insufficient, we do not need to appeal to Butlerian idealist arguments about the impossibility of a 'pre-discursive' biological reality; a classical sex/gender-distinction will do. If we follow Michèle Barrett – as I think we should – and insist 'that biological difference simply cannot explain the social arrangements of gender', it is easy to see what is wrong with Vogel's argument: what she demonstrates is that *humans with the capacity to bear children* are necessarily subjected to an extra level of oppression in capitalist society, not only because of their dependency upon others during the periods in which they are unable to work but also – insofar as they are wage labourers – because their temporary exit from wage labour gives rise to inequalities in the labour market.[17] But this is simply not the same as claiming that *women* are necessarily oppressed. The category of 'humans with the capacity to bear children' can also include trans men and/or queer people with uteruses, while it does not include many trans women.

At this point, we should note that assuming an overlap between the categories of 'humans equipped with a uterus' and 'women' might be justified if we limit our analysis to a particular historical situation in which the majority of those who belong in the first category identify and are identified by their surroundings as 'women'. When Ramas and Brenner assume such an overlap in their analysis of the incompatibility of child care and wage labour outside of the home in nineteenth-century British industry, for example, it might be justified on the grounds that it simply reflects the predominant social relations of gender at that historical point in time. In such a case, the overlap would have the theoretical status of an unexplained *presupposition*. In other words: *history* would be introduced in

---

Mies, *Patriarchy and Accumulation on a World Scale: Women in the International Division of Labour* (London: Zed Books, 1984), 23, 52; Vogel, *Marxism and the Oppression of Women*, 147.

16   Lewis, *The Politics of Everybody*, 125.

17   Michèle Barrett, *Women's Oppression Today: The Marxist/Feminist Encounter* (London: Verso, 2014), 76; see also Endnotes, 'The Logic of Gender', 76. The validity of this argument is also doubtful, however. The generational replacement of the labour force does not necessarily require everyone with a uterus to have children; it is possible, for example, to imagine a society in which a system of non-gender social distinctions and hierarchies would compel a subset of proletarians equipped with uteri to have a lot of children, while others would be expected to produce surplus value all of their lives on a par with all of those who do not have a uterus.

order to bridge the gap between the two categories, and therefore it would not be necessary to *explain* the overlap in order to analyse the relationship between capitalist production and gender. The problem is, however, that many Marxist feminists slide more or less directly from such analyses of particular historical situations to general claims about the *necessary* relationship between gender and capital, apparently without noticing that the methodological requirements for those two kinds of claims are radically different.[18] By vacillating between different levels of abstraction, they inadvertently 'ontologise' historically specific systems of gender rather than explain the relationship between capitalist production and the oppression of women. If one wants to argue that the oppression of women is a *necessary* feature of capitalism, the gap between the categories of 'women' and 'humans endowed with the capacity to bear children' has to be bridged *conceptually*, not *historically*.

There is, however, another, radically different argumentative strategy for bridging this gap and demonstrating that gender oppression is inherent in the logical core of capitalism – a methodologically sophisticated strategy whose defenders are certainly aware of the intricacies and pitfalls involved in defining concepts such as 'woman' and 'gender'. In fact, this solution consists in *redefining* gender. For Manning and the Endnotes collective, gender is nothing but 'the *anchoring* of a certain group of individuals in a specific sphere of social activities'.[19] In order to understand this position, it is useful to contrast it with the 'dual system' theory outlined by Heidi Hartmann in her classic essay on 'the unhappy marriage of Marxism and feminism'. Hartmann argued that Marxist categories are 'sex blind', by which she meant that they identify 'empty places' in a structure but 'do not explain why particular people fill particular places'.[20] This is the 'conceptual gap' Manning and Endnotes want to close by *redefining gender with reference to the indivisible remainder of reproductive tasks*: 'The categories "women" and "men" are nothing other than the distinction between the

---

18   See, for example, Eisenstein, 'Developing a Theory', 28; Silvia Federici, *Caliban and the Witch: Women, the Body, and Primitive Accumulation* (New York: Autonomedia, 2004), 17; Martha E. Giménez, 'Capitalism and the Oppression of Women: Marx Revisited', *Science and Society* 69, no. 1 (2005): 29; Maria Mies, *Patriarchy and Accumulation on a World Scale: Women in the International Division of Labour* (London: Zed Books, 1984), 170.

19   Endnotes, 'The Logic of Gender', 78.

20   Heidi Hartmann, 'The Unhappy Marriage of Marxism and Feminism: Towards a More Progressive Union', in *The Unhappy Marriage of Marxism and Feminism: A Debate on Class and Patriarchy*, ed. Lydia Sargent (London: Pluto Press, 1981), 10.

spheres of activity.'[21] In this way, the problem of how to determine the relationship between a set of activities and the identity of those who perform these activities simply disappears: women do not perform reproductive labour because they are women – rather, women are women because they perform reproductive labour. This argument was already latently present in Margaret Benston's pioneering 1969 article, which inaugurated the domestic labour debates: 'This is the work [i.e., unwaged household labour] which is reserved for women and it is in this fact that we can find the basis for a definition of women.'[22]

Is this, then, the conceptual bridge we were looking for? Unfortunately not: although Manning's and the Endnotes collective's rigorous analyses are very illuminating, their solution to the problem ultimately attempts to eliminate the problem by redefining its terms. This has a number of unfortunate implications. First, it implies that gender owes *its very existence* to the capitalist organisation of social reproduction. It thereby considerably increases the explanatory weight put on the analysis of reproductive labour; if Manning and Endnotes are right, we should be able to derive *all* dimensions of gender oppression from the split between production and reproduction. Second, if gender *as such* is a result of the capitalist mode of production, it cannot have a history prior to capitalism – which would be a peculiar claim. While we should avoid the ahistorical radical feminist concept of patriarchy, we should also avoid historicising gender to the point where it becomes impossible to speak of 'men' and 'women' prior to the advent of capitalism.

What Manning and Endnotes do is essentially to propose a new definition of gender which is quite different from what is usually meant by that concept, in daily language as well as in most feminist theory. Perhaps this is why Manning notes that

> it seems clear that the category woman is insufficient, and that a more dynamic concept such as 'feminized people' may serve both to emphasize the fact that it is a process and a relationship, and that the people in question are not always women.[23]

---

21   Manning, 'Closing the Conceptual Gap'; P. Valentine, 'The Gender Distinction in Communization Theory', *Lies: A Journal of Materialist Feminism* 1 (2012): 7.

22   Margaret Benston, 'The Political Economy of Women's Liberation', *Monthly Review* 71, no. 4 (2019), monthlyreview.org.

23   Manning, 'Closing the Conceptual Gap'.

Here, it becomes clear how the 'solution' proposed by Manning and Endnotes merely closes one gap by opening up another: if 'the people in question are not always women' – that is, if they can be men or gender non-conforming people – then what is the relation between these two levels? *Why do 'feminized people' tend to be 'women'?*

Method and Politics

We cannot define our way out of the question of the identity of those who perform the various kinds of labour required by capitalist (re)production. The upshot of the considerations presented so far in this chapter is that capitalist production is in principle compatible with a wide array of ways of organising the reproduction of labour power – or, put differently, that the analysis of capitalism in its ideal average does not allow us to say much about the specific way in which the reproduction of labour power has to be carried out. What we *can* conclude is that some of the activities required for the reproduction of labour power will most likely remain outside the immediate circuits of capital, and that someone will have to do this work. We cannot, however, conclude anything about the identity of the people to which these reproductive tasks will be assigned, or the social effects of this differentiation. As Barrett has pointed out, the attempt to derive gender differences and explain all aspects of the oppression of women on the basis of the analysis of the necessary presupposition of capital accumulation tends to slip into a functionalist and reductionist account of capital as an omnipotent subject creating the social differences it needs in order to function.[24] In order to understand the relationship between gender and capital, we have to take into account social forms which do not *arise* from the logic of capital, even if they are in practice completely entangled with the latter.

This position does not imply the claim that the relationship between capital and gender is purely contingent. My quarrel here is not with the claim that capitalism reproduces and fortifies gender oppression – a conclusion which has been convincingly demonstrated by many of the scholars cited in the preceding pages. The issue at stake here is how we *explain* this, or, more precisely, on *what levels of abstraction* the question of

---

24   Barrett, *Women's Oppression Today.*

the relationship between gender and capital should be posed. Rather than attempting to provide an answer to this question based on the analysis of the core structure of capitalism, I think we should follow scholars such as Barrett, Bhattacharya, Iris Young, and Cinzia Arruzza, and view the familiar binary and hierarchical system of gender as a social phenomenon which does not *originate* in the logic of capital, yet nevertheless reproduces and is reproduced by it.[25] Young puts it well:

> I am not claiming that we cannot conceive of a capitalism in which the marginalization of women did not occur. I am claiming, rather, that given an initial gender differentiation and a preexisting sexist ideology, a patriarchal capitalism in which women function as a secondary labor force is the only *historical* possibility.[26]

Or, to quote Arruzza's brilliant contributions to these debates:

> It is true that capitalist competition continually creates differences and inequalities, but these inequalities, from an abstract point of view, are not necessarily gender-related ... However, this does not prove that capitalism would not necessarily produce, as a result of its concrete functioning, the constant reproduction of gender oppression, often under diverse forms.[27]

Arruzza also suggests we understand this as a difference between two forms of necessity: while gender oppression might not be necessary for capitalism in the sense of being a 'logical precondition' of it, it is necessary in the sense that its historical existence has resulted in it becoming a 'necessary consequence' of capitalism.[28]

In the introduction, I explained that an analysis of the ideal average of the capitalist mode of production relies on two kinds of content: on the

---

25   Iris Marion Young, 'Beyond the Unhappy Marriage: A Critique of the Dual Systems Theory', in Sargent, *The Unhappy Marriage*, 62; Barrett, *Women's Oppression Today*, 249; Arruzza, 'Remarks on Gender'; Cinzia Arruzza, 'Logic or History? The Political Stakes of Marxist-Feminist Theory', *Viewpoint Magazine*, no. 4 (2015), viewpointmag.com; Tithi Bhattacharya, 'How Not to Skip Class: Social Reproduction of Labour and the Global Working Class', in *Social Reproduction Theory*, 87.

26   Young, 'Beyond the Unhappy Marriage', 62.

27   Arruzza, 'Remarks on Gender'.

28   Arruzza, 'Logic or History?'

one hand, transhistorical determinations common to all societies and, on the other, social forms which can be derived from the definition of capitalism. *Gender does not belong in either of these two categories.* Contrary to the implications of Vogel's analysis, it is not a natural, transhistorical fact. And contrary to the claims of Manning and Endnotes, it cannot be derived from the core structure of capitalism. Rather, gender is a historically constituted – that is, non-natural in the sense of non-necessary – social form whose existence cannot be explained solely by reference to the logic of capital. This means that we have to locate the analysis of the relationship between capital and gender on lower levels of abstraction defined by the integration of historically specific systems of gender into the analysis – defined, that is, by the theoretical integration of social forms which do not belong in either of the two categories just mentioned. In order to be truly comprehensive, such a theory would also have to include a theory of gender which would then allow us to explain why the capitalist separation between spheres of activity tends to overlap with a binary and hierarchical system of gender differences.

Some readers will accuse me of relapsing into a 'dual systems' perspective here, with my insistence that there is no logically necessary relationship between capital and gender – a position from which many Marxist feminists have been careful to distance themselves ever since Young's criticism of Hartmann in the early 1980s. I am not sure what to make of such a criticism, primarily because it is by no means clear what the terms 'dual system' and 'unitary' or 'single system' theory mean. The debate about these terms is, in several respects, a conceptual mess. Some authors understand 'dual system theory' as a claim about the *actual* relationship between class domination and the oppression of women; others construe it as a claim about the degree to which we can or should *theoretically* or *analytically* distinguish what *in reality* belongs together – and oftentimes, this quite fundamental difference is not really registered. Another confusing aspect of this debate concerns the widespread failure to distinguish between different levels of abstraction; it is one thing to claim, for example, that we can develop a very abstract account of the essence of capital without taking gender into consideration, and it is an entirely different thing to claim that we can analyse the basis of the power of capital in a particular situation without taking into account how it is connected with the reproduction of an oppressive system of gender. In that sense, it is perfectly possible to defend a 'dual system' approach on a high level of abstraction while insisting on a 'single system' or 'unitary' approach in concrete analyses. Finally, a third source of confusion is that many of these debates are couched in terms of the relationship between 'feminism' and 'Marxism', without clarifying what these terms mean: Is Marxism an academic discipline in itself, and if so, what is its specific object? Is it a philosophical system? Is it a method with which all social phenomena can be understood? Or is it a theory and critique of a historically specific mode of production, namely the capitalist?[29]

I do not find the abstract opposition between dual systems and a unitary approaches convincing or useful – partly because of the confusion surrounding these concepts, but also because it misrepresents what is required by an analytical apparatus capable of grasping the way in which capitalism relies upon and fortifies gender oppression. The degree to which we should strive after a unification of the conceptual apparatuses with which we comprehend gender and capital depends on *what* we want to examine, that is, it depends on the specific *object* of analysis, what *aspects* of this object we are interested in, and what *level of abstraction* the analysis operates on.[30]

The real issue at stake in these debates, however, is *political*. Many critics of dual systems theory prefer a unitary approach because it seems to provide us with a powerful basis for criticising the tendency among (certain kinds of) Marxists to de-prioritise struggles around gender because of a narrow-minded, masculinist ideal of revolutionary class struggle.[31] According to Young, the 'ultimate objection to any dual systems theory' is that it 'allows traditional marxism to maintain its theory of production relations, historical change, and analysis of the structure of

29   See Arruzza, 'Remarks on Gender'; Barrett, *Women's Oppression Today*, 28f; Johanna Brenner, *Women and the Politics of Class*, 59; Sara R. Farris, 'The Intersectional Conundrum and the Nation-State', *Viewpoint Magazine*, 2015, viewpointmag.com; Ferguson and McNally, 'Capital, Labour-Power, and Gender Relations', xxf; Hartmann, 'The Unhappy Marriage'; Heidi Hartmann, 'Summary and Response: Continuing the Discussion', in Sargent, *The Unhappy Marriage*; Manning, 'Closing the Conceptual Gap'; David McNally, 'Intersections and Dialectics: Critical Reconstructions in Social Reproduction Theory', in Bhattacharya, *Social Reproduction Theory*, 108; Valentine, 'The Gender Distinction'; Vogel, *Marxism and the Oppression of Women*, 28f; Young, 'Beyond the Unhappy Marriage'.

30   In a more recent contribution, the Endnotes collective seems to have changed their mind. See footnote 10 in Endnotes, 'Error', in *Endnotes 5: The Passions and the Interests* (London: Endnotes, 2020), 129f, where a position similar to the one defended here is presented.

31   Arruzza, *Dangerous Liaisons*; Arruzza, 'Logic or History?'

capitalism in a basically unchanged form'. In this way, it allows Marxists to continue to see 'the question of women's oppression as merely an additive to the main questions of marxism' – and, by extension, to see the struggle against the oppression of women as a struggle of secondary importance.[32] The idea seems to be that if we can demonstrate the necessary relationship between capitalism and the oppression of women, we have thereby demonstrated the revolutionary and anti-capitalist nature of feminist struggle and the necessity of viewing struggles against gender oppression as an inherent part of the struggle against capital. The question is, however, whether this is the right strategy for combatting narrow-minded conceptions of emancipatory politics. Should we not rather question the idea that political strategies can be immediately derived from abstract theory? Struggles against gender oppression are important because they are just that: struggles against oppression – not because of their logical relationship to the capital form. The 'dynamics of political struggle cannot', as Arruzza puts it, 'be directly deduced from theoretical observations on this level of abstraction'.[33]

Capital and Racism

Many of the confusions surrounding the discussions about the logical relationship between capital and gender can also be found in discussions about capital and other social differences, hierarchies, and forms of oppression. Take the example of racism. The popular point of view among radical scholars today seems to be that racism is a *necessary* element of the capitalist mode of production, meaning that the capitalist mode of production would be impossible without the existence of racialised hierarchies.[34] As with the corresponding argument about capitalism and

---

32   Young, 'Beyond the Unhappy Marriage', 49.

33   Arruzza, 'Logic or History?'

34   Himani Bannerji, 'Building from Marx: Reflections on Class and Race', *Social Justice* 32, no. 4 (2005); Chris Chen, 'The Limit Point of Capitalist Equality', in *Endnotes* 3, 202–23; Peter Hudis, 'Racism and the Logic of Capital: A Fanonian Reconsideration', *Historical Materialism* 26, no. 2 (2018): 199–220; Michael A. Lebowitz, 'The Politics of Assumption, the Assumption of Politics', *Historical Materialism* 14, no. 2 (2006): 29–47; F. T. C. Manning, 'On the Inner Laws of Capital and the Force That Decides', *Syndicate*, 2015, syndicate.network; F. T. C. Manning, 'Reply: Same Path, Different Weather?', *Syndicate*, 2015, syndicate.network; Michael A. McCarthy, 'Silent Compulsions: Capitalist Markets

gender oppression, this claim often functions as the basis for criticising certain narrow-minded conceptions of class struggle on the left.[35] This is an immensely important task: the dismissal of anti-racist struggles as divisive and aberrant 'identity politics' can unfortunately still be found among certain self-professed Marxists. The insistence on the necessary relationship between racism and capitalism is thus often accompanied by an implicit dichotomy according to which disagreement with this idea means that you have opted, in Manning's words, for 'the easy, well-trodden, obvious Marxist/leftist path'.[36] Things are not necessarily so simple, however. Disagreement with the claim that racism is a necessary precondition for capitalist production does not imply the claim that capitalism is 'indifferent' to processes of racialisation, nor that it would actually be possible for the capitalist system to break with its historical reliance on racism. Acknowledgement of the deep entanglement of racism and the valorisation of value does not oblige us to locate racism in the core structure of the capitalist mode of production. It is perfectly possible to hold that racism is a social phenomenon which does not *originate* in the capital form yet is conducive to and reproduced by the latter.

It should also be noted that it is not somehow more anti-racist to think that there is a necessary relationship between racism and capitalism. The difference between the position which holds that there is a necessary relationship between racism and capitalism and the position which denies this does not necessarily correspond to a difference in anti-racist and anti-capitalist strategy. After all, political strategy springs from concrete analyses of concrete situations, not from abstract analyses of concepts. So, when Alex Dubilet criticises David Harvey and writes, with reference to the Ferguson uprisings in 2014, that if 'we take our political prescriptions from a formal analysis of capital ... we seem to wind up somewhere completely on the sideline of the most intense mobilizations against the capitalist order of things that have occurred in the United States', our reply should be: yes, and that is why we should not take our political prescriptions from a formal analysis of capital.[37] That does not mean

---

and Race', *Studies in Political Economy* 97, no. 2 (2016); David R. Roediger, *Class, Race, and Marxism* (London: Verso, 2017).

35   See, for example, Bannerji, 'Building from Marx'; and Hudis, 'Racism and the Logic of Capital', 204.

36   Manning, 'Reply'.

37   Alex Dubilet, 'Dispossession, Uselessness, and the Limits of Humanism', *Syndicate*, 2015, syndicate.network.

that such a form of analysis is politically useless: indeed, it is the abstract analysis of concepts which makes it possible for us to develop a coherent and systematic theoretical apparatus which can then be used to produce strategically relevant analyses of concrete situations.

A much-discussed example of a failure to acknowledge this relationship between abstract theory and political strategy is found in Ellen Meiksins Wood's discussion of the relationship between class struggle and what she calls '*extra-economic* goods' such as 'gender-emancipation, racial equality, peace, ecological health, democratic citizenship'.[38] Citing the example of sexism, she argues that 'there is no specific structural necessity for, nor even a strong systemic disposition to, gender oppression in capitalism'. She then attempts to derive the 'strategic implication' that 'struggles conceived in purely extra-economic terms – as purely against racism or gender oppression, for example – are not in themselves fatally dangerous to capitalism', which means that 'they are probably unlikely to succeed if they remain detached from an anti-capitalist struggle'.[39] The crucial words here are 'purely' and 'in themselves'. Struggles are always concrete struggles undertaken in situations where they inevitably interact with hierarchies, tensions, and antagonisms in the specific conjuncture; in other words, *struggles are never 'pure'*, and for this reason, the question of what struggles are 'in themselves' is always an analytical abstraction. Put differently: *one never fights racism* – or anything else, for that matter – *'in itself'*. The degree to which struggles against racism threaten capital depends on the degree to which capital relies on racism in a particular conjuncture, and for this reason struggles against racism might very well be immediately anti-capitalist.[40]

In order to demonstrate that racism is a necessary presupposition of capitalist production, one would have to conceptually derive the existence of racial hierarchies from the capital form in the same way as one can derive the necessity of the split between proletarian life and its conditions from the generalisation of the commodity form. In other words, one would have to show that *the concept of a society in which social reproduction is governed by the valorisation of value* and *the concept of a society in which no such thing as racism existed* mutually exclude each other. No number

---

38   Ellen Meiksins Wood, *Democracy against Capitalism: Renewing Historical Materialism* (London: Verso, 2016), 264.

39   Ibid., 270.

40   See also Arruzza, 'Remarks on Gender'; and Arruzza, 'Logic or History?'

of empirical examples of the actual entanglement of racism and capitalism allows us to reach such conclusions. There is no question that capitalism, in Peter Hudis's words, 'first emerged as a world system through the anti-black racism generated by the transatlantic slave trade, and [that] it has depended on racism to ensure its perpetration and reproduction ever since.'[41] They question here is: How do we *explain* this? Can we explain the existence and nature of racism solely with reference to the logic of capital?

One popular strategy for substantiating the claim that there is a necessary relationship between racism and capitalism is to argue that it is meaningless to abstract from the historical fact that capitalism has always existed in a world deeply shaped by racism. Hudis's account provides a good example:

> To be sure, it is possible to conceive of the possibility that capitalism could have emerged and developed as a world system without its utilising race and racism. But historical materialism does not concern itself with what *could* have occurred, but with what *did* occur and *continues* to occur … Hence, the *logic* of capital is in many respects inseparable from its *historical* development.[42]

If taken to its logical conclusion, this argument has a number of consequences which I highly doubt its author would accept. What does it mean to say that 'the *logic* of capital is in many respects inseparable from its *historical* development'? The 'logic of capital' is obviously not something that exists separately from its 'historical development', but this is a point no one would deny. What Hudis seems to be saying, then, is that we cannot *conceptually* separate the logic of capital from its historical development – in other words, that the *real* entanglement of logic and history prohibits their *analytical* untangling. Such a claim, however, ignores the fact that *abstraction* is a fundamental feature not only of theory building, but also of concrete, empirical descriptions and even of human experience as such. Any given situation consists of an infinity of facts, and any description – or even just any meaningful experience – of any phenomenon involves abstraction, that is, the omission of irrelevant aspects of the phenomenon in question. This is a rather obvious epistemological point, and I assume that Hudis would agree. Taken at face value, the claim

---

41 Hudis, 'Racism and the Logic of Capital', 202.
42 Ibid., 203.

that the logic of capital is inseparable from its historical development means that we cannot even form a concept of the logic of capital; the only thing we can do is to record the facts of the empirical totality of capitalist development. After all, in order to form concepts and build theories, it is necessary to define an object of analysis by abstracting from irrelevant aspects of the empirical totality in which this object exists. In 'the analysis of economic forms neither microscopes nor chemical reagents are of assistance', as Marx notes in *Capital*: 'The power of abstraction must replace both.'[43] One of the ways in which this power of abstraction is usefully employed is to engage in counterfactual considerations and abstract from *actual* connections between various phenomena in order to examine how they might otherwise be related. If we deny the possibility of doing this, we inevitably fall prey to empiricism. If historical materialism was only concerned with 'what *did* occur and *continues* to occur', it would be reduced to a chaotic compilation of random facts.

Hudis is far from the only one who substitutes reference to the fact of real entanglement for conceptual argument. For instance, David McNally dismisses the discussion of whether or not there is a necessary relationship between capitalism and racism with these words:

> One cannot know such things in advance, on the basis of principles abstracted from concrete historical life. What we can say is that the actual historical process by which capitalism emerged in our world integrally involved social relations of race and racial domination.[44]

Another example is Himani Bannerji, who writes, 'As it stands, "race" cannot be disarticulated from "class" any more than milk can be separated from coffee once they are mixed, or the body divorced from consciousness in a living person.'[45] Of course we cannot actually separate the milk from the coffee once they are mixed; but that does not prevent us from conceptually distinguishing between them. Bannerji is completely right in her criticism of the tiresome distinctions between 'class struggle' and anti-racist 'identity politics', but there are better ways to undermine this than to insist that because two things are actually inseparable, we cannot or should not conceptually distinguish between them.

---

43   C1: 90.

44   McNally, 'Intersections and Dialectics', 107.

45   Bannerji, 'Building from Marx', 149.

The Production of Difference

In this chapter, I have argued that we cannot derive the existence of oppression based on gender or racialisation merely from an analysis of the core structure of capitalism. But what about other socially significant hierarchies and differences related to sexuality, religion, nationality, body forms, and so on? Or what about the relationship between capital and social differences in general? Can we say anything about this relationship on the level of abstraction on which this book operates?

I actually do think that there is a strong case to be made for the view that capital has an inherent and necessary tendency to nurture and reproduce social differences. Oppressive hierarchies based on gender, racialisation, religion, body forms, nationality, sexuality, and so on are conducive to the rule of capital on several levels of the capitalist totality, but in the end, it all boils down to the fact that antagonisms among proletarians tends to neutralise opposition to the power of capital. By organising the scissions of the capitalist totality – such as the split between production and reproduction, the split between wage labour and superfluity, or the split between sectors, job types, and wage levels – around social differences, capital fortifies its power: capitalists and governments find it easier to discipline and control proletarians, impose austerity measures, violently crack down on resistance, and so on. I therefore agree with Michael Lebowitz when he argues that 'the tendency to divide workers by turning their differences into antagonism and hostility' is 'an essential aspect of the logic of capital' – with the minor correction that it is not only 'workers' who are divided and subjected to capital.[46]

Although I think it is safe to say that capital will as a rule benefit from divisions among proletarians, we should also bear in mind that such antagonisms can, under certain circumstances, turn out to be a problem for capital: racist or sexist divisions among wage labourers can impede cooperation in the workplace, racist nationalism might lead to protectionist policies, and all sorts of cultural, religious, and national hostilities can spin out of control and result in civil war–like conflicts. The balancing act capital has to perform thus consists in nurturing antagonisms to such a degree that it prevents proletarians from forming a collective force yet does not create obstacles for the accumulation process.

---

46 Michael A. Lebowitz, 'The Politics of Assumption, the Assumption of Politics', *Historical Materialism* 14, no. 2 (2006): 39.

This is by no means a new insight. Contrary to a common misunder-standing, the Marxist notions of abstract labour and capital do not imply the claim that capitalism has a tendency to eradicate differences and trans-form everyone into homogeneous proletarians.[47] As I will come back to in my discussion of surplus populations in chapter thirteen, Marx famously held that racist attitudes towards the Irish among British workers were 'the secret of maintenance of power by the capitalist class'.[48] It was precisely the reproduction of racial difference which ensured the subjection of Irish immigrants to the regime of abstract labour.

Although it is possible to conclude that capital has an immanent and necessary tendency to reproduce social differences that can be mobilised in its favour, it is *not* possible to determine solely by means of a dialectical analysis of capitalism in its ideal average *what specific kind of difference* capital will place its bets on. Many critical scholars try at all costs to avoid this position because they think that it is incompatible with the effort to criticise narrow-minded traditional Marxist distinctions between revo-lutionary class struggle and 'identity politics'. But, as we have seen, this understandable concern is rather the result of the implicit acceptance of the idea that it is possible or desirable to derive political strategies from theoretical arguments developed on a very high level of abstraction.

The conclusions reached in this chapter tell us something important about the mute compulsion of capital: namely that it always operates in a world shot through with all sorts of antagonism and hierarchies which simultaneously strengthen and are strengthened by it. What the discussions in this chapter also remind us, however, is that we should avoid trying to explain everything with reference to the logic of capital. In order to really understand the relationship between racialisation and capital, for example, we need not only a theory of what capital is, but also a theory of what 'race' is – and the same goes for gender, sexuality, and so on. Because the purpose of this book is, once again, to develop a theory

---

47   This misunderstanding is shared by scholars such as Dipesh Chakrabarty, *Provincializing Europe: Postcolonial Thought and Historical Difference* (Princeton: Princeton University Press, 2007); Lisa Lowe, *Immigrant Acts: On Asian American Cultural Politics* (Durham, NC: Duke University Press, 1996); Brett Neilson, 'Five Theses on Understand-ing Logistics as Power', *Distinktion: Journal of Social Theory* 13, no. 3 (2012): 322–39; Roediger, *Class, Race, and Marxism*; Anna Tsing, 'Supply Chains and the Human Con-dition', *Rethinking Marxism* 21, no. 2 (2009): 148–76. For a critique, see Vivek Chibber, *Postcolonial Theory and the Specter of Capital* (London: Verso, 2013), chap. 6.

48   43: 475.

of the economic power of capital on the basis of an analysis of capitalism in its ideal average, such a project lies beyond its scope. We should keep in mind, however, that such an analysis of the core structure of capitalism only tells us something about *a part* of the mechanisms of the economic power of capital. This kind of analysis is, as Marx notes, 'right only when it knows its limits'.[49] And, here, we have reached the point 'where historical considerations must enter', at least as far as the relationship between capital and the production of difference goes.[50]

---

49   29: 505.
50   G: 460.

8

The Universal Power of Value

_____

In bourgeois society, separation is the determining factor.

–G. W. F. Hegel

In chapter six, I examined the mechanisms that force a part of the proletariat to go to the market to sell their capacity to work. As we saw, when
that happens, a *market relation* is established between the seller and the
purchaser of labour power. Between the worker and the capitalist, 'no
other relation exists than that of buyer and seller, no other politically or
socially fixed relation of domination and subordination'.[1] This is the basis
of the ideological representation of this relation as a voluntary contract
between free and equal proprietors. The analysis in chapter six of the class
domination presupposed by the commodity form allows us to see how
this apparently voluntary transaction is in reality 'coloured in advance',
in other words, how 'their relationship as *capitalist* and *worker* is the precondition of their relationship as *buyer* and *seller*'.[2] The worker is, in other
words, already subjected to capital *before* she goes to the market to sell
her labour power. But labour power is a peculiar commodity; it cannot
be separated from its bearer (the worker), and therefore its buyer has to
subjugate the worker in order to consume its use value. For this reason,
the worker is not only subjected to capital *before* she goes to market; once
she has sold her labour power,

_____

1 34: 95.
2 R: 1014f.

there comes into being, outside the simple exchange process, a relation of domination and servitude, which is however distinguished from all other historical relations of this kind by the fact that it only follows from the specific nature of the commodity which is being sold by the seller; by the fact, therefore, that this relation only arises here from purchase and sale, from the position of both parties as commodity owners.[3]

I will examine this 'relation of domination and servitude' – that is, the relation of the worker and the capitalist in the production process – in chapter ten. But there is even more to the economic power of capital; not only is the worker subjected to capital *before* she enters the market and *after* she leaves it; she is also subjected to the power of capital *while* she is there. The market is, in other words, not only a *result* and a *cause* of the power of capital: *it is itself one of its mechanisms*. It is the purpose of this as well as the following chapter to flesh out just how this dimension of the economic power of capital works.

Horizontal Relations

The concept of relations of production is widely recognised to be one of the key analytical categories of Marxist theory. As we saw in chapter two, orthodox historical materialism took relations of production to be the result of the development of the productive forces. Later generations of Marxists, following Marx himself, turned this scheme on its head – a change which made the concept of relations of production even more central. However, this concept is often used in too restrictive a sense. Althusser can serve as an example here: in his rendition of the fundamental concepts of the 'science of history' inaugurated by Marx, the notion of 'relations of production' refers to 'the one-sided *distribution* of the means of production between those holding them and those without them'; a relation which is the basis of 'relations of exploitation'.[4] In this conceptual configuration, the defining characteristic of a given set of relations of production is *the relation of the immediate producers to the means of production* and *the relation between those who control the means of production*

---

3   30: 106. See also C1: 280.
4   Louis Althusser, *On the Reproduction of Capitalism: Ideology and Ideological State Apparatuses* (London: Verso, 2014), 28f.

and those who do not. This is what Robert Brenner refers to as the '*vertical* class, or surplus extraction, relations between exploiters and direct producers'.[5] Such an understanding of the relations of production leads to the familiar definition of capitalist relations of production in terms of exploitation and class; in capitalism, the producers are separated from the means of production, which are centralised in the hands of a capitalist class, thus placing it in a position to appropriate surplus value produced by workers.

Now, what is wrong with such a description, one might ask? Is it not perfectly in line with the analysis of capitalist class domination in chapter six of this book? Indeed, it is – but it is also one-sided. What gets lost in this picture is the relation among producers, that is, what Brenner refers to as 'the *horizontal* relationships among the exploiters themselves and the direct producers themselves'.[6] Marx examines these horizontal relations on different levels of abstraction, which can be subsumed under two headlines: *value* and *competition*. In the theory of value, which serves as the point of departure in the systematic structure of *Capital*, Marx examines how labour is socially validated when production is organised privately and independently. In other words, he analyses the relation *between* the productive units rather than their *internal* structure. At a later point in the analysis, the 'private and independent producers' of which chapter one of *Capital* speaks turns out to be capitalist enterprises producing surplus value by exploiting labour. This important insight allows us to reconsider the relation between these units of production on a more concrete level of abstraction and reconceptualise the relation between them as a relation of *competition* – an absolutely crucial mechanism to understand if we want to unravel the workings of the economic power of capital.

The relations among producers take the form of market relations. Capitalism is a mode of production in which the market occupies a historically unprecedented role as the mechanism through which social reproduction

---

5   Robert Brenner, 'Property and Progress: Where Adam Smith Went Wrong', in *Marxist History-Writing for the Twenty-First Century*, ed. Chris Wickham (Oxford: Oxford University Press, 2007), 58.

6   Brenner prefers to speak of 'social property relations' rather than 'relations of production', partly because of the tendency to restrict the meaning of 'relations of production' to vertical class relations. Although Brenner is right in this criticism, I do not think we should avoid the concept. Instead, I follow Callinicos in viewing the horizontal and vertical relations as two constitutive elements of capitalist relations of production. See Brenner, 'Property and Progress', 58; see also Alex Callinicos, *Making History: Agency, Structure, and Change in Social Theory*, 2nd ed. (Leiden: Brill, 2004), 52.

is organised. Market relations cannot be understood solely on the basis of vertical class relations, even though there is a very close connection between these two sets of relations. The horizontal market relations among proletarians as well as among capitalists give rise to certain forms of power which cannot be derived from or reduced to the class domination examined in chapter six. These horizontal forms of power are the subject of this and the following chapter. I will begin with a discussion of Marx's theory of value, which demonstrates how the contradictory unity of *social* and *private* labour in capitalism results in a peculiar form of 'retroactive socialisation' (as Michael Heinrich terms it) which subjects *everyone*, regardless of their class status, to the abstract and impersonal power of the law of value. On this basis, we will then be able to specify the frequently ignored and misunderstood relation between the horizontal and vertical dimensions of capitalist relations of production.

Value Is Form

Marx presents his theory of value at the very outset of his analysis of the capitalist mode of production. A lot has been written about why Marx chose to begin with the analysis of the commodity, and, although I will not delve into a detailed discussion about Marx's method here, a few points of clarification are necessary.[7] First, I follow most contemporary commentators in rejecting the Engelsian reading of *Capital*, according to which the object of analysis in part one (chapters one through three) is a pre- or non-capitalist system of 'simple commodity production'.[8] *Capital* is about capitalism from the very first page.

---

7   Regarding the commodity as the point of departure, see Christopher Arthur, *The New Dialectic and Marx's Capital* (Leiden: Brill, 2004), 27ff; Jairus Banaji, 'From the Commodity to Capital: Hegel's Dialectic in Marx's *Capital*', in *Value: The Representation of Labour in Capitalism*, ed. Diane Elson (London: Verso, 2015), 14–45; Michael Heinrich, *Die Wissenschaft vom Wert: Die Marxsche Kritik der politischen Ökonomie zwischen wissenschaftlicher Revolution und klassischer Tradition* (Münster: Westfälisches Dampfboot, 1999), 173f; Michael Heinrich, *Wie das Marxsche 'Kapital' lesen? Leseanleitung und Kommentar zum Anfang des 'Kapital'*, vol. 1, 2nd ed. (Stuttgart: Schmetterling Verlag, 2009), 50ff; Jan Hoff, *Marx Worldwide: On the Development of the International Discourse on Marx since 1965* (Leiden: Brill, 2017), 241ff; and Patrick Murray, *Marx's Theory of Scientific Knowledge* (New York: Humanity Books, 1990), 141ff.

8   Ingo Elbe, 'Between Marx, Marxism, and Marxisms – Ways of Reading Marx's Theory', *Viewpoint Magazine*, 21 October 2013, viewpointmag.com; Søren Mau, 'The Transition to Capital in Marx's Critique of Political Economy', *Historical Materialism* 26,

Second, it is important to keep in mind that, although Marx is concerned with capitalism from the very first page, the kind of capitalism we
meet here is very different from the one we know by immediate experience.
Marx makes a lot of quite significant abstractions in his analysis of the
commodity form. For example, he abstracts from money until the end
of chapter one, from capital until chapter four, and from the existence of
labour power as a commodity until chapter five. In part one of *Capital*, he is
concerned with what he calls 'simple circulation', that is, an interconnected
whole of market transactions. On this level of abstraction, 'absolutely
no relations of dependence between the participants in exchange are
presupposed apart from those given by the process of circulation itself:
the exchangers are distinguished solely as buyers and sellers'.[9] In other
words, Marx initially considers only the relation *between* the units of
production, and not their *internal* relations. For this reason, classes are
completely absent from the analysis of the commodity form. At first glance,
it might seem futile to construct such an extremely abstract model, but
it is precisely this kind of abstraction that allows Marx to pin down the
necessary relations between the different moments of the capitalist totality
by dialectically deriving them from each other. And, as we will see later on
in this chapter, it is precisely such a procedure that allows us to determine
the exact relation between the vertical and the horizontal dimensions of
the capitalist relations of production.

Marx's theory of value was widely ignored or misunderstood until the
1960s, partly because it was deemed outdated by the theory of monopoly
capitalism, partly because some of the important texts were unavailable
(e.g., the *Grundrisse*, the *Urtext*, *Results of the Immediate Process of Production*, and the first edition of *Capital*), and partly because it was read
as an economic theory in a traditional sense.[10] One of the great merits
of value-form theory is to have demonstrated that Marx's theory of value

no. 1 (2018): 68–102; Nadja Rakowitz, *Einfache Warenproduktion: Ideal und Ideologie*
(Freiburg: ca ira, 2000).

    9   30: 36f.

    10   See Hans-Georg Backhaus, *Dialektik der Wertform: Untersuchungen zur marx-
schen Ökonomiekritik* (Freiburg: ca ira, 1997), 41ff; Simon Clarke, *Marx, Marginalism, and
Modern Sociology: From Adam Smith to Max Weber*, 2nd ed. (Basingstoke: Macmillan,
1991), 92ff; Lucio Colletti, *From Rousseau to Lenin: Studies in Ideology and Society* (New
York: Monthly Review Press, 1973), 76ff; Ingo Elbe, *Marx im Westen: Die neue Marx-
lektüre in der Bundesrepublik seit 1965* (Berlin: Akademie Verlag, 2008); Diane Elson, 'The
Value Theory of Labour', in *Value*, 116ff; Helmut Reichelt, *Neue Marx-Lektüre: Zur Kritik
sozialwissenschaftlicher Logik* (Freiburg: ca ira, 2013), 11f.

was never intended as a continuation of Ricardian political economy.[11] Marx was not an economist, *Capital* is not a work of economic theory, and the theory of value is not a refined version of the classical labour theory of value found in Smith and Ricardo. Marx's project was a *critique* of the entire field of political economy, and the theory of value is a critical analysis of social relations in a society in which social reproduction is mediated through the market.[12] One of Marx's recurring objections to classical political economy in general and Ricardo in particular is that it has completely neglected the *qualitative* aspect of value:

> Political economy has indeed analysed value and its magnitude, however incompletely, and has uncovered the content concealed within these forms. But it has never once asked the question why this content has assumed that particular form, that is to say, why labour is expressed in value, and why the measurement of labour by its duration is expressed in the magnitude of the value of the product.[13]

Marx is breaking new ground here; the question he asks is completely different from the one asked by political economy. To ask *why* labour takes the form of value-producing labour is to see value as a product of historically specific circumstances. Such a question is almost meaningless within the framework of the classical political economists, for whom the value form is simply presupposed as an unproblematic point of departure. From the point of view of political economy, what would have to be explained is not why social reproduction is organised by means

---

11   Some value-form theorists tend to exaggerate the novelty of their reading of Marx, however. Backhaus (*Dialektik der Wertform*, 16) and Reichelt (*Neue Marx-Lektüre*, 11), for example, essentially claim that no one had really understood *Capital* before they discovered the true essence of the theory of value in the 1960s, when they stumbled upon an old copy of the first edition of *Capital*. Although their reconstruction of Marx's critique of political economy was undoubtedly highly original, some of their fundamental points had already been at least partly made by Marxists such as Colletti, *From Rousseau to Lenin*; Raya Dunayevskaya, *Marxism and Freedom: From 1776 until Today*, 3rd ed. (London: Pluto Press, 1971); Henryk Grossman, *Works*, vol. 1, *Essays and Letters on Economic Theory* (Leiden: Brill, 2018); Karl Korsch, *Karl Marx* (Chicago: Haymarket, 2017); Evgeny B. Pashukanis, *Law and Marxism: A General Theory* (London: Pluto Press, 1983); I. I. Rubin, *Essays on Marx's Theory of Value* (Delhi: Aakar Books, 2008); and Kozo Uno, *Principles of Political Economy: Theory of a Purely Capitalist Society* (New Jersey: Atlantic Highlands, 1980).

12   Heinrich, *Die Wissenschaft vom Wert*, 25.

13   C1: 173f; see also 31: 399; and 32: 135, 318.

of the exchange of commodities, but rather why it has not *always* been like that.

These considerations allow us to see the hollowness of a common objection to Marx's analysis of the commodity: that he fails to *prove* that being a product of human labour is the 'third thing' shared by commodities, in other words, that the value of a commodity is determined by the socially necessary labour time necessary for its production.[14] This objection is premised on a failure to grasp the aim and meaning of the theory of value. As Marx explains in his famous letter to Ludwig Kugelmann from July 1868, in which he comments on a review of *Capital*:

> The chatter about the necessity of proving the concept of value arises only from complete ignorance both of the subject under discussion and of the method of science. Every child knows that any nation that stopped working, not for a year, but let us say, just for a few weeks, would perish. And every child knows, too, that the amounts of products corresponding to the differing amounts of needs demand differing and quantitatively determined amounts of society's total labour. It is self-evident that this *necessity* of the *distribution* of social labour in specific proportions is certainly not abolished by the *specific form* of social production; it can only change *its form of manifestation*. Natural laws cannot be abolished at all. The only thing that can change, under historically differing conditions, is the *form* in which those laws assert themselves. And the form in which this proportional distribution of labour asserts itself in a state of society in which the interconnection of social labour expresses itself as the *private exchange* of the individual products of labour, is precisely the *exchange value* of these products.[15]

The theory of value is, in other words, not intended to be an explanation of prices but rather to be a qualitative analysis of the organisation of social reproduction in capitalist society. The concept of value is meant to capture a specific form of *socialisation* of labour, that is, a historically specific way of coordinating production. The theory of value is from the very beginning a theory of the social form of labour, and the commodity is likewise defined as a product of labour from the first page of *Capital*; it is 'the simplest social form in which the product of labour presents itself

---

14   C1: 127.
15   43: 68.

in contemporary society'.[16] For this reason, it is, as Marx puts it so clearly in *A Contribution*, 'a tautology to say that labour is the *only* source of exchange value'.[17]

But precisely what does it mean to say that the theory of value is a theory of *the social form of labour in* capitalism, as many contemporary interpretations of Marx do? In what sense is the theory of value a theory of labour?[18] Obviously not in the sense of an examination of work conditions, technological aspects of the labour process, the differences between labour in various branches of production, and so on. The theory of value is not concerned with the concrete characteristics of the labour process, but rather with the social interconnection between the different parts of total social labour. To say that value is a concept designed to capture the social form of labour in capitalism thus means that it is designed to capture the specific manner in which individual acts of labour are socially validated and incorporated into a system of social production; the theory of value is, in other words, a theory of the *social interconnections between producers in the capitalist mode of production*.[19]

Value Is Domination

The characteristic thing about the social form of labour in capitalism is that it is simultaneously *social* and *private* (or *independent*). Its social character derives from the fact that it takes place within a division of labour, which means that people produce for each other rather than for their own consumption. As Marx emphasises in the letter to Kugelmann, a social division of labour presupposes a mechanism through which production

---

16   24: 544.

17   29: 276. Marx did not systematically distinguish between value and exchange value until the second edition of *Capital* (1872). Strictly speaking, the right word in this quote from *A Contribution* (1859) would be 'value' and not 'exchange value'. The same goes for the letter to Kugelmann.

18   Diane Elson argues that we should speak of 'the value theory of labour' rather than 'the labour theory of value', an idea which has recently been defended by William Clare Roberts (*Marx's Inferno: The Political Theory of* Capital [Princeton: Princeton University Press, 2017], 78ff). Dunayevskaya (*Marxism and Freedom*, 138) suggested the same terminological shift in 1958, although in a different sense.

19   This is not to say that there is no relation between the interconnection between producers on the one hand and the labour process on the other; on the contrary, the subjection of social reproduction to the law of value has tremendous impacts on the concrete character of the labour process, as we will see in chapter ten.

is coordinated and organised in order to achieve its aim – regardless of whether this aim is to meet human needs or to valorise value.[20] Production is, as we saw in chapter four, necessary for the reproduction of human life, and if society is to continue to exist, something has to be done in order to secure that at least the most basic needs of the producers will be met. Even when the aim of the total social production is the valorisation of value, it still has to secure the continuous existence of the producers in order to exist, which means that it has to secure the satisfaction of some human needs to a certain degree – otherwise it would simply perish. The immediate *aim* of capitalist production might be the valorisation of value, but the reproduction of labour power remains its necessary *condition*. An economic system based on a division of labour is a system of mutual dependence: if a group of producers spends all of its time making boots, it will be dependent upon someone else producing whatever they need in order to survive. And, if social reproduction, as a whole, is to take place, some kind of mechanism is needed in order to secure that a society does not end up with a lot of boots and no food. In capitalist society, that mechanism is the exchange of products of labour as commodities. The reason *why* this is so is that production is planned and carried out *privately* and *independently* by the individual units of production *before* it is socially validated, in other words, before these units find out whether their product actually fulfils a need of someone else within the division of labour. The products which end up as commodities on the market are 'the products of mutually independent acts of labour, performed in isolation', and for this reason, 'the labour of the private individual manifests itself as an element of the total social labour only through the relations which the act of exchange establishes between the products, and, through their mediation, between the producers'.[21] Capitalist social reproduction is therefore organised by means of a kind of 'retroactive socialisation' (*nachträgliche Vergesellschaftung*), as Heinrich puts it.[22]

---

20   The division of labour in question here is the overall social division of labour and not the division of labour within each unit of production – a distinction Marx missed in his early writings, where he also conflated the concepts of class and division of labour, leading him to conceive of communism as the abolition of the division of labour. He later gave up this idea and accepted the division of labour as a feature of human production as such. See Ali Rattansi, *Marx and the Division of Labour* (London: Macmillan, 1982), especially 56, 85, 93f, 128f.

21   C1: 132; C1: 165.

22   Michael Heinrich, 'Individuum, Personifikation und unpersönliche Herrschaft in

As previously mentioned, the point of departure of the theory of value is the commodity as the *dominant* social form of the products of labour; it is, then, 'not isolated acts of exchange, but a circle of exchange, a totality of the same, in constant flux, proceeding more or less over the entire surface of society; a system of acts of exchange'.[23] Such a situation, where social reproduction is mediated by commodity exchange, presupposes a certain regularity in the quantitative exchange relations between commodities. If it were possible for everyone to systematically accumulate wealth merely by repeating the same simple exchange over and over again (e.g., 1 chair = 50 eggs = 1 bicycle = 2 chairs = 100 eggs = 2 bicycle = 4 chairs, etc.), the market would break down, as nobody would want to engage in exchange.[24] Furthermore, if exchange relationships between different kinds of commodities fluctuated wildly in the short term (from exchange to exchange), it would be completely impossible to secure a living by producing for the market.[25] What explains this regularity? What is its point of reference? This is where labour enters the picture, since it is the only thing commodities have in common when we abstract from their use value – an abstraction which is carried out in the act of exchange itself.[26] When producers engage in exchange on the market, they thereby reduce their products – which are, by definition, different use values (if not, why exchange at all?) – to expressions of the same substance, namely *value*. By doing so, they also

Marx' Kritik der politischen Ökonomie', in *Anonyme Herrschaft: Zur Struktur moderner Machtverhältnisse*, ed. Ingo Elbe, Sven Ellmers, and Jan Eufinger (Münster: Westfälisches Dampfboot, 2012), 21. For further discussions of this contradictory unity of social and private labour, see Backhaus, *Dialektik der Wertform*, 51; Helmut Brentel, *Soziale Form und Ökonomisches Objekt: Studien zum Gegenstands- und Methodenverständnis der Kritik der politischen Ökonomie* (Wiesbaden: Springer Fachmedien Wiesbaden, 1989), 153ff; Clarke, *Marx, Marginalism, and Modern Sociology*, 101f; Colletti, *From Rousseau to Lenin: Studies in Ideology and Society*, 82f; Heinrich, *Die Wissenschaft vom Wert*, 207ff; Roberts, *Marx's Inferno*, 80f; Rubin, *Essays on Marx's Theory of Value*, 7ff.

23   G: 188.

24   Michael Heinrich, *An Introduction to the Three Volumes of Karl Marx's* Capital (New York: Monthly Review Press, 2012), 41.

25   Of course, wild market fluctuations happen all the time: people starve to death because a sudden economic crisis deprives them of the possibility of selling their labour power, and companies go bankrupt because demand for their product collapses. This is not, however, the normal condition in a capitalist economy, which is just another way of saying that so far, the generalisation of the commodity form has not led to the annihilation of humanity (although the looming biospheric catastrophe is threatening to realise such a scenario).

26   For a detailed breakdown of Marx's argument, see Heinrich, *Die Wissenschaft vom Wert*, 200ff.

reduce their own labour to the same kind of labour, namely *abstract*, value-producing labour. And, as Marx stresses, this 'reduction of different concrete private acts of labour to this abstraction of equal human labour is only accomplished through exchange, in which products of different acts of labour are in fact posited as equal'.[27]

Abstract labour is 'human labour pure and simple, the expenditure of human labour in general'.[28] Marx also defines abstract labour in a 'physiological sense' as the 'expenditure of human brains, muscles, nerves, hands, etc'.[29] Many scholars reject this physiological definition on the grounds that it explains a historically specific social form of labour with reference to transhistorical features of human labour. As Moishe Postone puts it: if 'the category of abstract human labour is a social determination, it cannot be a physiological category'.[30] However, as Kohei Saito has pointed out, this critique relies on an all-too-abstract opposition between the natural and the social.[31] Defining abstract labour in terms of 'expenditure of human brains, muscles, nerves, hands, etc.' does not imply that human labour is value producing *by virtue of* these transhistorical features; what Marx is trying to say is that these *transhistorical features* of human labour *acquire a historically unique social significance* in capitalism – a significance that cannot, however, be explained by reference to those transhistorical features.

In order to make this clearer, imagine a society in which a certain religious ritual was performed every time it snowed. Snow is a transhistorical phenomenon, yet it would not be possible to explain the religious ritual with reference to snow, considered as a purely natural phenomenon.

---

27   II.6: 41. This abstraction is thus, to use Sohn-Rethel's celebrated concept, a *real abstraction*. Alfred Sohn-Rethel, *Intellectual and Manual Labour* (New Jersey: Humanities Press, 1978), 20. Although Marx never used the term 'real abstraction' in exactly that form, the concept is clearly visible in several of his writings (see G: 303; 29: 272; 30: 55; R: 993; and C2: 185).

28   C1: 135.

29   C1: 137, 134.

30   Moishe Postone, *Time, Labor, and Social Domination: A Reinterpretation of Marx's Critical Theory* (Cambridge: Cambridge University Press, 2003), 145. See also Jacques Bidet, *Exploring Marx's* Capital: *Philosophical, Economic and Political Dimensions* (Leiden: Brill, 2007), 43; Werner Bonefeld, *Critical Theory and the Critique of Political Economy* (London: Bloomsbury, 2014), 121ff; Alex Callinicos, *Deciphering* Capital: *Marx's Capital and Its Destiny* (London: Bookmarks, 2014), 173; Heinrich, *Die Wissenschaft vom Wert*, 211ff; Heinrich, *Wie das Marxsche 'Kapital' lesen?*, 102; Heinrich, *An Introduction*, 50.

31   Kohei Saito, *Karl Marx's Ecosocialism: Capital, Nature, and the Unfinished Critique of Political Economy* (New York: Monthly Review Press, 2017), 107ff, 118f.

Insistence on the historical specificity and the social origins of such a religious ritual would not require us to deny that snow is a natural and transhistorical phenomenon. The same goes for abstract labour: in *all* human societies, labour is an 'expenditure of human brains, muscles, nerves, hands, etc.', but *only in capitalism* do temporal units of this expenditure of energy serve as the immediate basis of the organisation of social reproduction. In other words: the point of the definition of abstract labour in the physiological sense is that, as a result of a set of historically specific social relations, a transhistorical and natural process acquires a historically unique social function in the organisation of production. This is why Marx writes that 'within this world [i.e., the world of the commodities] the universal human character of labour forms its specific social character'.[32]

In order for the commodity to become the dominant social form of the products of labour, value has to acquire what Marx calls an 'autonomous' and 'independent' form; that is, it must incarnate itself into a specific commodity which is thereby transformed into *money*.[33] After having demonstrated the necessity of this doubling of the commodity into commodity and money, Marx goes on to analyse the different functions of money and the necessity of the transition from simple circulation (C–M–C) to the circulation of money and commodities as capital (M–C–M'). I will come back to this – particularly the analysis of the necessary transition to capital – in the next chapter, but for now I will set it aside for a moment in order to consider what the basic elements of the theory of value tell us about power in capitalism.

The fundamental insight of Marx's theory of value is that *the peculiar unity of social and private labour in capitalism transforms social relations among producers into a quasi-autonomous system of real abstractions imposing themselves on everyone by means of an impersonal and abstract form of domination.* When social relations among market-dependent producers comes to be mediated by the exchange of commodities, their access to their conditions of existence comes to be mediated by a market system in which the circulation of commodities and money generate compulsory

---

32   C1: 160.

33   29: 488; M: 633; V: 27; C1: 159, 180f. Regarding the necessity of money, see Backhaus, *Dialektik der Wertform*; Heinrich, *Die Wissenschaft vom Wert*, 220ff; Heinrich, *Wie das Marxsche 'Kapital' lesen?*, 104–62; Mau, 'The Transition to Capital', 72. See also Frank Engster's *Das Geld als Mass, Mittel und Methode: Das Rechnen mit der Identität der Zeit* (Berlin: Neofelis Verlag, 2014).

standards and demands that producers must meet in order to survive. In chapter six, we saw that the very existence of the capitalist market is the result of class domination, and in chapter ten we will see how the market transactions between the worker and the capitalist give rise to another relation of domination within the workplace. What the theory of value teaches us, however, is that the market not only *mediates* (and conceals) relations of domination – 'it is', in the words of William Clare Roberts, 'itself the exercise of an arbitrary power'.[34]

The movements of commodities and money on the market determine what producers must produce as well as when, how, and for how long they have to produce. In order to live, they will have to find a place in a predetermined division of labour, a place which might disappear suddenly. In order to hold on to a market share that allows them to survive, they will have to live up to a certain level of productivity. In order to avoid spending more time than what is socially necessary for the production of a commodity, they are forced to adopt certain techniques, technologies, organisational forms, and so on. If a producer introduces labour-saving technologies, other producers will have to follow suit, move to another branch, work more, or perish. In other words, the equalising pressures of the inherently unstable market set the conditions under which individuals gain access to what they need in order to live. Because mainstream economics treats the market as a system of voluntary transactions between free and equal individuals, it represents the equalising mechanisms of the market as a transmission of information needed by these individuals in order to make rational investment decisions. Marx's analysis allows us to see that what is actually transmitted by the market is not *information* but *compulsory commands* communicated through the movements of things. As Heinrich explains:

> The value of commodities is an expression of an overwhelming social interaction that cannot be controlled by individuals. In a commodity-producing society, people (all of them!) are under the control of things, and the decisive relations of domination are not personal but 'objective' (*sachlich*). This impersonal, objective domination, submission to 'inherent necessities', does not exist because things themselves possess characteristics that generate such domination, or because social activity

---

34   Roberts, *Marx's Inferno*, 58.

necessitates this mediation through things, but only because *people relate to things in a particular way – as commodities.*[35]

Roberts has criticised Heinrich as well as Postone for being 'quite vague about where this domination comes from and why it counts as domination'. He claims that because Heinrich 'understands objective domination as a relationship between people and things, he does not make it clear that the things in question only mediate relations with other people'.[36] This is, at least to a certain extent, convincing as a critique of Postone (to whom I will come back later in this chapter), but I do not think it adequately represents Heinrich's interpretation. He is quite clear that we are dealing with 'relations between human beings' hidden under what he (quoting Marx) calls a 'thing-like cover' (*dinglicher Hülle*).[37] Be that as it may, Roberts's point is still valid: the domination of value is a domination of people by people *mediated* by relationships between people and things.[38] Another way to put this is that the market is an *emergent property*; although it is, in the last instance, nothing but a totality of relations among human beings, it nevertheless detaches itself, to a certain degree, from these human beings and opposes them as an 'alien power', to use one of Marx's favourite expressions.

Marx's description of the abstract and impersonal domination of everyone by the value form is clearly reminiscent of the Feuerbachian critique of inversion in the early writings (examined in chapter three). In addition to the frequent use of the expression 'alien power', Marx also speaks of an 'inversion of subject and object', and explicitly compares religion and capital.[39] Such passages and expressions are sometimes quoted as

---

35   Heinrich, *An Introduction*, 75; see also Ingo Elbe, Sven Ellmers, and Jan Eufinger, 'Einleitung', in *Anonyme Herrschaft: Zur Struktur moderner Machtverhältnisse*, ed. Ingo Elbe, Jan Eufinger, and Sven Ellmers (Münster: Westfälisches Dampfboot, 2012), 7.

36   Roberts, *Marx's Inferno*, 91.

37   Heinrich, *Wie das Marxsche 'Kapital' lesen?*, 181; see also Michael Heinrich, 'Welche Klassen und welche Kämpfe? Eine Antwort auf Karl Reitters "Kapitalismus ohne Klassenkampf?"', *grundrisse: zeitschrift für linke theorie & debatte*, no. 11 (2004). Roberts's critique could also be extended to Robert Kurz, *Geld ohne Wert: Grundrisse zu einer Transformation der Kritik der politischen Ökonomie* (Berlin: Horlemann, 2012); Ingo Elbe, Sven Ellmers and Jan Eufinger, 'Einleitung'; and Anselm Jappe, *Die Abenteuer der Ware: Für eine neue Wertkritik* (Münster: Unrast Verlag, 2005).

38   See also Gerhard Hanloser and Karl Reitter, *Der bewegte Marx: Eine einführende Kritik des Zirkulationsmarxismus* (Münster: Unrast Verlag, 2008), 17. The authors make the exact same point in their critique of Stefan Breuer.

39   R: 990; 30: 110; C1: 772. See also 32: 409.

indications, or even proofs, that Marx never abandoned the humanist critique of alienation. In reality, however, they demonstrate the opposite. In the writings of 1843 and 1844, the alienated workers are confronted with their *own human essence* in the form of money or God (or the money-God). According to the theory of value, in contrast, it is *social relations* that confront members of bourgeois society as an alien power. The essence of the human being has, in other words, been replaced by social relations – precisely as the sixth thesis on Feuerbach announced. In addition to this, the social relations confronting commodity producers as an alien power are not something that one would want to reappropriate and actualise. The political horizon of the critique of inversion has thus developed from the reappropriation and realisation of an alienated essence to the abolition of autonomised social relations.

What Is Fetishism?

According to an increasingly popular reading of Marx's theory of value, the impersonal and abstract domination of value is captured in the concept of *fetishism*.[40] This reading diverges from the most common interpretation of the concept of fetishism, according to which the latter refers to an *ideological* naturalisation of social forms.[41] The earliest proponent of the nowadays-popular reading of the concept of fetishism was Isaak Rubin, who held that the 'theory of fetishism is, *per se*, the basis

---

40   In this section I rely heavily on Søren Mau, 'Den dobbelte fordrejning: fetichismebegrebet i kritikken af den politiske økonomi', *Slagmark: Tidsskrift for Idéhistorie*, no. 77 (2018).

41   See, for example, Shlomo Avineri, *The Social and Political Thought of Karl Marx* (Cambridge: Cambridge University Press, 1980), 118; Étienne Balibar, *The Philosophy of Marx* (London: Verso, 2014), 60f; Bidet, *Exploring Marx's Capital*, 260ff; Brentel, *Soziale Form und Ökonomisches Objekt*, 15; Nikolai Bukharin, *Historical Materialism: A System of Sociology* (New York: International Publishers, 1928), 237ff; Callinicos, *Deciphering Capital*, 150f; Terry Eagleton, *Ideology: An Introduction* (London: Verso, 1996), 84ff; Hanloser and Reitter, *Der bewegte Marx*, 30; David Harvey, *A Companion to Marx's Capital* (London: Verso, 2010), 41; Karl Kautsky, *Karl Marx' Oekonomische Lehren: Gemeinverständlich Dargestellt Und Erläutert* (Stuttgart: Verlag J. H. W. Dietz Nachf, 1912), 14; Pashukanis, *Law and Marxism*, 73; Postone, *Time, Labor, and Social Domination*, 70; Guido Starosta, *Marx's Capital: Method and Revolutionary Subjectivity* (Chicago: Haymarket, 2016), 142; Amy E. Wendling, *Karl Marx on Technology and Alienation* (London: Palgrave Macmillan, 2009), 54; Slavoj Žižek, *The Sublime Object of Ideology* (London: Verso, 2009), 19.

of Marx's entire economic system', and that the theory of fetishism is 'a general theory of production relations of the commodity economy'.[42] More recently, Heinrich has argued that 'commodity fetishism is no illusion, but a real phenomenon'.[43] Anselm Jappe likewise insists that 'for Marx, fetishism is not only an inverted representation of reality, but also an *inversion of reality itself*'.[44] What these authors claim is that fetishism refers not to the *ideological naturalisation* of a social practice but rather to *that practice itself*; or, with regards to commodity fetishism more specifically, not the ideological representation of value as a natural property of products of labour, but *the actual practice* of relating to each other through the exchange of products of labour.

If interpreters such as Rubin, Heinrich, and Jappe are right in these claims, it means that the concept of fetishism ought to occupy a central place in a theory of the economic power of capital. However, as a reading of Marx, I think this interpretation of the concept of fetishism is inaccurate – that is, it does not reflect Marx's use of the concept. Read as a suggestion for a new way of using this concept, I find it unnecessary. Before I go on to substantiate these claims, let me briefly clarify what it means to say that fetishism is a form of *ideology*, as I will do in the following pages. One of the commonplaces in the literature on fetishism is to emphasise that fetishism is not a matter of 'distorted perception', 'mere illusion', 'simple misrepresentation', or 'false consciousness'.[45] Such assurances display

---

42 Rubin, *Essays on Marx's Theory of Value*, 5f.

43 Heinrich, *Wie das Marxsche 'Kapital' lesen?*, 175.

44 Jappe, *Die Abenteuer der Ware*, 30. Similar interpretations can be found in Backhaus, *Dialektik der Wertform*, 46; Bonefeld, *Critical Theory*, 54; Dunayevskaya, *Marxism and Freedom*, 100; Nicholas Gray, 'Against Perversion and Fetish: The Marxian Theory of Revolution as Practical Demystification', *Studies in Social and Political Thought* 20 (2012); Wolfgang Fritz Haug, *Vorlesungen zur Einführung ins Kapital* (Köln: Pahl-Rugenstein Verlag, 1974), 166; John Holloway, *Change the World without Taking Power: The Meaning of Revolution Today* (London: Pluto Press, 2010), 49; Korsch, *Karl Marx*, 93f; Kurz, *Geld ohne Wert*, 33; Thomas Marxhausen, 'Die Entwicklung des Begriffs Fetischismus bei Marx', *Marx-Engels-Forschung* 22 (1988); Thomas Marxhausen, 'Die Theorie des Fetischismus im dritten Band des Kapitals', *Marx-Engels-Forschung* 25 (1988); Patrick Murray, *The Mismeasure of Wealth: Essays on Marx and Social Form* (Leiden: Brill, 2016), 39; and Roberts, *Marx's Inferno*, 86.

45 Eagleton, *Ideology*, 85; Harvey, *A Companion*, 41; Daniel Bensaïd, *Marx for Our Times: Adventures and Misadventures of a Critique* (London: Verso, 2009), 227; Roberts, *Marx's Inferno*, 86; Heinrich, *Wie das Marxsche 'Kapital' lesen?*, 174. See also Theodor W. Adorno, *Negative Dialectics* (New York: Continuum, 2007), 190; Louis Althusser et al., *Reading* Capital: *The Complete Edition* (London: Verso, 2015), 347; Balibar, *The*

an understandable effort to indicate a distance towards a certain vulgar Marxist understanding of ideology as a manipulative tool of the capitalist class which can be brushed away by critique and has no real basis in social reality. However, they also have the effect of making it seem as if an interpretation of fetishism as ideology must necessarily commit itself to such a poor notion of ideology. But this is not the case; the claim that fetishism is a matter of ideology does not imply the claim that ideology is an arbitrary illusion or a false consciousness which can be eradicated by critical analysis.

Let us take a look at Marx's use of the concept of fetishism. Since I am concerned with this concept in relation to the theory of value and, more generally, the critique of political economy, I will only consider his use of it in the writings from the *Grundrisse* onwards.[46] Here is the definition of fetishism in the second edition of volume one of *Capital*:

> In order, therefore, to find an analogy we must take flight into the misty realm of religion. There the products of the human brain appear [*scheinen*] as autonomous figures endowed with a life of their own, which enter into relations both with each other and with humans. So it is in the world of commodities with the products of human hands. I call this the fetishism which attaches itself to the products of labour as soon as they are produced as commodities, and is therefore inseparable from the production of commodities.[47]

What is Marx claiming here? For the religious mind, what is *in reality* a product of the human brain *appears* as autonomous figures with a life of their own – which they are *not*. Similarly with commodities: what

Philosophy of Marx, 60; Bonefeld, *Critical Theory*, 54; Holloway, *Change the World*, 49; Fredric Jameson, *Valences of the Dialectic* (London: Verso, 2009), 331; Postone, *Time, Labor, and Social Domination*, 62.

46   The concept already appears in Marx's writings from 1842 onwards (see 1: 147; and IV.1: 322). For discussions of the history of the concept and Marx's sources, see Alfonso Maurizio Iacono, *The History and Theory of Fetishism* (New York: Palgrave Macmillan, 2016); David McNally, *Monsters of the Market: Zombies, Vampires, and Global Capitalism* (Leiden: Brill, 2011), 201ff; William Pietz, 'The Problem of the Fetish, I', *RES: Anthropology and Aesthetics*, no. 9 (1985): 5–17; William Pietz, 'The Problem of the Fetish, II: The Origin of the Fetish', *RES: Anthropology and Aesthetics*, no. 13 (1987): 23–45; William Pietz, 'The Problem of the Fetish, IIIa: Bosman's Guinea and the Enlightenment Theory of Fetishism', *RES: Anthropology and Aesthetics*, no. 16 (1988): 105–24.

47   C1: 165. An almost-identical passage appears in the appendix to the first edition (A: 142f).

is *in reality* a set of social relations among human beings *appears* to be relations exclusively among commodities. Accordingly, Marx writes that '[Samuel] Bailey is a fetishist in that he conceives value ... as a *relation of objects to one another*'.[48] Value thus appears as a natural quality possessed by products of labour regardless of their social context – and *this is what fetishism is*.

An interpretation of Marx's use of the concept of fetishism cannot, however, base itself solely on this passage from *Capital*. If we look at other occurrences of the term in Marx's writings, they can be divided into two groups: first, there are a couple of short and ambivalent passages where 'fetishism' could, in principle, refer both to the ideological naturalisation of a social form and this social form itself. Two examples: 'bourgeois production must crystallise wealth as a fetish in the form of a particular thing'; 'in interest-bearing capital, the capital relation reaches its most externalised and fetish-like form'.[49] If we read these passages in connection with the second group of examples, however, it becomes evident that the interpretation of fetishism as ideology is more convincing. The clearest examples of this second group are when Marx writes about 'the fetishism of the political economists': 'the fetishism peculiar to bourgeois economics ... transform the social economic character that things achieve in the process of social production into a natural determination arising from the material nature of these things'.[50] Here, 'fetishism' obviously refers to an ideological form. It makes perfect sense, then, that Marx ends the section on fetishism in chapter one of *Capital* with quotes from economists who present value as 'a property of things'.[51] The interpretation of fetishism as ideology is also supported by passages where Marx associates it with terms like representing (*vorstellen*), viewing, believing, considering, or regarding (*anschauen*):

> The fetishist view peculiar to and springing from the essence of the capitalist mode of production, which considers *economic* form-determinations, such as being a *commodity* or being *productive* labour, as a property belonging to the material bearers of these form-determinations or categories in and of themselves.[52]

---

48   32: 334.

49   29: 387; M: 492; see also 32: 494; and A: 142.

50   R: 983, C2: 303; II.11: 176. See also G: 687; 29: 277; 32: 316, 334, 400; 33: 344; V: 39; and C1: 176.

51   C1: 177.

52   R: 1046. I have amended this translation quite heavily. The original reads: 'Die der

Here, it is again clear that fetishism is an ideological naturalisation of social forms. The 'fetish-worshipper', writes Marx, accepts the appearance (*Schein*) 'as something real' and 'actually believes that the exchange value of things is determined by their properties as things, and is altogether a natural property of things'.[53]

All of the passages just quoted quite unambiguously demonstrate that Marx uses the concept of fetishism in order to refer to an ideological naturalisation. There is one important passage in *Capital*, however, which does support the other reading – a passage which is almost always quoted in discussions of fetishism:

> To the producers, therefore, the social relations between their private labours appear as what they are, i.e., not as immediate social relations between persons in their work itself, but rather as thing-like [*sachliche*] relations between persons and social relations among things.[54]

Two things should be noted about this passage. First, Marx writes that social relations appear as thing-like relations between *persons* or as *social* relations among things. This contradicts the many passages where Marx describes fetishism as social relations which appears as *thing-like* relations or simply relations among *things*. In other words: in the passage just quoted, Marx claims that the *insight* that the relations among things are *in reality* relations between people is immediately a part of the *appearance* – whereas, in all of the other passages I have quoted in the preceding pages, it is precisely this insight which he claims is occluded by fetishism, that is, *not* included on the level of appearance. Second, it is remarkable that, whereas Marx usually emphasises the *difference* between essence and appearance, here he holds them to be *identical*. At the beginning of the section on fetishism in *Capital*, for example, he underlines that we need to analyse the commodity in order to see that it is not as 'extremely obvious' as it initially appears to be.[55] He also refers to the insight that

---

capitalistischen Productionsweise eigenthümliche, und aus ihrem Wesen entspringende fetischistische Anschauung, welche ökonomische Formbestimmtheiten, wie *Waare* zu sein, *productive* Arbeit zu sein etc, als den stofflichen Trägern dieser Formbestimmtheiten oder Categorien an und für sich zukommende Eigenschaft betrachtet' (II.4.1: 114f).

53   32: 317.
54   C1: 165f.
55   C1: 163.

exchange value (a relation between commodities) is nothing but the form
of appearance of value (a social relation) as a 'scientific discovery' – and,
as he explains elsewhere, 'all science would be superfluous if the form of
appearance of things directly coincided with their essence'.[56]

Why, then, did Marx write that social relations 'appear as what they
are'? It is not simply an inadvertent mistake; Marx rewrote the analysis of
the commodity many times, and the expression can also be found in the
French edition of *Capital* as well as in the first German edition, although
in a slightly different version.[57] My best guess is that it is a rhetorical figure
employed to emphasise that fetishism is not just a matter of contingent
and subjective confusion but is anchored in the everyday social practices
of capitalist society.

Based on these considerations, I think it is fair to conclude that Marx
regarded fetishism as an *ideological* form. That does not mean that he
regarded it as a result of the manipulation of the ruling classes, or that he
thought it would be possible to eradicate it simply by revealing its treacherous nature. On the contrary, Marx always makes sure to emphasise three
important things about fetishism: first, *everyone* – capitalists, economists,
proletarians, and so on – is subjected to it. Second, scientific analysis 'by
no means banishes the semblance of objectivity'.[58] Third, fetishism 'springs
from the peculiar social character of labour which produces commodities',
and not from an evil plan of the ruling classes.[59]

Fetishism is thus an *ideological* inversion of a *real* inversion. In capitalist
society, relations between people take the form of relations between things.
This does not mean that they stop being relations between people; it means
that social relations are *mediated* by relations among things. This is not
an ideological phenomenon, but a *practical* inversion which constitutes
the basis upon which the *ideological* inversion of fetishism arises – the
'becoming-invisible of mediations', as Gerhard Hanloser and Karl Reitter
call it.[60] In the section on fetishism in the first edition of *Capital*, Marx
explains this double inversion: 'Firstly, their relationship exists practically.
Secondly, however, because they are human beings, *their relationship
exists as a relationship for them*. The way in which it exists for them or

56   C1: 167; M: 766.
57   II.7: 54; V: 37.
58   C1: 167.
59   C1: 165.
60   Hanloser and Reitter, *Der bewegte Marx*, 30.

is reflected in their brain springs from the nature of the relationship itself.'[61]

The fact that Marx uses a term in a certain sense is hardly in itself an argument against other uses of it. We might, of course, choose to begin to use the concept of fetishism to refer to the practical inversion and invent a new term for its ideological representation. However, in order not to makes the terminology unnecessarily complicated by having to deal with two different senses of fetishism, and in order to be able to distinguish between the practical inversion of social relations and the ideological naturalisation of it, I prefer to follow what I take to be Marx's use of the concept of fetishism.[62]

Postone's Interpretation

One of the most influential and original attempts to provide a detailed and systematic account of the impersonal and abstract form of domination characteristic of capitalist societies is Moishe Postone's *Time, Labor, and Social Domination*. While I agree with his general description of capitalist domination and find many of his arguments compelling and illuminating, I also think that his account of the power of capital suffers

---

61   V: 36.

62   In order to conceptualise the practical and the ideological inversion a number of authors distinguish between *fetish-character* and *fetishism* or *fetish* and *fetishism*: Thomas Marxhausen, 'Zum Zusammenhang von Fetischismus, Entfremdung und Ideologie bei Marx', *Deutsche Zeitschrift für Philosohie* 35, no. 12 (1987); Thomas Marxhausen, 'Die Theorie des Fetischismus im dritten Band des *Kapitals*', *Marx-Engels-Forschung* 25 (1988); Thomas Marxhausen, 'Die Entwicklung des Begriffs Fetichismus bei Marx, *Marx-Engels-Forschung* 22 (1988); Hans G. Ehrbar, 'Glossary to Marx's *Capital* and Other Economic Writings', 2010, 214ff, available at http://content.csbs.utah.edu/~ehrbar/glossary.pdf; Riccardo Bellofiore, 'Lost in Translation: Once Again on the Marx-Hegel Connection', in *Marx's* Capital *and Hegel's* Logic: *A Reexamination*, ed. Fred Moseley and Tony Smith (Leiden: Brill, 2014), 177f; Chris Arthur, 'The Practical Truth of Abstract Labour', in *In Marx's Laboratory: Critical Interpretations of the* Grundrisse, ed. Riccardo Bellofiore, Guido Starosta, and Peter D. Thomas (Chicago: Haymarket, 2013), 117; and Guido Schulz, 'Marx's Distinction between the Fetish Character of the Commodity and Fetishism', *Studies in Social and Political Thought* 20 (2012). Some of them also claim that such a distinction can be found in Marx's text. Elsewhere, I have demonstrated that Marx does not make such a distinction, that it leads to contradictions or tautologies if applied to Marx's text, and that there are no good reasons for introducing it. See Mau, 'Den dobbelte fordrejning', 112ff.

from a number of shortcomings, the analysis of which will help to carry
the analysis of the economic power of capital further.

On 'its most fundamental level', the capitalist form of domination
identified by Marx does not, so Postone argues, 'consist in the domination
of people by other people, but in the domination of people by abstract
social structures that people themselves constitute'.[63] In his view, *class*
domination in capitalism is a *secondary* form of domination, an effect
of an underlying structural compulsion to which *everyone* is subjected.
Postone shares this idea with other value-form theorists, as I will discuss
in more detail in the next chapter. For now, though, I want to examine
Postone's interpretation of the concept of value, which he takes to express
'the very heart of capitalist society'.[64] One of the many errors of what he
calls traditional Marxism is to have conceived of value as a 'category of
the market' or a 'mode of distribution'.[65] According to such an interpretation, value is a social form which has to do only with what happens
after the production process, when the products of labour are distributed
through market exchange. Against this, Postone points out that value 'is
intrinsically related to a historically specific mode of production'.[66] The
organisation of social production on the basis of value has dramatic effects
on 'the concrete form of the labor process', as it sets in motion an 'abstract
temporal compulsion' which organises production 'according to the most
efficient possible use of human labor engaged in increasingly specialized
and fragmented tasks for the end of greater productivity'.[67] This perspective
allows Postone to undercut (what he perceives as) the traditional Marxist
view of the revolutionary overthrow of capitalism as 'a transformation of
the mode of distribution (private property, the market), but not of production'.[68] Against the 'affirmative attitude towards industrial production'
in traditional Marxism – the forces bursting through the fetters – Postone
emphasises that Marx's 'conception of emancipation includes the historical
overcoming of the labor process molded by capital'.[69]

Postone's emphasis on the effects of value on the labour process is an
important corrective to the techno-optimistic idea of capitalist production

---

63   Postone, *Time, Labor, and Social Domination*, 31.
64   Ibid., 25.
65   Ibid., 24, 8.
66   Ibid., 25.
67   Ibid., 353.
68   Ibid., 9.
69   Ibid., 9, 334.

as the germ of communism. Indeed, value as a social form is not just a matter of the connection between the units of production and the distribution of wealth, but also has to do with the concrete form of the labour process. His eagerness to avoid market-centred interpretations of value, however, leads him into a number of aporias and ambiguities. For instance, in his attempt to substantiate his claim that value is not a category of the market, he quotes the following passage from a 'crucially important section of the *Grundrisse*':[70] 'The exchange of living labour for objectified labour – i.e., the positing of social labour in the form of the contradiction of capital and wage labour – is the ultimate development of the *value-relation* and of production resting on value.'[71] He then offers this gloss:

> We have seen that value, as a category of wealth, generally has been conceived of as a category of the market; yet when Marx refers to 'exchange' in the course of considering the 'value relation' in the passages quoted,[72] he does so with regards to the capitalist process of production itself. The exchange to which he refers is not that of circulation, but of production – 'the exchange of living labour for objectified labour'.[73]

This is a puzzling interpretation. Why should we read 'the exchange of living labour for objectified labour' as a reference to the production process? And what does 'exchange of production' mean? Postone seems to regard this reading as self-evident. Could it be that he interprets this 'exchange' as what Marx refers to as the metabolism between humans and nature? There are three reasons why this is unlikely: first, Marx almost never uses the term exchange (*Austausch*) in reference to production.[74] Second, metabolism is not a relation between living and objectified

---

70   Ibid., 24.

71   G: 704.

72   The other passage is the headline of the section from the *Grundrisse* to which Postone refers: 'Contradictions between the *foundation* [Postone's emphasis] of bourgeois production (*value as measure*) and its development' (G: 704).

73   Postone, *Time, Labor, and Social Domination*, 24.

74   As far as I know, Marx only employs 'exchange' in this sense once, in a highly specific context and with the intention of underlining the *difference* between the exchange of commodities and the sphere of production (30: 358). In the MECW it is possible to find several passages where Marx writes about 'the exchange of matter between man and nature' (24: 553; 35: 53, 194), but this is simply a bad translation of *Stoffwechsel*.

labour, but rather a relation between labour, the instruments of labour, and the object of labour. Third, to understand 'the exchange of living labour for objectified labour' as metabolism would imply precisely the kind of transhistorical notion of labour Postone wants to avoid. Another, more likely possibility is that Postone takes 'objectified labour' to mean machinery. The exchange of living for objectified labour would then mean the interaction between labour and machinery in the sphere of production. But this is simply a misunderstanding of Marx's text. Again, why would Marx refer to this as an *exchange*? This choice of words seems to suggest that Marx is talking about a *market* relation – an interpretation that is also supported by several passages in which Marx makes it clear that 'objectified labour' refers to *money*. Two examples suffice: 'if a given value is exchanged for the value-creating activity, if objectified labour is exchanged for living labour, in short if money is exchanged for labour'; '*money* as the general form of *objectified labour* becomes the *purchaser* of labour-power'.[75] The passage quoted by Postone in support of his claim that value is not a category of the market thus actually says something entirely different, namely that the *market relation* between capital and labour is 'the ultimate development of the *value-relation*'. The reason for this is, as Marx explains elsewhere, that only with the commodification of labour power does it become possible for the commodity form to 'impose itself upon society as a whole'.[76]

No only does Postone want to correct market-centred conceptions of value and remind us that value is *also* connected to a specific mode of producing; he goes so far as to claim that

> although the market mode of circulation may have been necessary for the historical genesis of the commodity as the totalizing social form, it need not remain essential to that form. It is conceivable that another mode of coordination and generalisation – an administrative one, for example – could serve a similar function for this contradictory social form. In other words, once established, the law of value could also be mediated politically.[77]

---

75   30: 35; R: 1015; see also C1: 676, 713; R: 1009; and 30: 34.
76   C1: 733.
77   Postone, *Time, Labor, and Social Domination*, 291.

The theoretical consequences of this claim are overwhelming, and Postone does not really explain why such a scenario is 'conceivable'. The idea seems to be that the subjection of the labour process to abstract temporality and compulsory productivity increases could, in principle, be enforced by a state-like institution, even if it historically was the result of the market (i.e., the coordination of social production by means of exchange of the products of labour of private producers). This might very well be true, but would we still call such a society 'capitalist'? In an economic system without markets, there would be no commodities, no sale and purchase of labour power, no competition among private producers. If the law of value was mediated politically, as Postone claims it could be, how would producers be forced to live up to certain standards of productivity? Would that not mean that state coercion would come to replace the mute compulsion of the market? If so, in what sense would it still be a system of structural and impersonal domination, in other words, the kind of domination Postone holds to be an essential feature of capitalism?

What Postone does is essentially to re-define capitalism in a manner which bears little resemblance to Marx's conception. For Marx, value is a social form that results from the organisation of social production through the market. That does not mean that he conceives of value as merely a category of the market. Indeed, while value *arises* from the market-mediated relations *between* the units of production, that does not prevent it from having immense *effects* on what goes on *inside* of these units, that is, on the concrete character of the labour process. Changes within the sphere of production, in turn, act on the market. Marx always emphasises that 'the movement of capital is a unity of the process of production and the process of circulation'.[78] The causal relations between the sphere of circulation and the sphere of production run in both directions, and for that reason, we cannot reduce every aspect of capitalism to market relations. But the market still remains an *essential* feature of capitalism for Marx. In contrast to this, Postone's strong emphasis on the mode of production leads him to completely detach the latter from the mode of distribution, which then leads him to identify capitalism with a specific mode of producing, namely large-scale industrial production governed by abstract time. This allows him to do what sometimes seems to be the true aim of his project: to construct a conceptual apparatus capable of providing

---

78   33: 69; M: 49.

a critique of so-called actually existing socialism in the same terms as the critique of capitalism.[79] The price Postone pays for this, however, is a notion of capitalism which is simultaneously too broad and too narrow to have much analytical value: too broad because it detaches capitalism from the market and private property, and too narrow because it ends up identifying capitalism with large-scale industrial production, which is only one of the forms production can take on in capitalism.

---

79   Postone, *Time, Labor, and Social Domination*, 14.

9

Value, Class, and Competition

One of Moishe Postone's recurring criticisms of traditional Marxism is that it conceives of relations of domination in capitalism 'primarily in terms of class domination and exploitation'.[1] As we saw in chapter two, there has indeed been a strong tendency within Marxist theory to reduce the power of capital to the power of the capitalist class. The theory of value examined in the last chapter provides us with a rather different picture of domination in the capitalist mode of production. Recall Marx's answer to the question which political economy never asked: Why do the products of labour take the form of commodities endowed with value? Why does labour take the form of value-producing labour? Marx's answer: because social production is organised on the basis of the exchange of the products of labour of private and independent producers. Value becomes the mechanism through which economic activity is organised because the units of production are *separated from each other while still remaining dependent upon each other*. This explanation proceeds from the horizontal relations among the units of production, and nowhere is class domination or exploitation mentioned. These horizontal relations give rise to an abstract and impersonal form of domination to which *everyone* is subjected, regardless of their class position. In chapter six, however, we learned that the rule of capital presupposes the domination

---

1   Moishe Postone, *Time, Labor, and Social Domination: A Reinterpretation of Marx's Critical Theory* (Cambridge: Cambridge University Press, 2003), 7.

of proletarians by those who own or control the means of production – in other words, that certain vertical class relations of domination are a constitutive feature of capitalist relations of production. In the beginning of the last chapter, I stressed that both of these sets of relations – the horizontal and the vertical – are constitutive of capitalist relations of production. But what is the precise relation between these sets of relations? How is the universal domination of *everyone* by the value form related to the domination of *proletarians* by capitalists?

The Disappearance of Class

Marx's analysis of value as an expression of the horizontal relations among producers has led a number of scholars, including Postone, to downplay the significance of class domination and conclude that the domination of everyone by the value form is the most fundamental form of power in capitalism. One of the earliest examples of such an argument can be found in the writings of Theodor Adorno, who notes that 'everyone must subject themselves to the law of exchange if they do not want to perish, regardless of whether they are led by a "profit motive" or not'.[2] Although Adorno occasionally refers to class domination and emphasises that 'the exchange relation is, in reality, preformed [*präformiert*] by class relations', the dominant tendency in his work is to stress 'the universal domination of mankind by exchange value'.[3] This tendency to downplay the significance of class was taken over by Helmut Reichelt and Hans-Georg Backhaus, both of whom were students of Adorno. This is partly, however, due to the fact that they were more preoccupied with questions of method, dialectics, Marx's relation to Hegel, and the critique of bourgeois economics than with forms of domination.

Perhaps the most aggressive attack on the concept of class domination is found among the adherents of the critique of value (*Wertkritik*). According to Robert Kurz and Ernst Lohoff, 'the commodity form and

---

2 Theodor W. Adorno, 'Gesellschaft', in *Gesammelte Schriften*, vol. 8 (Frankfurt am Main: Suhrkamp, 1972), 14.

3 Theodor W. Adorno, 'Theodor W. Adorno on "Marx and the Basic Concepts of Sociological Theory"', trans. Verena Erlenbusch-Anderson and Chris O'Kane, *Historical Materialism* 26, no. 1 (2018): 158; Theodor W. Adorno, *Negative Dialectics* (New York: Continuum, 2007), 178.

the fetish incorporated in its productive core are the real essential categories [*die wirklichen Wesenskategorien*] of the capital relation – classes and class struggle are the surface appearances of this essence.'[4] In their view, the relation between capitalist and worker is merely a market relation between commodity owners, and the working class is accordingly nothing but the character mask of variable capital.[5] The same idea is defended by Stephan Grigat and Anselm Jappe, who hold the contradiction between 'value and the concrete social activities and needs' to be the 'real, fundamental contradiction' of capitalism, of which class antagonism is merely a *derived* form.[6] Jappe also claims that 'considered logically it is value that leads to the creation of classes.'[7] As mentioned earlier, Postone likewise regards class domination as 'a *function of* a superordinate, "abstract" form of domination.'[8] As Sven Ellmers has noted, the attempt to reduce class domination to a secondary or derived form of the universal domination of value relies – at least in the case of Kurz, Lohoff, and Jappe – on a peculiar misunderstanding of Marx's dialectical mode of presentation.[9] The fact that Marx proceeds from the analysis of the commodity and only introduces class later on, in part two of *Capital*, leads them to the conclusion that value is somehow more fundamental than class relations. What Marx's dialectical analysis reveals, however, is that a certain class structure was, in fact, a *necessary presupposition* from the very beginning. By deriving the necessity of the commodification of

---

4   Robert Kurz and Ernst Lohoff, 'Der Klassenkampf-Fetisch: Thesen zur Entmythologisierung des Marxismus', *krisis: Kritik der Warengesellschaft*, 1989, krisis.org.

5   Robert Kurz, *Geld ohne Wert: Grundrisse zu einer Transformation der Kritik der politischen Ökonomie* (Berlin: Horlemann, 2012), 77, 252, 289; Kurz and Lohoff, 'Der Klassenkampf-Fetisch'.

6   Stephan Grigat, *Fetisch und Freiheit: Über die Rezeption der Marxschen Fetischkritik, die Emanzipation von Staat und Kapital und die Kritik des Antisemitismus* (Frankfurt: ca ira, 2007), 208ff. Anselm Jappe, *Die Abenteuer der Ware: Für eine neue Wertkritik* (Münster: Unrast Verlag, 2005), 80ff, 95.

7   Jappe, *Die Abenteuer der Ware*, 76.

8   Postone, *Time, Labor, and Social Domination*, 126, 159. Emphasis added. See also Marcel van der Linden, *Workers of the World: Essays toward a Global Labor History* (Leiden: Brill, 2008), 39, where he refers to Kurz, Lohoff, and Postone when he declares that he follows 'those authors who give the value form, and not class contradictions, central place in their analysis of capitalism'.

9   Sven Ellmers, *Die formanalytische Klassentheorie von Karl Marx: Ein Beitrag zur 'neuen Marx-Lektüre'*, 2nd ed. (Duisburg: Universitätverlag Rhein-Ruhr, 2009), 46. See also Ingo Elbe's critique of Kurz, Lohoff and Postone: *Marx im Westen: Die neue Marx-lektüre in der Bundesrepublik seit 1965* (Berlin: Akademie Verlag, 2008), 514ff.

labour power from the commodity form through a series of intermediary steps, Marx demonstrates, in Ellmers's words, that 'the existence of classes is just as necessary for the universalisation of commodity production as the existence of private producers who are independent of each other'.[10] I have analysed this series of dialectical derivations in detail elsewhere, but, in order to be able to specify the relationship between the horizontal and the vertical aspects of the power of capital, it is necessary to briefly recapitulate the core of Marx's argument.[11]

No Value without Class

As mentioned earlier, Marx's analysis of the commodity form reveals that in order for it to become generalised, value must gain an independent and autonomous form of existence. This is what is apparently achieved with *money*. What Marx then goes on to demonstrate, however, is that money is in fact *not* capable of fulfilling this task as long as it is confined to the functions ascribed to it within simple circulation. When money and commodities circulate in the form $C–M–C$, money is only a 'vanishing mediation' between use values, which means that value 'is realized only in the moment of its disappearance'.[12] If money is withdrawn from circulation as a hoard in order to avoid this disappearance, however, it regresses to 'its metallic being, with its economic being annihilated'.[13] The upshot of this analysis of the contradiction of the money form is that value and commodities must circulate in the form $M–C–M$ in order for value to obtain an '*adequate existence*'; 'Its entry into circulation must itself be an element of its staying with itself [*Beisichbleiben*], and its staying with itself must be an entry into circulation.'[14] This form of circulation only makes sense if the second sum of money is larger than the first: $M–C–M'$. We have thereby obtained the concept of capital, but still only in the sense of a *form of circulation*, that is, as value '*maintaining and perpetuating itself in and through circulation*'.[15] Marx then poses the crucial question: How

10   Ellmers, *Die formanalytische Klassentheorie*, 46.
11   Søren Mau, 'The Transition to Capital in Marx's Critique of Political Economy', *Historical Materialism* 26, no. 1 (2018): 68–102.
12   G: 269, 260.
13   29: 479.
14   29: 488; G: 234.
15   G: 262.

is this form of circulation possible as more than an occasional fraud, given that the generalisation of the commodity form presupposes that the exchange of equivalents is the normal situation on the market? The well-known answer to this question is that such a situation requires the existence of a commodity whose very consumption is a source of value, in other words, that *labour power* is available on the market.[16] Since the consumption of labour power is labour itself, Marx can thereby derive capitalist *production* from capital as a form of *circulation*. The availability of labour power on the market presupposes, as we saw in the last chapter, the creation of the proletarian life cut off from its conditions. This carefully crafted dialectical analysis yields an important conclusion:

> Simple circulation is … an abstract sphere of the bourgeois process of production as a whole, which through its own determinations shows itself to be a moment, a mere form of appearance of some deeper process lying behind it, even resulting from it and producing it – industrial capital.[17]

Put differently, the *external* relations *between* the units of production, from which the theory of value proceeds, presuppose a certain *internal* organisation of these units, namely the production of surplus value on the basis of the exploitation of wage labour. The separation between the units of production presupposes the separation between the immediate producers and the means of production, or, the horizontal relations presuppose the vertical relations analysed in chapter six. Or, yet again, boiled down to the essentials: *value presupposes class*. Indeed, class domination is inscribed in the commodity form from the very first page of *Capital*.

Many value-form theorists acknowledge this necessary relation between value and class, yet many of them nevertheless continue to give priority to the universal domination of value in their accounts of capitalism. Ingo Elbe and Sven Ellmers both acknowledge the relation between value and class, and both of them criticise Kurz's reduction of class to a form of appearance of value – yet, in their introduction to a volume entitled *Anonymous Domination* (co-authored with Jan Eufinger), the existence

---

16   C1: 258ff.
17   29: 482.

of capitalist class domination is only mentioned in a footnote, whereas they put great emphasis on 'the domination of structures over all actors of bourgeois society'.[18] A similar tendency is visible in Michael Heinrich's work. In his magnum opus, *Die Wissenschaft vom Wert*, classes are scarcely mentioned except in the four pages explicitly devoted to the subject.[19] In his reply to Karl Reitter's critique of his conception of class struggle, he argues that class domination is a derived form of a more fundamental form of domination:

> The critique of political economy as Marx understood it after 1857 is in any case not 'substantially class analysis' [as Reitter claims], it consists rather in the analysis of economic form determinations, under which humans act, and which therefore also underlies the actions of classes [*die also auch den Aktionen der Klassen zugrunde liegen*].[20]

The 'form determinations' of which Heinrich speaks here presumably refer to the structures of domination implied by the commodity form, and Heinrich goes on to emphasise that the ruling classes are also subjected to this domination of things. In other places, however, Heinrich is clear about the fact that value is only possible on the basis of class domination.[21]

---

18 Elbe, *Marx im Westen*, 516; Ellmers, *Die formanalytische Klassentheorie*; Ingo Elbe, Sven Ellmers, and Jan Eufinger, 'Einleitung', in *Anonyme Herrschaft: Zur Struktur moderner Machtverhältnisse*, ed. Ingo Elbe, Sven Ellmers, and Jan Eufinger (Münster: Westfälisches Dampfboot, 2012), 8.

19 Michael Heinrich, *Die Wissenschaft vom Wert: Die Marxsche Kritik der politischen Ökonomie zwischen wissenschaftlicher Revolution und klassischer Tradition* (Münster: Westfälisches Dampfboot, 1999), 263–67; see also Michael Heinrich, 'Welche Klassen und welche Kämpfe? Eine Antwort auf Karl Reitters "Kapitalismus ohne Klassenkampf?"', *grundrisse: zeitschrift für linke theorie & debatte*, no. 11 (2004); Michael Heinrich, *An Introduction to the Three Volumes of Karl Marx's Capital* (New York: Monthly Review Press, 2012), 191; Michael Heinrich, 'Individuum, Personifikation und unpersönliche Herrschaft in Marx' Kritik der politischen Ökonomie', in Elbe, Ellmers, and Eufinger, *Anonyme Herrschaft*; Michael Heinrich, *Wie das Marxsche 'Kapital' lesen? Leseanleitung und Kommentar zum Anfang des 'Kapital'*, vol. 1, 2nd ed. (Stuttgart: Schmetterling Verlag, 2009), 181.

20 Karl Reitter, 'Kapitalismus ohne Klassenkampf? Zu Michael Heinrich, "Kritik der politischen Ökonomie"', *grundrisse: zeitschrift für linke theorie & debatte*, no. 11 (2004), grundrisse.net.

21 Heinrich, *An Introduction*, 91f.

Bringing Class Back In

Werner Bonefeld occupies a distinctive place in the value-form theoretical landscape in that he insists on the importance of the concept of class
in Marx's critique of capital. He explicitly refuses the 'courageous but
unsuccessful attempt to banish the class antagonism from the critique of
political economy' in the work of Postone and the *Neue Marx-Lektüre*.[22]
Bonefeld also acknowledges that a 'class of labourers with no independent access to the means of subsistence is the fundamental premise of
the capitalist social relations'.[23] The problem is, however, that Bonefeld
has a rather peculiar understanding of what class is. He tends to simply
subsume class relations under the fetishistic inversions of social relations,
as when he argues that 'at its best, Marx's critique of political economy
does not amount to a social theory of class. It amounts, rather, to a
critique of "capital" as a "social relationship between persons which is
mediated through things"'.[24] His texts are marked by a repetitive rhetoric
of 'inversion', 'perversion', 'reification', 'madness', 'absurdity', 'mystification', 'monstrosity', and 'irrationality', as well as the 'puzzling', 'occult',
'enchanted', and 'topsy-turvy' world of value – expressions and tropes
that all refer to fetishism and the universal domination of value. Some of
his statements about class are merely rhetorical variations on such tropes,
with 'fetish' or 'inversion' replaced with 'class': 'A critical theory of class
does not partake in the classification of people; it thinks in and through
society to comprehend its existing untruth'; 'Class … is a category of
a perverse form of social objectification'.[25] Bonefeld pays lip service to
the connection between value and class, but in the end, his analysis first
and foremost presents capitalism as a perverted system where the absurd
movements of economic things dominate everyone.

In his interpretation of *Capital* as a political theory concerned with
'the rule of capital as a complex and world-spanning system of domination', William Clare Roberts agrees with Heinrich, Elbe, and others that
'the impersonal domination embodied in the market is not a form of

---

22   Werner Bonefeld, 'On Postone's Courageous but Unsuccessful Attempt to Banish
the Class Antagonism from the Critique of Political Economy', *Historical Materialism*
12, no. 3 (2004): 103–24; Werner Bonefeld, *Critical Theory and the Critique of Political
Economy* (London: Bloomsbury, 2014), 7.

23   Bonefeld, *Critical Theory*, 11, 79.

24   Ibid., 101.

25   Ibid., 10, 114, 101f.

class domination. Instead, the dominant class in modernity, the class of capitalists, is as subject to this impersonal domination as are the laboring classes.'[26] At the same time, however, he underlines – with a quote from Marx – that this form of domination 'does not abolish class domination. Just as it encompasses and mediates a novel form of exploitation, the modern "domination of relationships" is also "transformed into certain personal relationships of dependence" within the workplace.'[27] This is indeed an important aspect of the relation between value and class, to which I will return in a moment. There are, however, two problems with Roberts's conception of the connection between value and class: first, his description of class domination in terms of exploitation taking place in the workplace overlooks the much more encompassing class domination presupposed by value (the form of class domination analysed in chapter six of this book); second, the idea that class domination is a 'transformed' form of the universal domination of all by value seems to hold on to the claim that the latter is *primary* in relation to the former.

It should, of course, be borne in mind that many of the authors discussed in the last couple of pages are – or at least have been until quite recently – swimming against the tide of the traditional Marxist reduction of the power of capital to the power of the capitalist class. Seen in that light, the strong emphasis on the mechanisms through which capital imposes itself on the social totality is a much-needed theoretical intervention. Indeed, the tendency to posit class domination as the ultimate ground of the rule of capital – or the tendency to regard the horizontal relations as an effect of the vertical – is found in many kinds of Marxism apart from orthodox historical materialism and Marxism–Leninism. A sophisticated defence of it can even be found in a major work of value-form theory, namely Helmut Brentel's *Soziale Form und ökonomisches Objekt*:

> Economic form should therefore be understood as the form of reflection and activity of a specific class opposition in relation to labour [Ökonomische *Form ist so als die Reflexions- und Betätigungsform eines spezifischen Klassensgegensatzes an der Arbeit zu begreifen*] … The doubled categories of bourgeois economics – use value and exchange

---

26   William Clare Roberts, *Marx's Inferno: The Political Theory of* Capital (Princeton: Princeton University Press, 2017), 1, 102.

27   Ibid., 102. The passage quoted by Roberts is from G: 164. Translation amended by Roberts.

value, commodity and money, concrete and abstract labour – are adequate expressions, consistent forms of reflection and mediation of the oppositions and antagonisms of wage labour and capital, the opposition of two social classes.[28]

This is the exact opposite position of the one taken by the authors discussed in the preceding pages, for whom class domination is a 'function' (Postone), a 'form of appearance' (Kurz, Lohoff), or a 'derived' (Jappe) or 'transformed' (Roberts) form of the deeper-lying domination embedded in value relations. This idea is also prevalent among autonomist Marxists, such as Harry Cleaver,[29] who holds that 'the commodity-form is the basic form of the class relation' or Reitter, whose critique of the disappearance of class in the works of Heinrich, Kurz, Postone, and others leads him towards the opposite extreme. On a lower level of abstraction – dealing with competition rather than value – John Weeks likewise insists that 'competition does not derive from the existence of many capitals ("companies"), but from the capital relation itself'.[30]

---

28   Helmut Brentel, *Soziale Form und ökonomisches Objekt: Studien zum Gegenstands- und Methodenverständnis der Kritik der politischen Ökonomie* (Wiesbaden: Springer Fachmedien Wiesbaden, 1989), 270.

29   Harry Cleaver, *Reading* Capital *Politically* (Leeds: Anti/Theses; Oakland: AK Press, 2000), 84. See Gerhard Hanloser and Karl Reitter, *Der bewegte Marx: Eine einführende Kritik des Zirkulationsmarxismus* (Münster: Unrast Verlag, 2008); Reitter, 'Kapitalismus ohne Klassenkampf?'; Karl Reitter, 'Vorwort', in *Karl Marx: Philosoph der Befreiung oder Theoretiker des Kapitals? Zur Kritik der 'Neuen Marx-Lektüre'*, ed. Karl Reitter (Wien: Mandelbaum Verlag, 2015); Karl Reitter, 'Rubin, Backhaus und in Anschluss Heinrich – Wegbereiter der Neuen Marx-Lektüre: Oder was mit dem Vorwurf des "Naturalismus" an die Adresse von Marx eigentlich transportiert wird', in *Karl Marx*; Karl Reitter, '"There Is a Tendency to Fetishize the Fetish": An Interview with Karl Reitter', *Viewpoint Magazine*, 6 October 2015, viewpointmag.com. See also the contributions to the volume edited by Reitter, especially Jürgen Albohn, 'Eine kurze Kritik der Wertkritik'; Tobias Brugger, 'Die ideologische Lesart der Neuen Marx-Lektüre als Totengräber radikaler Kritik'; Andreas Exner, 'Zur Relevanz von klassenteoretischen Analysen heute: Reflexionen einer wertformkritischen Perspektive'.

30   John Weeks, *Capital and Exploitation* (Princeton: Princeton University Press, 1981), 151.

Distinct, yet Interrelated

Both of these positions are, in my view, incorrect: *class cannot be reduced to an effect of value relations, nor can value be reduced to a result of class domination.* What, then, is the relation between the horizontal and vertical dimensions of the capitalist relations of production? We already know that *value presupposes class*; this is what we learned from Marx's dialectical derivation of the concept of capital from the immanent contradictions of simple circulation. The opposite is not true, however: *the separation between the producers and the means of production does not presuppose value.* Put differently: it is perfectly possible to conceive of a situation in which the immediate producers are separated from the means of production but where there is no production for the market.[31] Imagine a mode of production in which the immediate producers are separated from the means of production and the ruling class is organised into several independent units. Rather than producing for the market, however, these units would produce for themselves (i.e., for the consumption of the ruling classes as well as that of the workers). Workers would be paid in kind and provided with housing, health care, and so on by their employer. They would be free to choose their own employer, and depending on the supply of labour power, the employers would compete for workers by offering them better working conditions, working hours, quality of housing, and so on. What this thought experiment tells us is that a relation of exploitation based on the dispossession of the immediate producers does not necessarily imply that the ruling class is split into interdependent units of production relating to each other through a market. *Value presupposes class, but class does not presuppose value.*

This conclusion might seem to support the idea that class domination is primary, but this is not the case. To claim that class is a *presupposition* or a *condition* of value is not to claim that value is an immediate *effect* of class domination. As the thought experiment in the preceding paragraph demonstrated, value cannot be derived from the separation between the producers and the means of production. Class domination is, in other words, a *necessary* yet *insufficient* condition of value. Although the relationship between the horizontal and the vertical relations is not symmetrical,

---

31   Endnotes, 'Error', in *Endnotes 5: The Passions and the Interests* (London: Endnotes, 2020), 119.

since the latter is the precondition of the former, they nevertheless retain a certain logical autonomy from each other in the sense that they are *irreducible*; neither of them can be said to be an effect of the other. The same goes for the mechanisms of domination which spring from them. *The horizontal and the vertical relations constitutive of the capitalist relations of production must therefore be recognised as two interrelated yet distinct sources of the power of capital.*

In order to understand the economic power of capital, however, it is not enough to point out the logical irreducibility of the horizontal and the vertical relations. We also need to consider how their interaction affects the mechanisms of domination springing from them. The insight that horizontal relations among market agents presuppose class domination allows us to see these relations from a new (class) perspective: it '*dispels* the illusion [*Schein*] of *relations between commodity owners*' by revealing that the apparent equality between market agents was merely the result of abstracting from everything that takes place outside of the act of exchange:[32]

> The two people who face each other on the marketplace, in the sphere of circulation, are not just a *buyer* and a *seller*, but *capitalist* and *worker* who confront each other as *buyer* and *seller*. Their relationship as *capitalist* and *worker* is the presupposition [*Voraussetzung*] of their relationship as *buyer and seller*.[33]

However, as Marx immediately goes on to add, the class relation does not – contrary to the claims of those who regard class domination as a derived form – spring 'directly from the nature of the commodity, i.e., that no one immediately produces the products they need in order to live, so that each producer produces a specific product as a *commodity* which he then sells in order to acquire the products of others'.[34] The market relation between the worker and the capitalist reveals itself to be nothing but a '*mediating form*' of the '*subjugation by capital*'; it demonstrates that

---

32   R: 1063.

33   R: 1015; see also 10: 589f.

34   R: 1015. Note that Ben Fowkes's translation of this passage – which is admittedly difficult to translate into readable English – is somewhat confusing. See the original in MEGA2 II.4.1: 89f.

in reality, the worker belongs to capital *before* he has sold himself to the capitalist. His *economic* bondage is at once *mediated through, and concealed by*, the periodical renewal of the act by which he sells himself, his change of individual wage-masters [*Lohnherrn*], and the oscillations in the market-price of his labour.[35]

Capitalist class domination – that is, the vertical relations between the exploiters and the exploited – is mediated by the horizontal relations among the units of production. Put differently: *proletarians are subjected to capitalists by means of a mechanism of domination which simultaneously subjects everyone to the imperatives of capital*. At the same, the 'subjection [*Unterordnung*] of the worker to the product of labour, the [subjection of the] value-creating power to value' is, as Marx explains in a manuscript for the second book of *Capital*, 'mediated (appears in) through the *relation of compulsion and domination* between the capitalist (the personification of capital) and the worker'.[36] This is what gives capitalist class domination its distinctive impersonal and abstract character, and this is why it is so misguided to equate class domination as such with personal relations of domination or to oppose it to 'abstract' domination, as Kurz, Jappe, and Postone do.[37]

We now know that the market is *itself* a mechanism of domination, and that it also *relies* on class domination. But, as I mentioned briefly at the beginning of this chapter, there is even more to it. Not only do the capitalist and the worker *enter* the market in different ways and for different reasons (the capitalist in order to make a profit, the worker in order to survive); they also *leave* it in significantly different ways. After the exchange, the 'buyer takes command of the seller' in the production process, and yet another 'relation of domination and servitude' comes into existence.[38] So, while it is certainly true that the capitalist is 'just as much under the yoke of the capital-relation as is the worker', it is crucial to add that *the universal domination of the market affects workers and*

---

35   C1: 724. Emphasis added.

36   II.11: 21f, 572.

37   See Kurz, *Geld ohne Wert*, 77, 252, 289; Jappe, *Die Abenteuer der Ware*, 82, 87; Postone, *Time, Labor, and Social Domination*, 30, 126, 159. See also R: 1032; Elbe, *Marx im Westen*, 516.

38   30: 106.

capitalists in fundamentally different ways.[39] Ellen Meiksins Wood puts it well: 'What the "abstract" laws of capitalist accumulation compel the capitalist to do – and what the impersonal laws of the labour market enable him to do – is precisely to exercise an unprecedented degree of control over production.'[40] In other words, the mutual mediation of the horizontal and the vertical relations of domination gives rise to *another dimension of class domination*, namely relations of domination *within the workplace*. This is the subject of chapter ten. Yet, before we get to that, we have to go through the horizontal relations once more, but this time in another and more concrete form: as *competition*.

Systematic Confusion

The transition from simple circulation to capitalist production in the second part of *Capital* marks a shift of focus from what happens *between* the units of production to what takes place *inside* of them in the production process. That does not mean, however, that everything which needs to be said about the horizontal relations can be found in the first part of *Capital*. Here, it is important to bear in mind that the dialectical progression of categories in *Capital* (and similar writings) is not a linear series in which every category is constructed, rounded off, and closed down before we move on to the next. Against such a 'building block' approach, as David Harvey calls it, we should insist on what Endnotes refer to as the 'bi-directionality of systematic dialectics.'[41] What this means is that there is always a retroactive constitution of meaning at play in the development of categories; we thus have to continually reinterpret earlier categories in the light of subsequent conceptual developments. This is what the concept of competition accomplishes in relation to the concept of value: they refer to the same relations, namely the horizontal relations among market agents – only on different levels of abstraction. What initially, in the first chapters of *Capital*, appear simply as private and independent producers

---

39   30: 399.

40   David Harvey, *The Limits to Capital* (London: Verso, 2006), 2f; Ellie Meiksins Wood, *Democracy against Capitalism: Renewing Historical Materialism* (London: Verso, 2016), 41.

41   Endnotes, 'The Moving Contradiction: The Systematic Dialectic of Capital as a Dialectic of Class Struggle', in *Endnotes 2: Misery and the Value Form* (London: Endnotes, 2010), 116.

are later revealed to be capitalist companies exploiting wage labour. With this insight in mind, we can then revisit the horizontal relations and re-conceptualise them as *competition* between capitalist companies as well as between proletarians who sell their labour power.

Although Marx discusses competition in the *1844 Manuscripts*, it was not until the *Auseinandersetzung* with Proudhon in 1846–47 that he really began to appreciate its crucial role in capitalist society. This development is reflected in *The Poverty of Philosophy*, where he argues that competition '*implements* the law according to which the relative value of a product is determined by the labour time needed to produce it'.[42] This phrasing resembles a conclusion Marx would later come to regard as absolutely crucial, namely that competition *executes* the laws of capital but does not *create* them. In spite of this, however, Marx by and large follows political economy at this stage in his development; he assumes competition to be an unproblematic analytical point of departure, regarding it as a kind of prime mover that explains the dynamics of capitalism. In *Wage Labour and Capital*, for example, he suggests that the movement of wages as well as the development of the productive forces can be explained with reference to competition.[43] A decisive breakthrough occurs in the *Grundrisse*, where Marx realises that competition does not explain the laws of movement of capital; it merely *executes* them in the form of 'reciprocal compulsion'.[44] This leads him to draw an analytical distinction between *capital in general* and *many capitals* or *competition*, a distinction he employs as an architectural principle for the 'book on capital' in his six-book plan.[45] The analysis in the *Grundrisse* nevertheless leaves much to be desired, and Marx makes important headway when he returns to the topic in the *1861–63 Manuscripts*. In these manuscripts, we find the first analysis of the relation between competition and the production of relative surplus value, as well as Marx's first attempt to explain the distribution of surplus value and the formation of a general rate of profit on the basis of competition. The insights yielded by this analysis also allow him to unravel the ways in which competition provides the basis for ideological obfuscations of the inner mechanisms of capitalist production. The *1861–63 Manuscripts*

---

42 6: 135. Emphasis added.
43 Heinrich, *Die Wissenschaft vom Wert*, 181.
44 G: 651; see Heinrich, *Die Wissenschaft vom Wert*, 182.
45 Roman Rosdolsky, *The Making of Marx's 'Capital'* (London: Pluto Press, 1977), 41ff.

are also where the distinction between 'capital in general' and the 'many capitals' begins to break down.[46] The insights of the *1861–63 Manuscripts* are then refined in the *1864–65 Manuscript* for the third book of *Capital*, which seems to be Marx's last substantial discussion of competition, apart from a few passages in volume one of *Capital*.[47]

One of the unresolved issues in Marx's critique of political economy is the question of where to introduce competition in the systematic structure of the theory. The concept crops up here and there, sometimes prefaced with a comment about how 'it is not our intention here to consider the way in which the immanent laws of capitalist production manifest them-selves in the external movement of the individual capitals,' but that 'we may' nevertheless 'add the following comments' – followed by 'comments' which are not only quite substantial, but even *necessary* for the further development of the argument.[48] Several scholars have rightly pointed out that intra-branch competition has an explanatory role in the chapters on relative surplus value in the first volume of *Capital*.[49]

In a certain sense, however, competition is actually present from the very beginning of *Capital* – not in the banal sense that the dialectical unfolding of categories implies that everything is always present from the beginning but in the sense that the horizontal relations among producers in chapter one is, as I have already explained, nothing other than what is later termed 'competition'. Marx seems to suggest as much in the *Ergän-zungen und Veränderungen* to the second edition of *Capital*, where he notes that the general level of 'intensity' and 'skills' determining socially necessary labour time is regulated by competition.[50] Since the capital

---

46   Alex Callinicos, *Deciphering* Capital: *Marx's* Capital *and Its Destiny* (London: Bookmarks, 2014), 139f; Michael Heinrich, 'Capital in General and the Structure of Marx's *Capital*', *Capital and Class* 13, no. 2 (1989): 63–79; Heinrich, *Die Wissenschaft vom Wert*, 185ff.

47   See Joachim Bischoff and Christoph Lieber, 'Konkurrenz und Gesellschaftkritik: Mehrwert und Profitratensteuerung im Marxschen Forschungs- und Darstellungsproz-ess ('Heft Ultimum')', in *Kapital und Kritik: Nach der 'neuen' Marx-Lektüre*, ed. Werner Bonefeld and Michael Heinrich (Hamburg: VSA, 2011).

48   C1: 433; see Jacques Bidet, *Exploring Marx's Capital: Philosophical, Economic, and Political Dimensions* (Leiden: Brill, 2007), 145; Callinicos, *Deciphering* Capital, 141f.

49   See Bidet, *Exploring Marx's Capital*, 145; Callinicos, *Deciphering* Capital, 140; Diane Elson, 'The Value Theory of Labour', in *Value: The Representation of Labour in Capitalism*, ed. Diane Elson (London: Verso, 2015), 168; Maria Daniela Giammanco, 'Competition and Technical Progress in Marx: Two Different Perspectives', *History of Economic Ideas* 10, no. 2 (2002): 73.

50   II.6: 31.

form has not been introduced at this point, it is assumed that the aim of exchange is use value, and for this reason, we are not exactly dealing with competition in the full sense of the term. Nevertheless, the equalising function of exchange in chapter one clearly resembles the kind of equalisation mechanisms revealed by the analysis of competition.[51]

The overall systematic structure of Marx's treatment of competition thus seems to look something like this: it first appears implicitly in the theory of value, but only in its general function as a mechanism of equalisation which regulates social production. It then appears as *intra*-branch competition, later in volume one, in order to help explain the production of relative surplus value and the tendency towards a rising organic composition of capital. Even later in the same volume, it crops up again in order to explain the concentration and centralisation of capital. In the third book, it first appears as *inter*-branch competition in order to explain the formation of a general rate of profit and the objective basis of ideological mystification. Finally, the interaction of intra- and inter-branch competition – in other words, the combination of the tendency of rising organic composition of capital with the distribution of surplus value – explains the tendency of the rate of profit to fall (or so Marx thinks – more on this in chapter thirteen). In a significant passage in the manuscript for the third book of *Capital* (written before volume one), Marx writes that 'the actual movement of competition, etc., lies outside of our plan, and we only need to present the internal organisation of the capitalist mode of production in its ideal average, so to speak'.[52] Although it is not entirely clear what Marx means by 'the actual movement', I think the most convincing reading is that it refers to empirical or historical analysis.[53] On this interpretation, all of the aspects of competition referred to in this paragraph belong to the analysis of capitalism in its ideal average.

The Executor

So, what is competition? In its broadest sense, it is a relation between two social agents striving to obtain the same goal: 'whoever says competition

---

51   See Bidet, *Exploring Marx's* Capital, 141; Patrick Murray, *The Mismeasure of Wealth: Essays on Marx and Social Form* (Leiden: Brill, 2016), 167.

52   M: 898; see also 33: 101.

53   See Heinrich, 'Capital in General and the Structure of Marx's Capital'.

says common aim,' as Marx writes in *The Poverty of Philosophy*.[54] For this reason, and contrary to what a number of scholars argue, the relation between capital and labour is not a relation of competition.[55] The worker and the capitalist are engaged in two very different projects; whereas the worker finds herself 'in the relation of simple circulation' and 'only receives money as *coin*, i.e., merely a transitory form of the means of subsistence', the capitalist is accumulating capital.[56] Competition is an *intra*-class relation which exists among capitalists as well as among workers – or, put differently: competition is a relation between sellers, regardless of the kind of commodities they offer.

As previously noted, Marx emphasises that competition 'executes the inner laws of capital; makes them into compulsory laws towards the individual capital, but … does not invent them. It realizes them.'[57] This means that capital cannot be understood *solely* on the basis of the horizontal relations among producers, but it also means that it cannot be understood *without* reference to these relations – after all, they are the mechanism by means of which the laws of capital are *realised*. Competition is 'the inner *nature* of capital, its essential character, appearing in and realized as the reciprocal interaction of many capitals with one another, the inner tendency as external necessity'.[58] Capital can therefore 'only exist as many capitals', and in this sense, the relation between capitals is in fact nothing but 'the relation of capital to itself'.[59]

Competition is a universalising mechanism, a transmitter of compulsory commands expressed in the language of prices. Producers are free to produce whatever they want (within boundaries set by law or custom), and purchasers are free to choose who they want to buy from, so producers are forced to react to prices set by other producers. In a certain sense, competition is a deeply Platonic mechanism: it treats every particular capital as

---

54   6: 193. 'This striving is competition' (31: 264). 'Competition' derives from the Latin *competere*, which means to strive in common.

55   See, for example, Paul Burkett, 'A Note on Competition under Capitalism', *Capital and Class* 10, no. 3 (1986): 192–208; Paresh Chattopadhyay, 'Competition', in *The Elgar Companion to Marxist Economics*, ed. Ben Fine, Alfredo Saad Filho, and Marco Boffo (Cheltenham: Edward Elgar, 2012), 74; Giammanco, 'Competition and Technical Progress', 70; Weeks, *Capital and Exploitation*, 155.

56   G: 288; 30: 104.

57   G: 752, 552; 33: 72, 102.

58   G: 414; 33: 75; C1: 381, 739.

59   G: 414; G: 650.

the immediate incarnation of *capital as such*, very much in the same way as the idealist philosopher mistakes particular fruits for the incarnation of *the Fruit as such*, as ridiculed by Marx in *The Holy Family*.[60] The crucial difference is, of course, that whereas the abstractions of the idealist philosopher are purely intellectual, the abstraction enforced by competition takes place in social reality; capital is an 'abstraction in actu'.[61] Individual capitals are merely representatives of the abstract logic of capital which confronts them as an alien power: *what the individual capital meets when it confronts a competitor is nothing but its own essence disguised as another individual capital.*

The universalising mechanisms of competition take place on multiple levels of the capitalist totality. Competition within branches of production (intra-branch competition) results in differentiation as well as equalisation. It differentiates by forcing individual capitals to constantly strive to cut costs in order to secure a surplus profit – in other words, to allow a particular capital to run ahead of its competitors. The very same process also, however, forces other capitals within that branch to follow suit, thereby engendering a new compulsory level of productivity. In addition to this, competition between different branches of production (inter-branch competition) secures the formation of a general rate of profit through migration of capital between these branches. Inter- as well as intra-branch competition, then, are universalising mechanisms generating social averages which individual capitals must live up to if they want to survive.[62] The same is true of wages, which are also subjected to the equalising movements of the market, even if they are not exclusively or directly determined by them. 'The competition among workers is', as Marx notes, 'only another form of competition among capitals'.[63] Or, as Michael Lebowitz explains: 'When workers compete among themselves, they press in the *same direction* as capital.'[64] When *capitals* compete, they are confronted by their *own* essence. When *workers* compete, however, they are confronted with the essence of *capital*.

---

60   4: 58ff.

61   C2: 185.

62   On the difference and relation between intra- and inter-branch competition, see Callinicos, *Deciphering* Capital, 142f; Chattopadhyay, 'Competition', 41.

63   G: 651.

64   Michael Lebowitz, *Beyond* Capital: *Marx's Political Economy of the Working Class*, 2nd ed. (London: Palgrave Macmillan, 2003), 83.

Another aspect of the universalising pressure of competition is its role in the expansion of capitalist relations of production.[65] Already in the *Manifesto*, Marx and Engels identified 'cheap prices' as 'the heavy artillery with which it [the bourgeoisie] batters down all Chinese walls'.[66] Expansion takes two forms: *extensive* expansion, that is, the incorporation of larger parts of the global population into the circuits of capital; and *intensive* expansion, namely the integration of larger parts of social life into the circuits of capital. Insofar as competition 'conceptually ... is nothing other than the inner *nature of capital*', we can also conclude that 'the tendency to create the *world market* is directly given in the concept of capital itself'.[67]

Hostile Brothers

At first glance, competition seems to be a splintering or a centrifugal force, something which separates and isolates: it forces capitals to differentiate themselves, to run ahead of others. Competition among workers likewise forces the individual worker to accept a lower wage or to be more compliant than other workers, with the consequence that labour 'confronts capital as the labour of the individual labour capacity, of the *isolated worker*'.[68] In this sense, competition is a differentiating force which secures the subjection of individuals to capital by means of a kind of divide et impera strategy. On closer examination, however, it turns out that, like the other separation constitutive of the capitalist mode of production – that of life and its conditions – the *separation of capitals as well as workers into competing units is only the basis of a certain connection and constitution of a unity*. As Marx and Engels explain in *The German Ideology*, 'Competition *separates* individuals from one another, not only the bourgeois but still more the workers, in spite of the fact that it *brings them together*.'[69] *Competition is a unity of split and unity*, or, to speak Hegelese, it is the practical implementation of the identity of identity and difference. *It is the very split among capitals as well as among*

---

65   C2: 190; M: 347f.

66   6: 488.

67   G: 414; G: 408; see also Simon Clarke, 'Marx and the Market' (Center for Social Theory, UCLA, 1995), 26, homepages.warwick.ac.uk/~syrbe/pubs/LAMARKW.pdf.

68   34: 129.

69   5: 75; I.5: 91. Emphasis added.

workers that gives rise to the universalising mechanisms which secure capital's existence as a totality – it is, in other words, the split which transforms the power of capital into more than a simple aggregation of the power of individual capitals. Capital is 'a social power', and competition is the mechanism which brings about this unity; in competition, 'the individual has an effect only as a part of a social power, as an atom in the mass, and it is in this form that competition brings into play the social character of production and consumption'.[70] Competition is thus simultaneously a 'bellum omnium contra omnes' as well as the war of capital against the social totality.[71]

This unifying dynamic tells us something important about how the vertical and horizontal dimensions of capitalist relations of production mediate each other. Competition is a class-transcending form of power, but at the same time, it strengthens the *class* character of the power of capital because it unifies competing capitalists as 'hostile brothers, [who] divide among themselves the loot of other people's labour'.[72] This division of the loot among various fractions of capital – the distribution of surplus value – also tells us something important about exploitation and the power of capital.

In the Marxist tradition, it is common to view the relation of exploitation as the cornerstone of the power of capital. Briefly put, the existence of exploitation is often taken as proof of the existence of a relation of domination. But what exactly is exploitation in capitalism? Often, exploitation is understood as a relation between the *individual* capital and its employees. However, such an understanding of exploitation fails to take into account the distribution of surplus value, thereby reducing the analysis to the framework of the first volume of *Capital*, where Marx generally abstracts from the mechanisms that spread surplus value among different factions of the capitalist class. What the theory of the distribution of surplus value teaches us is that *exploitation is a relation situated on the level of the social totality*, or that *labour is exploited by capital as such, rather than by individual capitalists*. The formation of a general rate of profit and the splitting of profit into rent, interest, and profit of enterprise means that the surplus value produced by workers ends up all over the place in the capitalist class (and, through taxation, in the hands of the state). Competition is

---

70   6: 499; M: 303.
71   C1: 477.
72   31: 264.

the mechanism through which this distribution takes place, and hence the mechanism through which the exploitative relation is elevated to a relation at the level of the social totality.

Competition should thus be understood as one of the mechanisms of the economic power of capital. It is an *abstract, universal,* and *impersonal* form of domination to which *everyone* is subjected. The ideological nature of bourgeois notions of free competition, free trade, and free market thereby becomes clear. The market has never been the 'the absolute mode of existence of free individuals'; in fact, a market can never be free, unless we are talking about the freedom of capital.[73] In Marx's words: 'It is not individuals who are set free by free competition; it is, rather, capital which is set free.'[74] The so-called individual freedom involved in market transactions is in reality

> the most complete suspension of all individual freedom, and the most complete subjection of individuality under social conditions which assume the form of objective powers, even of overpowering objects [*sachlichen Mächten, ja von* übermächtigen *Sachen*] – of things independent of the relations among individuals themselves.[75]

'Free' competition is thus a mode of domination, a 'means of compulsion' (*Zwangsmittel*), a set of social relations in which market agents impose 'the rule of capital' on each other through 'reciprocal compulsion'.[76] There are at least three dimensions of the unfreedom of the market. First: as we saw in chapter six, a certain form of class domination is needed in order to secure workers' appearance on the market as sellers of labour power in the first place. In other words: *the market is unfree because it presupposes domination.* In this chapter, we have seen that the unfreedom of the market goes deeper than that. Not only does the capitalist market *rely* on relations of domination; *it is itself nothing but a form of domination.* This is the second dimension of the unfreedom of the market. In a crucial passage in the *Grundrisse* previously quoted in chapter six, Marx points out that 'state coercion' was necessary in the early days of capitalism in order to 'transform the propertyless into *workers* at conditions advantageous for

---

73   G: 649.
74   G: 650.
75   G: 652.
76   31: 275; G: 652, 651.

capital', since at this stage of capitalist development, these conditions 'are not yet forced upon the workers by competition among one another'.[77] In other words, competition has the same function as violence had in the original creation of capitalism, and competition is an absolutely crucial part of the mute compulsion of economic relations. But there is even more to it. As previously noted, workers are not only dominated *before* they show up on the market and *while* they are there; they are also subjected to the power of capital *after* they leave the market and enter 'the hidden abode of production'. This is the third dimension of the unfreedom of the market. Competition is a *class-transcending* form of power, but *not only does it presuppose class domination; it also strengthens and intensifies it,* since it forces the capitalist to discipline and subjugate workers within the sphere of production. This is the subject of the next chapter.

---

77 G: 736.

PART III
Dynamics

10

The Despotism of Subsumption

In the preceding chapters, I have presented a somewhat static picture of the capitalist mode of production – a sort of synchronic analysis of the essential social relations presupposed by the subjection of social production to the logic of valorisation. This analysis enables us to see why the power of capital takes the form of the mute compulsion of economic relations. But there is more to it than that. Capitalist relations of production set in motion certain dynamics, or 'laws of motion', which express themselves on all levels of the economic totality, from the most minute processes in the workplace to global restructurings of capital flows.[1] These dynamics will be the subject of this as well as the rest of the chapters that make up part three of this book.

I will begin with an examination of what takes place inside of the workplace, where the power of capital assumes the form of the power of the capital*ist*.[2] The central category here is the 'real subsumption' of labour – a concept designed to capture the way in which capital continually remoulds the social and material aspects of the production process. In chapters eleven and twelve, I will then go on to expand the concept of subsumption in two directions: first, I will discuss the subsumption of nature and how this affects the economic power of capital; second, I will

---

1   C1: 92.
2   This includes salaried managers who act as 'personifications' of capital. See 33: 486 and Michael Heinrich, *An Introduction to the Three Volumes of Karl Marx's* Capital (New York: Monthly Review Press, 2012), 193.

suggest that we understand capital's global restructuring of production –
for example by increasing the international division of labour – in terms
of real subsumption. In these chapters, I will also look at two examples of
how real subsumption enhances the power of capital: the development of
agriculture since the 1940s and the so-called revolution in logistics which
began to unfold in the 1970s. In chapter thirteen, I will consider two
crucial dynamics of the accumulation of capital: the creation of a relative
surplus population and the crisis-ridden nature of capitalist production.

The shift to a dynamic perspective on the economic power of capital
allows us to cast new light on some of the social relations discussed in
earlier chapters. What appeared then as *conditions* of capitalist production
will now reveal itself to simultaneously be its *results*. The power of capital
exhibits a peculiar, circular form: the *effects* of capitalist relations of production are also *causes* of those same relations. Or, in Hegelese: capital
posits its own presuppositions. '*Every moment* [*which is*] *a presupposition
of production* [*is*] *simultaneously its result*', as Marx put it in his attempt
to summarise the *Grundrisse* manuscript in headlines.[3] In this and the
following chapters, we will try to understand this paradoxical circularity
of the power of capital, and the important conclusion it yields: *one of the
sources of the power of capital is the very exercise of this power.*

A Unity of Anarchy and Despotism

Let us begin by examining relations of domination within the workplace.
Recall that we are concerned here with the analysis of capitalism in its
ideal average, which means that we are only concerned with relations of
power within the workplace insofar they are implied by the core structure
of capitalism. In real life, there are of course a wide variety of sources,
expressions, and forms of domination in the workplace.

From the perspective of the market, there is no essential difference
between the buyer and the seller of labour power: like every other market
relation, theirs is just a voluntary transaction between market agents.
The peculiar thing about labour power as a commodity, however, is that,
unlike most other commodities, it cannot be separated from its seller.
When its buyer wants to realise its use value (i.e., consume it), it thus
involves domination and the confiscation of a part of the seller's life.[4]

3   II.2: 283; G: 717.
4   33: 493.

In this manner, the very *equality* of the seller and the buyer of labour power is the basis of their *inequality* as soon as they enter the sphere of production, where 'the buyer takes command of the seller, to the extent that the latter himself enters into the buyer's consumption process with his person as a worker'.[5] This transition from the sphere of circulation to the sphere of production thus involves a change in 'the physiognomy of our *dramatis personae*', as Marx puts it in *Capital*: the seller becomes a worker, and the buyer a capitalist.[6] Capitalist production is thus a unity of the 'anarchy' of the sphere of circulation and the 'despotism' of the sphere of production.[7]

Power hierarchies within the workplace represent an anomaly for neo-classical economists, who can only understand power as a consequence of imperfect competition. Some economists, such as Armen Alchian and Harold Demsetz, even deny the existence of such power hierarchies by interpreting interpersonal relations within the firm as nothing but a concealed form of voluntary market transactions.[8] Such a position is, as I pointed out in the introduction, only possible on the condition that we abstract from the class domination necessary for the existence of a labour market. As soon as we dispense with this abstraction, it becomes possible to see relations between workers, capitalists, and managers for what they really are: relations of domination.

As I noted in my survey of Marx's terminology in chapter one, when he deals with relations of domination within the sphere of production, he often resorts to concepts, expressions, and metaphors related to the military or authoritarian forms of political power – as when he writes that the worker is subjected to 'the thoroughly organised despotism of the factory system and the military discipline of capital'.[9] He often describes capitalist management as 'purely despotic' and the workplace hierarchy as comparable to 'a real army'.[10] The point of using this kind of language is of course to highlight the glaring contradiction between bourgeois ideology

---

5   30: 106.

6   C1: 280; see also 30: 106; and R: 989.

7   C1: 477; 30: 310; M: 943.

8   Armen A. Alchian and Harold Demsetz, 'Production, Information Costs, and Economic Organization', *American Economic Review* 62, no. 5 (1972): 777–95. See Giulio Palermo, 'The Economic Debate on Power: A Marxist Critique', *Journal of Economic Methodology* 21, no. 2 (2014), for an overview and compelling critique of these debates within mainstream economics.

9   34: 29

10   C1: 450.

and the brutal realities of life in the factories. It is, as Marx puts it in the *1861–63 Manuscripts*,

> precisely the *apologists of the factory system*, such as *Ure*, the apologists of this complete de-individualisation of labour, confinement in barrack-like factories [*Einkasernirung*], military discipline, subjugation to the machinery, regulation by the stroke of the clock, surveillance by overseers, complete destruction of any development in mental or physical activity, who vociferate against infringements of individual freedom and the *free* movement of labour at the slightest sign of state intervention.[11]

Marx is mostly concerned with industrial production in eighteenth- and nineteenth-century Britain, and he provides substantial empirical evidence in support of his claims about the authoritarian rule of industrial capitalists. Here, however, we have to ask: On what level of abstraction are Marx's descriptions of capitalist management situated? Are they only valid for a historically and geographically specific variant of capitalist production, as Michael Burawoy has argued, or do they tell us something about the core structure of capitalism?[12]

Management practices have obviously changed a lot since Marx's time, at least in certain sectors of the leading capitalist economies. Since the 1970s, the old-fashioned authoritarian and despotic form of management has gradually been replaced by seemingly egalitarian network-based forms of empowering management accompanied by an ideology of authenticity and innovation.[13] The Hobbesian boss who treats workers as homogeneous cogs in the machine has given way to the casual manager who treats employees as friends, encouraging them to express themselves and bring their personal quirks and emotions with them on the job. If contemporary capitalism increasingly relies on forms of creative, affective, and immaterial

---

11   33: 491.

12   Michael Burawoy, *The Politics of Production: Factory Regimes under Capitalism and Socialism* (London: Verso, 1985).

13   See Luc Boltanski and Eve Chiapello, *The New Spirit of Capitalism*, trans. Gregory Elliott (London: Verso, 2018); Peter Fleming, *Authenticity and the Cultural Politics of Work: New Forms of Informal Control* (Oxford: Oxford University Press, 2009); Frédéric Lordon, *Willing Slaves of Capital: Spinoza and Marx on Desire*, trans. Gabriel Ash (London: Verso, 2014); Andrew Sturdy, Peter Fleming, and Rick Delbridge, 'Normative Control and Beyond in Contemporary Capitalism', in *Working Life: Renewing Labour Process Analysis*, ed. Paul Thompson and Chris Smith (Basingstoke: Palgrave Macmillan, 2010), 113–35.

labour which are difficult to reconcile with old forms of hierarchical control, as Michael Hardt, Antonio Negri, and Carlo Vercellone suggest, does that mean that Marx's description of relations of domination within the workplace is outdated?[14]

Two important things should be noted here. The first is that we should understand the transition from traditional or Fordist to postmodern or post-Fordist forms of management as a change in the *form* of domination rather than a decrease in the degree of domination. Domination is inscribed in the very essence of the relationship between the employer and the employee. Competitive pressure forces capitalists to live up to certain standards in order to stay in business, and for this reason, it is not entirely up to the capitalists to choose how they treat their employees and what management strategies they use. Competitive pressures thus act as external constraints on how much freedom employees can be granted. 'Capitalists cannot,' as Vivek Chibber puts it, 'leave it to their employees to work at an intensity consistent with profit maximization.'[15] They have to 'institutionalize direct authority on the shop floor, or within the office, as an intrinsic component of work organization.'[16] This authority can, however, take many different forms. Acting like an absolutist monarch is one strategy, and in certain settings, this might be the most profitable thing to do. In other contexts, however, it might be more profitable to offer employees free mindfulness classes (as Google does), cultivate an emotional attachment to the company brand, grant employees a certain degree of autonomy (flexible hours, work from home, etc.), or encourage them to express themselves through their job.[17] These are merely different ways of securing the same goal: the production of surplus value.[18]

---

14   Michael Hardt and Antonio Negri, *Commonwealth* (Cambridge, MA: Belknap, 2011). Carlo Vercellone, 'From Formal Subsumption to General Intellect: Elements for a Marxist Reading of the Thesis of Cognitive Capitalism', *Historical Materialism* 15, no. 1 (2007): 13–36.

15   Vivek Chibber, *Postcolonial Theory and the Specter of Capital* (London: Verso, 2013), 117.

16   Ibid., 117.

17   See Boltanski and Chiapello, *The New Spirit of Capitalism*; Trent Cruz, 'Creative Management: Disciplining the Neoliberal Worker' (PhD diss., University of Western Ontario, 2016), available at https://ir.lib.uwo.ca/cgi/viewcontent.cgi?article=5862&context =etd; Fleming, *Authenticity and the Cultural Politics of Work*; Peter Fleming and Andrew Sturdy, '"Just Be Yourself!"', *Employee Relations* 31, no. 6 (2013); Sturdy, Fleming, and Delbridge, 'Normative Control and Beyond in Contemporary Capitalism'.

18   See also Heinrich, *An Introduction*, 114f.

The second important thing to note here is that we should not underestimate the extent to which authoritarian management practices like those examined by Marx are not only still very common but have even spread in the neoliberal era, where many of the victories won by workers' movements in the first half of the twentieth century have been rolled back. In the production centres of the global South and the informal sector throughout what Mike Davis calls the 'planet of slums', despotic management is the still the order of the day.[19] It is also widespread in low-wage jobs in the rich countries. A few examples borrowed from Elizabeth Anderson's recent critique of authoritarian management in the United States: Walmart 'prohibits employees from exchanging casual remarks while on duty, calling this "time theft"'; Apple 'inspects the personal belongings of their retail workers'; and Tyson Foods 'prevents its poultry workers from using the bathroom'.[20]

Interpersonal or Impersonal?

Marx's use of a vocabulary and imagery associated with military command and pre-capitalist forms of political rule also poses another important question: what is the precise relation between the authority of the capitalist within the workplace and the abstract and impersonal domination examined in the preceding chapters? Marx's description of the capitalist as 'the factory Lycurgus' – a reference to the legendary lawgiver of Sparta – and his use of words like 'despotism' and 'autocracy' seems to suggest that the power of the capitalist is similar to the power of pre-capitalist rulers.[21] In capitalism, Marx explains, the 'power of the Egyptian and Asiatic kings or the Etruscan theocrats in the ancient world

---

19   Mike Davis, *Planet of Slums* (London: Verso, 2017).

20   Elizabeth Anderson, *Private Government: How Employers Rule Our Lives (and Why We Don't Talk about It)* (Princeton: Princeton University Press, 2017), xix, 135ff. Anderson's critique contains some good insights and examples, but her opposition between despotism in the workplace and the allegedly egalitarian spirit of the market is pure ideology. The despotism of the workplace is, as we have seen, an *effect* of the anarchy of the market, not its opposite.

21   C1: 550. 'In the factory code, the capitalist formulates his autocratic power over his workers like a private legislator, and purely as an emanation of his own will' (C1: 549f). In another passage from *Capital*, Marx compares 'the directing authority' of the production process to a conductor of an orchestra (C1: 448f). In that passage, however, he is discussing direction and coordination in an entirely general sense, i.e., independently

has … passed to capital and therewith the capitalists'.[22] If that is the case, however, in what sense can we say that the power of capital is *abstract* and *impersonal*? Is the power of the capitalist not a very *concrete* and *interpersonal* form of domination?

Let us approach this question through a brief detour. In his critique of the Subaltern Studies Group, Chibber argues that Ranajit Guha and Dipesh Chakrabarty misunderstand the relationship between interpersonal coercion and the impersonal power of economic relations. Guha and Chakrabarty hold that Indian colonial capitalism failed to produce the bourgeois forms of power dominant in Europe. Accordingly, they contrast the violent and personal authority of managers in colonial capitalism to the 'the body of rules and legislation' and the hegemonic bourgeois culture of European capitalism.[23] Rather than dissolving traditional communal bonds, they argue, colonial capitalism reinforced caste hierarchies by mobilising them in the effort to dominate workers. Chibber points out – correctly, in my view – that this misrepresents capitalist authority in nineteenth-century Europe, which was often extremely violent and coercive.[24] Chibber furthermore demonstrates that the reproduction or even strengthening of caste hierarchies in the Indian context is strikingly similar to the many ways in which Western capitalists have profited from racial, gendered, national, cultural, and religious divisions within the working class. As we saw in chapter seven, capitalists will always find it rational (i.e., favourable for the valorisation of value) to utilise differences and antagonisms among workers, regardless of the historical and geographical context.[25]

What is more important for our purposes, however, is Chibber's claim that 'the drive to dominate labor above and beyond the impersonal coercion of economic relations is indeed generic to capitalism, and that there is therefore no reason to exclude interpersonal domination from the category of "bourgeois relations of power"'.[26] According to him, capital 'has never been content to rely on the "dull compulsion of economic relations" to

---

of its capitalist form. The image of an orchestra could thus be read as the communist alternative to the militaristic and despotic capitalist. See also 30: 263.

22   30: 260.
23   Chakrabarty, quoted in Chibber, *Postcolonial Theory*, 105.
24   Chibber, *Postcolonial Theory*, 120ff.
25   Ibid., 117ff.
26   Ibid., 112.

enforce its diktat'; it has rather always been 'rational for capital to sustain and reinforce power relations resembling those of the feudal past'.[27] In other words: the despotic authority of the capitalist within the workplace demonstrates that the reproduction of capitalism relies on a *combination* of historically novel forms of *impersonal* domination and *(inter)personal* relationships of domination similar to those found in pre-capitalist social formations.

Chibber is right in arguing that a despotic form of domination within the workplace is fully compatible with the impersonal pressures of capital, but his descriptions of the despotic authority of the capitalist as a form of *personal* power similar to pre-capitalist forms of authority is misleading. In the manuscripts for the third book of *Capital*, Marx insists that the 'authority that the capitalist assumes in the immediate production process … is essentially different from the forms assumed by authority on the basis of production with slaves, serfs etc'.[28] The reason why they are 'essentially' different is that the authority of capitalists 'accrues to its bearers only as the personification of the conditions of labour vis-à-vis labour itself'; or, as Marx puts it elsewhere: 'The capitalist only holds power as the *personification of capital*.'[29] The relationship between the worker and the capitalist is, as we saw in chapter six, not a result of a personal relation of dependence but the result of a market transaction: 'What brings the seller into a relationship of dependency is', as Marx explains in the *Results of the Immediate Process of Production*, 'solely the fact that the buyer is the owner of the conditions of labour. There is no fixed political and social relationship of supremacy and subordination.'[30] This 'subordination' is thus 'only of an *objective* nature'; in other words, it is not grounded in the specificity of the persons involved in the relationship.[31] As Marx puts it in a passage which I also quoted in chapter six: 'The slave is the property of a particular *master*; the worker must indeed sell himself to capital, but not to a particular capitalist.'[32]

---

27   Ibid., 123f.

28   M: 943; see also 30: 94.

29   M: 943; see also R: 989; 34: 122; R: 1053f; 34: 123; and C1: 450.

30   R: 1025f; see also 1021.

31   34: 96.

32   R: 1032; see also 9: 203. According to William Clare Roberts, this conception of the power of the capitalist is directly contained in Marx's concept of despotism – Marx inherited this from Hegel, for whom it referred to 'a specific form of tyranny in which constant flux in the person of the despot did nothing to disturb the overall structure of

Contra Chibber, the authority of the capitalist in the sphere of production is thus not a form of *personal* power, at least not in the sense in which the power of a feudal lord or a slave-owner is personal. It might be argued that the power of the capitalist is 'personal' in the sense that its exercise can be attributed to an identifiable person (the manager), in contrast to competitive pressures which express themselves in prices rather than work instructions. But this merely obscures the crucial difference between the authority of the capitalist and the power of pre-capitalist exploiters: whereas the feudal peasant or the slave is subjected to the rule of a particular person, the capitalist worker is subjected to the capitalist class as such. *The authority of the capitalist within the workplace is merely the form of appearance of the impersonal power of capital.* It was this 'depersonalization' of the notion of exploitation, as William Clare Roberts calls it, that allowed Marx to move beyond the moralistic critique of capitalists, according to which the origins of this relation of domination is to be sought for in their flawed character. *The despotism of the workplace is nothing but the metamorphosis of the impersonal and abstract compulsion resulting from the intersection of the double separation constitutive of capitalist relations of production.*

Subsumption: Formal and Real

Now that the relation between the despotism of the workplace and the wider structures of economic power in capitalism has been clarified, we can broach the question of what capitalists actually *do* with the power granted them by their position in the capitalist system. This is what the concept of *subsumption* is intended to capture. Marx seems to have adopted this concept from Hegel, for whom it referred to 'the *application* of the universal to a particular or singular posited *under* it'.[33] Since capital is, as I explained in chapter one, a sort of empty and universal form into which all kinds of different activities, processes, and things

---

society'. See William Clare Roberts, *Marx's Inferno: The Political Theory of Capital* (Princeton: Princeton University Press, 2017), 167.

33   G. W. F. Hegel, *The Science of Logic* (Cambridge: Cambridge University Press, 2010), 555; see Endnotes, 'The History of Subsumption', in *Endnotes 2: Misery and the Value Form* (London: Endnotes, 2010), 137; Andrés Sáenz De Sicilia, 'The Problem of Subsumption in Kant, Hegel and Marx' (PhD diss., Centre for Research in Modern European Philosophy, Kingston University, 2016).

can be absorbed, it makes perfect sense that Marx utilised the concept of subsumption in his attempt to understand what happens to a labour process when capital takes hold of it. The term crops up here and there, in a very general sense, in many of Marx's writings, including some of his early work. The more specific and precise concept of the *subsumption of labour under capital* begins to appear in the *Grundrisse* and then becomes increasingly central to Marx's analysis during his first thoroughgoing empirical and historical study of modern industrial production in the *1861–63 Manuscripts*.[34]

The concept of subsumption is sometimes used to refer to everything that is governed, or even just affected, by the logic of capital; in contemporary radical thought it is not uncommon, for example, to come across expressions such as 'the subsumption of life', 'the subsumption of society', or 'the subsumption of subjectivity'. I will discuss such attempts to extend the notion of subsumption later in this chapter. But first, I want to examine Marx's use of it.

The first thing to note is that in Marx's writings, 'subsumption' refers to the *labour process*, in other words, to the way in which production is subsumed under the logic of capital. Subsumption is *formal* when it 'does not imply a fundamental change in the real nature of the labour process' – that is, when capital takes over a labour process whose technical and organisational structure is a result of *non-capitalist* logics.[35] In formally subsumed production, capital has simply taken over labour processes 'as it finds them available in the existing technology, and in the form in which they have developed on the basis of non-capitalist relations of production'.[36] The transition from non-capitalist production to formally subsumed production is thus only a matter of *property relations*; capitalist production within specific branches is, at least in the initial stages, perfectly able to 'exist without causing the slightest alteration of any kind in the mode of production or the social relations within which production takes place'.[37]

Since the labour process 'remains unchanged' under formal subsumption, its capitalist form 'may be easily dissolved'; in other words, a transition from formally subsumed capitalist production to non-capitalist

---

34   G: 586, 700. Rob Beamish, *Marx, Method, and the Division of Labor* (Urbana: University of Illinois Press, 1992).

35   R: 1021; see also G: 586f; 30: 64, 92, 279; and C1: 425.

36   30: 92.

37   30: 262.

production would not require a reorganisation of the production process.[38] However, this changes when subsumption becomes *real* – which happens when capital 'radically remoulds' the 'social and technological conditions' of the labour process, that is, when *capital as a social form materialises itself*.[39] The capitalist production process has a dual nature, corresponding to the dual nature of the commodity: it is simultaneously a material process transforming raw materials into use values and a process of valorisation creating surplus value for a capitalist.[40] Real subsumption is the process whereby one of these aspects (the valorisation process) meshes with or intervenes in the other (the material character of the labour process); in other words, *it is the becoming-substance of form*.[41] Marx also refers to this as the 'specifically capitalist mode of production'.

There are two main causes of real subsumption, corresponding to the two fundamental separations constitutive of capitalist relations of production.[42] First, the resistance of workers: capitalists are continuously forced to reorganise the labour process (deploying new technologies, new forms of control and surveillance, new divisions of labour, new managerial structures, etc.) in order to deprive workers of the opportunity to exploit vulnerabilities in the technological and organisational setup of the production process. An example: the effort to intensify automation in the American automobile industry in the early 1950s was to a large degree a response to many years of militant struggle, as chronicled by James Boggs in *The American Revolution*.[43]

The second main cause of real subsumption is the pressure of competition, which forces individual capitals to live up to certain productivity standards. Since each of these can act as a cause of real subsumption in the

---

38   30: 279.

39   34: 30.

40   C1: 283ff.

41   30: 140, 279.

42   In any concrete situation, there might be an infinity of possible causes, such as the idiosyncrasies and quirks of individual capitalists. Here, however, we are only concerned with those causes which form a part of the core structure of capitalism, that is, those that demonstrate how real subsumption is, in Arthur's words, 'logically implicit in the concept of capital'. See Christopher Arthur, *The New Dialectic and Marx's Capital* (Leiden: Brill, 2004), 76; Endnotes, 'The History of Subsumption', 150.

43   James Boggs, *The American Revolution: Pages from a Negro Worker's Notebook* (New York: Monthly Review Press, 2009). See also Beverly J. Silver, *Forces of Labor: Workers' Movements and Globalization Since 1870* (Cambridge: Cambridge University Press, 2003), chap. 2.

absence of the other, it is possible to separate them analytically. In reality, however, they are closely related, even if their relation can take many different forms, depending on the context. Insofar as resistance leads to a decrease in the rate of surplus value, it can intensify competition, which in turn provides capitalists with a stronger incentive to discipline their workers, intensify work, speed up and streamline production, introduce new technology, and so on. Insofar as worker resistance succeeds in dampening the frenetic pace of technological change imposed on capitalists by competition, however, it can also, as David Harvey explains, put 'a floor under competition' and thus 'help stabilize the course of capitalist development'.[44] Strong resistance in one branch might cause capital to flow into other branches, thus affecting the inter-branch competition. An example of a process of real subsumption resulting from both competitive pressures and worker resistance is the transition from water-powered mills to coal-fired steam-engines in the British textile industry in the second quarter of the nineteenth century – a process driven by a convergence of a crisis of overproduction and a wave of strikes and riots.[45]

It is often assumed that the aim of technological and organisational changes in capitalism is to increase productivity.[46] While it is true that productivity is an important – and perhaps the most popular – weapon in the competitive struggle among capitals, and that the historically unprecedented dynamism of capitalist production has resulted in mind-boggling rates of productivity growth compared to earlier modes of production, it is always important to bear in mind what the ultimate aim of capitalist production is *the production of surplus value.* The aim of real subsumption is not productivity increases per se, but to increase productivity *in a form compatible with capitalist relations of production.* We should therefore not be surprised to find that the history of capitalism is filled with examples of technologies and organisational arrangements which were chosen despite the fact that cheaper and more productive alternatives were available. The steam-engine won out over water-powered mills in nineteenth-century British industry not because it was cheaper or more productive, but because water technologies were incompatible

---

44   David Harvey, *The Limits to Capital* (London: Verso, 2006), 117.

45   Andreas Malm, *Fossil Capital: The Rise of Steam Power and the Roots of Global Warming* (London: Verso, 2016), chap. 4.

46   Harry Braverman, *Labor and Monopoly Capital: The Degradation of Work in the Twentieth Century* (New York: Monthly Review Press, 1974), 173ff.

with competitive relations among firms and the antagonism between capitalists and workers.[47] Similarly, the transition from 'putting out' systems
to the factory system in nineteenth-century British industry was driven
by the need to secure the control by the capitalists over the work process
rather than the quest for technical superiority; as Marx notes, 'the social
function of hierarchical work organization is not technical efficiency, but
accumulation'.[48] In the post-war boom in US industry, record-playback
technology was likewise outmatched by numerical-control technology,
partly because the operation of the former required skilled workers – and
to leave skills in the hands of workers is always, as I will come back to,
a risk for capital.[49] What this tells us is that real subsumption is not just
a matter of technical efficiency; it is a *power technique*, a mechanism for
reproducing the capitalist relations of production.

Corporeal Calibration

Once capital takes hold of a labour process, it sets in motion what Harry
Braverman calls 'the Babbage principle: break it up into its simplest
elements'.[50] The production process is a socio-material process which
consists of raw materials, energy, skills, knowledge, and instruments
(tools or machines), which are combined within a certain division of
labour and organisational structure. All of these different elements of
the labour process can be subjected to changes in the process of real subsumption. In the implementation of such changes, capital is 'constantly
compelled to wrestle with the insubordination of the workers'.[51]

The separation between life and its conditions may force the proletarian to show up on the market and sell their labour power, but it does not
automatically guarantee their subjection to the demands of the manager;
'hence the complaint that the workers lack discipline runs through the
whole of the period of manufacture'.[52] The 'need for discipline and super-

---

47   Malm, *Fossil Capital*.

48   Stephen A. Marglin, 'What Do Bosses Do? The Origins and Functions of Hierarchy in Capitalist Production', *Review of Radical Political Economics* 6, no. 2 (1974): 62.

49   David F. Noble, *Forces of Production: A Social History of Industrial Automation*
(New York: Knopf, 1984), chap. 7.

50   Braverman, *Labor and Monopoly Capital*, 82. See also C1: 617.

51   C1: 490.

52   C1: 490; Malm, *Fossil Capital*, 128.

vision' gives rise to a distinctively capitalist function within the production process, namely the 'labour of superintendence' undertaken by 'over-lookers' who 'represent the capitalist towards the workers'.[53] In addition to effects of workers knowing that they are being monitored, systematic surveillance is also what provides the capitalists with the knowledge they need in order to optimise the labour process and break what industry triumphalist Andrew Ure called 'the refractory hand of labour'.[54] The paradigmatic example of this is the classic Taylorist time-and-motion study, where every movement of the working body is monitored and used as data in order to increase productivity. Such studies are becoming more and more efficient and easy with the development of new digital technologies – to cite two recent examples: in 2013, it was reported that workers at a Tesco distribution centre in Ireland were forced to wear electronic armbands tracking their work performance, and in early 2018, Amazon patented a wristband which not only tracks the movements of the workers but also directs them by means of vibration.[55]

Another disciplinary tool popular among capitalists – found in formally as well as in really subsumed labour processes – is to pit workers against each other by nurturing or creating hierarchies and antagonisms among them related to differences in nationality, gender, racialisation, differing wage levels, religion, age, seniority, and so on.[56] However, capitalists sometimes have to be careful with this strategy, since it can backfire by impeding cooperation and lead to conflicts among workers that end up being harmful for the capitalists. In other words, capitalists must aim to keep a level of antagonism among workers strong enough to keep them from forming a collective force but weak enough to not make cooperation too troublesome.

One of the most important methods for 'the suppression of any claim by labour to autonomy' is the introduction of new technology.[57] Demon-

---

53   33: 486; C1: 449f; see also Michel Foucault, *Discipline and Punish: The Birth of the Prison* (London: Penguin, 1991), 174f.

54   C1: 564.

55   Olivia Solon, 'Amazon Patents Wristband That Tracks Warehouse Workers' Movements', *Guardian*, 1 February 2018, theguardian.com; Kevin Rawlinson, 'Tesco Accused of Using Electronic Armbands to Monitor Its Staff', *Independent*, 13 February 2013, independent.co.uk.

56   Michael A. Lebowitz, 'The Politics of Assumption, the Assumption of Politics', *Historical Materialism* 14, no. 2 (2006): 29–47.

57   30: 340.

strating how machinery is a 'powerful weapon for suppressing strikes', Marx argues that it 'would be possible to write a whole history of the inventions made since 1830 for the sole purpose of providing capital with weapons against working class revolt'.[58] Capitalists are able to use labour-saving technology in this way because they possess what Robert Brenner describes as 'perhaps the most effective means yet discovered to impose labour discipline in class-divided societies': the threat of dismissal.[59] The ability of machinery to 'produce a surplus working population' increases competition among workers, thereby making it easier for capitalists to make workers 'submit to the dictates of capital'.[60] A further disciplinary effect of machinery is its ability to calibrate and direct the movements of human bodies; as Marx explains, the 'compulsion of the workshop … introduces simultaneity, regularity and proportionality into the mechanism of these different operations, in fact first combines them together in a uniformly operating mechanism'.[61] This aspect of machinery provides us with a good example of why the notion of economic power is necessary if we are to understand how capital imposes its logic on social life: the power bequeathed to capitalists by machinery cannot be grasped in terms of the violence/ideology couplet, but is rather a form of power which addresses the subject indirectly by altering its material environment. Foucault puts it well:

> This subjection is not only obtained by the instruments of violence or ideology; it can also be direct, physical, pitting force against force, bearing on material elements, and yet without involving violence; it may be calculated, organized, technically thought out; it may be subtle, make use neither of weapons nor of terror and yet remain of a physical order.[62]

The ability of capitalists to exert such a 'micro-physics of power' through the insertion of human bodies into the mechanical infrastructure of production is greatly enhanced by certain forms of energy. 'As long as the

---

58   C1: 562f.
59   Robert Brenner, 'The Social Basis of Economic Development', in *Analytical Marxism*, ed. John Roemer (Cambridge: Cambridge University Press, 1986), 31.
60   C1: 532.
61   30: 271; see also 30: 259.
62   Foucault, *Discipline and Punish*, 26.

motive force proceeds from human beings (and indeed animals too) it can,' as Marx explains, 'only physically function for a certain portion of the day'.[63] Compared to the versatile, flexible, unremitting, and submissive nature of coal and oil, animate power is a troublesome, unreliable, and irregular source of energy. 'A steam-engine etc., needs', as Marx notes, 'no rest. It can continue operating for any length of time' and is therefore well suited for ensuring that the worker adapts their 'own movements to the uniform and unceasing motion of an automaton'.[64] Energy thus plays a key role in guaranteeing the worker's 'subordination to the system of machinery as a whole'.[65] As Andreas Malm notes, the coupling of machinery to motive forces deriving from what he calls 'the stock' (primarily coal and oil) allows for coercion to 'take a step back', since the exercise of power is now partly relegated to the system of machinery.[66] Machinery is thus not only an *effect* of the power of capital; it is also one of its *sources*.[67]

The Rule of Abstract Time

The regularity, uniformity, and continuity imposed on working bodies by means of capitalist technology is an indispensable part of the *temporal* aspect of capitalist domination. We have already touched upon the temporality of mute compulsion in chapter six, where we saw how capital mobilises the future and the past in order to subjugate the present. Within the workplace, the power of capital introduces yet another dimension of its inherent temporality.

One of the conclusions reached by Marx during his study of the history of technology in 1863 was that the clock formed an important part of the material basis for early capitalist industry: 'What, without the clock, would be a period in which the value of the commodity, and therefore the labour time necessary for its production, is the decisive factor?'[68] The clock is, as

---

63   30: 332.

64   30: 332; C1: 546.

65   33: 489. See also 30: 269, 342; 32: 419; 33: 488f, 491, 497; and 34: 29, 98, 102.

66   Malm, *Fossil Capital*, 310.

67   Ibid., 311; see also Elmar Altvater, 'The Social and Natural Environment of Fossil Capitalism', in *Coming to Terms with Nature*, ed. Leo Panitch and Colin Leys (London: Merlin Press, 2006), 37–60; Matthew T. Huber, *Lifeblood: Oil, Freedom, and the Forces of Capital* (Minneapolis: University of Minnesota Press, 2013), chap. 1.

68   33: 403; 41: 450.

Lewis Mumford notes, 'not merely a means of keeping trach of the hours, but of synchronising the actions of men'.[69] What the clock measures is an *abstract* kind of time – in other words, a sequence of empty, homogeneous blocks measured in units completely detached from the rhythms of nature and human activity. Mumford explains it well:

> The clock ... dissociated time from human events and helped to create the belief in an independent world of mathematically measurable sequences: the special world of science. There is relatively little foundation for this belief in common human experience: throughout the year the days are of uneven duration, and not merely does the relation between day and night steadily change, but a slight journey from East to West alter astronomical time by a certain number of minutes. In terms of the human organism itself, mechanical time is even more foreign: while human life has regularities of its own, the beat of the pulse, the breathing of the lungs, these change from hour to hour with mood and action, and in the longer span of days, time is measured not by the calendar but by the events that occupy it. The shepherd measures from the time the ewes lambed; the farmer measures back to the day of sowing or forward to the harvest.[70]

With the exception of medieval monasteries and towns, the abstract time measured by the clock was not a significant part of social life before the advent of capitalism.[71] Generally speaking, inhabitants of pre-capitalist worlds only knew time as something defined by the duration of certain *events* or *actions* – it was a 'task-oriented' form of time, as E. P. Thompson put it in his classic study of time and capitalist work discipline. The relevant units referred to common experiences of everyday life, like the time it takes to cook rice, say a prayer, cook an egg, or urinate.[72] Time

---

69 Lewis Mumford, *Technics and Civilization* (Chicago: University of Chicago Press, 2010 [1934]), 14.

70 Ibid., 15.

71 Jacques Le Goff, *Time, Work, and Culture in the Middle Ages* (Chicago: University of Chicago Press, 1980); Moishe Postone, *Time, Labor, and Social Domination: A Reinterpretation of Marx's Critical Theory* (Cambridge: Cambridge University Press, 2003), 202ff; E. P. Thompson, 'Time, Work-Discipline, and Industrial Capitalism', *Past and Present* 38 (1967): 56–97.

72 Thompson, 'Time, Work-Discipline, and Industrial Capitalism', 60; Postone, *Time, Labor, and Social Domination*, 201.

was also defined by religious rituals and – especially in rural areas – the rhythms of nature.[73] This was a world of what Moishe Postone calls concrete time – that is, time as a *dependent* variable in the sense that it was dependent upon what takes place in time.[74]

We should be careful not to fall into the trap of idealising pre-capitalist forms of temporality. Working in concrete time is not, as Malm points out, 'all joy and reward: it can be just as stressful, excessive, disciplined and punishing as any other. When a peasant sees the clouds gathering on the horizon, he may have to work without rest for a whole day'.[75] Nothing is easier than to bemoan the alienating nature of abstract time and write a Heideggerian hymn to the wisdom of the farmer who has no clocks but knows the rhythms of nature like the back of his hand. However, pre-capitalist temporality is neither more authentic nor any less socially determined than any other form of time. The problem with abstract time is not that it is contrary to nature, but that it is a *means of oppression*.

Capitalist production does not sit well with concrete time. For one thing, the generalisation of the commodity form means that the exchange of materialised expressions of abstract temporal units of human labour becomes the mechanism through which social life is reproduced. But the rule of abstract time is not just a consequence of the role of exchange in capitalism; it is also the result of the real subsumption of labour, which requires the calibration of the human body to the regularity of machinery. 'Temporal regularity' is, in Mumford's words, the 'first characteristic of modern machine civilisation'.[76] Capitalism thus gives rise to a form of production in which 'time penetrates the body and with it all the meticulous controls of power'.[77] In order to do so, capital must diminish the irregularities of nature, for example by substituting coal and oil for water, wind, or solar energy. Capitalists purchase labour power for a determinate amount of time, which means that labour 'has to occur during that time – not when the weather is right, or when the sun has risen, or when the worker happens to be in the mood for hard labour'.[78] The tension between concrete time and the logic of capital is therefore one of the main

---

73   Le Goff, *Time, Work, and Culture in the Middle Ages*, 48f.
74   Postone, *Time, Labor, and Social Domination*, 201.
75   Malm, *Fossil Capital*, 304.
76   Mumford, *Technics and Civilization*, 269.
77   Foucault, *Discipline and Punish*, 152.
78   Malm, *Fossil Capital*, 303.

reasons why capitalist production originally became, and still is, deeply dependent upon fossil fuels.[79]

The Restructuring of Skills

One of the consequences of real subsumption is a tendency towards *deskilling* of labour power. The possession of skills has always provided workers with a powerful basis of resistance. Deskilling makes it easier to replace workers, hence increasing the competition among them, and for this reason, it is not only an effect of the power of capital but also one of its sources. One way to deskill labour is to reorganise the division of labour within the production process; by transforming a complex labour process into a number of simple tasks – think of Adam Smith's famous pin factory – capitalists are able to replace expensive and recalcitrant skilled workers with cheap, unskilled ones, who are generally easier to discipline because they are easy to replace.[80] Another way to deprive workers of skills, as mentioned earlier, is to introduce new technology. A good example is provided by Richard Sennett's analysis of technological changes in an American bakery. In the late 1990s, Sennett returned to a bakery he had studied more than two decades earlier and found that the skills of the bakers had been replaced by computers: 'Now the bakers make no physical contact with the materials or the loaves of bread, monitoring the entire process via on-screen icons.'[81] Another example is the self-acting mule, one of the most important technologies of the industrial revolution, which was invented in the 1820s with the aim of eradicating the need for skilled spinners.[82] Although reorganisation of the division of labour and technological development can take place independently of each other, they are often closely connected. The introduction of new technologies often results in what Braverman calls 'the separation of conception from execution', in other words, the separation of labour and the

---

79   Ibid.

80   C1: 455ff; 33: 388; Ali Rattansi, *Marx and the Division of Labour* (London: Macmillan, 1982), 143ff.

81   Richard Sennett, *The Corrosion of Character: The Personal Consequences of Work in the New Capitalism* (New York: Norton, 1999), 68.

82   Robert C. Allen, *The British Industrial Revolution in Global Perspective* (Cambridge: Cambridge University Press, 2009), 208.

knowledge necessary for carrying out this labour.[83] Workers are thus divided into a mass of unskilled workers on the one hand, and a small group of highly skilled workers, such as engineers, scientists, designers, or programmers, on the other. The paradoxical effect of technological development under capitalism is thus, in Braverman's words, that 'the more science is incorporated into the labor process, the less the worker understands of the process'.[84] Or, as Marx puts it in the *1861–63 Man-uscripts*: '*Knowledge thus becomes independent* of labour and enters the service of capital.'[85]

In his classic *Labor and Monopoly Capital*, Braverman famously defends what has become known as 'the deskilling thesis', according to which capitalist production implies a long-term tendency to deskill the work-force. Although Braverman acknowledges that this is accompanied by a process of polarisation, wherein knowledge tends to become centralised in a layer of high-skilled workers, he insists that deskilling is indeed the general tendency of capitalist production for the majority of workers.[86] This idea has been the subject of countless discussions – empirical as well as theoretical – within the field of labour process analysis ever since Braver-man published his groundbreaking analysis.[87] In the early 1980s, Harvey concluded that 'evidence suggests that this [i.e., deskilling] has been the direction in which capitalism has been moving, with substantial islands of resistance here and innumerable pockets of resistance there'.[88] Some twenty years later, in the context of discussions about lean production, Tony Smith concluded that 'the deskilling thesis has not been definitively falsified, either in its general or in its specific application to lean produc-tion. But neither has it been conclusively established.'[89]

---

83   Braverman, *Labor and Monopoly Capital*, 114.

84   Ibid., 425.

85   34: 57. See also 30: 276, 304; 33: 364; 34: 32, 124, 126; R: 1055; and C1: 548f.

86   Braverman, *Labor and Monopoly Capital*, 424ff.

87   For overviews of these debates, see Tony Elger, 'Valorisation and "Deskilling": A Critique of Braverman', *Capital and Class* 7 (1979): 58–99; Harvey, *The Limits to Capital*, 106–19; David Knights and Hugh Wilmott, 'Introduction', in *Labour Process Theory*, ed. David Knights and Hugh Wilmott (Basingstoke: Macmillan, 1990), 1–45; Craig R. Littler, 'The Labour Process Debate: A Theoretical Review 1974–1988', in *Labour Process Theory* (Basingstoke: Macmillan, 1990), 46–94; Peter Meiksins, 'Labor and Monopoly Capital for the 1990s: A Review and Critique of the Labor Process Debate', *Monthly Review* 46, no. 6 (1994): 45; Tony Smith, *Technology and Capital in the Age of Lean Production: A Marxian Critique of the 'New Economy'* (Albany: State University of New York Press, 2000), chap. 2.

88   Harvey, *The Limits to Capital*, 119.

89   Smith, *Technology and Capital*, 48.

Since then, discussions about the so-called post-industrial 'knowledge economy', the 'information revolution', or – in the critical version of this diagnosis – 'cognitive capitalism' and 'biopolitical production' have led to a resurgence of an old critique of Braverman, namely that capitalism also contains an immanent tendency towards *upskilling*.[90] The well-educated knowledge worker elevated by these critics to be the paradigmatic figure of contemporary capitalism is, however, only found among a vanishing layer of the global workforce, most of which is located in leading capitalist economies. Outside of these, low-skilled industrial and agricultural labour, and all kinds of informal work, is still the norm. Most new jobs in rich countries such as the United Kingdom and the United States 'are in low-skill, low-wage parts of the service sector'.[91] Rather than a dynamic and upskilling knowledge economy, the direction in which contemporary capitalism seems to be moving is towards what the Endnotes collective has called a 'post-industrial wasteland' populated by informally employed surplus populations and, to quote Jason E. Smith's trenchant analysis of this dynamic, 'workers parked in low-productivity service work, exchanged against sub-subsistence wages'.[92]

My aim here is not, however, to defend Braverman's deskilling thesis. In fact, the discussions about whether or not there has been an empirically detectable trend towards deskilling in the course of the history of capitalism have been a red herring. Rather than reading Marx's analysis of deskilling as an empirical prediction, we should follow Harvey and read it as an attempt to disclose 'what it is that workers are being forced to cope *with* and to defend *against*'.[93] In other words: Marx's claims about capital's inherent tendency to dispossess workers of their skills is not a claim about an inevitable historical trend but an identification of the direction in which capital is pushing. Whether or not this will result in a tendency towards

90 Vercellone, 'Formal Subsumption'; Hardt and Negri, *Commonwealth*; Paul Thompson and Chris Smith, 'Debating Labour Process Theory and the Sociology of Work', in *Working Life: Renewing Labour Process Analysis*, ed. Paul Thompson and Chris Smith (Basingstoke: Palgrave Macmillan, 2010), 15f.

91 Thompson and Smith, 'Debating Labour Process Theory', 15; See also Jason E. Smith, 'Nowhere to Go: Automation, Then and Now', 2 pts., *Brooklyn Rail*, March–April 2017, brooklynrail.org.

92 Endnotes, 'A History of Separation', in *Endnotes 4: Unity in Separation* (London: Endnotes, 2015), 156; Smith, 'Nowhere to Go'; Endnotes and Aaron Benanav, 'Misery and Debt: On the Logic and History of Surplus Populations and Surplus Capital', in *Endnotes 2: Misery and the Value Form* (London: Endnotes, 2010), 37ff.

93 Harvey, *The Limits to Capital*, 113.

deskilling depends on the relative strength of capital in relation to other social forces (primarily forces of labour). This reading also provides us with an answer to a common critique of Marx (and Braverman), namely that he treats workers as passive objects of capitalist domination, underestimating worker resistance and its ability to slow, halt, and reverse deskilling pressures.[94] What this overlooks is that Marx's critique of political economy was, as Michael Lebowitz puts it, 'never intended as the complete analysis of capitalism'; it is rather an analysis of 'capital – its goals and its struggles to achieve those goals'.[95]

Another reason why the preoccupation with the deskilling thesis as an empirical prediction is a red herring is that it fails to realise that 'what is on capital's agenda is not', as Harvey puts it, 'the eradication of skills per se but the eradication of *monopolisable* skills'.[96] A process of general upskilling is therefore fully compatible with capitalism and can take place alongside a process of eradication of monopolisable skills. Capital is not interested in deskilling as such, but only in deskilling as a tool of domination – a point often missed by critics of deskilling, who replace Marx's critique of domination with a romantic critique of deskilling as such, based on vague ideals of wholeness and original unity. For an example of the importance of distinguishing between skills per se and monopolisable skills, consider recent debates about the 'emotional labour' required by many workers in the burgeoning service sector. As feminist critics have rightly pointed out, many of the service sector jobs usually regarded as requiring no or few skills actually involve several complex emotional and social skills, which are often rendered invisible by being presented as the natural abilities of the women who perform this labour.[97] As Jonathan Payne points out,

---

94 Meiksins, 'Labor and Monopoly Capital for the 1990s'.

95 Michael Lebowitz, *Beyond* Capital: *Marx's Political Economy of the Working Class*, 2nd ed. (London: Palgrave Macmillan, 2003), viii, ix.

96 David Harvey, *Seventeen Contradictions and the End of Capitalism* (London: Profile Books, 2014), 119f. See also Kendra Briken et al., 'Labour Process Theory and the New Digital Workplace', in *The New Digital Workplace: How New Technologies Revolutionize Work*, ed. Kendra Briken et al. (London: Palgrave, 2017), 4.

97 Sharon C. Bolton, 'Conceptual Confusions: Emotion Work as Skilled Work', in *The Skills That Matter*, ed. Chris Warhurst, Irena Grugulis, and Ewart Keep (London: Palgrave, 2004); Susan Durbin and Hazel Conley, 'Gender, Labour Process Theory, and Intersectionality: *Une Liason Dangereuse*', in *Working Life: Renewing Labour Process Analysis* (Basingstoke: Palgrave Macmillan, 2010); Arlie Russell Hochschild, *The Managed Heart: Commercialization of Human Feeling* (Berkeley: University of California Press, 2012).

however, the problem is that there is often 'no real shortage of those able to perform the kind of "skilled" emotion work required in the bulk of low-end service jobs'.[98]

'A Unity Which Rules over Them'

Not only does the capitalist division of labour within the workplace tend to eradicate monopolisable skills; it also leads to an increasing *specialisation* of tasks. These two aspects are obviously closely related, since a common method of deskilling is to break up a production process into a number of simple and specialised tasks. It is possible, however, to dissolve a production process into several independent tasks without making these tasks simpler, and for this reason specialisation and deskilling should be conceptually separated. The specialisation as well as the deskilling involved in real subsumption are examples of what is perhaps the most fundamental dynamic of the material restructuring of social reproduction set in motion by capital: *separate in order to reconnect, fracture in order to reassemble, atomise in order to integrate.* In chapter six, I explained how capital drives a wedge between life and its conditions in order to reconnect them through the cash nexus. In chapter eight, I discussed how the generalisation of the commodity form dissolves pre-capitalist methods for coordinating social production in order to re-establish the connection between different parts of the total social labour through the market. The analysis of real subsumption reveals how a similar process takes place within the production process. Through deskilling and specialisation, capital 'seizes labour-power by its roots' and transforms it into *a potential whose condition of actualisation is the mediation of valorising value*.[99]

> If, in the first place, the worker sold his labour-power to capital because he lacked the material means of producing a commodity, now his own individual labour-power withholds its services unless it has been sold to capital. It will continue to function only in an environment which

---

98   'What's Wrong with Emotional Labour?', SKOPE Research Paper 65 (University of Warwick, 2006), 22. See also Durbin and Conley, 'Gender, Labour Process Theory and Intersectionality', 188ff.

99   C1: 481.

first comes into existence after its sale, namely the capitalist's workshop. Unfitted by nature to make anything independently, the manufacturing worker develops his productive activity only as an appendage of that workshop. As the chosen people bore in their features the sign that they were the property of Jehovah, so the division of labour brands the manufacturing worker as the property of capital.[100]

The valorisation of value thus becomes 'a real condition of production'.[101] In the *1861–63 Manuscripts*, Marx describes this dimension of capital's power by drawing a useful distinction between the *objective* and the *social* conditions of labour – a distinction which corresponds to the double nature of human production as a social and a natural process.[102] In chapter six, we saw how capital's appropriation of the *objective* conditions of labour is a crucial basis of its economic power. With the real subsumption of labour, however, the dispossession of the worker is taken a step further: now capital also appropriates the *social* conditions of labour. What I described in chapter six as the *transcendental* plane of the power of capital – its capacity to transform itself into the condition of possibility of social life – can now be understood as a result of this *double dispossession* of the *objective* as well as the *social* conditions of production. Real subsumption makes the worker 'one-sided, abstract, partial', 'disconnected [and] isolated', with the consequence that their labour power 'becomes powerless when it stands alone'.[103] The unification of these partial and disconnected workers into a single *Gesamtkörper* takes place under the command of capital, which becomes 'as indispensable as that a general should command on the field of battle'.[104] The cooperation of workers is thus no longer '*their* being, but the *being* of capital':[105]

Nor is it a relation which belongs to them; instead, they now belong to it, and the relation itself appears as a relation of capital to them. It is not their reciprocal association, but rather a unity which rules over them, and of which the vehicle and director is capital itself. Their own

---

100   C1: 482.
101   C1: 448.
102   30: 279f; 5: 43.
103   30: 279; C1: 357; 34: 123f. See also 32: 402; 33: 479; and R: 1055.
104   C1: 448f.
105   G: 585.

association in labour – cooperation – is in fact a power alien to them; it is the power of capital which confronts the isolated workers.[106]

The ability of the logic of valorisation to socially and materially reconfigure the production process is premised upon the power granted to capitalists by the relations of production examined in the preceding chapters. In this sense, real subsumption is an *effect* of the power of capital. But, as we have seen, *the very exercise of this power tends to reproduce it*, and for that reason, *the capitalist production process is not only the production of commodities endowed with surplus value – it is at the same time the production of power.*

The Total Subsumption of Everything?

In Marx's writings, the concepts of formal and real subsumption refer exclusively to the labour process. Several thinkers have proposed to extend these concepts in various directions. Jacques Cammatte and Antonio Negri both claim that *real* subsumption has been superseded by the *total* subsumption of labour or – in Negri's case – the *total* subsumption of *society*. Hardt and Negri talk about the real subsumption of 'the social *bios*', Jason Read and Matthew Huber talk about the real subsumption of *subjectivity*, and Fredric Jameson holds that capitalism has reached a stage where 'everything has been subsumed'.[107] Such claims are usually based on the idea that capitalism has reached a stage where 'there is no longer anything outside it', where 'capital has taken hold of every detail and every dimension of existence' or where 'capitalism,

---

106   30: 261; see also G: 470f, 587; 30: 262, 269; and 34: 30.

107   Jacques Camatte, *Capital and Community* (New York: Prism Key Press, 2011), 109. Antonio Negri, *Marx beyond Marx: Lessons on the Grundrisse* (New York: Pluto Press, 1992), 114, 131, 142; Antonio Negri, 'Twenty Theses on Marx: The Interpretation of the Class Situation Today', in *Marxism beyond Marxism*, ed. Saree Makdisi, Cesare Casarino, and Rebecca E. Karl (New York: Routledge, 1996), 159. Michael Hardt and Antonio Negri, *Empire* (Cambridge, MA: Harvard University Press, 2003), 25. Jason Read, *The Micro-Politics of Capital: Marx and the Prehistory of the Present* (Albany: State University of New York Press, 2003), 18. Huber, *Lifeblood*, 18. Fredric Jameson, *Representing Capital: A Reading of Volume One* (London: Verso, 2011), 71. See also Étienne Balibar, 'Towards a New Critique of Political Economy: From Generalized Surplus Value to Total Subsumption', in *Capitalism: Concept, Idea, Image: Aspects of Marx's Capital Today*, ed. Peter Osborne, Éric Alliez, and Eric-John Russell (London: CRMEP Books, 2019).

as ideology, practice, and economy, has penetrated all dimensions of social life'.[108]

While such statements can be rhetorically useful in certain contexts, their analytical value is close to none. It might very well be that there is nothing on this earth which is not somehow *affected* by capital, but that is not the same as saying that everything has been subsumed under capital or that capital has taken hold of all dimensions of social life. The social as well as natural world is shaped by innumerable forces which do not derive from the logic of capital – not only because these forces have been able to keep the logic of capital at bay but also because capital is not a supervillain seeking to rule the entire world. The aim of capitalist production is surplus value, and, as long as norms, practices, ideologies, natural processes, lifestyles, and so on do not interfere with this aim, there is no reason why capital would want to eradicate or change them. Capital is much more strategic than that; as long as it is able to keep a firm grip on the fundamental conditions of social reproduction, it does not need to meticulously control everything. Take the example of the reproduction of labour power. One of the peculiar things about labour power is that although it is a commodity, 'it is not produced capitalistically', as Lise Vogel puts it.[109] Whatever the precise reasons for this, it is remarkable that capitalism is – or at least has been so far – perfectly compatible with relinquishing direct control over a process which is an absolutely indispensable condition of its existence.[110] That does not mean that the reproduction of labour power takes place 'outside' of capitalism or is unaffected by it; rather, it means that the reproduction of labour power and the production of (other) commodities take place inside of capitalism in different ways. Our conceptual apparatus should be able to reflect such real differences, but this is precisely what is obscured by claims about the total subsumption of everything. The commodity-producing labour process has a special status for capital since, as Endnotes explain, it '*is* the immediate production process of capital. Nothing comparable can be

---

108   Jameson, *Representing Capital*, 71; The Invisible Committee, *Now* (South Pasadena, CA: Semiotext(e), 2017), 84; Read, *The Micro-Politics of Capital*, 1.

109   Lise Vogel, *Marxism and the Oppression of Women: Toward a Unitary Theory* (Chicago: Haymarket, 2014), 157.

110   Tithi Bhattacharya, 'How Not to Skip Class: Social Reproduction of Labour and the Global Working Class', in *Social Reproduction Theory: Remapping Class, Recentring Oppression*, ed. Tithi Bhattacharya (London: Pluto Press, 2017), 81.

said of anything beyond the production process, for it is only production which capital directly claims as its own.'[111] The sphere of production is the stronghold of the power of capital, and although the logic of valorisation spreads from there like ripples in a pond, it has no need to subsume other spheres of society in a similar manner.

At this point, it should also be noted that subsumption takes on very different forms in various sectors and branches of production. Real subsumption has always been most intense in manufacturing, while agriculture remained quite resistant to it until the mid-twentieth century, after which it accelerated at a rapid pace (more about this in the next chapter). Many (though not all) service sector jobs are difficult, if not impossible, to subject to real subsumption – a circumstance which is, as Jason E. Smith and Endnotes have demonstrated, quite important for understanding the dynamics of contemporary capitalism, as it explains why they are left behind by outsourcing and automation.[112] Many of these service sector jobs might never undergo a transition from formal to real subsumption. Such differences between the pace and dynamics of subsumption in various branches and sectors are difficult to discern if the concept of subsumption becomes a synonym for capital's power in a broad sense.

These considerations allow us to see why it is also misguided to use the concepts of formal and real (and total) subsumption as the basis of a periodisation of the history of capitalism, as suggested by Vercellone, Negri, Cammatte, and *Théorie Communiste*.[113] Use of the concepts of formal and real subsumption to characterise different historical phases of the development of the capitalist totality obscures the two important conclusions we have just reached: first, that capital's relation to the sphere of production is quite different from its relation to other moments of the social totality; second, that *within* the sphere of production, there are very important differences with regards to the pace and dynamics of subsumption in various branches and sectors.

For these reasons, we should stick to Marx's concept of subsumption as referring to the way in which the logic of capital relates to the social and material structure of the production process. This is neither a case of

---

111   Endnotes, 'The History of Subsumption', 149.
112   Smith, 'Nowhere to Go'; Endnotes, 'A History of Separation', 155ff.
113   Vercellone, 'Formal Subsumption'; Negri, 'Twenty Theses on Marx'; Camatte, *Capital and Community*. See Endnotes, 'The History of Subsumption' for a good critique.

conceptual conservatism nor a denial of the profound ramifications of the logic of capital beyond the sphere of production. It is, rather, an insistence on conceptual clarity: in order to understand the power of capital, we need a conceptual apparatus which is able to reflect capital's differing attitudes to the various moments of the social totality.

11

The Capitalist Reconfiguration of Nature

At the end of the last chapter, I argued that in order to maintain the analytical usefulness of the concept of subsumption, we should keep using it in the same way as Marx did, namely as a concept designed to capture capital's relation to the concrete material and organisational structure of the production process. There are no rules without exceptions, however. There is at least one extension of the concept of subsumption which has proven very fruitful: its application to the relationship between capital and nature. In a certain sense, this is more a shift of perspective than an extension of the concept beyond its original meaning. As Marx is always careful to point out, labour is 'the manifestation of a force of nature', and as such the subsumption of *labour* is also immediately the subsumption of *nature*.[1] Labour power is embedded in the human body, which has its own natural rhythms and does not automatically adhere to the demands of capital. The naturalness of labour power represents an *obstacle* to capital accumulation – a fact that comes out particularly clearly in the analysis of the struggle over the length of the working day in volume one of *Capital*: in its 'blind and measureless drive, its werewolf hunger for surplus labour, capital oversteps not only the moral but even the merely physical limits of the working day'.[2] The boundless logic of valorisation makes it impossible for capital to sustain its own natural conditions,

---

1   24: 81.
2   C1: 375.

which is why the state is forced to step in and regulate the working day. It thus makes perfect sense that Paul Burkett identifies a 'model of environmental crisis' in Marx's analysis of the struggle over the length of the working day.[3]

The Real Subsumption of Nature

As Andreas Malm has forcefully demonstrated, labour and (the rest of) nature share 'an ineradicable *autonomy* from capital' which stems from the fact that both are 'ontologically prior' to capital and governed by logics which do not originate in capital.[4] This is especially – but not exclusively – true of *organic* processes: 'capitalist production has not yet', as Marx notes it in the *1861–63 Manuscripts*, 'succeeded, and never will succeed in mastering these [organic] processes in the same way as it has mastered purely mechanical or inorganic chemical processes'.[5] The ineradicable autonomy of nature is an obstacle for capital, and for this reason capitalist production sets in motion a structural pressure to iron out the bumps of nature, or, put differently, to inaugurate a process of *real subsumption of nature*. As Malm eloquently puts it: 'Capital cannot do without the stranger of nature, so it chases it and seeks to subordinate it, integrate it into a disciplinary regime and make its most erratic impulses redundant'.[6] In this process, capital attacks not only labour (as a natural process), but all aspects of the production process in which the autonomy of nature rears its head.

But what exactly do we mean by the 'subsumption of nature'? The concept was first introduced by Burkett in his 1999 *Marx and Nature*, but the first attempt to specify its meaning and evaluate its analytical potential can be found in a 2001 paper by William Boyd, W. Scott Prudham, and Rachel A. Schurman.[7] According to them, subsumption of nature (whether formal or real) is a process which takes place only in extractive

---

3   Paul Burkett, *Marx and Nature: A Red and Green Perspective* (Chicago: Haymarket, 2014), 12, 133ff.

4   Andreas Malm, *The Progress of This Storm: Nature and Society in a Warming World* (London: Verso, 2018), 197; Andreas Malm, *Fossil Capital: The Rise of Steam Power and the Roots of Global Warming* (London: Verso, 2016), 309ff.

5   33: 291.

6   Malm, *The Progress of This Storm*, 201.

7   Burkett, *Marx and Nature*, 67.

industries and agriculture (what they refer to as 'nature-based industries').[8] Furthermore, real subsumption of nature can only be said to
take place in a subset of these industries, namely those based on *biological*
processes:

> The key to understanding the distinction between formal and real
> subsumption of nature lies in the difference between biological and
> nonbiological systems and the unique capacity to manipulate biolog-
> ical productivity. The *real subsumption of nature* refers to systematic
> increases in or intensification of biological productivity (i.e. yield,
> turnover time, metabolism, photosynthetic efficiency) – a concept that
> obviously applies only to those biologically based sectors that operate
> according to a logic of cultivation.[9]

So, whereas production based on non-biological systems is forced to
operate according to a 'logic of extraction', in which nature is only formally
subsumed – a process similar to the production of absolute surplus value –
industries based on biological systems are able to really subsume nature
in a manner similar to the production of relative surplus value. Boyd et
al. also argue that with the transition from formal to real subsumption,
capital begins to circulate *through* nature rather than *around* it.[10]

Boyd et al. certainly capture some important aspects of capital's relation
to nature (especially the difference between its relation to non-biological
and biological processes), but their concept of real subsumption of nature
is ultimately too narrow, leading them to lose sight of a number of important effects of capital on nature. In order to see why, let us begin with the
distinction between capital circulating *around* versus circulating *through*
nature. On its most elementary level, capital is *value in motion*, a motion
in which value undergoes a series of transubstantiations: when commodities and money circulate in the form of capital, they are reduced to
mere forms of an identical substance, namely value.[11] This is why Marx
concludes that the 'different modes in which the values existed were a pure

---

8   William Boyd, W. Scott Prudham, and Rachel A. Schurman, 'Industrial Dynamics
and the Problem of Nature', *Society and Natural Resources* 14, no. 7 (31 August 2001):
562.
9   Ibid., 564.
10   Ibid., 565.
11   C1: 255f.

semblance; value itself formed the constantly self-identical essence within their disappearance'.[12] In other words, capital always circulates 'through' the material bearers of its circuit, whether these bearers are natural or not. Seen from this perspective, capital never circulates 'around' anything at all. On a more concrete level, we might also question the adequacy of this distinction on the basis of a simple consideration of traditional agricultural production. What are seeds growing in the field of a seventeenth-century capitalist farmer if not an example of capital circulating 'through' nature? Or what about the transformation of grass into milk in the stomach of a cow in traditional dairy production? Fruits intended for sale growing on a tree in an orchard? The production of silk by silk worms? In his discussion of the distinction between production time and working time in the manuscripts for the second book of *Capital*, Marx provides several such examples: fermentation of wine, drying pottery, bleaching and ripening of corn. In processes such as these, capital is, Marx explains, 'handed over to the sway of natural processes'.[13]

A more fundamental problem with the analysis presented by Boyd et al. is the assumption that the subsumption of nature only takes place in 'nature-based' industries. With this restriction, we are left with no conceptual tools to understand the relationship between capital and nature in other sectors and branches. Boyd et al. claim that 'the defining feature of nature-based industries is that they *confront nature directly* in the process of commodity production'. But could we not say the same thing about manufacturing? There, capital confronts nature directly in several ways: as working bodies with a set of natural dexterities, needs, capacities, and limits; as energy (electricity, oil, gas, coal, water, wind, etc.); and, at least in some parts of industry, as chemical processes integrated in the production process. According to Marx, it is

> mass production – cooperation on a large scale, with the employment of machinery – that first subjugates [*unterwirft*] the *forces of nature* on a large scale – wind, water, steam, electricity – to the direct production process, converts them into *agents of social labour*.[14]

---

12   G: 312.
13   C2: 316f.
14   34: 31f; see also 30: 321; C1: 509.

From Water to Coal to Oil

Capital has always had to wrestle with the autonomy of nature in man-ufacturing, and over time it has secured a number of fateful victories which have allowed it to gain a higher degree control over nature. A good example of this is the shift from water power to steam in the British textile industry, as described in Malm's magisterial study.[15] The flow of water needed in order to power the mills was irregular and tied to specific loca-tions, often in rural areas, where a combination of an insufficient supply of labour and large investments in fixed capital tended to empower workers. The shift to coal-fired steam-engines changed all of that: now the motive force could be turned on and off at will (in contrast to water running in a canal), the power supply could easily be regulated, energy could be stored and transported, and factories could relocate to urban areas with a high level of competition for jobs among proletarians. In short: whereas water remained 'quasi-autonomous and immune to real subsumption', coal allowed capitalists to achieve a much-higher degree of control over nature within the production process, which in turn provided them with a powerful weapon in the struggle against labour.[16] What took place in the shift from water to coal in the British textile industry was thus, in Malm's words, a process of 'real subsumption of labour by means of really sub-sumed nature' – a phrasing which has the virtue of highlighting the close relationship between the subsumption of nature and that of labour, and which thereby also highlights the reason why the subsumption of nature is an important element in the economic power of capital.[17] Coal was a *weapon*, a means of cracking down on rebellious workers; the subsump-tion of nature was a method for tightening capital's grip on social life.

For a while, it worked well. But at some point, around the turn of the twentieth century, reliance on coal became a problem for capital as it enhanced the power of workers located in the strategically important and 'interconnected industries of coal mining, railways docking and shipping', as Timothy Mitchell puts it.[18] So, what did the forces of capital do? They took a further step in the real subsumption of nature by shifting to *oil*, which,

---

15   Malm, *Fossil Capital.*
16   Ibid., 313.
17   Ibid., 309.
18   Timothy Mitchell, *Carbon Democracy: Political Power in the Age of Oil* (London: Verso, 2013), 23.

in contrast to coal, 'flowed along networks that often had the properties of a grid, like an electricity network, where there is more than one possible path and the flow of energy can switch to avoid blockages or overcome breakdowns.'[19] As Malm explains, such examples demonstrate that 'when capital desperately seeks to restructure the labor process and put it on a more profitable footing, nothing can be more useful than a truly revolutionary power technology. It is the battering ram, the generalizable device with which capital destroys resistance and swings into renewed expansion.'[20]

The subsumption of nature is thus a crucial part of the economic power of capital. This subsumption is formal when capital merely utilises a natural process without altering its form, and it becomes real when capital actively intervenes in natural processes in order to suppress the autonomy of nature and accommodate these processes to the demands of valorisation – a process which, contrary to what Boyd et al. claim, takes place in all sectors and branches of capitalist production.

The Real Subsumption of Agriculture

In the remaining sections of this chapter, I want to examine an important example of how real subsumption has strengthened the economic power of capital: the intensification of capital's grip on agricultural production since the 1940s. In my analysis of real subsumption so far, I have by and large followed Marx in his focus on *industrial* production. Although the kind of modern industry examined in *Capital* was still marginal in Marx's time (at least on a global level), he correctly identified it as the spearhead of capital's offensive. The prominence given to industrial capital in Marx's writings is sometimes used as an argument for the idea that as a theoretical framework, the critique of political economy is only relevant for analyses of industrial – and not agricultural – production. According to ecosocialists such as Ted Benton, Marx's promethean fascination with capitalist industry led him to construct his theories on the model

---

19   Ibid., 38; see also Matthew T. Huber, *Lifeblood: Oil, Freedom, and the Forces of Capital* (Minneapolis: University of Minnesota Press, 2013).

20   Andreas Malm, 'Long Waves of Fossil Development: Periodizing Energy and Capital', in *Materialism and the Critique of Energy*, ed. Brent Ryan Bellamy and Jeff Diamanti (Chicago: MCM' Publishing, 2018), 172; see also Tom Keefer, 'Fossil Fuels, Capitalism, and Class Struggle', *Commoner*, no. 13 (2009): 15–21.

of industrial labour, with the consequence that they are unfit for understanding agriculture.[21] Such claims have been thoroughly rebutted by John Bellamy Foster and Paul Burkett, who have convincingly demonstrated that Marx's critique of political economy is not only very attentive to the ecological destruction wrought by capitalist agriculture in Marx's own time, but also that it remains an unsurpassed theoretical framework for understanding the biospheric crisis created by contemporary capitalism.[22] The agricultural chemist Justus von Liebig's critique of the robbery of soil fertility in modern agriculture had a profound influence on Marx, and, as Kohei Saito's recent study of Marx's notebooks has documented, Marx continued to work on the ecological aspects of his critique of political economy in the period following the publication of the first volume of *Capital* in 1867.[23]

There is a good reason why Marx did not have much to say about real subsumption of labour and nature in agriculture: it barely existed in the nineteenth century. Despite being the birth site of capitalism, agriculture remained highly recalcitrant to real subsumption well into the twentieth century. To be sure, the specialisation of production and concentration of land associated with the emergence of capitalist agriculture in England did lead to substantial productivity gains (which became the basis for urbanisation and the industrial revolution), but these were mostly achieved using equipment and techniques inherited from the Middle Ages.[24] Compared

---

21 Ted Benton, 'Marxism and Natural Limit: An Ecological Critique and Reconstruction', *New Left Review* 178 (1989): 51–86.

22 John Bellamy Foster, *Marx's Ecology: Materialism and Nature* (New York: Monthly Review Press, 2000); Burkett, *Marx and Nature*. For their most recent defence, see John Bellamy Foster and Paul Burkett, *Marx and the Earth: An Anti-Critique* (Leiden: Brill, 2016). As Malm points out, however, they sometimes 'take the Marx they like best and claim that no other Karl can be found'. Andreas Malm, 'Marx on Steam: From the Optimism of Progress to the Pessimism of Power', *Rethinking Marxism* 30, no. 2 (2018): 173. For a more balanced view, see Andreas Malm, 'For a Fallible and Lovable Marx: Some Thoughts on the Latest Book by Foster and Burkett', *Critical Historical Studies* 4, no. 2 (2017): 267–75.

23 Kohei Saito, *Karl Marx's Ecosocialism: Capital, Nature, and the Unfinished Critique of Political Economy* (New York: Monthly Review Press, 2017).

24 See Robert C. Allen, *The British Industrial Revolution in Global Perspective* (Cambridge: Cambridge University Press, 2009), 57ff; Aaron Benanav, 'A Global History of Unemployment: Surplus Populations in the World Economy, 1949–2010' (PhD diss., UCLA, 2015), 116ff; Robert Brenner, 'The Agrarian Roots of European Capitalism', in *The Brenner Debate*, ed. T. H. Aston and C. H. E. Philpin (Cambridge: Cambridge University Press, 1987), 308ff; David B. Grigg, *The Transformation of Agriculture in the West*

to manufacturing, where technological development raced ahead, agriculture remained stagnant. Even in an advanced capitalist economy such as France at the end of World War II, 'nearly half the population still lived in localities of fewer than two thousand inhabitants and consumed food from their farms or neighboring ones in ways reminiscent of the Middle Ages'.[25] Or, as Eric Hobsbawm once put it: 'For 80 percent of humanity the Middle Ages ended suddenly in the 1950s'.[26]

The late eighteenth and the nineteenth centuries witnessed a number of technological innovations, most notably the steel plough and the steam-powered thresher machine, but agriculture still 'remained highly resistant' to real subsumption.[27] One of the main problems, as mentioned earlier, was soil fertility.[28] From the 1940s onwards, this as well as other obstacles was overcome by a dramatic process of real subsumption, aptly summarised by Richard Lewontin and Jean-Pierre Berlan:

> In 1910 farmers gathered their own seeds from last year's crop, raised the mules and horses that provided traction power, fed them on hay and grains produced on the farm, and fertilized the fields with the manure they produced. In 1986 farmers purchase their seed from Pioneer Hybrid Seed Co., buy their 'mules' from the Ford Motor Company, the 'oats' for their 'mules' from Exon, their 'manure' from American Cyanamid, feed their hogs on concentrated grain from Central Soya, and sow their next corn crop with the help of a revolving loan from Continental Illinois Bank and Trust Co.

Since the 1940s, they conclude, agriculture has 'become completely penetrated by capital' and has changed almost beyond recognition.[29]

(Oxford: Blackwell, 1992), 33, 47; Marcel Mazoyer and Laurence Roudart, *A History of World Agriculture: From the Neolithic Age to the Current Crisis* (London: Earthscan, 2006), 355f; Tony Weis, *The Global Food Economy: The Battle for the Future of Farming* (London: Zed Books, 2007), 172f; Ellen Meiksins Wood, *The Origin of Capitalism: A Longer View* (London: Verso, 2002), 103.

25   Christopher Mills Isett and Stephen Miller, *The Social History of Agriculture: From the Origins to the Current Crisis* (New York: Rowman & Littlefield, 2016), 257.

26   Eric Hobsbawm, *The Age of Extremes: The Short Twentieth Century, 1914–1991* (London: Abacus, 1995), 288.

27   Benanav, 'A Global History of Unemployment', 122ff; Grigg, *The Transformation of Agriculture*, 48.

28   Benanav, 'A Global History of Unemployment', 121.

29   Richard Lewontin and Jean-Pierre Berlan, 'Technology, Research, and the Penetration of Capital: The Case of U.S. Agriculture', *Monthly Review* 38, no. 3 (1986).

This development is the result of three closely related processes: first, a set of technological changes related to mechanisation, fertilisers, and biotechnological manipulation of plants and animals; second, an organisational restructuring related to new divisions of labour; and third, an increasing and ever-tighter subjection of agriculture to market forces as a result of the so-called green revolution, the logistics revolution, and the structural adjustment programmes of the 1980s. Let us take a closer look at these three trends, beginning with the technological changes.

Agricultural Technologies

In the first decade of the twentieth century, the German chemists Fritz Haber and Carl Bosch developed a method for artificially fixating nitrogen from atmospheric gasses (the so-called Haber-Bosch process). Nitrogen is one of the essential soil nutrients needed for plants to grow (and for life in general), and the inability to come up with effective methods for fixating it in a form which plants can absorb was a crucial barrier for the attempts to increase land productivity in the nineteenth and early twentieth centuries.[30] The development of the Haber-Bosch process was therefore 'a break-through of world-historical significance', as Aaron Benanav puts it, as it made possible the production of synthetic fertilisers, which in turn led to tremendous productivity gains.[31] The rapid dissemination of synthetic fertilisers after World War II effectively overcame the barriers to productivity increases inherent in traditional, organic methods for restoring soil fertility.

Around the same time, another immensely important technological development gathered pace, namely the mechanisation and automation of production processes made possible by the introduction of tractors, combine harvesters, and other machines which radically reduced the need for animal traction as well as human labour.[32] To cite just one example, geographer Bret Wallach reports that

---

30 Benanav, 'A Global History of Unemployment', 117ff.

31 Ibid., 126; Weis, *The Global Food Economy*, 55f.

32 See Benanav, 'A Global History of Unemployment', 134ff; Richard Lewontin, 'The Maturing of Capitalist Agriculture: Farmer as Proletarian', in *Hungry for Profit: The Agribusiness Threat to Farmers, Food, and the Environment*, ed. Fred Magdoff, John Bellamy Foster, and Frederick H. Buttel (New York: Monthly Review Press, 2000), 97; Lewontin and Berlan, 'Technology, Research, and the Penetration of Capital'; Mazoyer and Roudart, *A History of World Agriculture*, chaps. 9, 10.

James G Boswell II, until his death in 2009 one of the biggest cotton producers in the United States, had once employed 5,000 cotton pickers. In his lifetime they were replaced by a hundred machine operators who picked Boswell's 150,000 California acres.[33]

As Benanav notes, these two crucial technological breakthroughs – synthetic fertilisers and mechanisation – amounted to 'a double revolution [which] transformed farms and feed-lots into *open-air factories*'.[34] Agriculture finally caught up with industry – or rather, it gradually *became* a branch of industry – and the wave of real subsumption resulted in massive growth of productivity as well as ecological destruction. The double revolution led to increasing specialisation and the spread of monocultural production, which in turn made farming vulnerable to pests, thereby making it necessary to develop new forms of pesticides.[35] As political ecologist Tony Weis explains, 'The rise of agro-chemicals revolutionized the control of insects, weeds and fungi, replacing the need for on-farm diversity and labour-intensive ecological management with a new normative objective: biological standardization.'[36]

Alongside the development and dissemination of synthetic fertilisers and mechanisation, another revolutionary leap forward in the ability to subjugate the refractory hand of nature took place in the field of *biotechnology*. This was partly a result of the need to develop plants that were not only capable of absorbing large amounts of synthetic fertiliser but also fitted the new machines used for harvesting and threshing.[37] Humans have always altered nature through selective breeding of plants and animals, so in a certain sense biotechnology is as old as agriculture itself (or, in the form of domestication of animals, even older). Nevertheless, the biotechnological advances achieved in the course of the first half of the twentieth century represent a profound rupture in the history of plant breeding. This is where we find some of the most stunning examples of the real subsumption of nature. In a process similar to the replacement of craft knowledge with science in nineteenth-century industrial production,

---

33   Bret Wallach, *A World Made for Money: Economy, Geography, and the Way We Live Today* (Lincoln: University of Nebraska Press, 2015), 203f.

34   Benanav, 'A Global History of Unemployment', 114.

35   Ibid., 139; Lewontin, 'The Maturing of Capitalist Agriculture', 97.

36   Weis, *The Global Food Economy*, 57.

37   Mazoyer and Roudart, *A History of World Agriculture*, 386ff.

plant breeding went from being a farming practice to a highly complicated, scientific undertaking. At first, this research was – at least in the United States, which was at the forefront of this development – mainly financed and conducted by the state. With time, however, plant breeding became completely dominated by agrobusinesses.[38] Today, farmers are compelled to buy seeds from transnational corporations (agro-TNCs) such as Monsanto in order to remain competitive.

In its attempt to commercialise plant breeding, capital has always had to struggle with a powerful expression of the annoying autonomy of nature: *the ability of plants to reproduce*. This ability completely undermines the dependence of farmers upon seed companies: as Lewontin explains, if a seed grows into a plant with the ability to reproduce, 'the seed company has provided the farmer with a free good'.[39] The double nature of the plant as a product *and* a means of production thus represents a serious biological obstacle for capital.[40] In his impressive study of the political economy of the seed, Jack Kloppenburg notes that 'capital has pursued two distinct but intersecting routes' to overcome this barrier.[41] One option is to simply impose the commodity form on seeds by means of legislation. By obtaining patent rights on seeds and installing DNA fingerprints in them, agrobusinesses can legally prevent farmers from exploiting their ability to reproduce, despite it being technically possible.

Another option – pursued by capital with great success – is to genetically modify seeds in order to make their reproduction impossible. This was first achieved with the development of hybrid plants in the 1930s. Although hybrid plants do have the ability to reproduce, their progeny 'exhibits a considerable reduction in yield'.[42] Farmers are therefore obliged to return to seed companies every year, meaning that hybridisation has 'opened to capital a whole new frontier of accumulation'.[43] As it turns out, however, that hybridisation has a number of technical limitations, chief among which is that the method cannot be applied to a number of important crops, such as soybeans and wheat.[44]

---

38 Jack Ralph Kloppenburg, *First the Seed: The Political Economy of Plant Biotechnology, 1492–2000*, 2nd ed. (Madison: University of Wisconsin Press, 2004).
39 Lewontin, 'The Maturing of Capitalist Agriculture', 98.
40 Kloppenburg, *First the Seed*, 10f.
41 Ibid., 11.
42 Ibid., 93; see also Lewontin, 'The Maturing of Capitalist Agriculture', 98f.
43 Kloppenburg, *First the Seed*, 11.
44 Lewontin, 'The Maturing of Capitalist Agriculture', 99.

Another major step in the commercialisation of seeds was the development and widespread adoption of genetically modified crops from the 1990s onwards – the most well-known example being the soybean developed by Monsanto, which is the only available seed that can survive exposure to their herbicide Roundup.[45] In this way, farmers are forced to buy seeds and chemicals from agro-TNCs.

A further step in the real subsumption of nature was achieved with the development of so-called genetic use restriction technology (GURT), or 'terminator' technology, as it is sometimes called: *seeds which produce completely sterile plants.* The first patent for such 'suicide seeds' was issued in 1998, but so far the technology has been so controversial that its use has been politically blocked.[46] Not surprisingly, however, there is a continued interest in and development of this technology in agrobusiness – a fact which demonstrates that at least some corporations believe that the ban will eventually be lifted.[47] In contrast to hybridisation, terminator technology is applicable to all crops, meaning that if this technology is ever put to use, 'at one blow, the problem of capitalist seed production … has been solved', as Lewontin puts it.[48] Farmers would then be completely dependent upon seed companies.

These biotechnological 'improvements' provide us with an excellent and concrete example of how the mute compulsion of capital is enhanced by the material restructuring of processes necessary for social reproduction to take place – in this case, the material restructuring of the biological properties of plants. As Kloppenburg explains, a seed is essentially

a packet of genetic information, an envelope containing a DNA message. In that message are encoded the templates for the subsequent development of the mature plant. The content of the code crucially shapes the manner in which the growing plant responds to its environment. Insofar as biotechnology permits specific and detailed 'reprogramming'

---

45   Weis, *The Global Food Economy*, 73ff; Kloppenburg, *First the Seed*, chap. 11.

46   See Kloppenburg, *First the Seed*, 319ff; Weis, *The Global Food Economy*, 75; Lewontin, 'The Maturing of Capitalist Agriculture', 100f; Luca Lombardo, 'Genetic Use Restriction Technologies: A Review', *Plant Biotechnology Journal* 12, no. 8 (2014): 995–1005.

47   Lombardo, 'Genetic Use Restriction Technologies'.

48   Lewontin, 'The Maturing of Capitalist Agriculture', 102; Gerad Middendorf et al., 'New Agricultural Biotechnologies: The Struggle for Democratic Choice', in Magdoff, Foster, and Buttel, *Hungry for Profit*, 112.

of the genetic code, *the seed, as embodied information, becomes the nexus of control over the determination and shape of the entire crop production process.*[49]

Here, the real subsumption of nature becomes palpable. Similar to the way in which the capitalist division of labour tends to create workers whose labour power is useless outside of the mediations of capital, *commercial biotechnology aims to inscribe the logic of valorisation into the genetic code of the seed, so that the plant cannot grow without the mediations of capital.* Biotechnology thus provides a good example of the relation between economic and coercive power. As long as plants can reproduce, capital has to rely on patent rights, and thereby the coercive power of the state. The case of hybrid seeds, GMOs, and terminator technology demonstrates how the economic power of capital can replace the violence of the state by means of technology. If suicide seeds are ever released, it would, as Weis eloquently puts it, 'shift the *seed as commodity* from a more tenuous *scientific-legal conception*, where it can be contested in various ways (e.g. saving seeds, challenging patents), to a *biophysical attribute* whereby their annual purchase is simply irresistible'.[50] Here, we see one dimension of what it means to say that mute compulsion is a form of power which operates by means of the restructuring of the material conditions of social reproduction; *capitalist biotechnology inscribes the logic of valorisation into the biophysical structure of plants.* It thereby becomes unnecessary for agrobusinesses to inspect fields and (threaten to) sue farmers; instead, they simply *relegate their power to the seeds.* Note that this is not just some kind of techno-dystopian scenario; hybrid seeds achieved this already in the 1930s, GMO crops accelerated the materialisation of the commodity form in the 1990s, and the only thing that prevents a truly nightmarish rollout of terminator technology is resistance.

The real subsumption of nature by means of biotechnology has been most dramatic in the field of plant engineering, but it also takes place in the bodies of animals in meat and dairy industries. Breeding, growth hormones, genetic engineering, and antibiotics have substantially increased productivity in livestock production. For example, cows produce more milk than ever before, and production time for farmed salmon has been

---

49 Kloppenburg, *First the Seed*, 201.
50 Weis, *The Global Food Economy*, 75.

reduced from three years to a year and a half.[51] Perhaps the most spectac-
ular example is broilers. As Raj Patel and Jason W. Moore explain:

> Today's birds are the result of intensive post-World War II efforts
> drawing on genetic material sourced freely from the most profitable
> fowl. That bird can barely walk, reaches maturity in weeks, has an over-
> size breast, and is reared and slaughtered in geologically significant
> quantities.[52]

The productivity gains achieved in crop production freed up land for
animal feed, which in turn led to cheapening of meat and what Weis calls
the 'meatification' of diets in the second half of the twentieth century,
'implying a near-doubling of the meat consumption in the average diet of
every single person on earth amid a soaring human population.'[53] As with
the production of crops, this development has dramatically increased the
dependency of producers upon providers of external inputs.

Agricultural Divisions of Labour

The *second* major process which has revolutionised agriculture since
the middle of the twentieth century is a thoroughgoing restructuring of
the division of labour. Until well into the twentieth century, agriculture
remained a 'closed system' in which farms generally produced their own
means of production.[54] The technological developments described in the
preceding paragraphs changed that completely, since it made farming
dependent upon inputs which had to be bought on the market: machinery, fuel, seeds, fertilisers, pesticides, antibiotics, growth hormones, and
so on. Marx anticipated this development in a remarkably prescient
passage in the *Grundrisse*:

---

51   Eric Holt-Giménez, *A Foodie's Guide to Capitalism: Understanding the Political
Economy of What We Eat* (New York: Monthly Review Press, 2017), 79.

52   Raj Patel and Jason W. Moore, *A History of the World in Seven Cheap Things: A
Guide to Capitalism, Nature, and the Future of the Planet* (Oakland: University of California Press, 2017), 3. See also Weis, *The Global Food Economy*, 60.

53   Weis, *The Global Food Economy*, 17.

54   Benanav, 'A Global History of Unemployment', 123.

If agriculture itself rests on scientific activities – if it requires machinery, chemical fertilizer acquired through trade, seeds from distant countries etc., and if rural, patriarchal manufacture has already vanished … then the machine-making factory, external trade, crafts etc., appear as *needs* for agriculture … in this case, agriculture no longer finds the natural conditions of its own production within itself, naturally, arisen, spontaneous, and ready at hand, but these exist as an independent industry separate from it.[55]

As Marx goes on to add, 'this pulling-away of the natural ground from the conditions of every industry, and *this transfer of its conditions of production outside of itself*, into a general context' is an immanent tendency of capital.[56] Indeed, this is precisely what took place at an accelerating pace throughout the twentieth century.

As Lewontin points out, this development makes it necessary to distinguish between *farming* and *agrobusiness*.[57] Farming is 'the physical process of turning inputs like seed, feed, water, fertilizers, and pesticides into products like wheat, potatoes, and cattle on a specific site, the farm, using soil, labor, and machinery'. Agrobusiness, on the other hand, is a broader category which, in addition to farming, includes all of the processes which precede and follow farming (production of inputs and processing of outputs). Farming is, by nature, quite impervious to the logic of capital. Despite enlisting science in its service, capital has never been able to completely eliminate the irregularities of nature – far from it. Turnover times are generally difficult to reduce, and things like the weather, the climate, and diseases cause sudden interruptions that are very difficult to prevent. Additionally, agricultural production is spatially fixed, requires large investments of sunk capital, provides limited opportunities for economies of scale, and requires labour processes that are difficult to monitor and control.[58] For these and other reasons, the farming part of

---

55   G: 527.
56   G: 528. Emphasis added.
57   Lewontin, 'The Maturing of Capitalist Agriculture', 94f.
58   Ibid., 95. For discussions of these and other obstacles to the logic of capital posed by the nature of agriculture, see Kloppenburg, *First the Seed*, 27ff; Susan A. Mann and James M. Dickinson, 'Obstacles to the Development of a Capitalist Agriculture', *Journal of Peasant Studies* 5, no. 4 (1978): 466–81; Patrick H. Mooney, 'Labor Time, Production Time and Capitalist Development in Agriculture: A Reconsideration of the Mann-Dickinson Thesis', *Sociologia Ruralis* 22, nos. 3–4 (1982): 279–92; Michael Perelman, 'Obstacles to the

agricultural production is not, in fact, very attractive for capitalists. The strategy pursued by capital has therefore been to empty farming of as many aspects of the production process as possible, in order to turn them into industrial production processes. Farmers are thereby reduced to a kind of subcontractor or 'putting out' worker, who might own their means of production but are nevertheless completely dominated by the agrobusinesses who provide them with inputs and purchase their outputs.[59] Farming is still dominated by small producers, but they have gradually been reduced to an ancillary in a system of production dominated by input-producing companies on the one hand and distributors, retailers, and food-processing companies on the other.[60] The deeply paradoxical thing here is that what must count as one of the very most crucial processes in the reproduction of social life, namely farming, has been reduced to a kind of leftover task – troublesome but regrettably necessary. The nature of capitalism thereby becomes plain for everyone to see; as Marx illustrates, 'Here, production appears only as necessary mediation, in reality a necessary evil for the purpose of making money.'[61]

The Global Expansion of Capitalist Agriculture

The third major trend in capital's restructuring of agriculture over the course of the last century is its global expansion. All over the world, and especially in the global South, traditional forms of subsistence farming have been replaced by industrialised production for the market. Enormous numbers of people who were hitherto at least partially shielded from the market are now exposed to its vagaries.[62] The creation of such market dependence has taken many forms, among them 'the promise of higher incomes … the pulverization of holdings through population

---

Development of a Capitalist Agriculture: A Comment on Mann and Dickinson', *Journal of Peasant Studies* 7, no. 1 (1979): 119–21.

59   Lewontin, 'The Maturing of Capitalist Agriculture', 105.

60   Weis, *The Global Food Economy*, 29, 70ff, 81; Lewontin and Berlan, 'Technology, Research, and the Penetration of Capital'; Jasper Bernes, 'The Belly of the Revolution', in Bellamy and Diamanti, *Materialism and the Critique of Energy*, 352.

61   II.11: 31.

62   Farshad Araghi, 'The Great Global Enclosure of Our Times: Peasants and the Agrarian Question at the End of the Twentieth Century', in Magdoff, Foster, and Buttel, *Hungry for Profit*; Benanav, 'Global History of Unemployment'.

growth, or expropriation by landlords', in Benanav's words.[63] As in early modern England, violence has often played the most prominent role in this, for example in the form of US-backed military coups against governments planning to introduce progressive land reforms.[64]

One of the most important drivers of proletarianisation of peasants in the global South was the so-called green revolution of the 1950s and '60s. Led by the US government and the Ford and Rockefeller Foundations, this 'revolution' exported the industrial agricultural model based on high-yield crops, hybrid seeds, irrigation, synthetic fertiliser, pesticides, and machinery to countries in Latin America, Asia, and, to a lesser extent, Africa.[65] Peasants were thereby made dependent upon commercial inputs, and production was redirected towards export of cash crops and livestock products.[66] Smallholders without the resources to make this transition were wiped out.[67] The green revolution thus resulted in a considerably tighter integration of peasants of the global South into the world market and therefore also a considerable increase in the reach of the economic power of capital.

When considering the dynamics of the agricultural sector, it is always important to bear in mind what is commonly referred to as Engel's law, after the statistician Ernst Engel: namely the fact that people tend to spend a smaller part of their income on food as their income rises – in other words, that there is a low income elasticity of demand for agricultural products.[68] Combined with the immense productivity increases brought about by the global industrialisation of agriculture, this tendency led to a persistent pattern of falling prices of agricultural goods throughout the twentieth century.[69] This, in turn, increased competitive pressures among farmers, who had already been enmeshed in what Weis calls 'complex and ever more despatialized corporate webs'.[70] 'The price mechanism,

---

63 Benanav, 'A Global History of Unemployment', 111.

64 Weis, *The Global Food Economy*, 97f.

65 Harry M. Cleaver, 'The Contradictions of the Green Revolution', *American Economic Review* 62, no. 1/2 (1972): 177–86; Vandana Shiva, *The Violence of the Green Revolution: Third World Agriculture, Ecology, and Politics* (London: Zed Books, 1991); Weis, *The Global Food Economy*, 106ff; Kloppenburg, *First the Seed*, 157ff.

66 Araghi, 'The Great Global Enclosure', 149.

67 Holt-Giménez, *A Foodie's Guide to Capitalism*, 48; Weis, *The Global Food Economy*, 108.

68 Benanav, 'A Global History of Unemployment', 141ff.

69 Ibid., 140ff.

70 Weis, *The Global Food Economy*, 162.

that juggernaut of the capitalist mode of production, smashed its way through the agricultural sector, irrespective of the policy regime in place', as Benanav aptly puts it.[71] Many countries of the global South were forced to take on enormous debts, which – combined with the 'Volcker Shock' of 1979 – set the scene for the so-called structural adjustment programs (SAPs) of the 1980s, by means of which capital's grip on the global food system was tightened even more.[72] Under the direction of the International Monetary Fund and the World Bank, 'a similar package of reforms was', as Weis explains, 'stamped upon every debtor nation, generally including: trade and investment liberalization; export promotion; currency devaluation; fiscal austerity; price and wage deregulation; the privatization of state services and enterprises; and the assurance of private property rights'.[73] SAPs accelerated tendencies that were already well underway, partly as a result of the green revolution.[74] Around the same time, the revolution in logistics – which I will examine in the next chapter – contributed greatly to securing the conditions for global competition in agriculture. 'Food is logistical now, too', as Jasper Bernes notes. 'Under the coordinative power of the supermarket system, food travels farther than before. But even where source and destination are proximate, the logistics of agricultural inputs – from seeds, to fertilizers, to machinery – are themselves complex and likewise dependent upon long supply chains for their production'.[75] The globalisation of industrial agriculture was institutionalised with the establishment of the World Trade Organisation in 1995 and the effectuation of the Agreement on Agriculture, the aim of which is, in the words of Weis, 'to entrench and extend the rights of transnational capital'.[76]

In my run-through of the real subsumption of agriculture, I have focussed on those aspects which are most relevant as examples of how the economic power of capital works. It should also be noted, however,

---

71   Benanav, 'A Global History of Unemployment', 173.

72   See Araghi, 'The Great Global Enclosure of Our Times', 150; Mazoyer and Roudart, *A History of World Agriculture*, 471ff; Benanav, 'A Global History of Unemployment', 172ff.

73   Weis, *The Global Food Economy*, 118.

74   Benanav, 'A Global History of Unemployment', 171f.

75   Bernes, 'The Belly of the Revolution', 348.

76   Weis, *The Global Food Economy*, 129. See Philip McMichael, 'Global Food Politics', in Magdoff, Foster, and Buttel, *Hungry for Profit*; Weis, *The Global Food Economy*, chap. 4; Sophia Murphy, 'Free Trade in Agriculture: A Bad Idea Whose Time Is Done', *Monthly Review* 61, no. 3 (2009), monthlyreview.org.

that this development has led to immense ecological destruction in the form of pollution, reduction of biodiversity, soil erosion, unforeseen consequences of genetic modification, and tremendous increases of greenhouse gas emissions from petrol-fuelled machinery, transportation, synthetic fertiliser, and the meatification of diets.[77] Another important consequence of the agricultural trends of the last century is the massive and global displacement of rural populations, large parts of which have ended up as un- or underemployed informal workers in the ever-growing urban slums of the global South – a topic to which I will return in chapter thirteen, although on a higher level of abstraction.[78]

In order to understand how the trends described in the preceding pages affect the power of capital, it is important to bear in mind that agriculture has a unique status in all forms of societies. Regardless of how small a percentage of GDP it accounts for, or how small a part of total social labour it requires, agriculture remains the sector in which the most basic necessities of life are produced. It possesses a qualitative significance stemming from the fact that 'humans must be in a position to live in order to be able to "make history"', as Marx and Engels put it.[79] The abolition of agriculture would require the extermination of something like 90 per cent of the global population, so it seems safe to say that agriculture, and especially farming, has become a necessary part of the metabolism of human societies and nature.[80] When capital seizes hold of agriculture and subjects it to real subsumption, it significantly tightens its grip on social reproduction. The logic of capital existed for thousands of years until it managed to enmesh itself in crops, animals, and the soil. As Ellen Meiksins Wood stresses, it was not until the market managed to penetrate the production of food that capitalism proper was born.[81] Despite the agrarian origins of capitalism, agricultural production remained resistant to real subsumption for centuries. While capital recorded many victories in its struggle against nature in eighteenth- and nineteenth-century industry, the autonomy of plants, animals, the soil, the climate, and the weather proved difficult to break. Once real subsumption got going, however, its pace and results

---

77 See Patel and Moore, *A History of the World*, chap. 5; Simon Pirani, *Burning Up: A Global History of Fossil Fuel Consumption* (London: Pluto Press, 2018), 72f, 88ff; Shiva, *The Violence of the Green Revolution*; Weis, *The Global Food Economy*, 28ff.

78 Benanav, 'A Global History of Unemployment', chap. 3.

79 5: 41.

80 Mazoyer and Roudart, *A History of World Agriculture*, 19.

81 Wood, *The Origin of Capitalism*, 97.

have been mind blowing. Capital has remoulded agricultural production on all levels, from the biophysical structure of seeds to international treatises securing the uninhibited reign of agrobusinesses. Biotechnological manipulation has inscribed the commodity form in the raw material of production, and all over the world farmers have been hurled onto a world market sustained by planetary supply chains, financial flows, and international institutions. The violent system of colonialism has been replaced by the subjugation of the global South to Western agro-TNCs by means of the mute compulsion of global markets. 'Agriculture as we know it now is saturated with market relations', as Bernes puts it.[82] Recall what Marx identified as the crucial thing about formal and real subsumption and power: formal subsumption 'may be easily dissolved'.[83] Not so with real subsumption. It would have been much easier to make the transition from capitalist to non-capitalist agricultural production a hundred years ago than it is today – and for this reason, the real subsumption of nature and labour in agriculture represents an incredibly important basis of the power of capital in our time.

---

82   Bernes, 'The Belly of the Revolution', 355.
83   30: 279.

12

Logistical Power

Capital is, by definition, expansive. Immanent determinations of capital, including this expansive drive, are, as we learned in chapter nine, forced upon individual capitals by their competitive relation to each other. Competition compels capitals to seek new outlets for their commodities, and thereby also to strive 'beyond every spatial barrier'.[1] Or, as Marx and Engels famously put it in the *Manifesto*: 'The need of a constantly expanding market for its products chases the bourgeoisie over the whole surface of the globe.'[2] However, capital's tendency to tear down spatial barriers is not only a matter of finding new outlets for commodities. It is also a way of curbing proletarian power: increasing mobility of capital is equivalent to a fusion of labour markets, which increases competition among workers and thereby makes it easier to discipline them. 'All improvements in the means of communication', Marx explains, 'facilitate the competition of workers in different localities.'[3] In addition to this, the ability to relocate production, and thereby jobs, also puts pressure on the state: in order to avoid unemployment, loss of tax revenues, and increases in public expenditures, states are compelled to secure a so-called business-friendly environment. In short: *mobility is power*, and means of transportation and communication are *weapons*.[4]

---

1 G: 524.
2 6: 487.
3 6: 423.
4 C1: 579.

Capital is always on the run – not only from disobedient workers, disobedient governments, and disobedient nature, but also from itself. That is
to say, it is constantly in flight from its tendency to overproduction, which
acts as a powerful impetus towards the expansion of markets. We should
be careful, however, to avoid the claim that the ideal world of capital is a
frictionless space of absolute mobility. Relative immobility of *labour power*
is often advantageous for capital, since it is easier to suppress wages if the
unemployed are unable to migrate. In the case of spatially fixed production,
however, a highly mobile labour force will often be beneficial for capital,
especially if demand for labour varies with the seasons. For certain forms
of agricultural production (e.g., fruit production), the ideal labour force is
thus a free-floating surplus population of migrants. In short, 'the fundamental tensions and ambivalences on the part of capital' generate, as David
Harvey puts it, 'countervailing influences over the geographical mobility
of labour-power, independently of the will of the workers themselves'. So,
while the logic of capital requires *money and commodities* to move freely,
it sometimes requires the movement of *labour power* to be constrained.

Capital is a movement in which value alternately takes on the form of
money and commodities. In recent years, a vast amount of literature has
been devoted to the study of how the global mobility of money has shaped
the neoliberal epoch. Combined with new information technologies,
financial deregulation, and easy credit, the exhaustion of the post-war
boom led to a financialisation of the global economy, which is now dominated by an ever-growing financial sector in which enormous amounts
of obscure financial instruments are incessantly traded by algorithms.
The literature on financialisation has uncovered many important aspects
of contemporary capitalism, including the encroachment of finance on
everyday life by means of consumer credit, mortgages, and student debt.
It has also, however, contributed to the dissemination of the popular idea
that contemporary capitalism has disappeared into an immaterial ether
of symbols, information, signs, and algorithms. What often gets lost in
discussions about financialisation is the acceleration in the circulation of
physical commodities which has taken place alongside the acceleration
of the circulation of money.[5] Neoliberal financialisation is, of course,
a very significant feature of contemporary capitalism, but it is only one

---

5   Martin Danyluk, 'Capital's Logistical Fix: Accumulation, Globalization, and the
Survival of Capitalism', *Environment and Planning D: Society and Space* 36, no. 4 (2018):
632.

aspect of it. Another and equally important aspect is the so-called logistics revolution, which began around roughly the same time as the wave of financialisation, as the 'hidden counterpart' of the latter.[6]

Marx on Logistics

Before examining the logistics revolution, however, I first want to take a brief look at Marx's thoughts on what is today known as logistics. The first thing to notice is that, from very early on in his writings, Marx was very attentive to the global nature of capitalism and its connection to colonialism and world trade.[7] Marx was also very attentive to developments in transportation and communication – which is not surprising, given that he lived in a time where 'the necessary tendency of capital to strive to equate circulation time to 0' expressed itself in the spread of railways, steamboats, and telegraphs.[8]

Transportation occupies a peculiar position in the systematic structure of Marx's critique of political economy. In the various drafts for his unfinished project, Marx mostly deals with transportation in the sections devoted to the *circulation* of capital. At the same time, however, he consistently stresses that transport is a part of the *production process*.[9] The rationale behind this categorisation is that the *location* of a commodity is a part of its use value: a product is not really a commodity until it is actually available on the market.[10] For this reason, Marx argues that the production process encompasses everything that is today called the supply chain, including warehousing, distribution, and retail.[11]

Transportation is thus 'the continuation of a production process *within* the circulation process and *for* the circulation process'.[12] This process takes place in *time* and *space*. One of the peculiarities of capitalism, however, is that it reduces spatiality to 'a merely *temporal* moment'.[13] Space is reduced

---

6   Jasper Bernes, 'Logistics, Counterlogistics and the Communist Prospect', in *Endnotes 3: Gender, Class and Other Misfortunes* (London: Endnotes, 2013), 182f.

7   See, for example, 5: 69f; I.5: 81ff; 6: 485ff; and C1: 918f.

8   G: 629; see also C2: 326ff; 32: 419f; and C1: 506ff.

9   G: 534; 33: 38; 34: 145; II.4.1: 203; C2: 135.

10   G: 534, 635, 672; 32: 421.

11   33: 41.

12   C2: 229.

13   II.4.1: 203.

to time in the sense that distance matters for capital only because it takes time to cross it, which is why Marx notes that 'the spatial determination itself here appears as a *temporal determination* [*Zeitbestimmung*]'.[14] Capital's tendency to reduce turnover time therefore takes the form of an 'annihilation of space through time'.[15] Note that this is not only a matter of *speed*, but also of a certain *regularity* of time. Capital not only needs transport to be fast; it also needs it to be regular, reliable, and scheduled.

Marx's attentiveness to the way in which capital's expansive drive acts as a powerful pressure for developing new and improved means of transport and communication is a useful reminder that recent phenomena such as containerisation, intermodalism, and just-in-time production are nothing but contemporary incarnations of a dynamic as old as capitalism itself. In *Capital*, Marx quotes a London factory owner to illustrate the ramifications of railways and telegraphs:

> The extension of the railway system throughout the country has tended very much to encourage giving short notice. Purchasers now come up from Glasgow, Manchester, and Edinburgh once every fortnight or so to the wholesale city warehouses which we supply, and give small orders requiring immediate execution, instead of buying from stock as they used to do. Years ago we were always able to work in the slack times so as to meet the demand of the next season, but now no one can say beforehand what will be in demand then.[16]

If capital is to be mobile, it needs an *infrastructure*: roads, canals, rails, ports, airports, and so on. Such projects require large investments of sunk capital and are usually too risky or unprofitable to be attractive for individual capitals. Infrastructure forms a part of what Marx called the *general* conditions of production, in contrast to the conditions of *particular* capitals or fractions of capital. Capital has to shift such burdens 'on to the shoulders of the state,' since the latter is the only institution that possesses 'the privilege and will to force the totality'.[17] An early example of

---

14 Ibid.
15 G: 524.
16 Ibid.
17 G: 531. See David Harvey, *The Limits to Capital* (London: Verso, 2006), 378ff. The concepts of infrastructure and the 'general conditions of production' were central in the German state derivation debates of the 1970s. See, for example, Elmar Altvater, 'Some Problems of State Interventionism', in *State and Capital: A Marxist Debate*, ed.

this is the construction of canal systems in the United States in the 1820s and '30s, where new steamboats and growth in trade required investments too costly and risky for individual capitals to undertake.[18]

To sum up, three characteristics of Marx's analysis of logistics stand out. First, it locates the source of the drive to improve transportation and communication technology in capitalist relations of production. Second, it throws light on the relation between capital and the state by pointing out that capital relies on certain conditions of production which cannot be secured by individual capitals. Third, it breaks with the view of logistics as simply a matter of cost reduction; that is, it views logistics as a *weapon*, a mechanism of domination.

The Logistics Revolution

Only a brief look at the history of capitalism is required in order to see its intimate connection with the annihilation of space through time. Initially, capitalist production based itself on transport technology developed under pre-capitalist modes of production. Without the improvement in ship design achieved in the fifteenth and sixteenth centuries, for example, Western colonisation would have been difficult, if not impossible. During the eighteenth century, ocean freight rates declined dramatically due to technological as well as organisational changes.[19] The nineteenth century witnessed the emergence of means of transportation and communication which had 'no precedent for regularity, for the capacity to transport vast quantities of goods and numbers of people, and above all, for speed: the railway, the steamship, the telegraph'.[20] The opening of the Suez Canal in 1869 and the Panama Canal in 1914 significantly contributed to the

John Holloway and Sol Picciotto (London: Edward Arnold, 1978); Joachim Hirsch, 'The State Apparatus and Social Reproduction: Elements of a Theory of the Bourgeois State', in Holloway and Picciotto, *State and Capital*; Dieter Läpple, *Staat und Allgemeine Produktionsbedingungen, Grundlagen zur Kritik der Infrastrukturtheorien* (Berlin: VSA, 1973).

18   Alfred Dupont Chandler, *The Visible Hand: The Managerial Revolution in American Business* (Cambridge: Belknap, 2002), 33f.

19   C. Knick Harley, 'Ocean Freight Rates and Productivity, 1740–1913: The Primacy of Mechanical Invention Reaffirmed', *Journal of Economic History* 48, no. 4 (1988): 851–76; Douglass North, 'Ocean Freight Rates and Economic Development 1750–1913', *Journal of Economic History* 18, no. 4 (1958): 537–55.

20   Eric Hobsbawm, *The Age of Capital: 1848–1875* (London: Abacus, 2004), 68.

eradication of spatial barriers to world trade. Meanwhile, the invention and dissemination of the internal combustion engine led to the proliferation of trucking, which became a serious competitor to railways from the 1920s onwards.[21]

Despite all of these important advances, there was still considerable room for improvements in the transport sector by the middle of the twentieth century. The field of business logistics slowly began to emerge in the United States in the 1950s and '60s, but the incentive to systematically reduce costs and increase productivity in transport was dampened by the relative high profit rates in the post-war boom.[22] Moving freight by ship in the 1950s 'was still a hugely complicated project', as break-bulk cargo had to be loaded and unloaded manually by gangs of unionised dock workers.[23] The situation began to change in the 1970s, as the post-war boom came to an end while waves of social unrest spread in the leading capitalist countries. Intensified competition, labour militancy, and falling rates of profit provided businesses with powerful incentives to seek new ways to discipline labour and cut costs, and one of the results of this endeavour was the so-called logistics revolution.

But what *is* logistics? As Charmaine Chua notes, 'It is not altogether clear how one should define the vast behemoth that has come to be known as "logistics".'[24] The term usually refers to 'the management of the entire supply chain',[25] and, in this sense, it can refer to a distinctive branch of industry – that is, companies specialising in logistics – or a set of activities within companies, or both. In his essay on contemporary logistics, Jasper Bernes describes it as

---

21   Edna Bonacich and Jake B. Wilson, *Getting the Goods: Ports, Labour and the Logistics Revolution* (Ithaca, NY: Cornell University Press, 2008), 96f; Marc Levinson, *The Box: How the Shipping Container Made the World Smaller and the World Economy Bigger*, 2nd ed. (Princeton: Princeton University Press, 2016), 205.

22   W. Bruce Allen, 'The Logistics Revolution and Transportation', *ANNALS of the American Academy of Political and Social Science* 553, no. 1 (1997): 108; Deborah Cowen, *The Deadly Life of Logistics: Mapping Violence in Global Trade* (Minneapolis: University of Minnesota Press, 2014), chap. 1.

23   Levinson, *The Box*, 21.

24   Charmaine Chua, 'Logistical Violence, Logistical Vulnerabilities: A Review of *The Deadly Life of Logistics: Mapping Violence in Global Trade* by Deborah Cowen', *Historical Materialism* 25, no. 4 (2017): 169.

25   Bonacich and Wilson, *Getting the Goods*, 3.

the active power to coordinate and choreograph, the power to conjoin
and split flows; to speed up and slow down; to change the type of commodity produced and its origin and destination point; and, finally, to
collect and distribute knowledge about the production, movement and
sale of commodities as they stream across the grid.[26]

As is often pointed out in the critical literature on this topic, modern
logistics in part originates in the military, where the coordination of the
flow of supplies to the front has been a concern at least since armies
became so large that the traditional plundering of local populations
became an unfeasible strategy for the provision of food and other necessities.[27] The historical connection between military and commercial
logistics is expressed clearly in what is perhaps the most important piece
of technology in modern logistics: the standard container. The early
development of what eventually became one of the most salient symbols
of globalisation began in the United States in the mid-1950s, but it was
only after the American military decided to use it to clean up the logistical chaos of the Vietnam War that the containerisation of world trade
began to accelerate. Restructuring the global system of transportation to
make it fit the container was a huge task requiring enormous investments
in ports and ships, deregulation of the transport sector and standardisa-
tion of container designs. Once this infrastructure was in place, however,
the scene was set for a revolution in transportation. The rise in oil prices
throughout the 1970s prevented the container from unfolding its full
potential, but from the end of the decade, a sharp decrease in international shipping costs began.[28] This trend continued to accelerate in the
1980s, when the deregulation of the American transport industry gave
rise to so-called intermodal transportation – that is, direct transfers of
containers between ships, trucks, and trains, which makes it possible to
transport cargo without having to repackage.[29]

The logistics revolution has profoundly changed the landscape of global
production. Today, more than 80 per cent of the volume and more than

---

26 Bernes, 'Logistics, Counterlogistics and the Communist Prospect', 180.

27 Martin Van Creveld, *Supplying War: Logistics from Wallenstein to Patton* (Cambridge: Cambridge University Press, 2004).

28 Levinson, *The Box*, 341.

29 Bonacich and Wilson, *Getting the Goods*, 53; Levinson, *The Box*, 351; Cowen, *The
Deadly Life of Logistics*, 41ff.

70 per cent of the value of global trade is transported by ship.[30] Every day, enormous amounts of commodities flow through increasingly automated mega-ports; in 2017, a staggering 40,230,000 containers' worth of goods (measured in twenty-foot equivalent units, TEUs) were handled by the busiest port in the world: the port of Shanghai.[31] In 1973, when containerisation was already well underway, American, Asian, and European container ships transported 4 million TEUs. Ten years later, this number had tripled to 12 million.[32] In 2017, the total number of TEUs flowing through the ports of the world reached an astounding 709 million.[33] Despite chronic overcapacity, shipping companies continue to build ever-larger ships in order to face up to the intense competition in the sector. Economist and historian Marc Levinson notes that in 2005, a ship with a capacity of 8,000 TEUs was 'considered unusually large'.[34] In 2022, the largest ships reached a capacity of 24,000 TEUs. These ships are unloaded in enormous deep-water ports where longshoremen have been replaced with automated vehicles and cranes stacking containers equipped with unique ISO codes.[35] These ports, many of which are partly or completely privatised, compete for ships and 'behave more or less like private, profit-making corporations'.[36]

As a result of these trends, the historically quite radical and militant dockworkers' unions have been seriously weakened. Sociologists Edna Bonacich and Jake B. Wilson summarise the impact of the logistics revolution on workers in this way: 'increased contingency, weakened unions, racialization, and lowered labor standards'.[37] This is true not only of dockworkers but also of workers in railway and trucking industries. The real significance of the logistics revolution, however, lies not in its impact on the shipping industry viewed in isolation but in its effects on the entire structure of the global economy.[38] Containerisation and intermodalism

---

30   UNCTAD, *Review of Maritime Transport 2017* (UNCTAD, 2017), x.

31   Ibid., 73.

32   Cowen, *The Deadly Life of Logistics*, 57.

33   UNCTAD, *Review of Maritime Transport*, 71.

34   Levinson, *The Box*, 388.

35   Ibid., 372ff.

36   Bonacich and Wilson, *Getting the Goods*, 55.

37   Ibid., 15. See also Cowen, *The Deadly Life of Logistics*, 41ff; Thomas Ehrlich Reifer, 'Labor, Race, and Empire: Transport Workers and Transnational Empires of Trade, Production, and Finance', in *Labor versus Empire: Race, Gender, and Migration*, ed. Gilbert G. Gonzalez et al. (New York: Routledge, 2004).

38   Levinson, *The Box*, 330.

was, along with computerisation, a crucial precondition for the emergence and dissemination of just-in-time production: cheap, fast, and precise transportation made it possible for manufacturers to move away from the traditional, vertically integrated company structure with large inventories of raw materials and finished products ('just-in-case' production) in order to focus on their core operations in a network of horizontally integrated production.[39]

Marx's claim that transportation should be regarded as a part of the production process has never been as relevant as it is today, when intermediate products make up the bulk of internationally traded goods. Commodities are, as geographer Deborah Cowen puts it, 'manufactured *across logistics space* rather than in a singular place'.[40] This constant flow of commodities has reduced inventory levels, and the remaining warehouses and distribution gradually replace workers with robots handling palleted goods bearing barcodes and RFID tags.[41] The modern supply chain has also led to a shift of power from producers to large retailers, who systematically collect data in order to closely monitor customers and control the entire supply chain.[42]

---

39   Tony Smith, *Technology and Capital in the Age of Lean Production: A Marxian Critique of the 'New Economy'* (Albany: State University of New York Press, 2000); Bernes, 'Logistics, Counterlogistics, and the Communist Prospect', 78; Bonacich and Wilson, *Getting the Goods*, 4; Levinson, *The Box*, 356ff.

40   Cowen, *The Deadly Life of Logistics*, 2.

41   Bonacich and Wilson, *Getting the Goods*, 123ff; Levinson, *The Box*, 358.

42   Bonacich and Wilson, *Getting the Goods*, 6ff. See also Guido Starosta, 'Global Commodity Chains and the Marxian Law of Value', *Antipode* 42, no. 2 (2010): 433–65; and Guido Starosta, 'The Outsourcing of Manufacturing and the Rise of Giant Global Contractors: A Marxian Approach to Some Recent Transformations of Global Value Chains', *New Political Economy* 15, no. 4 (2010): 543–63. For an analysis of Walmart, see Jesse LeCavalier, *The Rule of Logistics: Walmart and the Architecture of Fulfillment* (Minneapolis: University of Minnesota Press, 2016). The rise of retailer power is overlooked by Neilson, who claims that supply chains imply 'a decentralization of the decision-making practices that apply to strategy and tactics'. Brett Neilson, 'Five Theses on Understanding Logistics as Power', *Distinktion: Journal of Social Theory* 13, no. 3 (2012): 328. While the move away from vertically integrated firms to modern lean production has involved a form of diffusion of functions, this has not led to a decentralisation of power. We should, rather, follow Bennett Harrison and talk of 'the "concentration without centralisation" of corporate authority'. Quoted in Bernes, 'Logistics, Counterlogistics, and the Communist Prospect', 179.

Logistics as Violence

In recent years, a growing body of critical literature has emphasised the intimate connection between logistics and power.[43] It is becoming increasingly clear that logistics is 'the invisible heart of the new geography of power in the global economy', as sociologist Thomas Reifer puts it.[44] Much of this literature is, however, hampered by a number of weaknesses relating to their focus as well as their theoretical framework. Many studies focus more or less exclusively on the impact of the logistics revolution *within* the logistics sector itself, in other words, how it has undermined the power of workers employed in this sector or how it has led to a shift of power from producers to retailers.[45] This is certainly an important part of the story, but if we want to understand the true extent of the impact of the logistics revolution on the balance of forces on a more general level, we also have to take into consideration its effects *outside* of the sector itself. Some of these studies focus more specifically on capital's increasing reliance on racialised and female low-wage workers in this sector.[46] For instance, anthropologist Anna Tsing argues that 'supply chain capitalism' relies on 'social-economic niches' which are 'reproduced in performances of cultural identity'.[47] This leads her to rehearse an old criticism of Marxism popular in postcolonial theory, namely that workers in contemporary supply chain capitalism are unable to 'negotiate the wage in the manner imagined in much of both Marxist and neo-classical economics: that is, as abstract "labor", without the obstacles of these "cultural" factors'.[48] As Vivek Chibber has demonstrated, this is simply a misreading of Marx's analysis. The concept of abstract labour has nothing to do with

---

43   Charmaine Chua et al., 'Introduction: Turbulent Circulation: Building a Critical Engagement with Logistics', *Environment and Planning D: Society and Space* 36, no. 4 (2018): 621.

44   Reifer, 'Labor, Race, and Empire', 18.

45   Edna Bonacich, 'Pulling the Plug: Labor and the Global Supply Chain', *New Labor Forum* 12, no. 2 (2003); Bonacich and Wilson, *Getting the Goods*; Cowen, *The Deadly Life of Logistics*; Reifer, 'Labor, Race, and Empire'; Anna Tsing, 'Supply Chains and the Human Condition', *Rethinking Marxism* 21, no. 2 (2009): 148–76.

46   Reifer, 'Labor, Race, and Empire', 15, 23f; Tsing, 'Supply Chains and the Human Condition'; Bonacich and Wilson, *Getting the Goods*; Jake Alimahomed-Wilson, *Solidarity Forever? Race, Gender, and Unionism in the Ports of Southern California* (Lanham: Lexington Books, 2016).

47   Tsing, 'Supply Chains and the Human Condition', 171.

48   Ibid., 158.

the cultural identity of workers, and Marx's claim about the universalising drive of capital does not in any way imply the claim that capital tends to eradicate cultural differences.[49] In fact, as we saw in chapter seven, Marx's analysis of capital demonstrates why it is always advantageous for capital to reproduce and utilise cultural identities and hierarchies. It also demonstrates that this production of difference – which Tsing erroneously perceives as an example of the irrelevance of the Marxian analysis of capitalism – is not specific to the logistics sector. In other words, the analysis of the reproduction of cultural identities among workers employed in the logistics sector actually tells us something about the logic of capital as such, but it tells us nothing about *logistics* specifically.

As previously mentioned, many critical scholars of the logistics revolution emphasise the proximity between military and commercial logistics.[50] They variously interpret the military origins of modern logistics as an indication of the 'precarity of the distinction between "civilian" and "military"', 'the militarization of society', the 'intersection between U.S. military and corporate power', or 'the intimate relationship between state violence and commercial trade in the modern era'.[51] Although such claims seem to be motivated by good intentions – namely to undermine the idea of international trade as a peaceful execution of voluntary market transactions – they rely on questionable assumptions and inadvertently obscure the nature of the power executed by means of logistics. These problems can be summed up in three points. First, while it may be true that business logistics did not emerge as a concept and an independent field until the post–World War II era, the systematic effort to improve transportation and secure an effective management of supply chains have, as previously noted, been a part of capitalism from the very beginning. The preoccupation with the martial origins of logistics leads some scholars to convey the impression that capitalism has no history of revolutionising the means of transportation prior to the 1950s, when logistics migrated from the military to the business world. Second, the *origin* of a technology does not necessarily tell us anything about its function and effects when transposed from one social

---

49   Vivek Chibber, *Postcolonial Theory and the Specter of Capital* (London: Verso, 2013), chap. 6.

50   Reifer, 'Labor, Race, and Empire'; Neilson, 'Five Theses'; Cowen, *The Deadly Life of Logistics*.

51   Cowen, *The Deadly Life of Logistics*, 4; Neilson, 'Five Theses', 323; Reifer, 'Labor, Race, and Empire', 25; Chua et al., 'Introduction', 620.

context to another. Take money as an example: it existed for thousands of years before capitalism emerged, but once that happened, the social role of money fundamentally changed. To argue that the commercial adoption of a technology originating in the military signals a militarisation of society is to subscribe to an essentialist understanding of technology in which origin always determines function and effect, regardless of the social context. Third, as I will come back to, logistics should be understood as a part of the *economic power* of capital. Military power is perhaps *the* paradigmatic form of the *violent, coercive power* of the state. The attempt to understand the logistics of capital through the lens of warfare obscures the difference between the violent logic of military power and the mute compulsion of capital.

Logistics as Biopolitics

Another problem with many of the critical approaches to the power of logistics is the widespread inability to identify the driving force behind the logistics revolution, that is, to explain *why* it took (and still takes) place.[52] Everyone more or less agrees that it has something to do with 'capitalism', 'the market', or 'commercial interests', but these terms are rarely explained or defined. This lacuna seems to be partly a result of the theoretical frameworks through which these scholars try to decipher the phenomenon of logistics. One popular framework is Foucault's notion of biopolitics. Among its exponents, Brett Neilson and Ned Rossiter claim that logistics is a 'biopolitical technology central to managing the movement of labour and commodities'.[53] Niccolò Cuppini, Mattia Frapporti, and Maurilio Pirone likewise hold that logistics is 'a complex biopolitical apparatus … a *dispositif* that produces subjectivity'.[54] However, they never really explain why, nor what it means. As we saw in chapter six, biopolitics is a concept intended to capture the way in which the modern state assumes the task of managing the biological body of the population.

---

52   Danyluk, 'Capital's Logistical Fix', 631.

53   Brett Neilson and Ned Rossiter, 'Still Waiting, Still Moving: On Labour, Logistics and Maritime Industries', in *Stillness in a Mobile World*, ed. David Bissell and Gillian Fuller (New York: Routledge, 2010).

54   Niccolò Cuppini, Mattia Frapporti, and Maurilio Pirone, 'Logistics Struggles in the Po Valley Region: Territorial Transformations and Processes of Antagonistic Subjectivation', *South Atlantic Quarterly* 114, no. 1 (2015): 122.

It is not immediately clear what this has to do with capitalist logistics, which is concerned with *commodities* rather than *people* and controlled by *capital* rather than *the state*. One might argue, as does Cowen, that insofar as social reproduction has become dependent upon global supply chains, logistics is 'not only about circulating *stuff* but about sustaining life'.[55] This is certainly true, but it does not tell us anything specifically about logistics; on the contrary, the same could be said of virtually all aspects of the capitalist economy. If we take this as evidence of the 'biopolitical' nature of logistics, we end up with a very broad and impoverished concept of biopolitics.

Another way to support the interpretation of logistics as a biopolitical apparatus might be to focus on the tension between the flow of commodities and the flow of people, as does Craig Martin when he points out that global supply chains aim at 'the *curtailment* of movement for unsanctioned flows ... whilst also *facilitating* the movement of sanctioned flows'.[56] In this reading, the same technology which secures the seamless flow of things also poses a threat for border regimes since it can be exploited by those that capital and the state want to keep immobile. The logistics revolution has thus compelled states to develop new ways of controlling the flow of people across borders.[57] Controlling migration is certainly one of the characteristic biopolitical tasks of the modern state, so perhaps this provides a basis for the claim about the link between logistics and biopolitics?[58] I do not think so. While it seems reasonable to conclude that modern logistics has led to an *intensification* of biopolitical control of migration, this does not merit the conclusion that logistics is *itself* a biopolitical apparatus. After all, logistics did not emerge as a method for state control of the population; rather, the need for improved means of controlling migration is *a by-product* of the logistics revolution.

Some scholars have attempted to throw some Marxist categories into the Foucauldian mix. Unfortunately, the results have not been impressive. Neilson, for one, argues that logistics plays a 'pivotal role' in 'negotiating' the 'distinction between abstract and living labor', a distinction he

---

55   Cowen, *The Deadly Life of Logistics*, 3.

56   Craig Martin, 'Desperate Mobilities: Logistics, Security and the Extra-Logistical Knowledge of "Appropriation"', *Geopolitics* 17, no. 2 (2012): 359.

57   Cowen, *The Deadly Life of Logistics*, chaps 2, 4.

58   Michel Foucault, *The History of Sexuality*, vol. 1, *The Will to Knowledge* (London: Penguin, 1998), 140; Cowen, *The Deadly Life of Logistics*, 196–231.

attributes to Marx.[59] In his view, logistics tends 'to eliminate the gap between living and abstract labor'.[60] This makes absolutely no sense: for Marx, abstract labour *is* living labour. The counterpart to living labour is dead labour, which refers to products of labour, especially those employed as instruments, such as machines and tools. In capitalism, living labour has a double nature: it is simultaneously concrete labour producing use values and abstract labour producing value. Abstract labour is thus *an aspect of living labour* in capitalism.

Logistics as Mute Compulsion

This is not to say that there is nothing valuable in the critical literature on logistics. On the contrary, many of the studies I have cited – especially the work of Cowen and Bonacich and Wilson – offer very important insights, despite the flaws just described.[61] In addition to this, two critical studies of the logistics revolution stand out as particularly relevant for our purposes: those of Jasper Bernes and Martin Danyluk.[62] Both of them identify the logic of capital – and not a martial or biopolitical logic – as the driving force behind the logistics revolution. This enables them to *explain* why there is a systematic drive to revolutionise the means of transportation and communication in the capitalist mode of production, and it also enables them to avoid depicting this drive as something which emerged only after World War II. Bernes and Danyluk are also capable of explaining why the logistics revolution happened when it did: the economic crisis resulting from the exhaustion of the post-war boom alongside increasing labour militancy made it necessary for capital to launch an assault on labour by orchestrating what Harvey calls a 'spatial fix'.[63] Both of them also underline that logistics is not just a matter of reducing costs but also of securing the domination of workers – not only of those employed in the logistics sector, but of workers in *all* sectors. As

---

59   Neilson, 'Five Theses', 330f; Neilson and Rossiter, 'Still Waiting, Still Moving'.

60   Neilson, 'Five Theses', 336.

61   Cowen, *The Deadly Life of Logistics*.

62   Bonacich and Wilson, *Getting the Goods*; Bernes, 'Logistics, Counterlogistics, and the Communist Prospect'; Danyluk, 'Capital's Logistical Fix'.

63   Danyluk, 'Capital's Logistical Fix', 640ff; Harvey, *The Limits to Capital*, 431ff; see also Beverly J. Silver, *Forces of Labor: Workers' Movements and Globalization Since 1870* (Cambridge: Cambridge University Press, 2003).

Bernes explains, 'The sophisticated, permutable supply chains make it possible for capital to seek out the lowest wages anywhere in the world and to play proletarians off of each other. Logistics was therefore one of the key weapons in a decades-long global offensive against labour.'[64]

What I want to add to this is an interpretation of the logistics revolution in light of the theory of the economic power of capital developed in the preceding chapters. This allows us to specify what *kind of* power is at stake here. What the logistics revolution has permitted capital to do is to bolster its grip on society without using direct violence and ideology. As I have emphasised several times, my claim is neither that capital relies *exclusively* on the mute compulsion of economic relations nor that it ever could. This also applies to logistics. Infrastructure projects, for example, have often involved the violent dispossession of those who live where someone wants to build an airport or a highway. Increasing mobility also allows capital to relocate production to countries where violent suppression of labour militancy is more common. Once infrastructural and logistics systems are in place, however, they enable capital to replace violence and ideology with economic power – that is, they allow capital to restructure the material conditions of social reproduction in a manner which tightens its grip on society as a whole. This restructuring has at least three dimensions.

First: capital's power over *workers* is strengthened by the increase in the capacity to relocate production or change subcontractors. This power is not grounded in the capacity of capitalists to employ physical violence; nor is it a case of ideological power. It is, rather, grounded in the ability to relocate production, and thereby to fire workers – in other words, to break the fragile link between proletarian life and its conditions. Capitalism is founded upon the insertion of the logic of valorisation into the gap between life and its conditions, and what the spatial flexibility bestowed upon capital by global supply chains does is enhance capital's ability to master this vital link.

Second: spatial flexibility leads to fusions and expansions of markets, and thereby also to the intensification of competition among capitals as well as among workers. Logistics thus acts as an *intensifier* of the form of domination springing from the horizontal relations of production. What this tells us is that the logistics revolution has not only enhanced the power of *capitalists over workers*; it has also strengthened the power of *capital over everyone*.

---

64   Bernes, 'Logistics, Counterlogistics, and the Communist Prospect', 186.

Third: by restructuring the international division of labour, capital digs deeper into the transcendental level of social reproduction. In chapter ten, we saw how the real subsumption of labour implies an increasing division of labour within the workplace, with the consequence that capital supplements its appropriation of the *objective* conditions of labour with the appropriation of the *social* conditions of labour. A similar process takes place on a global level and has been significantly accelerated by the logistics revolution. Similar to the way in which capital 'seizes labour-power by its roots' within the workplace, it seizes local, regional, or national economies by their roots and subjects them to the familiar process of fracture and reassembly: it breaks up production processes and sectors into pieces. spreading their fragments all over the globe in order to reunite them through planetary supply chains.[65] The consequence of this is that the conditions necessary for social reproduction to take place on a local or regional level might be scattered all over the world, with the means for their mediation under the firm control of capital. Logistics thus allows capital to supplement its appropriation of the *objective* and *social* conditions of labour with the appropriation of the *spatial* or *geographical* conditions. This amounts to a kind of *real subsumption*, yet on the level of the global totality rather than on the level of the workplace. As Cowen points out, the 'process mapping' used in supply chain management 'might be understood as a *rescaled motion study* in the interest of *transnational* efficiency.[66] It works at multiple scales: from the scale of the worker's body to the intermodal system, aiming to calibrate the former to the latter'. And as we know, real subsumption makes it more difficult to dissolve the stranglehold of capital. Increasing geographical integration of networks of production makes it tremendously difficult to break with capitalism since it increases the scale on which such a transformation would have to take place. As Bernes notes, the logistics revolution tends to create a situation in which 'any attempt to seize the means of production would require an *immediately global* seizure'.[67]

These three mechanisms of domination, created or intensified by the logistics revolution, all spring from capital's ability to restructure the material conditions of social reproduction. In other words: they are a part of the economic power of capital. All of them are simultaneously a *result*

---

65   C1: 481.

66   Cowen, *The Deadly Life of Logistics*, 109.

67   Bernes, 'Logistics, Counterlogistics, and the Communist Prospect', 197.

of this power and one of its *sources*, that is, they display the same circular structure as the mechanisms of domination examined in chapters ten and eleven. *Logistics and the infrastructure on which it relies are essentially methods for carving the logic of capital into the crust of the earth.*

Choke Points

However: 'where capital goes, conflict goes', as Beverly Silver reminds us.[68] As virtually all critical studies of logistics stress, the logistics revolution has not just strengthened the power of capital – it has also made it more *vulnerable*. In 2012, Barack Obama launched a 'National Strategy for Global Supply Chain Security' with what sounded almost like an invitation: 'As the global supply chain becomes more complex and global in scope, it is increasingly at risk from disruptions including natural hazards, accidents, and malicious incidents … even localized disruptions can escalate rapidly.'[69] Recent years have seen an increase in protests directly attacking the 'choke points' of capital, a trend which has led some scholars and activists to proclaim blockades and sabotage to be the paradigmatic tactics of anti-capitalist resistance in the twenty-first century.[70]

---

68   Silver, *Forces of Labor*, 41.

69   White House, 'Fact Sheet: National Strategy for Global Supply Chain Security', whitehouse.gov, 2012, available at obamawhitehouse.archives.gov.

70   For examples of such protests and discussions of their strategic perspectives, see Alimahomed-Wilson, *Solidarity Forever?*; Jake Alimahomed-Wilson and Immanuel Ness, eds., *Choke Points: Logistics Workers Disrupting the Global Supply Chain* (London: Pluto Press, 2018); Angry Workers of the World, 'Further Comments on Organisation', libcom. org, 15 August 2014; Bernes, 'Logistics, Counterlogistics, and the Communist Prospect'; Jasper Bernes, 'The Belly of the Revolution', in *Materialism and the Critique of Energy*, ed. Brent Ryan Bellamy and Jeff Diamanti (Chicago: MCM' Publishing, 2018); Bonacich, 'Pulling the Plug'; Chua, 'Logistical Violence, Logistical Vulnerabilities'; Rossana Cillo and Lucia Pradella, 'New Immigrant Struggles in Italy's Logistics Industry', *Comparative European Politics* 16, no. 1 (2018): 67–84; Joshua Clover, *Riot. Strike. Riot: The New Era of Uprisings* (London: Verso, 2016); Cuppini, Frapporti, and Pirone, 'Logistics Struggles'; Degenerate Communism, 'Choke Points: Mapping an Anticapitalist Counter-Logistics in California', libcom.org, 21 July 2014; Jeff Diamanti and Mark Simpson, 'Five Theses on Sabotage in the Shadow of Fossil Capital', *Radical Philosophy* 2, no. 2 (2018); Kim Moody, *On New Terrain: How Capital Is Reshaping the Battleground of Class War* (Chicago: Haymarket, 2018); Out of the Woods, 'Disaster Communism Part 3: Logistics, Repurposing, Bricolage', libcom.org, 22 May 2014; *Short-Circuit: A Counterlogistics Reader*, n.d., available at https://desarquivo.org/sites/default/files/short_circuit_a_counterlogistics_reader. pdf; Silver, *Forces of Labor*; Society of Enemies, 'Blockading the Port Is Only the First of

Among the best-known examples are the Occupy movement's blockade of the Port of Oakland in 2011, the International Longshore and Warehouse Union strike on May Day in 2015 (also at the Port of Oakland) in solidarity with Black Lives Matter, strikes at Amazon warehouses, and the G20 protests in Hamburg in 2017 under the slogan 'Shut Down the Logistics of Capital!'. As the US strategy for global supply chain security demonstrates, governments are well aware of this tactical predilection. All over the world, ports, trucks, highways, railways, sea routes, ships, containers, trains, distribution centres, and warehouses are controlled and protected by an increasingly militarised security apparatus.[71] Does this invalidate my analysis of logistics as something which enhances the power of capital? Should we rather think of capital's reliance on global supply chains as a sign of its *weakness*, that is, as a corner of the ring into which resistance has forced it to retreat? Not at all. While it is certainly true that every shift of strategy on the part of capital gives rise to new vulnerabilities and that every basis for its power is therefore simultaneously a basis for the resistance to this power, it is also true that *vulnerability* is not the same as *weakness*; vulnerability is only *potential* weakness, and there is nothing that guarantees the realisation of this potential. Historically, there are many examples of workers who have successfully taken advantage of being located in strategically important parts of the economy, such as coal miners or railway workers.[72] So far, however, the logistics revolution has failed to produce a general enhancement of proletarian power. While there have been successful examples of proletarians who have managed to take advantage of the vulnerabilities created by global supply chains and just-in-time production in recent years, it seems fair to conclude that the neoliberal era has generally enhanced the power of capital at the expense of the power of anti-capitalist forces, and that the

Many Last Resorts', libcom.org, 7 April 2011; Nick Srnicek and Alex Williams, *Inventing the Future: Postcapitalism and a World without Work* (London: Verso, 2015); The Invisible Committee, *To Our Friends* (Los Angeles: Semiotext(e), 2015); Alberto Toscano, 'Logistics and Opposition', *Mute* 3, no. 2 (August 2011), metamute.org; Alberto Toscano, 'Lineaments of the Logistical State', *Viewpoint Magazine*, 28 September 2014, viewpoint-mag.com; Transnational Social Strike Platform, ed., *Logistics and the Transnational Social Strike* (Fall 2017 Journal), transnational-strike.info; … ums Ganze!, 'G20 Hamburg: Blast the Chain. Bring the Harbor to a Halt', *Plan C*, 11 June 2017, weareplanc.org.

71   Cowen, *The Deadly Life of Logistics*, chaps 2, 4.

72   Timothy Mitchell, *Carbon Democracy: Political Power in the Age of Oil* (London: Verso, 2013); Silver, *Forces of Labor*.

logistics revolution has been a central strategic element in the neoliberal counter-offensive.

A different but related question is whether or not the contemporary networks of infrastructure and logistics can be 'repurposed' or 'reconfigured' to other ends than the accumulation of capital. Beginning with a critique of the 'romantic vision of communitarian sabotage' advanced by the Invisible Committee, Alberto Toscano has defended the idea that there are no a priori reasons to declare logistical technologies 'dialectically irrecuperable'.[73] Nick Srnicek and Alex Williams expand on this idea and argue that 'an efficient and global logistics network' will be an essential ingredient in the creation of a sustainable, flexible, and highly automated post-capitalism.[74] At the other extreme, we find the romantic insurrectionism of the Invisible Committee, which leaves little room for the 'reappropriation' of anything that does not organically spring from existential bonds within a revolutionary cell.[75] A nuanced argument against 'the reconfiguration thesis' is presented by Bernes, who reminds us that the 'fixed capital of the contemporary production regime is designed for the extraction of maximum surplus value; each component part is engineered for insertion into *this* global system'.[76] In other words, we should always remember that the *use value* of some technologies might correspond to a need which exists *only* in a capitalist society – and according to Bernes, this is precisely the case with capital's logistics. This does not mean that a post-capitalist society would not be able to use parts of this system or some of the technologies involved.[77] Considered as a totality, however, it is 'a system in which extreme wage differentials are built into the very infrastructure. Without those differentials, most supply-chains would become both wasteful and unnecessary'.[78]

Note that this dispute concerns *logistics* technology, not technology *as such*. As Toscano emphasises, he and Bernes 'broadly agree that there is no a priori way to simply declare certain features of capitalist production and circulation as allowing for communist uses. The test is a practical

---

73 Toscano, 'Lineaments of the Logistical State'; Srnicek and Williams, *Inventing the Future*, 150f.

74 Srnicek and Williams, *Inventing the Future*, 150f.

75 The Invisible Commitee, *To Our Friends*, chaps. 3, 7; The Invisible Committee, *Now* (South Pasadena, CA: Semiotext(e), 2017), 84f.

76 Bernes, 'Logistics, Counterlogistics, and the Communist Prospect', 194.

77 Ibid., 201.

78 Ibid., 194.

and political one.'[79] Despite their generally optimistic view on technology, Srnicek and Williams also hold that 'there is no a priori way to determine the potentials of a technology'.[80] This leads me to the general question of the relation between social relations and technology – a question we have encountered several times throughout the preceding chapters. One of the important tasks of the analysis of the real subsumption of labour and nature is to reveal the poverty of productive force determinism. Techno-logical development is determined by social relations. As Andreas Malm puts it, with reference to the advent of steam: 'The relation chose the force, not vice versa.'[81] The history of capitalism is full of 'roads not taken', to use David Noble's phrase: historical junctures where certain technologies were abandoned, not because they were less productive, but because they were incompatible with capitalist relations of production.[82] In these cases, capitalist relations of production *hindered* the development of the pro-ductive forces; technologies were left behind *despite* being cheaper, more productive, or more effective, or all of these things at the same time.[83]

It is not enough, however, to get the *direction* of the causal relation between forces and relations right. We also have to clarify the *strength* of this link, in other words, how tightly bound technologies are to the social relations of which they are the results. The task here is to avoid two well-trodden positions: on the one hand, the view that technologies are essentially neutral, in the sense that even though they are outcomes of specific sets of social relations, they can always be put to use in other social contexts; and, on the other hand, the techno-pessimistic view according to which technologies will always carry with them the social relations out of which they emerged, so that their use will inevitably re-erect those social relations. In opposition to both of these positions, we should insist that this question cannot be answered on the level of technology in general.

---

79   Toscano, 'Lineaments of the Logistical State'.

80   Srnicek and Williams, *Inventing the Future*, 152.

81   Andreas Malm, 'Marx on Steam: From the Optimism of Progress to the Pessi-mism of Power', *Rethinking Marxism* 30, no. 2 (2018): 176.

82   David Noble, *Forces of Production: A Social History of Industrial Automation* (New York: Knopf, 1984).

83   For examples, see Jack Ralph Kloppenburg, *First the Seed: The Political Economy of Plant Biotechnology, 1492–2000*, 2nd ed. (Madison: University of Wisconsin Press, 2004), chap. 5; Andreas Malm, *Fossil Capital: The Rise of Steam Power and the Roots of Global Warming* (London: Verso, 2016), chap. 6; Stephen A. Marglin, 'What Do Bosses Do? The Origins and Functions of Hierarchy in Capitalist Production', *Review of Radical Political Economics* 6, no. 2 (1974): 60–112; Noble, *Forces of Production*, chap. 7.

As Melvin Kranzberg puts it: 'Technology is neither good nor bad; nor is it neutral.'[84] *Some* technologies can be applied in social contexts other than the ones in which they emerged. Many medical technologies, for example, would be useful in a post-capitalist society despite being the outcome of the quest for profit. Other technologies are so intimately linked to capitalist property relations that it is extremely difficult to see how they could possibly be of any use in a non-capitalist context. An example is the suicide seeds discussed in chapter eleven, the sole purpose of which is to secure that farmers are cut off from control over the crops they grow. Here, we can really say that '*relations of production are within the productive forces*', as Raniero Panzieri puts it.[85] Suicide seeds would not have any use value whatsoever in a post-capitalist world. The case of suicide seeds is a good example of what technological development under capitalism is all about – not only because it unambiguously demonstrates the causal primacy of the relations of production but also because it demonstrates another important fact which should always be borne in mind when thinking about technology and capitalism: that the logic of capital, no matter how omnipotent it may seem, is only *one* social force among many. If this were not the case, the use of suicide seeds would have been widespread by now.

The Production of Capitalism

In this and the two preceding chapters, we have discovered something important about the economic power of capital: namely that it is partly *a result of its own exercise*. The economic power of capital stems not only from the relations of production but also from the social and material reconfigurations resulting from those relations. Indeed, when capitalist production first emerged on the stage of history, it did so in a world shaped by non-capitalist social logics. It had to base itself on political institutions, customary arrangements, technologies, divisions of labour,

---

84 'Technology and History: "Kranzberg's Laws"', *Bulletin of Science, Technology, and Society* 15, no. 1 (1995): 5. See also Endnotes, 'Error', in *Endnotes 5: The Passions and the Interests* (London: Endnotes, 2020).

85 Raniero Panzieri, 'Surplus Value and Planning: Notes on the Reading of "Capital"', in *The Labour Process and Class Strategies*, ed. Conference of Socialist Economists (London: Conference of Socialist Economists, 1976), 12.

cultural forms, and international relations inherited from a world where the valorisation of value was not the 'all-dominating economic power' it later became. Initially, capital was a social *form* imposed on *pre-capitalist content*. As soon as its grip on the conditions of social life was established, however, this form revealed itself to possess a strong propensity to *materialise* itself, to transcend its own formality and incarnate itself in a mesh of limbs, energies, bodies, plants, oceans, knowledges, animals, and machines – a process which continues to constantly reshape the world to this day. This is what the concept of *real subsumption* captures. It is far from frictionless, and among the most important of the many obstacles capital encounters are *labour* and *nature*, both of which possess an ineradicable autonomy with which capital has struggled for centuries.

For a long time, the hot spot of this struggle was the industrial shop floor, where the power of capital metamorphosed into the despotic authority of the capitalist manager. Through the introduction of machinery and the restructuring of the division of labour, capital began to gnaw itself into the bodies of workers in order to secure their submission to the profit imperative and its accompanying regime of discipline and abstract time. In the twentieth century, after having struggled with autonomy of plants, animals, the soil, and the weather for hundreds of years, capital finally managed to subject agriculture to a process of real subsumption similar to what took place in manufacturing during the nineteenth century. Once again, capital enlisted the help of science in its effort to crack open the biophysical structure of seeds and the bodies of animals in order to secure a steady flow of profit. When the post-war boom came to a close as a result of its own immanent contradictions, capital swung into action on a global scale by launching a revolution in the means of transportation and communication. By accelerating the process of real subsumption on the level of the global totality of production, capital moved closer to creating a world in which profitability is the condition of life.

On the basis of the analysis of real subsumption in this and the two preceding chapters, we can revisit what I referred to at the beginning of chapter ten as the 'circularity' of the power of capital. In the first volume of *Capital*, Marx provides a sequence of answers to the question of *what* gets produced in the capitalist production process. On the basis of part one, which deals with simple circulation, we can conclude that capitalist production is the production of *commodities*. After having introduced the concept of capital, Marx is able to specify that capitalist production 'is not merely the production of commodities, it is, by its very essence, the production of surplus-value'.[86] Then, after examining the production of relative surplus value, which requires the real subsumption of labour, Marx is able to conclude that as a 'process of reproduction', capitalist production 'produces not only commodities, not only surplus-value, but it also produces and reproduces the capital-relation itself' – or, as he puts it in the *1861–63 Manuscripts*, in the most compressed version of this insight, 'the *capital-relation* generates the *capital-relation*' – with a crucial addition: 'on an increased scale'.[87] For this reason, Marx approvingly cites Simonde de Sismondi's description of capital as a *spiral*.[88] The power of capital thus has a circular structure:

> Presuppositions, which originally appeared as conditions of its becoming – and hence could not spring from its *action as capital* – now appear as results of its own realization, reality, as *posited by it* – not as *conditions of its arising, but as results of its existence.*[89]

What circulates in millions of shipping containers or grows in eroding soils pumped with synthetic fertiliser and Monsanto seeds is thus not only commodities but also capitalist relations of production. *Capitalist production is the production of capitalism.* This insight demonstrates that the economic power of capital is in its essence *dynamic*: if we take into account only the relations of production, we overlook an important source of this power, namely the *dynamics* set in motion by these relations. In this and the two preceding chapters, we have examined one particular aspect of these dynamics: the socio-material remoulding of production. But as we will see in the next and final chapter, there is more to say about these dynamics.

---

86   C1: 644.
87   C1: 724, 34: 187; see also R: 1065; and 30: 115.
88   G: 266, 620, 746; 32: 153; C1: 727, 780.
89   G: 460.

13

Surplus Populations and Crisis

The dynamics examined in the previous chapters are all expressions of more or less *constant* pressures in the capitalist mode of production. The incentive to push forward with the real subsumption of labour and nature might be stronger in periods with rising proletarian militancy or intense competition, but it is always there. In this chapter, I want to take a closer look at a set of dynamics which exhibits a different trajectory: capital's tendency to create a relative surplus population and its tendency to undermine itself in the form of crises. In contrast to real subsumption, both of these tendencies tend to follow a cyclical pattern. Similar to the real subsumption of labour and nature, however, they are simultaneously *results* and *sources* of the power of capital. Both of these tendencies should likewise be regarded as belonging to the core structure of the capitalist mode of production. For these reasons, an account of the economic power of capital has to include a consideration of both.

The General Law of Capitalist Accumulation

In chapter twenty-five of the first volume of *Capital*, Marx argues that capitalism necessarily leads to a continuous generation of a relative surplus population.[1] As David Harvey explains, Marx constructs two models of

---

1   C1: 794.

accumulation in this very long chapter.[2] In the first model, he abstracts from the development of the productive forces in order to demonstrate how capital necessarily generates a certain level of unemployment, independently of changing productivity levels. The argument is fairly simple: as accumulation proceeds, an increasing demand for labour eventually leads to rising wages. However, this will also cause accumulation to slow down and hence cause a drop in the demand for labour power, leading to a decline in wages. In other words: the 'mechanism of the capitalist production process removes the very obstacles it temporarily creates'.[3] What emerges from this movement is a cyclical pattern in which a certain level of unemployment is maintained in order to secure wage levels compatible with a certain level of profitability: 'The rise of wages is therefore confined within limits that not only leave intact the foundations of the capitalist system, but also secure its reproduction on an increased scale.'[4] The relative surplus population is, as Marx explains, 'the background against which the law of the demand and supply of labour does its work'. Here, capital 'acts on both sides', as Marx puts it: the accumulation of capital determines not only the *demand* for labour power but also its *supply*, since unemployment levels are expressions of the needs of accumulation.[5]

Marx distinguishes between three forms of existence of this relative surplus population, which he considers to be a necessary condition of capitalist production: the *floating* surplus population, that is, workers belonging permanently to the labour force but temporarily under- or unemployed; the *latent* surplus population, in other words, proletarians who are not regularly a part of the workforce but can be drawn into wage labour when capital needs them (Marx cites the example of rural populations, but we could also mention domestic workers or proletarians on public benefits);[6] and finally, the *stagnant* surplus population, which is the lowest strata of the working class: those who have 'extremely irregular employment' but, unlike the latent surplus population, generally do not have access to means of subsistence outside of the wage relation.[7] Taken

---

2   David Harvey, *The Limits to Capital* (London: Verso, 2006), 158f; *A Companion to Marx's* Capital (London: Verso, 2010), 268ff.

3   C1: 770.

4   C1: 771.

5   C1: 792f.

6   Aaron Benanav, 'A Global History of Unemployment: Surplus Populations in the World Economy, 1949–2010' (PhD diss., UCLA, 2015), 13.

7   32: 186; C1: 796; C1: 792ff.

together, these different subgroups within the relative surplus population make up what Marx calls the industrial reserve army.

In his second model of accumulation, Marx considers the effects of productivity increases on unemployment, concluding that in the long run, the relative surplus population tends to grow. This is what he refers to as the 'general law of capitalist accumulation'.[8] Again, the argument is quite simple: competition forces individual capitals to increase productivity by introducing labour-saving technology, and, as these technologies become generalised across sectors or the entire economy, the technical composition of capital increases. Assuming that the falling demand for labour as a result of increasing productivity is stronger than the rising demand of labour as a result of the expansion of production, the capitalist economy as a whole will, in the long run (i.e., across multiple business cycles), shed more workers than it will absorb. Ever-larger segments of the relative surplus population will thus become '*absolutely redundant*' for the valorisation of value.[9]

'Like all other laws', the general law of capitalist accumulation 'is modified in its working by many circumstances'.[10] Marx acknowledges the possibility that the growth of capitalist production might in principle be so strong that the relative surplus population will contract rather than expand; but he insists that in the long run, the opposite will happen. As Michael Heinrich points out, however, Marx does not really explain why 'the redundancy effect of the rise in productivity outbalances the employment effect of accumulation'.[11] Note that this is not a matter of determining the relation between a tendency arising from the logic of capital and a counter-tendency arising from some other social logic; it is, rather, a question of determining the relative strength of two tendencies immediately contained in the concept of capital: on the one hand, the necessity of expanding production and, on the other hand, the expulsion of living labour from the production process. Marx does not produce an

---

8   C1: 794ff.

9   Endnotes and Aaron Benanav, 'Misery and Debt: On the Logic and History of Surplus Populations and Surplus Capital', in *Endnotes 2: Misery and the Value Form* (London: Endnotes, 2010), 29.

10   C1: 798.

11   Michael Heinrich, *An Introduction to the Three Volumes of Karl Marx's* Capital (New York: Monthly Review Press, 2012), 127; Michael Heinrich, *Die Wissenschaft vom Wert: Die Marxsche Kritik der politischen Ökonomie zwischen wissenschaftlicher Revolution und klassischer Tradition* (Münster: Westfälisches Dampfboot, 1999), 323f.

argument to back up the assumption that the latter will necessarily be stronger than the former in the long run, and for this reason, the '*tendency of a growing* industrial reserve army assumed by Marx cannot be strictly substantiated as a claim'.[12]

Marx's analysis of the effects of accumulation on the proletariat has often been misunderstood as a claim about the necessary decline in the living standard of the working class, in a purely quantitative sense – what is often referred to as the 'immiseration thesis'.[13] Throughout the twentieth century, the theory of surplus population was mostly either discarded as irrelevant or rejected as a false prediction, even by many Marxists.[14] It seemed particularly irrelevant from the vantage point of the post-war boom, when rising productivity and rising real wages went hand in hand. It turned out, however, that these 'golden years' were quite exceptional. After a couple of decades of neoliberal counter-offensive, Marx's theory of surplus population has become the object of renewed interest, and in recent years a number of studies have demonstrated its acute relevance.[15] In his study of the history of global unemployment since 1950, Aaron Benanav demonstrates how a combination of de-industrialisation, de-agrarianisation, and population growth has created an enormous global surplus population: according to his estimate from 2015, it 'numbers around 1.3 billion people, accounting for roughly 40 percent of the world's workforce. By contrast, only about 33 percent of the world's workforce is employed in the non-agriculture formal sector'.[16] In 2011, David Neilson and Thomas Stubbs estimated that the global surplus population 'is set to grow further in the medium-term future' and pointed out that it is 'distributed in deeply unequal forms and sizes across the countries of the world'.[17] The majority of the proletarians excluded from the circuits

---

12   Heinrich, *An Introduction*, 126; see also Harvey, *The Limits to Capital*, 160ff.

13   Endnotes, 'An Identical Abject-Subject?', in *Endnotes 4: Unity in Separation* (London: Endnotes, 2015), 282f; Endnotes and Benanav, 'Misery and Debt', 33f; Heinrich, *An Introduction*, 127f.

14   Aaron Benanav and John Clegg, 'Crisis and Immiseration: Critical Theory Today', in *The SAGE Handbook of Frankfurt School Critical Theory*, ed. Beverly Best, Werner Bonefeld, and Chris O'Kane (London: SAGE, 2018), 1629–48.

15   Fredric Jameson, *Representing* Capital: *A Reading of Volume One* (London: Verso, 2011), 71.

16   Benanav, 'A Global History of Unemployment', 25.

17   David Neilson and Thomas Stubbs, 'Relative Surplus Population and Uneven Development in the Neoliberal Era: Theory and Empirical Application', *Capital and Class* 35, no. 3 (2011): 451.

of capital are racialised populations, immigrants, and inhabitants of the global South. In the global South, they are forced to get by as informal workers in ever-growing slums, and in the United States, the surplus population is managed by policing and mass incarceration with vastly disproportionate impacts on black communities.[18] It turns out, then, that Marx's general law of capitalist accumulation actually provides a rather precise account of the forces at play in the neoliberal era. Perhaps Marx's predictions were, as Benanav and John Clegg suggest, only wrong when it comes to *timing*.[19]

An *empirical* validation of Marx's predictions does not, however, tell us anything about the necessary relationship between the accumulation of capital and the growth of the surplus population. The issue at stake here is not whether or not capitalism involves a secular tendency for the surplus population to grow, but how we *explain* such a tendency. The general law of capitalist accumulation cannot be substantiated as a claim about the core structure of capital, and this means that if we can empirically verify the existence of such a tendency, we cannot explain it solely with reference to the logic of capital (even if this remains a crucial *part* of the explanation).[20] Things stand a bit differently with the *first* model of accumulation, however, since this is formulated independently of claims about productivity growth. What we are able to conclude on the basis of an analysis of the ideal average of the capitalist mode of production, then, is that a surplus population is a necessary condition of capitalist production, and that capital itself gives rise to cyclical dynamics which

---

18   Mike Davis, *Planet of Slums* (London: Verso, 2017); Ruth Wilson Gilmore, *Golden Gulag: Prisons, Surplus, Crisis, and Opposition in Globalizing California* (Berkeley: University of California Press, 2006); Jan Rehmann, 'Hypercarceration: A Neoliberal Response to "Surplus Population"', *Rethinking Marxism* 27, no. 2 (2015): 303–11. See also Joshua Clover, *Riot. Strike. Riot: The New Era of Uprisings* (London: Verso, 2016), chap. 8; Endnotes, 'An Identical Abject-Subject?'; Sara R. Farris, 'Femonationalism and the "Regular" Army of Labor Called Migrant Women', *History of the Present* 2, no. 2 (2012): 184–99; Sara R. Farris, 'Migrants' Regular Army of Labour: Gender Dimensions of the Impact of the Global Economic Crisis on Migrant Labor in Western Europe', *Sociological Review* 63, no. 1 (2015): 121–43.

19   Benanav and Clegg, 'Crisis and Immiseration: Critical Theory Today'.

20   Many commentators accept Marx's assumptions without further ado. See, for example, Simon Clarke, *Marx's Theory of Crisis* (Basingstoke: Macmillan, 1994), 254ff; Endnotes, 'An Identical Abject-Subject?'; Endnotes and Benanav, 'Misery and Debt'; Ben Fine and Alfredo Saad-Filho, *Marx's Capital*, 5th ed. (London: Pluto Press, 2010), 83f; William Clare Roberts, *Marx's Inferno: The Political Theory of Capital* (Princeton: Princeton University Press, 2017), 181f.

ensure its continuous existence. When rising wages begin to threaten profits, competitive pressures force accumulation to slow down or compel capitalists to introduce labour-saving technology. The result is a rise in the supply of labour power and a drop in wages, which leads to the restoration of the conditions of accumulation.

Surplus Populations as a Mechanism of Domination

Most discussions of capital's tendency to uncouple proletarians from the circuits of capital tend to focus on its *causes* and its negative impacts on proletarian lives. Here, I am interested in something else, namely the fact that it 'greatly increases the power of capital'.[21] It does so first of all by intensifying competition among workers, which has several advantages for capital.[22] 'The pressure of the unemployed compels those who are employed to furnish more labour' – in other words: the easier it is for employers to replace workers, the easier it is to discipline them.[23] In this way, competition among workers tend to enhance the power of the employer within the workplace. In addition to this, an environment of increasing competition for jobs is also fertile ground for turning divisions among workers into antagonisms such as racism or nationalism – which helps to prevent proletarians from confronting capital collectively. The figure of the job-stealing immigrant, for example, seems to have been a relatively stable ideological formation throughout large parts of the history of capitalism, including in contemporary Europe and the United States. Marx analyses a concrete example of such a dynamic in his writings on Ireland. Recall that the Irish were regarded as a 'race' in Marx's time.[24] Due to hunger, industrialisation, centralisation of land holdings,

---

21   32: 180.

22   32: 441.

23   C1: 793. Jason E. Smith provides a recent example: 'While in most economic slumps productivity tends to drop off rapidly, with output falling faster than jobs can be shed, in the opening round of the recent crisis [i.e., the global crisis of 2008] something else happened entirely. Firms on average registered modest *gains* in productivity, despite the hostile climate. Yet they did so despite rapid *drop-offs* in output: total output was shrinking, but payrolls were being slashed even faster. The uptick in productivity, in this case, was likely due not to technical innovations, but to longer, more stressful, days on the job for those who kept them.' Jason E. Smith, 'Nowhere to Go: Automation, Then and Now', part 1, *Brooklyn Rail*, March–April 2017, brooklynrail.org.

24   Theodore W. Allen, *The Invention of the White Race*, vol. 1; *Racial Oppression*

and the conversion of tillage into pasture, a large number of people migrated from Ireland in the nineteenth century.[25] A part of this relative surplus population ended up as the lowest stratum of the proletariat in English industrial towns.[26] In Marx's view, the ruling classes benefitted tremendously from the tensions between English workers and racialised immigrant workers:

> The *English bourgeoisie* has ... divided the proletariat into two hostile camps ... in *all the big industrial centres in England* there is profound antagonism between the Irish proletarian and the English proletarian. The average English worker hates the Irish worker as a competitor who lowers wages and the *standard of life*. He feels national and religious antipathies for him. He regards him somewhat like the *poor whites* of the Southern States of North America regarded black slaves. This antagonism among the proletarians of England is artificially nourished and kept up by the bourgeoisie. It knows that this scission is the *true secret of maintaining its power.*[27]

This is just one example of how the generation of a surplus population strengthens the power of capital by giving rise to and consolidating all kinds of antagonisms among proletarians.[28] This tells us something about the relation between different forms of power: in this case, the mute compulsion of accumulation is the ground upon which racist, nationalist, and religious ideology flourish.

As previously mentioned, capital 'acts on both sides at once' in the supply and demand for labour. This does not, however, prevent 'capital and its sycophants, political economy' from condemning trade unions as 'the infringement of the "eternal" and so to speak "sacred" law of supply

---

and Social Control, 2nd ed. (London: Verso, 2012), 27ff; Kevin B. Anderson, *Marx at the Margins: On Nationalism, Ethnicity, and Non-Western Societies*, 2nd ed. (Chicago: Chicago University Press, 2016), chap. 4.

25   11: 528ff; 20: 5f; 21: 189ff.

26   See Engels's description of the living conditions of Irish proletarians in Manchester in *The Condition of the Working Class in England* (4: 361).

27   21: 88, 120.

28   See also Sara R. Farris, 'Social Reproduction and Racialized Surplus Populations', in *Capitalism: Concept, Idea, Image. Aspects of Marx's Capital Today*, ed. Peter Osborne, Éric Al-liez, and Eric-John Russell (London: CRMEP Books, 2019).

and demand'.[29] Neither does capital hesitate to employ direct violence in order to establish the mechanism of supply and demand in the first place:

> As soon as (in the colonies, for example) adverse circumstances prevent the creation of an industrial reserve army, and with it the absolute dependence of the working class upon the capitalist class, capital, along with its platitudinous Sancho Panza, rebels against the 'sacred' law of supply and demand, and tries to make up for its inadequacy.[30]

What Marx suggests here is that violent dispossession and the mechanisms by which accumulation secures the continuous existence of a surplus population should be regarded as two different ways of regulating the supply of labour power available to capital. Once the producers have been violently separated from access to means of subsistence outside of the circuits of capital, the mechanisms of accumulation take over; economic power replaces direct coercion.[31] The dynamic through which a relative surplus population is created and reproduced thereby 'rivets the worker to capital more firmly than the wedges of Hephaestus held Prometheus to the rock'.[32]

The Causes of Crises

As Marx explains, capitalism has always been haunted by 'an epidemic that, in all other epochs, would have seemed an absurdity – the epidemic of over-production'.[33] The debates about the nature of capitalist crises have been going on non-stop for more than a century and have produced a vast amount of literature.[34] Most of these debates revolve around the question of what *causes* crises: Is it the restricted consumption of the

---

29   C1: 793.

30   C1: 794.

31   See also chapter 33 of *Capital*, vol. 1, and the passage from the *Grundrisse* – quoted in chapter three – where Marx points out how 'state coercion' is replaced with competition (G: 736).

32   C1: 799.

33   6: 490.

34   For overviews, see Clarke, *Marx's Theory of Crisis*, chaps. 1, 2; Ernest Mandel, *Late Capitalism* (London: New Left Books, 1976), chap. 1; Anwar Shaik, 'An Introduction to the History of Crisis Theories', in *U.S. Capitalism in Crisis*, ed. Union for Radical Political

working class, disproportionality between sectors, overaccumulation of capital, or overproduction of commodities? Although there is no consensus about the precise causal mechanisms, all Marxists seem to agree that crises are not the result of contingent and external shocks to the economy; they stem, rather, from the inherently contradictory nature of capitalist production. The 'true barrier to capitalist production is', as Marx puts it, '*capital* itself'.[35]

In what follows, I will mostly be concerned with the *effects* of crises, or rather a subset of the latter, namely those effects which have an impact on the economic power of capital. However, it is not possible to simply circumvent the question of causes, so before we move on to discuss the effects, let me offer a couple of signposts and briefly sketch out how the position defended in the following relates to the debates about the causes of crises. As do most contemporary scholars, I regard underconsumptionist crisis theory as belonging to the graveyard of Marxist theory, alongside productive force determinism, analytical Marxism, and other dead ends. While it was very popular in the first half of the twentieth century, the theory finds few defenders today. Underconsumptionist crisis theory relies on the very basic misunderstanding that consumption is the motive force of capitalism. Indeed, if 'capitalism depended on the consumption needs of the working class, it would', in the words of Simon Clarke, 'be not merely crisis-prone but its very existence would be impossible'.[36]

Another important variant of Marxist crisis theory is disproportionality theory, that is, the idea that a crisis arises from disproportionalities between different branches of production. The problem with this theory is that it offers no explanation as to why disproportionalities arise in the first place and that it does not explain why disproportionality leads to a *general* crisis instead of just local crises in certain branches – which is actually the mechanism through which disproportionalities are usually removed.[37]

Since the 1970s, most Marxist theories of crisis have taken as their point of departure the law of the tendency of the rate of profit to fall. This law hinges on the assumption that in the long run, the organic composition of capital will rise rapidly enough to outpace its countervailing force, namely

Economics (New York: Economics Education Project of the Union for Radical Political Economics, 1978).

35   M: 359.

36   Clarke, *Marx's Theory of Crisis*, 206.

37   Ibid., 204.

a rise in the rate of surplus value. But, as Heinrich has demonstrated, there are some serious problems with this assumption.[38] Boiled down to its essentials, the problem can be stated this way:

> Regardless of how we express the rate of profit, it is always a relation between two quantities. The *direction* of movement for these two quantities (or parts of these two quantities) is known. That, however, is not sufficient; the point is, *which of the two quantities changes more rapidly* – and we do not know that.[39]

What is at stake here is, once again, what we can and what we cannot conclude on certain levels of abstraction. What Heinrich argues – convincingly, in my view – is that we cannot demonstrate the existence of a *necessary* tendency of the rate of profit to fall on the basis of an analysis of the ideal average of the capitalist mode of production. This conclusion does not imply the denial of the *possibility* that the profit rate might fall precisely in the manner predicted by the 'law'. Nor does it even imply the denial that such a tendential fall of rate of profit has taken place throughout the history of capitalism.[40] It merely implies that the long-term tendencies of the profit rate is an empirical question which cannot be deduced from the analysis of the core structure of capitalism.[41]

---

38   Heinrich, *Die Wissenschaft vom Wert*, 327ff; Heinrich, *An Introduction*, 149ff; Michael Heinrich, 'Heinrich Answers Critics', mronline.org, 1 December 2013; Michael Heinrich, 'Crisis Theory, the Law of the Tendency of the Profit Rate to Fall, and Marx's Studies in the 1870s', *Monthly Review* 64, no. 11 (2013), monthlyreview.org; Michael Heinrich, 'The "Fragment on Machines": A Marxian Misconception in the *Grundrisse* and Its Overcoming in *Capital*', in *In Marx's Laboratory: Critical Interpretations of the Grundrisse*, ed. Riccardo Bellofiore, Guido Starosta, and Peter D. Thomas (Chicago: Haymarket, 2014).

39   Heinrich, 'Crisis Theory'.

40   As many have pointed out, the idea that the profit rate had a long-term tendency to decline was completely uncontroversial in Marx's time. It is thus reasonable to assume that Marx regarded his task as that of providing an explanation of a well-established empirical fact.

41   For other good critical discussions of the law of the tendency of the rate of profit to fall from which I have drawn inspiration, see Riccardo Bellofiore, 'The Long Depression: A Critique of, and a Dialogue with, Michael Roberts on the Marxian Theory of Crisis, and Its Relevance Today', *History of Economic Thought and Policy*, no. 1 (2018): 115–26; Clarke, *Marx's Theory of Crisis*, chaps. 5, 7, 9; Harvey, *The Limits to Capital*, 176ff; David Harvey, 'Crisis Theory and the Falling Rate of Profit', in *The Great Financial Meltdown: Systemic, Conjunctural or Policy Created?*, ed. Turan Subasat (Cheltenham: Edward Elgar, 2016); G. A. Reuten, ' "Zirkel Vicieux" or Trend Fall? The Course of the Profit

Where does this leave us? The good news is that we do not need the law of tendency of the rate of profit to fall in order to have a coherent Marxist theory of crisis, or to derive the necessary tendency to over-production. In order to see why, it is necessary to recall that the aim of capitalist production is profit – an aim which is forced upon individual capitals by competition. For any individual capital, the possibilities for making a profit are not restricted by the size of the market, since individual capitals always have the possibility of capturing market shares from their competitors. In other words, from the perspective of the individual capital, the expansion of production, insofar as it allows this individual capital to undercut its competitors, is immediately also an expansion of the market. On the level of the totality, however, this leads to a general overproduction. A crisis therefore arises from the contradiction between what is rational from the point of view of the *individual* capital and what is rational from the point of view of the capitalist system as *a whole*. Clarke sums up this dynamic well:

> Once the capitalist has taken command of production, the characteristic way in which the capitalist appropriates a profit is not by responding to fluctuations in demand for the product, but by introducing new and more productive methods of production in order to reduce his costs below those of his competitors. The capitalist who is able to reduce his costs is not confined by the limits of his share of the market, but can expand his production without limit in the anticipation of undercutting his competitors.[42]

Rate in Marx's *Capital III*', *History of Political Economy* 36, no. 1 (2004): 163–86; Peter D. Thomas and Geert Reuten, 'Crisis and the Rate of Profit in Marx's Laboratory', in Bellofiore, Starosta, and Thomas, *In Marx's Laboratory*; John Weeks, *Capital and Exploitation* (Princeton: Princeton University Press, 1981). See also Kohei Saito, 'Profit, Elasticity and Nature', in *The Unfinished System of Karl Marx: Critically Reading Capital as a Challenge for Our Times*, ed. Judith Dellheim and Frieder Otto Wolf (Cham: Palgrave Macmillan, 2018); and the rejoinders to Harvey and Heinrich by Callinicos: Alex Callinicos, *Deciphering Capital: Marx's Capital and Its Destiny* (London: Bookmarks, 2014), chap. 6; Alex Callinicos and Joseph Choonara, 'How Not to Write about the Rate of Profit: A Response to David Harvey', *Science and Society* 80, no. 4 (2016): 481–94; Guglielmo Carchedi and Michael Roberts, 'A Critique of Heinrich's, "Crisis Theory, the Law of the Tendency of the Profit Rate to Fall, and Marx's Studies in the 1870s" ', *Monthly Review Press* (blog), 1 December 2013, monthlyreview.org; Michael Roberts, 'Monocausality and Crisis Theory: A Reply to David Harvey', in *The Great Financial Meltdown: Systemic, Conjunctural or Policy Created?*, ed. Turan Subasat (Cheltenham: Edward Elgar, 2016).

42   Clarke, *Marx's Theory of Crisis*, 281.

For this reason, capitalist production necessarily results in crises of overproduction. This is a mode of explanation firmly rooted in the fundamental contradiction of capitalism, namely the contradiction between use value and value. In the capitalist mode of production, the production of useful things is subordinated not only to the production of value, but to the *valorisation* of value, and the mute compulsion of competition forces individual capitals to produce without regard for the limits of the market, like a stuck gas pedal in a car heading towards a cliff.[43] As Clarke notes, the fact that 'opportunities to achieve a surplus profit by the introduction of new methods of production ... are unevenly developed between the various branches of production' has the consequence that the most dynamic sectors will take the lead in this collective race into the abyss.[44] For this reason, disproportionality is a common feature of crises and might be the *immediate* cause of a crisis, even if it is not its *ultimate* cause (as disproportionality theories hold).

As I will come back to in the following sections, a crisis is not only the point at which accumulation is interrupted; it is also a mechanism by means of which capital *re-establishes the conditions of another round of accumulation*. An understanding of crises along the lines sketched out here therefore requires us to reject the idea of secular crises; 'permanent crises do not exist', as Marx put it in a critique of Adam Smith.[45] What the theory of crisis demonstrates is not the inevitable collapse of capitalism but rather, in the words of Clarke, 'the permanent instability of social existence under capitalism'.[46]

The limits of what an analysis of the capitalist mode of production in its ideal average can tell us come out particularly clearly in the theory of crisis. On this level of abstraction, we can conclude that capitalist production necessarily generates periodic crises of overproduction; what we cannot derive, however, is the specific mechanisms which trigger a crisis. While we can say something about its ultimate or underlying cause – overproduction – we cannot identify the immediate or proximate causes of concrete crises without taking into account the specific and contingent details of the situation.[47]

---

43 A similar view is defended by Heinrich in *Die Wissenschaft vom Wert*, chap. 8.5; *An Introduction*, 172ff; and 'Crisis Theory'.

44 Clarke, *Marx's Theory of Crisis*, 283.

45 32: 128.

46 Clarke, *Marx's Theory of Crisis*, 280.

47 Ibid., 285; Heinrich, *Die Wissenschaft vom Wert*, 356f; Heinrich, *An Introduction*, 174f.

Crisis as a Source of Power

Crises have often had mesmerising effects on revolutionaries. In his study of the 1848 revolutions in *Class Struggles in France*, Marx drew the conclusion that the economic crisis of 1847 had 'hastened the outbreak of the revolution'. On this basis, he and Engels became convinced that a '*new revolution is possible only in consequence of a new crisis. It is, however, just as certain as this crisis.*'[48] In the following years, Marx constantly looked for signs of this coming crisis, which he anticipated several times in his articles in the *New York Tribune*.[49] When a global financial crisis finally broke out in the autumn of 1857, he and Engels were euphoric. 'The American crisis – its outbreak in New York forecast by us in the November 1850 *Revue* – is beautiful', Marx wrote to Engels in October 1857.[50] A couple of weeks later, he confessed that 'never, since 1849, have I felt so cosy as during this outbreak'.[51] Engels agreed, replying that

> physically, the crisis will do me as much good as a bathe in the sea; I can sense it already. In 1848 we were saying: Now our time is coming, and so in a certain sense it was, but this time it's coming properly; now it's a case of do or die.[52]

The crisis of 1857 provided Marx with an occasion to finally write down the results of his economic studies while continuing to write articles about the crisis for the *New York Tribune* as well as compiling a comprehensive logbook about the development of the crisis.[53] He was eager to 'at least get the outlines [*Grundrisse*] ready before the *déluge*', as he wrote to Engels.[54] In the so-called fragment on machines in *Grundrisse*, written around February or March 1858, Marx announced the inevitable breakdown of

---

48   10: 52, 135; see also 497, 510.

49   See Clarke, *Marx's Theory of Crisis*, chap. 4; Heinrich, *Die Wissenschaft vom Wert*, 346; and Michael R. Krätke, 'The First World Economic Crisis: Marx as an Economic Journalist', in *Karl Marx's* Grundrisse: *Foundations of the Critique of Political Economy 150 Years Later*, ed. Marcello Musto (London: Routledge, 2008), 162–8; Marcello Musto, *Another Marx: Early Manuscripts to the International* (London: Bloomsbury, 2018), chaps. 3, 4.

50   40: 191.

51   40: 199.

52   40: 203.

53   40: 214, 226; IV.14; Krätke, 'The First World Economic Crisis'; Michael R. Krätke, 'Marx's "Books of Crisis" of 1857-8', in Musto, *Karl Marx's* Grundrisse, 169–75.

54   40: 217.

'production based on exchange value'.[55] But the *déluge* never came; the global crisis turned out to be relatively short lived, and the high hopes Marx and Engels had placed in the crisis were left unfulfilled. As Peter Thomas and Geert Reuten have shown, this led Marx to reconsider his conception of crisis when he returned to the subject in various manuscripts written between 1861 and 1865: the 'eschatological theory of crisis' formulated in the *Grundrisse* gave way to a new conception of crisis as a normal phase of cycles of accumulation.[56] Such a perspective was already somewhat visible in the *Grundrisse*, where Marx wrote that crises 'violently lead it [capital] back to the point where it can go on without committing suicide'. However, he immediately goes on to add that 'these regularly recurring catastrophes lead to their repetition on a higher scale, and finally to its violent overthrow'.[57] What Marx suggests here is the existence of a cyclical pattern evolving around a secular decline.

Marx's abandonment of a theory of crisis as the meltdown of capitalism precipitating its revolutionary overthrow led him to formulate a number of insights which are relevant for a theory of the economic power of capital. Put briefly, Marx moved from a conception of crisis as a *crisis of* the power of capital to an understanding of crisis as a *part of* the power of capital. In this view, a crisis is 'a necessary violent means for the cure of the plethora of capital', a mechanism by means of which capital *avoids* breakdown.[58] Rather than a question about the *causes* of crises, this has to do with the *effects* or the *political meaning* of crises. Although many commentators have noted this aspect of Marx's analysis, discussions about Marxist crisis theory tend, as previously noted, to focus on the causes of crises rather than their effects. Furthermore, they fail to integrate this

---

55 G: 705.

56 Thomas and Reuten, 'Crisis and the Rate of Profit in Marx's Laboratory', 326. For similar analyses of the development in Marx's understanding of crisis, see Clarke, *Marx's Theory of Crisis*, chaps. 3–7; Heinrich, *Die Wissenschaft vom Wert*, 345ff, 2014; and Reuten, ' "Zirkel Vicieux" or Trend Fall?'. Marx's declining health forced him to stop working on the *Grundrisse* in April 1858 ('Obviously I overdid my nocturnal labour last winter', he writes to Engels [40: 310]). After spending May and June recovering, he finally succeeded in writing up a part of his critique in a form which could be published (after drafting the *Urtext* in August–October 1858). The result, *A Contribution to the Critique of Political Economy*, was finished in January 1859. He then went on to spend large parts of 1859 and 1860 on the feud with Karl Vogt, until he finally returned to his studies in 1861. This explains the gap of approximately four years in Marx's writings on crisis (1858–62).

57 G: 750.

58 33: 105.

dimension of crises into a wider analysis of the strategies through which capital reproduces its sway over social life.

Crises are not only a result of the mute compulsion of competition; they are also a *source* of this power.[59] Faced with the risk of falling prey to a frothing market in times of crisis, capitalists have to step up their competitive game by all means available to them: they must intensify work, discipline workers, cut costs (including wages), introduce new technology, find new outlets for their commodities, and so on. In a crisis, companies will often find it hard to finance large investments, so they tend to focus on strategies which do not require new investments, such as the intensification of work, reduction of superfluous costs, or jettisoning of the least profitable parts of their business. Increased competition also intensifies the expansive nature of capitalist production by forcing capitalists to look for new markets as a response to overproduction.

However, not all capitals make it in this struggle. Bankruptcies and downsizing – and the gloomy prospects of making investments in general – result in the 'violent annihilation of capital not by circumstances external to it, but rather as a condition of its self-preservation.'[60] As Marx explains in the *1861–63 Manuscripts*, such annihilation can take two forms: the *physical destruction* of means of production, whereby 'their use value and their exchange value go to the devil'; and *depreciation*, where only value, and not use value, is lost.[61] Depreciation and destruction 'purge excess capital from the economy', thereby setting the stage for a new upswing.[62] Furthermore, surviving capitalists can usually buy means of production from downsized or bankrupted companies at a bargain, thereby lowering the value composition of capital and increasing the rate of profit.[63] The annihilation of capital is especially hard on branches where overproduction is particularly acute, and for this reason crises also tend to abolish disproportionalities.[64] 'The crisis itself may', in Marx's words, 'be a form of equalisation [*Ausgleichung*].'[65]

---

59   M: 365; Clarke, *Marx's Theory of Crisis*, 239, 242.

60   G: 749f.

61   32: 127.

62   David McNally, *Global Slump: The Economics and Politics of Crisis and Resistance* (Oakland: PM Press, 2011), 82.

63   Harvey, *The Limits to Capital*, 200ff.

64   Heinrich, *Die Wissenschaft vom Wert*, 354; Joachim Hirsch, 'The State Apparatus and Social Reproduction: Elements of a Theory of the Bourgeois State', in *State and Capital: A Marxist Debate*, ed. John Holloway and Sol Picciotto (London: Edward Arnold, 1978), 74.

65   32: 151.

A crisis also intensifies competition among *workers*, and, as we know from chapter nine, competition among workers is a mechanism through which the laws of capital are realised.[66] As accumulation slows down, the relative surplus population grows, creating a downward pressure on wages. The employed workers 'have to accept a fall in wages, even beneath the average; an operation that has exactly the same effect for capital as if relative or absolute surplus-value had been increased'.[67] In addition to this, intensification of competition also makes it a lot riskier to resist the real subsumption of labour. This leads to an increase in the rate of surplus value. It is thus no coincidence, for example, that Taylorism was developed in the crisis-ridden American steel industry during the Great Recession of the late nineteenth century.[68]

A Method of Resolution

By means of these mechanisms – annihilation of excess capital, expansion of markets, downward pressure on wages, and an increase in the rate of surplus value – a crisis removes its own (proximate) causes and prepares the way for a new round of accumulation: 'A crisis is always the starting-point of a large volume of new investment.'[69] It is thus a 'method of resolution', a moment of what Marx refers to in the French edition of *Capital* as *les cycles renaissants* – 'rejuvenating cycles' – of capital accumulation.[70] Crises are 'momentary, violent solutions for the existing contradictions, violent eruptions that re-establish the balance [*Gleichgewicht*] that has been disturbed'.[71] As Heinrich emphasises, this should not be understood as a restoration of an equilibrium in the sense of bourgeois economics, since *it is precisely the 'balance' which in and of itself generates its breakdown*.[72] We are not, in other words, dealing with an equilibrium that can only be disturbed by factors external to it.

Here, we approach the limit of what we can say about the way in which crises enhance the power of capital on the level of abstraction at which this

---

66   Harvey, *The Limits to Capital*, 202; McNally, *Global Slump*, 82.

67   M: 363.

68   Eric Hobsbawm, *The Age of Empire: 1875–1914* (London: Abacus, 2002), 44.

69   C2: 264.

70   M: 362; II.7: 557.

71   M: 358.

72   Heinrich, *Die Wissenschaft vom Wert*, 354f, 369.

analysis is situated. Like the approximate *causes* of crises, their immediate effects depend on a host of factors which cannot be deduced from the core structure of capitalism. So, what *can* we say at this level of abstraction? First, we can conclude that the fundamental social relations underlying the capitalist mode of production set in motion a dynamic which inevitably drives the economy into crises of overproduction. Second, we can also conclude that capitalism is extremely crisis *prone*, meaning that it is extremely *vulnerable* to external shocks. Third, we can also demonstrate that a crisis generates mechanisms – depreciation, falling wages, and so on – which *restore the conditions of accumulation*. In drawing such conclusions, we abstract – as I explained in the introduction – from historical circumstances which are only *externally* related to the core structures of capitalism. This means that the kind of dynamics described in this chapter should not be understood as empirical predictions of inevitable future trends. Rather, the laws of capital executed by competition are, 'like all economic laws', *tendencies*, that is, laws 'whose absolute implementation is paralysed, held up, retarded and weakened by counteracting factors'.[73] As in the case of the tendency to deskilling discussed in chapter ten, the analysis of the dynamics of accumulation and crisis on this level of abstraction depicts the structural pressures stemming from the basic social relations of capitalist society. At any given point, a proletarian uprising or a natural disaster might of course bring about an abrupt 'disintegration of the whole shit'.[74] But, until that happens, the dynamics of capital accumulation will be a force to reckon with.

A crisis also has important effects on the relationship between capital and the state. This issue lies beyond the scope of this book, but let me nevertheless offer some brief remarks in order to indicate how important it is to keep this dimension in mind when thinking about the impact of a crisis on the balance of forces. The state's reaction to a crisis depends on a lot of different factors: the immediate cause and nature of the crisis, the location of a state in the global system of production as well as international alliances, the balance of forces between classes, access to natural resources and energy, and so on. Given that all capitalist states depend on the accumulation of capital, however, it is possible to pinpoint certain structural pressures to which most states will likely find themselves subjected in times of crisis. First and foremost, crises put pressure on states

73   M: 286, 339.
74   43: 25.

to help capital, and this can happen in countless ways. States can support expansion of markets through imperialism or international agreements; they can guarantee access to cheap credit, crack down on social protests, invest in infrastructure, lower corporate taxes, privatise public assets, and so on.

The history of capitalist crises is filled with examples of states employing a combination of such strategies in order to help profitability recover. In the 1830s and '40s, for example, the crisis in the British cotton industry put pressure on the government to repeal the Corn Laws, since they held up wages. This was at least one of the factors which eventually led to the repeal of the tariffs in 1846.[75] The Great Recession of the late nineteenth century likewise pushed states to support expansion through colonialism; according to Eric Hobsbawm, 'it is quite undeniable that the pressure of capital in search of more profitable investment, as of production in search of markets, contributed to policies of expansion – including colonial conquest'.[76] Fast-forward a century, to the crisis of the 1970s, and we find a number of the strategies just mentioned: deregulation of international trade and finance, cheap credit, tax cuts, investments in infrastructure, and repression of unions – all of which were preconditions for the neoliberal quasi-recovery of the 1980s.[77]

Some of these strategies can have contradictory effects, reflecting the contradictory pressure on the state: on the one hand, states are under pressure to facilitate, or at least not stand in the way of, the restoration of profitability; on the other hand, they must also avoid the kind of social instability which easily arises if capital is allowed to run amok in its destructive fury. An example of this is the provision of cheap credit; on the one hand, it dampens the crisis, but on the other, it also prolongs it by putting capitals with one foot in the grave in a debt respirator. As several scholars have pointed out, this is exactly what happened in the 1970s; 'the same expansion of credit that ensured a modicum of stability also held back recovery' by 'making possible the survival of those high-cost,

---

75 Eric Hobsbawm, *The Age of Revolution: Europe 1789–1848* (London: Abacus, 2003), 57f.

76 Hobsbawn, *The Age of Empire*, 45.

77 Robert Brenner, *The Boom and The Bubble: The US in the World Economy* (London: Verso, 2002); Robert Brenner, *The Economics of Global Turbulence: The Advanced Capitalist Economies from Long Boom to Long Downturn, 1945–2005* (London: Verso, 2006); David Harvey, *A Brief History of Neoliberalism* (Oxford: Oxford University Press, 2005); McNally, *Global Slump*.

low-profit firms that perpetuated over-capacity and over-production'.[78] Something similar happened in the wake of the crisis of 2008, where the United States 'established itself as liquidity provider of last resort to the global banking system'.[79] Aside from bailing out banks and flooding the economy with cash, governments in leading capitalist economies also assisted capital in overcoming the crash through austerity, tax cuts, police repression, removal of legal barriers to precarity in the labour market, sale of public property at a bargain, handovers of power to technocrat governments or, in the case of China, massive public investments.[80] As German chancellor Angela Merkel explained in 2011, it was a question of organising 'parliamentary codetermination in such a way that it is nevertheless market conforming' – a project which, of course, entails the acknowledgement that 'elections cannot be allowed to change economic policy', as Merkel's finance minister Wolfgang Schäuble put it.[81]

Negation as Condition

By now it should be clear why crises should be regarded as one of the impersonal and abstract power mechanisms through which capital imposes itself on social life. Crises are perhaps *the* best example of the *impersonal* character of the economic power of capital; as an outcome of anarchic yet patterned myriads of individual actions, a crisis is the systemic effect par excellence. When a crisis hits, it becomes clear just how much a society in which social reproduction is governed by the valorisation of value is a society which has lost control. *No one is in control, and there is no centre from which power radiates; instead, capitalist society is ruled by social relations morphed into real abstractions whose opaque movements we call 'the economy'* – 'like the sorcerer, who is no longer able to control the powers of the nether world whom he has called up by his

---

78   Brenner, *The Economics of Global Turbulence*, 157; see also Benanav and Clegg, 'Crisis and Immiseration'; McNally, *Global Slump*, 83.

79   Adam Tooze, *Crashed: How a Decade of Financial Crises Changed the World* (Allen Lane, 2018), 9; Robert Brenner, 'What Is Good for Goldman Sachs Is Good for America: The Origins of the Current Crisis'(working paper, Institute for Social Science Research, UCLA, 2009).

80   David Harvey, *Marx, Capital and the Madness of Economic Reason* (London: Profile Books, 2017), chap. 9; Tooze, *Crashed*, chap. 10.

81   Quoted in Tooze, *Crashed*, 396, 522.

spells'.[82] In times of crisis, it becomes clear just how much capitalism has surrendered life to the vagaries of the market.

A crisis is a temporary *solution* to the inherent and ineradicable contradictions of accumulation; it is capital's attempt to flee its own shadow. Capital survives by *internalising its own partial negation*: it has to annihilate a part of itself in order to carry on with the valorisation of value. The logic of valorisation thus includes within itself its own negation, 'not by circumstances external to it', as Marx puts it, 'but rather as *a condition of its self-preservation*'.[83] One of the ways in which a crisis helps to restore profitability is by *intensifying* the mechanisms of domination which are also operative *outside* of times of crisis. Competition, downward pressure on wages, unemployment, real subsumption: all are completely normal parts of all phases of an accumulation cycle. Crises do not *create* these mechanisms; if competition *executes* them, as we saw in chapter nine, a crisis is the compressed and temporary *intensification* of them.

One way to think of the relation between crisis and power is therefore to see crises as levers of the mechanisms of domination examined in the preceding chapters. Crises intensify capital's expansive drive; they compel capital to draw more and more people and activities into its circuit by means of privatisation and accumulation by dispossession, or through the commodification of activities which have hitherto remained outside the direct command of capital. In this way, crises tend to expand and fortify the form of class domination we examined in chapter three. This also leads to a strengthening of the mechanisms of domination described in chapter four, as the expansion of capitalist class domination increases competition and market dependence, imposing the commodity form on new spheres of life. Finally, by tightening the grip on individual capitals, crises also accelerate the real subsumption of labour and nature as capitalists struggle to survive the massacre on the market. In addition to these *intensifications* of mechanisms which operate throughout all phases of accumulation cycles, crises also have their own specific power mechanism: the annihilation of capital.

I want to emphasise that the analysis of the role of crises in the reproduction of capitalism presented here does not imply the claim that crises can be reduced to a kind of internal self-regulation of the capitalist system. My claim is not that crises always and everywhere lead to rehabilitation,

---

82   6: 489.
83   G: 749f. Emphasis added.

expansion, and strengthening of the power of capital. My claim is, rather, that the *immanent* tendency of crises is to set in motion powerful dynamics which, *if left unchecked*, tend to restore and expand the power of capital. Whether or not these dynamics will prevail depends on a number of factors, chief among which is the balance of forces in the concrete conjuncture. Similarly, my analysis does not imply the view that a crisis can never be a sign of the weakness of the power of capital, nor that a crisis can never bring about unique revolutionary openings. There are plenty of examples of revolutionary struggles being accelerated by crises in the history of capitalism. A crisis of capital is always also a crisis of proletarian reproduction, and therefore also a situation in which the incompatibility between the convulsions of accumulation and the need for a secure and stable life achieves its most glaring expression. No wonder, then, that crises tend to result in social unrest and struggle. At the same time, however, the history of capitalist crises seems to suggest that a crisis often leads to a weakening of revolutionary forces. The first global capitalist crisis in 1857 was followed by a wave of capitalist expansion, as was the Great Recession of the late nineteenth century, in spite of a rapidly growing and self-confident labour movement. The results of the Great Depression of 1929 were more ambiguous; working-class insurgency proliferated in the 1930s but was eventually crushed by fascism and, after World War II, by a massive capitalist expansion, often led by social democratic governments. The peaks of anti-capitalist resistance have often taken place in contexts marked not by economic crisis but by *war* – as was the case with the Paris Commune in 1871 and the revolutionary sequence of the late 1910s – or, in the case of the late 1960s, relative prosperity. The crisis of the 1970s undermined rather than accelerated anti-capitalist resistance; as Benanav and Clegg put it, 'The era of a deep crisis of capitalism has been accompanied by an even deeper crisis in the practical opposition to capitalism.'[84]

But what about the most recent crisis? There is no question that the global crisis of 2008 opened up a new cycle of struggles. Movements against anti-austerity – and neoliberalism more generally – have spread across Europe, reaching a dramatic and ultimately disappointing head in Greece in 2015. In the global South, especially in India, South Africa, and China, recent years have witnessed a surge in the number and impact

---

84   Benanav and Clegg, 'Crisis and Immiseration', 1634.

of strikes and riots. In addition to this, there have been a number of important struggles which might not be explicitly anti-capitalist but are nevertheless often connected to the crisis and its impacts, contributing to the widespread feeling that something – or perhaps everything – is about to collapse: the Black Lives Matter movement, the Arab Spring, the Movement of the Squares, #MeToo and other feminist movements, the escalating climate justice movement, riots, and the Yellow Vests movement in France. Despite this massive wave of social unrest, which is unlike anything seen since the 1970s, we cannot unequivocally conclude that the power of capital has been weakened. Although it might be a bit too early to draw conclusions, it seems more likely that the opposite is the case: that the crisis has strengthened the power of capital. Concentration of wealth has accelerated, global inequality has skyrocketed, public assets have been privatised, austerity has been imposed, taxes have been cut, and wages have declined – in short, capital has largely succeeded in pushing through many of its core objectives. We should, as Endnotes point out in their survey of the crisis and class struggles of 2011–13, 'guard against the tendency to mistake the crisis of this mode of production for a weakness of capital in its struggle with labour. In fact, crises tend to *strengthen* capital's hand.'[85]

The functionaries and ideologues of capital know this. In 2010, the International Monetary Fund urged policymakers to 'seize the moment and act boldly'.[86] The European Central Bank declared that 'the crisis has clearly shown that there is no alternative to structural reforms'.[87] In 2014, the then president of the European Commission, José Manuel Barroso, summed up the crisis management of the preceding six years in the following way: 'The crisis ended up giving us the political momentum to make changes that before the downturn had been unattainable – some of those changes were even unthinkable.'[88] In a similar vein, free marketeer Milton Friedman famously argued that

> only a crisis – actual or perceived – produces real change. When that crisis occurs, the actions that are taken depend on the ideas that are

---

85 Endnotes, 'Holding Pattern', 29.

86 International Monetary Fund, *Regional Economic Outlook, October 2010, Europe, Building Confidence* (Washington, DC: International Monetary Fund, 2010), 1.

87 European Central Bank, *Annual Report 2014* (Frankfurt: European Central Bank, 2014), 40, available at ecb.europa.eu/pub/pdf/annrep/ar2014en.pdf.

88 'President Barroso's Speech on the European Semester', European Commission, 2014, http://europa.eu/rapid/press-release_SPEECH-14-38_en.htm.

lying around. That, I believe, is our basic function: to develop alternatives to existing policies, to keep them alive and available until the politically impossible becomes politically inevitable.[89]

Friedman wrote this in 1962, when many still believed that Keynesianism had found a way of neutralising the crisis tendencies of capitalism. By the mid-1970s, however, the crisis Friedman hoped for had arrived, and he was able to implement many of his neoliberal ideas as an advisor to the likes of Augusto Pinochet, Margaret Thatcher, and Ronald Reagan.[90] The forces of capital know very well that a crisis is a splendid opportunity to strengthen capital's grip on social life. We communists should also take heed of that.

---

89   Milton Friedman, *Capitalism and Freedom* (Chicago: Chicago University Press, 2002 [1962]), xiv.

90   See Naomi Klein, *The Shock Doctrine: The Rise of Disaster Capitalism* (London: Penguin, 2008).

Conclusion

Human beings have to work if they want to live. Or, more precisely: *some* of them have to work. Given certain natural conditions, human individuals generally have the capacity to produce more than what is necessary for their own survival, and for that reason, the reproduction of a community of human beings does not necessarily require *everyone* to work. Human societies have always included people who are temporarily or permanently unable to work: some are ill, some are disabled, injured, too young or too old, and so on. Therefore, human societies always have to find a way to make some people work for others, or, put differently: to find a way of organising surplus labour and distribute its results. There is nothing inherently oppressive about this. Surplus labour is simply a necessity, and even a communist mode of production would have to figure out a way to secure the survival of those who are unable to work.

The capacity to perform surplus labour might be a condition of possibility of the existence of humanity as such, but it has a gloomy downside: it is also what makes *class society* possible. In order to actualise this possibility, some people have to find a way to force others to work for them. How does one do that? How does a group of people establish itself as a ruling class and reproduce the social relations that allow them to exploit a class of producers?

Throughout most of human history, ruling classes have generally relied on a combination of ideology and violence. Ideology affects how people perceive the world they inhabit, what they take to be just and unjust, necessary and contingent, natural and artificial, divine and human, inevitable and permutable. Such ideas and intuitions function as coordinates for action, and for this reason, ideology can be an important source of power for ruling classes. Violence is usually a bit more straightforward and palpable: most of us try to avoid pain, injury, and death, and for this reason the threat of violence is often an effective motivating force.

The earliest large-scale class societies in ancient Mesopotamia were, in the words of James C. Scott, 'based systematically on coerced, captive human labor'.[1] According to Scott, it 'would be almost impossible to exaggerate the centrality of bondage, in one form or another, in the development of the state until very recently'.[2] Slavery was similarly the basis of the Qin dynasty and the early Han dynasty in China, as well as ancient Greece and the Roman Empire. Feudal society was also 'violent at its very basis', as Christopher Isett and Stephen Miller put it.[3] In these pre-capitalist class societies, ruling classes employed violence in order to extract surplus labour from producers.[4] Producers were mostly *personally unfree*, which means that they did not have the right to withdraw from the exploitative relation and that an attempt to do so would, at least under normal circumstances, involve great difficulties and risks.

In the course of the sixteenth and seventeenth centuries, a set of social relations which increasingly allowed ruling classes to extract surplus

1   James C. Scott, *Against the Grain: A Deep History of the Earliest States* (New Haven: Yale University Press, 2017), 180.

2   Ibid., 155.

3   Christopher Isett and Stephen Miller, *The Social History of Agriculture: From the Origins to the Current Crisis* (New York: Rowman & Littlefield, 2016), 40.

4   On the role of violence in the reproduction of pre-capitalist class relations, see M: 777; Perry Anderson, *Passages from Antiquity to Feudalism* (London: New Left Books, 1974), chap. 1; Robert Brenner, 'The Agrarian Roots of European Capitalism', in *The Brenner Debate*, ed. T. H. Aston and C. H. E. Philpin (Cambridge: Cambridge University Press, 1987); Robert Brenner, 'Agriarian Class Stucture and Economic Development in Pre-Industrial Europe', in Aston and Philphin, *Brenner Debate*; Robert Brenner, 'Property and Progress: Where Adam Smith Went Wrong', in *Marxist History-Writing for the Twenty-First Century*, ed. Chris Wickham (Oxford: Oxford University Press, 2007), 64f; G. E. M. De Ste. Croix, *The Class Struggle in the Ancient Greek World: From the Archaic Age to the Arab Conquests* (Ithaca, NY: Cornell University Press, 1989); Spencer Dimmock, *The Origin of Capitalism in England, 1400–1600* (Leiden: Brill, 2014), chap. 3; Isett and Miller, *Social History of Agriculture*, 17ff, 32, 40; Scott, *Against the Grain*, chap. 5; Ellen Meiksins Wood, *The Origin of Capitalism: A Longer View* (London: Verso, 2002), 55f; Ellen Meiksins Wood, *Democracy against Capitalism: Renewing Historical Materialism* (London: Verso, 2016), chap. 1.

labour from peasants without having to resort to violence began to emerge. Peasants were separated from the land and forced to sell their labour power to farmers, who then sold their products as commodities in competitive markets with the aim of making a profit. The pursuit of wealth in its monetary form – an activity which had previously been relegated to the margins of society – began to infiltrate the entire social fabric, and capital eventually became 'the all-dominating economic power'.[5] Bringing about this state of affairs required a lot of violence, but, once it had been established, it was possible to replace some of this violence with the 'mute compulsion of economic relations'. The emergence of the capitalist mode of production did not, then, lead to an *evacuation* of power from the economy; it rather signalled a new configuration of power in which the coercive power required to guarantee property relations was centralised in the hands of the state and thereby formally separated from the organisation of production and the extraction of surplus labour, which now became organised by means of an abstract and impersonal form of domination. This historically novel way of structuring the reproduction of social life turned out to be tremendously tenacious, versatile, and infused with a fiercely expansionary drive. Today, four centuries later, it is more entrenched than ever before.

In this book, I have attempted to construct a systematic conceptual framework for understanding one of the ways in which the life of society becomes subordinated to the valorisation of value. Let me try to summarise. Like all other organisms, human beings have to maintain a constant exchange of matter with the rest of nature. The unique thing about the specifically human version of this metabolism is that it is inherently fragmented, flexible, and underdetermined; because of their peculiar corporeal organisation, human beings have no immediately given or necessary way to relate to the rest of nature. The characteristic thing about the human metabolism with the rest of nature is thus an *absence of necessity*, or perhaps more precisely, a unity of necessity and contingency: a metabolism *has* to be established, but its social form is never simply given.

The capitalist mode of production is the first mode of production in history to fully exploit the ontological precarity of the human metabolism. Whereas pre-capitalist modes of surplus extraction were based on the

---

5   G: 107.

intimate connection between the producers and the means of production, capital secures its grip on society by introducing a twofold cleavage of the human metabolism in order to govern the temporary reconnection of what has thus been separated.

The first cleavage is the creation of the proletarian, that is, a naked life separated from its conditions, to which it can only gain access through capital's mediation. With this biopolitical fracture, in which the control over the conditions of the life of society is centralised in the hands of the capitalist class, it becomes possible for the latter to force proletarians to give up a part of their life to capital, without having to resort to violence. Instead, capitalists can rely on proletarians' own will to live in order to be able to charge the interest on the transcendentally indebted life of the proletarian known as surplus value. Class domination thereby inserts itself on a transcendental level, where the valorisation of value becomes the condition of possibility of social reproduction.

The second cleavage is the horizontal splitting of producers into competing units of production which relate to each other through the market. The organisation of social reproduction by means of the exchange of products of labour produced by independent and private producers transforms social relations among people into real abstractions, which then confront them as alien powers. In turn, these horizontal relations give rise to a set of mechanisms through which the logic of capital transcends class differences and imposes itself on the social totality as such.

The economic power of capital must be grasped as a result of the mutual traversal of these two constitutive splits, which engenders a twofold subjection: the subjection of *proletarians* to *capitalists* and the subjection of *everyone* to *capital*. Neither of these can be reduced to the other, because they spring from two distinct and irreducible sets of social relations. Capital's mute compulsion is the result of their mutual mediation of each other: proletarians are subjected to capitalists by means of a set of mechanisms which simultaneously subjects everyone to the logic of valorisation, and vice versa. The 'muteness' of capital's power thus reveals itself to be a result of a set of historically specific relations of production in which the human capacity to infuse materiality with relations of domination has been exploited to a degree never seen before in human history.

Relations of production are not capital's only source of power, however. Seen as a continuous process, capitalist production reveals itself to possess a curious ability to transform its *preconditions* into its *results of its own movement*; it posits its own presupposition. Capitalist relations of production set in motion a number of dynamics which are simultaneously *results and sources* of the power of capital. This paradoxical circularity operates on multiple levels of the capitalist totality, from the microscopic manipulation of plant DNA to the restructuring of international divisions of labour.

Within the workplace, competitive pressure and proletarian resistance force the personifications of capital to employ their despotic power and discipline workers, introduce new technologies, and restructure the division of labour. By means of this real subsumption of labour, capital gnaws into the bodies of workers in order to calibrate them to the abstract temporality of capitalist production and make sure that they gradually become useless outside of capital's mediations. The same dynamic is visible in capital's relation to the rest of nature, whether energy sources, animals, soil, or plants. Capitalist production implies an unremitting drive to break the refractory hand of nature.

Real subsumption also takes place outside of the workplace, on national, regional, and global levels. By annihilating space through time and creating a logistical empire welded to its logic, capital gains a mobility which it uses as a powerful weapon against rebellious proletarians and foot-dragging governments. Through its restructuring of the international division of labour, capital adds another dimension to its transcendental power by supplementing its appropriation of the *objective* and *social* conditions of labour with its *spatial* or *geographical* conditions.

Everywhere it goes, capital thus launches its characteristic modus operandi on all levels of the capitalist totality: fracture, pulverise, split, and cleave in order to collect, connect, assemble, and reconfigure by weaving the valorisation of value into the transcendental fabric of social reproduction.

The circularity of mute compulsion power also comes out clearly in capital's necessary tendency to generate a relative surplus population as well as in its recurring negation of itself in the form of crises. Both of these dynamics, which tend to follow a cyclical pattern, intensify the mechanisms of mute compulsion; the existence of a relative surplus population increases competition among proletarians, and a crisis increases competitive pressures on capitals, thereby forcing them to strengthen their effort to discipline workers and intensify the real subsumption of labour, nature, and international networks of production.

The mute compulsion of capital, then, is the result of a particular set of social relations and a particular set of dynamics set in motion by those relations. Taken together, the examination of these relations and dynamics explains why capitalist society is dominated by an expansive logic of valorisation that imposes itself on society not only by means of violence and ideology but also by inscribing itself into the material composition of social reproduction.

The economic power of capital is a complex apparatus of domination whose mechanisms operate on all levels of the capitalist mode of production. The purpose of this book has been to zoom in on this specific form of power in order to systematically distinguish it from coercive and ideological power, and to identify its sources and mechanisms. In order to fixate this as an object, it has been necessary to purify it by abstracting from everything which is not logically implied by it. Such abstractions are necessary in order to build theories, but, in order for theories to become strategically relevant for the practical effort to abolish the world of capital, the opposite movement also has to occur. The purpose of building abstract theories of capital is not just to produce insights which are true in a purely passive and traditional sense, but rather to assist the revolutionary effort to create communism. Contrary to what many intellectuals may be led by their guilty conscience or vanity to believe, the role of theory in such an endeavour is bound to be very limited. '*Ideas* can never lead beyond an old world order but only beyond the ideas of the old world order', as Marx once put it.[6] What theories like the one developed in this book *can* do, however, is develop concepts which can be employed on lower levels of abstraction in order to produce strategically relevant conjunctural analyses. Because the struggle against capital does not take place in a theoretical laboratory, it never confronts the mute compulsion of capital as it has been described in this book. In the messy reality in which struggles occur, the economic power of capital is always completely entangled with coercive and ideological domination and social forms, logics, and dynamics which do not arise from the capital form. We should always keep in mind that theories developed on high levels of abstractions cannot and should not provide us with answers to the question of what must be done – but also that this does not mean that such theories are politically useless. Political action must always spring from what Lenin called 'the very gist, the living soul, of Marxism', namely the 'concrete analysis of a

---

6   4: 119.

concrete situation';[7] in order to undertake such analyses, however, we need carefully constructed concepts, and this is what theory provides. My hope is thus that, combined with other relevant theories and a sensitivity towards the specificity of the conjuncture, the systematic scrutiny of the concept of mute compulsion offered in this book will be able to make a contribution – however slight – to the dismantling of the destructive, oppressive, and nightmarish system known as the capitalist mode of production and thereby to the creation of the conditions of possibility of a free life – also known as *communism*.

---

7   Lenin, 'Kommunismus', in *Collected Works*, vol. 31 (Moscow: Progress Publishers, 1974).

Acknowledgements

Since I began working on *Mute Compulsion* in 2016, I have received a lot of help and support from a large group of very kind, patient, and erudite people. First of all, I want to thank Sebastian Budgen and the rest of the staff at Verso for their great work with the book.

Mute Compulsion is based on a PhD thesis defended at the University of Southern Denmark in 2019. I want to thank my supervisor Anne-Marie Søndergaard Christensen for her critical and supportive supervision. I also want to thank the staff at the Department for the Study of Culture and the PhD committee.

I am extremely grateful to have so many clever comrades to discuss important stuff with. Nicolai Von Eggers, Nicklas Weis Damkjær, Esben Bøgh Sørensen, Janaína de Faria, Mathias Hein Jessen, Mikkel Flohr, Dominique Routhier, Eskil Halberg, Kresten Lundsgaard-Leth, Hans Erik Avlund Frandsen, Susanne Possing, Rasmus Christian Elling, Marie Louise Krogh, Jon Rostgaard Boiesen (RIP), Daniel Valentin Kjer, Mark Søgaard Lie, Tone Grosen Dandanell, Bjarke Skærlund Risager, Saman Atter Motlagh, Lotte List, Henrik Jøker Bjerre, Jeannette Søgaard Lie, Signe Leth Gammelgaard, Magnus Møller Ziegler: thank you.

I have profited immensely from discussions with all the good people who took time out of their own busy schedules to read parts of my manuscript: Magnus Møller Ziegler, William Clare Roberts, Eskil Halberg, Andreas Jensen, Signe Leth Gammelgaard, Niels Albertsen, Andreas Malm, Janaína de Faria, Jonas Larsen, Dominique Routhier, Mathias

Hein Jessen. Thank you for your comments, criticisms, questions, and suggestions. A special thanks to Anna Cornelia Ploug, who read the entire manuscript in its longest version and has had an enormous influence on this book, and to Nicolai von Eggers, who read large parts of my earliest drafts. Another special thanks to Michael Heinrich for his generous critique and support, and for writing a wonderful foreword for the book.

Appendix: Cited Volumes of Marx and Engels's *Collected Works*

Vol.	Title	Written	Pages
1	Proceedings of the Sixth Rhine Province Assembly. First Article. Debates on Freedom of the Press and Publication of the Proceedings of the Assembly of the Estates	Apr. 1842	132–81
	The Leading Article in No. 179 of the *Kölnische Zeitung*	Jul. 1842	184–202
	Proceedings of the Sixth Rhine Province Assembly. Third Article. Debates on the Law on Thefts of Wood	Oct. 1842	224–63
	Letter to Arnold Ruge	Mar. 1843	398–402
3	Contribution to the Critique of Hegel's Philosophy of Law	Mar.–Aug. 1843	3–129
	Letters from *Deutsch-Französische Jahrbücher*	Mar.–Sep. 1843	133–45
	On the Jewish Question	Aug.–Dec. 1843	146–75
	Contribution to the Critique of Hegel's Philosophy of Law. Introduction	Dec. 1843–Jan. 1844	175–87
	Critical Marginal Notes on the Article 'The King of Prussia and Social Reform. By a Prussian'	Jul. 1844	189–206
	Comments on James Mill, *Éléments d'économie politique*	First half of 1844	211–28
	Economic and Philosophic Manuscripts of 1844	Apr.–Aug. 1844	229–348
4	*The Holy Family, or Critique of Critical Criticism. Against Bruno Bauer and Company*	Aug.–Nov. 1844	5–211
	Draft of an Article on Friedrich List's Book *Das nationale System der politischen Oekonomie*	Mar. 1845	265–94
5	Theses on Feuerbach	Spring 1845	3–5

Index